Lost Years

Lost Years

BUSH, SHARON,
AND FAILURE IN THE
MIDDLE EAST

MARK MATTHEWS

NATION BOOKS
NEW YORK
WWW.NATIONBOOKS.ORG

Copyright © 2007 Mark Matthews

Published by
Nation Books
A Member of the Perseus Books Group
116 East 16th Street, 8th Floor
New York, NY 10003

Nation Books is a co-publishing venture of the Nation Institute and the
Perseus Books Group

Books published by Nation Books are available at special discounts for
bulk purchases in the United States by corporations, institutions, and
other organizations. For more information, please contact the Special
Markets Department at the Perseus Books Group, 2300 Chestnut Street,
Suite 200, Philadelphia, PA 19103, or call (800) 255-1514,
or e-mail special.markets@perseusbooks.com.

Library of Congress Cataloging-in-Publication Data is available

ISBN-10: 1-56858-332-X
ISBN-13: 978-1-56858-332-7

10 9 8 7 6 5 4 3 2 1

Book design by Pauline Neuwirth, Neuwirth & Associates, Inc.

To Sarah

CONTENTS

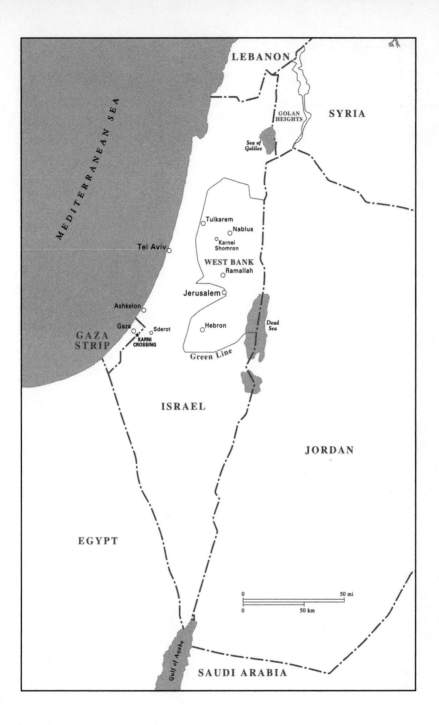

Significant Players

United States

George W. Bush, president of the United States

Dick Cheney, vice president

Colin Powell, secretary of state

Condoleezza Rice, national security adviser,
later secretary of state

Donald Rumsfeld, secretary of defense

Richard Armitage, deputy secretary of state

Douglas J. Feith, undersecretary of defense for policy

Dov Zakheim, Pentagon comptroller

Edward S. Walker Jr., assistant secretary of state for
Near Eastern affairs

Bill Burns, ambassador to Jordan, assistant secretary of state for
Near Eastern affairs

David Welch, assistant secretary of state for international
organization affairs; later ambassador to Egypt, assistant secretary
of state for Near Eastern affairs

Martin Indyk, U.S. ambassador to Israel; assistant secretary of state
for Near Eastern affairs

Daniel Kurtzer, U.S. ambassador to Egypt; ambassador to Israel
(Indyk's successor)

Elliott Abrams, senior director for Near Eastern affairs, National
Security Council, later deputy national security adviser

Marine General (Retired) Anthony Zinni, special envoy

AARON MILLER, longtime peace-process negotiator,
State Department

JOHN WOLF, U.S. special envoy

GEORGE MITCHELL, former Senate Democratic leader, diplomatic
troubleshooter, led inquiry into the al-Aqsa Intifada

FRED ZEIDMAN, U.S. Holocaust Memorial Council, GOP
fundraiser

MATTHEW BROOKS, executive director, Republican Jewish Coalition

MALCOLM HOENLEIN, executive vice president, Conference of
Presidents of Major American Jewish Organizations

ISRAEL

ARIEL SHARON, prime minister of Israel
(incapacitated January 2006)

EHUD OLMERT, deputy prime minister

DAVID IVRY, Israeli ambassador to the United States

DANNY AYALON, Israeli ambassador to the United States (Ivry's
successor)

DOV WEISGLASS, Sharon's adviser and chief of staff

EFRAIM HALEVY, head of Mossad; chairman of the National
Security Council

SHALOM TURGEMAN, diplomatic adviser to the prime minister

MAJOR GENERAL GIORA EILAND, chairman of the National
Security Council

ZALMAN SHOVAL, former Israeli ambassador to the United States;
member of Knesset; adviser to Sharon

RAANAN GISSIN, adviser to Sharon; foreign press spokesman

AVI DICHTER, head of Shin Bet, Israeli security service; later public
security minister

BRIGADIER GENERAL MICHAEL HERZOG, senior aide to the
minister of defense; later visiting military fellow at the Washington
Institute for Near East Policy

YEHUDA LANCRY, ambassador to the United Nations

DAN GILLERMAN, ambassador to the United Nations

PALESTINE

YASSER ARAFAT (died November 2004), chairman of the Palestine Liberation Organization; president of the Palestinian Authority

MAHMOUD ABBAS (ABU MAZEN), prime minister (2003); elected as Arafat's successor

MOHAMMED DAHLAN, adviser to Arafat and Abbas; former head of preventive security force, Gaza

SAEB EREKAT, peace process negotiator, spokesman, diplomatic adviser to Arafat and Abbas

NASSER AL-QIDWA, Palestinian representative to the United Nations; later foreign minister

MAEN AREIKAT, head of the Palestinian Negotiations Affairs Department

DIANA BUTTU, attorney with the Palestinian Negotiations Support Group

OTHER

JAMES WOLFENSOHN, former World Bank president; Quartet representative on Israel's Gaza disengagement

KOFI ANNAN, secretary general of the United Nations

KIERAN PRENDERGAST, UN undersecretary general for political affairs

TERJE ROED-LARSEN, UN representative for the Middle East peace process

MIGUEL MORATINOS, Middle East representative for the European Union; later foreign minister of Spain

MARWAN MUASHER, foreign minister of Jordan

NABIL FAHMY, ambassador of Egypt to the United States

QUARTET: the United States, the European Union, Russia, and the United Nations

PREFACE

GEORGE W. BUSH inherited a bleak but by no means hopeless Middle East landscape from Bill Clinton. His Democratic predecessor's risky attempt to conclude an Israeli-Palestinian peace at Camp
David in the summer of 2000 had failed, leading nine weeks later to the
outbreak of the second intifada. By the time Bush was sworn in on January 20, 2001, three and a half months of violence had deepened
hatred and fear between Israelis and Palestinians and caused a humanitarian emergency in the occupied territories, while spreading disillusionment, on both sides, with the peace process begun at Oslo in 1993
and pessimism among the departing Clinton team. Israelis, having lost
all faith in Palestinians' willingness to coexist alongside them, were
ready to elect Ariel Sharon, whose brazen military record assured them
of a tough response to Palestinian attacks.

Yet the level of violence then was mild compared with what would
come later. The Islamist militant groups Hamas and Islamic Jihad were
for the most part still keeping suicide attacks in check. Fewer than fifty
Israelis had died, and most attacks against Israelis had occurred inside
the occupied territories, not in Israel proper. The Israeli border had not
yet been virtually sealed off to Palestinian workers. Israeli and Palestinian
negotiators meeting at the Egyptian resort at Taba were continuing to

narrow gaps over the most serious obstacles to peace—the return of a certain number of refugees to Israel, and how Jerusalem and its holy sites would be controlled.

That was a pivotal moment. Two peoples were causing each other increasing pain, yet the peace process still showed faint signs of life. A determination by the new Republican president to pick up the pieces and persevere in the United States' traditional mediating role would have sent an important signal of hope to the majorities on both sides, who, though angry and distrustful, still longed for peace.

This book is the story of that missed opportunity and many others that were to follow. It draws from more than a dozen years' experience in reporting on American policy toward the Middle East, two years of on-the-ground reporting and subsequent visits, and dozens of interviews with a variety of participants from the United States, Israel, Europe, the United Nations, and the Arab world. The story revisits the people who played important roles in the key turning points of the past half-dozen years, setting the scene and offering, at times, fresh insights.

Throughout his first term and well into his second, Bush engaged in the Middle East peace process episodically and without success, allowing it to be sidetracked by U.S. military adventures, eruptions of Israeli-Palestinian violence and terror, and the tug-of-war among his subordinates over American priorities. By the time Sharon was incapacitated by a stroke on January 4, 2006, a bloody five-year impasse had robbed the two peoples of any prospect for reconciliation in the near term and plunged Palestinian society into a sink of nihilism, poverty, and clan warfare.

The terror attacks of September 11 exposed the Middle East's multiple pathologies as a threat to the United States and the West. These pathologies included religious fanaticism, fractured societies, backward education systems, moribund economies, and a wide gulf between the rulers and the ruled. They couldn't all be tackled at once. But a serious, sustained effort to solve the Arab-Israeli conflict could have lanced one of the most important sources of bitterness, while reducing suspicion of U.S. intentions. Instead, Bush hoped an invasion of Iraq and establishment of a stable democracy there would serve as a model for dramatic change throughout the region. What he got by neglect of the peace process and the catastrophic war in Iraq was a Middle East in even worse shape, defined by human misery, rising insecurity, spreading hatred, and shrinking U.S. influence.

The tragic irony of the story is that Bush sincerely wanted peace in the Holy Land and correctly diagnosed some of the key problems that stood in the way of that peace. He called more prominently and explicitly than his predecessor for a viable Palestinian state on contiguous territory. Perhaps more important, symbolically, he injected the name used by Palestinians and their supporters—Palestine—into official American parlance. He repeatedly demanded a halt to the growth of Jewish settlements in occupied territory, embraced Palestinian moderates, and pressed for reform of Palestinian governance, finances, and security services.

Ariel Sharon himself represented an opportunity that Bush failed to seize. Stubbornly hawkish, possessed of a dark and narrow view of the Arab world, and less than a model of probity in his political and business affairs, Sharon nonetheless brought valuable strengths. He commanded the Israeli political scene as had only a handful of Israeli leaders before him, displaying a mastery of tactics, timing, and coalition management. Although his popularity rose and fell with the national mood, Sharon's commitment to Israel's security was widely trusted by his countrymen. He was a pragmatist, not an ideologue. And when he made a solemn commitment, particularly one that was important to the United States, he usually kept it.

There is little doubt that, had Bush pressed him into peace talks, Sharon would have staked out uncompromising positions. He would have rejected a return to the 1967 line that much of the world views as a de facto border between Israel and a future Palestine; he would have opposed return of the refugees displaced by the 1948 war and their descendants to their original homes and villages in Israel, and he would have demanded Israeli sovereignty over Jerusalem, which both sides claim as their capital. He would likely have buttressed these well-known positions with preconditions, insisting on a halt to Palestinian violence before talking about substance. Then he would have bargained. He knew how much the Israeli public valued strong ties with Washington. Had Bush been intent on pursuing peace, Sharon would have had to show good faith. He recognized that Israel would have to make painful concessions. He was ready, when he thought the moment right, to abandon the settlers' movement and relinquish all of the Gaza Strip—even the strategic high ground of Netzarim, overlooking a future Palestinian port, and supervision of the border with Egypt. He acknowledged that the Israeli occupation and control over Palestinian lives was unsustainable. What's more, he wanted to be the one to draw Israel's final borders.

Bush didn't put Sharon's pragmatism and flexibility to the test. Instead, he allowed the Israeli prime minister to seize the initiative. A serious peace process that would lead ultimately to a two-state solution never got under way. Bush never persuaded Sharon that such a process was in Israel's interest. "You couldn't do that absent the president being very firm with Ariel Sharon, and the president would not be firm," Richard Armitage, deputy secretary of state in Bush's first term, told me. Never before was an American administration so willing to accept the approach of a right-wing government in Israel. Far from pushing Israel in the direction of peace, Bush, over time, became increasingly tolerant of Sharon's tactics of siege, mass arrests, targeted assassinations, and closure—tactics that gave Israel a short-term advantage over terrorists but fed support for violence even among the Palestinian mainstream. Rather than offering hope, Israel's withdrawal from Gaza ended up creating an impoverished, unsupervised prison in which inmates preyed on one another. Mutual hostility between Israelis and Palestinians continued without respite, and violence became the two parties' main form of discourse. As of this writing, the conflict that broke out in 2000 has killed more than four thousand Palestinians and one thousand Israelis.

Compared with Iraq, the Israeli-Palestinian conflict presented important ingredients for an American success in the Middle East. It offered known players and a detailed diplomatic history, replete with proposals for solving the toughest issues, examples of success, and lessons on what pitfalls to avoid. Washington's community of Middle East experts, though often at odds with each other, offered a vast storehouse of knowledge, as did scholars at universities across the United States and in Europe. The experience of Bush's father was instructive. George H. W. Bush deeply offended members of the American Jewish community by appearing to question their loyalty at a time when he was exerting strong pressure on Israel to negotiate. This was a mistake any successor would want to avoid repeating. Yet he and his secretary of state, James A. Baker III, also provided a compelling example of how to achieve a diplomatic breakthrough in the Middle East. To them, the reward of direct Arab-Israeli peace talks stood at the end of a minefield of explosive obstacles. Carefully and systematically, over months, they moved along this minefield, defusing each of these obstacles, before bringing Israel to the negotiating table with its Arab adversaries in Madrid. The elder Bush improved the strategic environment for Israel in other ways: by containing Saddam Hussein, facilitating a massive influx of immigrants from the former Soviet Union, and winning repeal of a UN General Assembly resolution that equated Zionism and racism. As the State Department's longtime Middle East adviser Aaron Miller put it in an interview, "They were actually delivering things to the Israelis of real consequence."

The younger Bush saw little point in the kind of painstaking diplomacy practiced by either his father or Bill Clinton. By his own account, Bush drew a meaningful lesson from Clinton's experience: he learned that Yasser Arafat wasn't worth his time. "Listen, I always felt—first of all, I looked at the history of Mr. Arafat. Now, I saw what he did to President Clinton. There was no need to spend capital, unless you had an interlocutor who could deliver the Palestinian people toward peace," he told NBC news anchorman Tom Brokaw during an interview aboard Air Force One on April 25, 2003. Arafat became, in Bush's description, the chief impediment to peace and a reason for the United States to avoid involvement.

Arafat was an undeniable problem: he was a dissembler with one foot in violence. He skated to the edge of destruction, for himself and for his people's dreams, apparently thinking that by doing so he could get a better deal than the one offered verbally at Camp David. The Clinton team's ultimate, bitter disillusionment with him was a measure of its earlier misplaced faith.

Successful U.S. mediation does not depend on trust. It requires a shrewd measure of the interests, strengths, and weaknesses of both sides and reliable methods to monitor and enforce agreements. Arafat, like Sharon, brought useful strengths. He had an instinctive grasp of the popular mood among Palestinians and personified their struggle. Among the aides and cronies in his orbit were competent realists who had shown themselves in the past to be capable of carrying out commitments with his support. The several years leading up to Camp David were relatively tranquil ones, thanks largely to U.S.-monitored security cooperation between Israeli and Palestinian agencies.

The challenge for peace brokers was to empower Palestinian realists while not trampling on Arafat's iconic status. Once Bush humiliated Arafat and placed him beyond the pale, the old leader reacted in a way that could have been predicted: jealously protecting his prerogatives, he overruled or jettisoned the realists—most importantly, Mahmoud Abbas.

If the purpose of the peace process was only to secure rights and a better life for Palestinians, then Bush might have been justified in using Arafat's behavior as an excuse for abandoning the United States' mediating role. But helping Palestinians was never the main purpose. If the Palestinians were living next to a country that did not have such close and important ties to the United States, they never would have commanded as much American attention as they did. As Henry Kissinger famously put it in a different context, diplomacy isn't social work. And if it were, the genocide in Darfur would have triggered a stronger world response.

The purpose of the peace process was, first, to ensure Israel's long-term security. Israelis have endured too many decades of living under threat, surrounded by hatred. The United States long ago assumed a responsibility to keep Israel safe, to maintain its qualitative edge in weaponry, and to act as protector of last resort. But recent history has shown that U.S.-supplied bulldozers, attack helicopters, and F-16s can't, by themselves, provide a satisfactory level of security against a people fighting occupation. Used too often or too clumsily, these weapons fuel and prolong the hostility of Israel's adversaries, who in turn find new ways of inflicting damage.

Bush seemed to acknowledge as much when he spoke with Brokaw in 2003: "My view is, is that the only way for there to be peace and for the survival of Israel and for the hope of the Palestinian people is for two states living side by side in peace."

Peace between Israel and the Palestinians would not suddenly make Israel welcome in the Middle East. But it would remove a major cause of the widespread hostility toward the Jewish state, which persists even in the two countries, Jordan and Egypt, that have full diplomatic relations with Israel. It's not an original thought, but the conflict acts like an obstruction blocking wider progress in the region. It provides a platform for Muslim militants to agitate for an Islamic state and gives autocratic rulers an excuse to repress democrats and dissidents.

A second aim of the peace process was to help stabilize the most explosive and threatening part of the globe—and one that, by virtue of its underground oil wealth, is vital to the industrialized world. Stability would work to the advantage of both the United States and Israel. Extremists would be deprived of a major recruitment tool. Iran's ability to enlist allies in its fight against the United States would likely be more difficult.

In the zero-sum prism through which many people view U.S. policy toward the Middle East, Bush is seen as the most pro-Israel American president ever. Not only did he grant Israel broad latitude in combating Palestinian militants, but he was seen to be moving U.S. policy toward the Israeli position in the all-important calculus of final borders, refugees, and the status of Jerusalem.

Michael B. Oren, a respected historian at the Shalem Center in Jerusalem, said in an interview: "The Bush administration has ushered in a revolution in U.S.-Israel relations. It's a revolution that's happening at all levels. For the five decades in U.S.-Israel relations before Bush, American policy toward Israel and the core issue of the Arab-Israeli conflict [was] remarkably consistent, regardless of who was in the White House, Republican or Democrat."

Bush shifted or reversed the policy of previous presidents on these core issues, he said. In West Jerusalem, the United States is preparing ground for a new embassy, signaling that it will recognize Jerusalem as

Israel's capital. "The fact that the administration has come out and said Israel is the Jewish state and will remain the Jewish state—that's code. That's code for 'refugees won't be coming back in any large numbers.'" Bush has said Israel has the right to defend itself against terrorism, he added. And on territory, "Bush has flipped around the formula. If in the past the Arabs got territory before they gave peace, clearly now the Arabs have to give peace before they get any territory." Plus, "Bush is the first president since Johnson to say that Israel does not have to go back to the 1967 borders. . . ."

Oren's rundown highlights a key problem that has shadowed Israeli-Palestinian relations for years and severely undermined negotiations through much of the 1990s: every move toward or away from peace is observed through the prism of these all-important final-status issues and is seen as undercutting the claims of one side or the other. Oren's description of policy shifts under Bush obscures several important points: no peace will be lasting unless it balances the needs and inter-ests of both sides. As long as Israelis fear walking in Jerusalem, the Holy City won't give them the spiritual comfort they long for and deserve—regardless of what neighborhoods are sovereign Israeli territory. As long as Palestinian refugees remain scattered in camps across the region, they will be a source of instability and unrest. And if a durable peace can be achieved and ultimately bring about reconciliation, the precise lines of the border will fade in importance. The fact is that the territory occupied by both Israel and Palestine will be so small that an imper-meable barrier between the two would likely be unrealistic.

In other important ways, it could be argued that Bush was not such a good friend to Israel. Israel's strategic environment in some respects grew worse under his presidency. Because of the chaos in Iraq, the United States now has less leverage over Iran, which is viewed by Israel as an existential threat. Not only has Iran's ally Hezbollah regained its bearings in Lebanon, but Iran has gained a foothold in the West Bank and Gaza with the help of the Hamas-led government.

Israel was not helped by having its best friend and protector over-stretched militarily, bogged down in an unpopular war, and out of sync with much of the world in its approach to the Middle East. Bush's isolation on the question of the peace process became starkly evident in August 2006, at the annual summit of the Group of 8, representing the world's industrialized democracies and Russia. The G-8's communiqué on that summer's short, inconclusive war between Israel and Hezbollah contained a subtle repudiation of American policy: the leaders agreed that the "immediate crisis" stemmed from "efforts by extremist forces to destabilize the region." But they clearly stated: "The root cause of the problems in the region is the absence of a comprehensive Middle East peace."

By early 2007, a year after Ariel Sharon entered a coma at age seventy-seven and disappeared from the political stage, President Bush began to shift gears. Despite a Palestinian agreement on a unity government that joined Mahmoud Abbas's Fatah party with the militant Hamas movement, Secretary of State Condoleezza Rice went ahead and sponsored a three-way meeting between President Abbas and Israeli Prime Minister Ehud Olmert. She insisted that they talk about a "political horizon"—meaning the final-status issues that Israel and the United States had long kept off the table. Rice recognized that this was necessary to show the Palestinians they didn't need violence to gain a viable state. She explained to reporters that "this is something that people have been saying to us and I think they're right. Without a political horizon it is going to be difficult to show why this course, the course of Abu Mazen [Mahmoud Abbas], is better than other courses that others may try to get them [the Palestinians] to follow." Belatedly taking a cue from Bush's father and Bill Clinton, she pledged the administration to an ongoing effort: "[I]t takes hard work, it takes patience, it takes perseverance, it takes getting up, you know, after a bad day and trying to make a better day," she said in Jerusalem. "And that's what I'm going to do. So as long as I'm secretary of state, that's what I'm going to do. And that's what the president wants me to do, and I think the parties want me to do it, too. ... I'm not in this for—you know, to say oh, well, that's too hard or that's too complicated. It's always complicated in the Middle East." Left unsaid was that Olmert and Abbas were both too weak politically to take major risks for peace and that time was running out on the Bush presidency. It was probably too late to recoup from failure.

1

REPAIR WORK

■ 1990s ■

ON NOVEMBER 9, 1994, the day after winning his first election as governor of Texas, George W. Bush walked into his campaign's Houston headquarters and spotted Fred Zeidman, a friend, Republican fundraiser, devoted supporter of Israel, and advocate for Bush in the Jewish community. What he said struck Zeidman as strange, given its timing.

"The very first thing he said to me, after I congratulated him on being elected governor, was, 'Now let's go to Israel.' He wanted to go to Israel." Zeidman recalled his own surprise nearly a dozen years later, sitting in the Washington office he then occupied as chairman of the United States Holocaust Memorial Council. "He's always had this absolute passion for Israel. And I said, 'Great, no problem, we'll arrange it,' and then I immediately called Matt Brooks [who headed what is now called the Republican Jewish Coalition]. I said, 'The governor wants to go to Israel.'"

Zeidman wasn't alone in believing that Bush had a special feeling for the Jewish state. Through words and actions over the next decade, Bush would persuade a number of American Jews and Israelis of his rock-solid commitment to protecting Israel and, in tandem with that, to securing the future of the Jewish people.

Over time, the sheer repetition of the pledges of support for Israel, condemnations of anti-Israel terrorism, and willingness to defend Israel against nuclear threats from Iran would make them a part of Bush's public persona. Explaining why he supported Bush's reelection as president in 2004, former New York City mayor Edward Koch, a Democrat, said, "There's no question that George W. Bush . . . is the most supportive president in terms of support for Israel and its security needs."

How much of Bush's attitude stemmed from political calculation is hard to know, because the man is almost indistinguishable from the politician. As the scion of a political dynasty, Bush absorbed politics from early manhood and became one of the shrewdest political practitioners of his generation. Throughout his career, he has displayed a knack for emphasizing those parts of his life or character that carried political appeal among constituencies whose support he seeks. Bush's plainspoken drawl draws from his early boyhood in Midland, Texas, rather than the elite East Coast accents and speech patterns heard among relatives and at prep school and college. Similarly, he communicates his Christian faith in a way that makes him appear to be the soul mate of the Republican Party's growing base of conservative evangelical believers, rather than what he is—a member of the mainline and relatively liberal United Methodist denomination.

But for a man seeking to redeem his family's political stature, what Bush told Zeidman wasn't strange. Just two years had passed since Bush had seen his father defeated by Bill Clinton in a campaign dominated by the early 1990s economic recession, but also haunted by a bitter confrontation in 1991 between the elder Bush and American supporters of Israel. George H. W. Bush, president between 1988 and 1992, had the least comfortable relationship with Israel's government of any American president since Dwight Eisenhower. Determined to achieve a breakthrough in ending a half-century of Arab-Israeli conflict, he engaged in a months-long tug-of-war with the Israeli government, dominated by the right-wing Likud Party, which was then still determined to expand Jewish settlement in the Gaza Strip, West Bank, and East Jerusalem, all territories occupied by Israel in the 1967 war. To Bush, the settlements represented a serious obstacle to peace. Faced with defiance from then–Prime Minister Yitzhak Shamir, the elder Bush resorted to financial pressure, first delaying and then attaching restrictions on the loan guarantees Israel was seeking to house hundreds of thousands of Jews arriving from the former Soviet Union.

When, in September 1991, the Israel lobby attempted an end run, dispatching hundreds of its American supporters to Capitol Hill, Bush took them on as well. Summoning the news media, he portrayed himself as "one lonely little guy down here" up against "powerful political forces" and "something like a thousand lobbyists." As top aides winced, he said, "I think the American people will support me."

He recounted what his administration had done for Israel: "Just months ago, American men and women in uniform risked their lives to defend Israelis in the face of Iraqi Scud missiles, and indeed, Desert Storm, while winning a war against aggression, also achieved the defeat of Israel's most dangerous adversary. And during the current fiscal year alone, and despite our own economic problems, the United States provided Israel with more than $4 billion in economic and military aid, nearly $1,000 for every Israeli man, woman, and child, as well as with $400 million in loan guarantees to facilitate immigrant absorption." He didn't mention that Israel, going against its military doctrine of swift and fierce retaliation, had bowed to pressure from the White House and avoided any response to the Scud attacks.

Bush aides felt especially peeved at Ariel Sharon, who, as housing minister, not only pressed ahead full tilt with settlement construction but publicly opposed American plans for an international peace conference that would open direct negotiations between Israel and Arabs. Sharon said Bush was falling into an "Arab trap" aimed at stopping immigration to Israel.

The pressure from the elder Bush worked. The pro-Israel lobby retreated. Brent Scowcroft, the president's national security adviser, felt Bush had sent a "useful signal" that he wouldn't be deterred by lobbyists, however powerful. The U.S. administration prevailed in launching a peace process that ultimately led to an Israeli-Palestinian breakthrough in 1993 and an Israeli-Jordanian peace treaty the following year.

But many American Jews never forgave the president for the tone of his remarks, which to them came painfully close to questioning their patriotism and reviving the anti-Semitic stereotype of an all-powerful, manipulative interest group. His harsh words undercut the goodwill he might deservedly have won for helping hundreds of thousands of Soviet Jews and thousands more Ethiopians to move to Israel; defeating and seriously weakening one of Israel's worst Arab enemies, Saddam Hussein; and campaigning to undo the infamous 1975 United Nations General Assembly resolution that labeled Zionism a form of racism.

"When the president stood up and said, I think incorrectly, in the loan guarantees, 'I'm one guy here against a thousand lobbyists,' no matter what he did from there, he could never do any right," Matthew Brooks, head of the Republican Jewish Coalition, said in a 2005 interview. Significantly, Brooks could quote the former president's stinging words almost verbatim a decade and a half after they were uttered.

Israel's ambassador to Washington during that period, Zalman Shoval, also felt the White House lash after complaining publicly, in an interview with Reuters correspondent Alan Elsner in early 1991, that his country was getting the "runaround" on U.S. financial aid. The ugliest episode of that period was a furor over a quote attributed to Secretary of State James A. Baker III in a newspaper column by former New York mayor Koch. Koch wrote: "When Baker was criticized recently at a meeting of high-level White House advisers for his belligerent attitude toward Israel, he responded, 'F— 'em. They [the Jews] didn't vote for us.'" The account was vehemently denounced as "garbage" by Baker's spokeswoman, but a similar quote was reported by New York Times columnist William Safire, who claimed to have two high-level sources who'd heard it. To many Israelis and American backers of Israel, the words accurately summed up the Bush-Baker attitude—even if they were never uttered. As Ehud Olmert, then a cabinet minister, told Israel Radio, "I can only judge the issue by the report and its denial. I have no way of knowing whether he said such words or not. I have no doubt that the current administration is not sympathetic to Israel and does not count on the support of the Jews in the U.S. domestic political arena."

While the Jewish electorate is too small to be decisive in most national elections, it can be an important factor in a close contest because of a few swing states with relatively large Jewish populations. Jews vote in high numbers and play an active and important fundraising role in both the Republican and Democratic parties. By the fall of the following year, the elder Bush's reelection campaign was in trouble, the victim of a slow start, bad organization, and, most important, a weak national economy. Struggling to repair the damage he had caused in the Jewish community, he told a B'nai B'rith convention in September 1992, "There may even be issues where you and I will take opposing sides and things may get hot and words may be exchanged. In the past, I'll never forget this one, some remarks of mine were, I felt, misinterpreted. I have gone on the record expressing my regret for any pain those words caused. Again I want to make it clear, I support, I endorse, and I deeply believe in the God-given right of every American to promote what they believe. It is your right as an individual. It's more than a right. It's your duty as an American citizen." He also reflected the personal hurt he felt in being labeled an anti-Semite. "[T]o accuse those who may come to different conclusions on one or another public issue of harboring anti-Semitism is to cheapen the term. That is dangerous. That is deeply wrong. And when those words, without justice, have been aimed at me, I can tell you, they cut right to the heart."

This late repair effort failed. From winning 30 percent of the Jewish vote in 1988, Bush dropped to 12 percent when he lost to Bill Clinton four years later, a change widely attributed to the White House clash with the pro-Israel lobby. Neither the elder Bush nor his son has said much publicly about the dispute with Israel and its political ramifications. But George H. W. Bush told an audience at Tufts University in 2003: "I remember refusing to give Israel loan guarantees for settlements, if they continued to build settlements in the occupied territories. I said, 'We're not going to do it.' And I paid a hell of a price for it. . . ."

The lesson was not lost on his son. Scowcroft recalled, "I came to the conclusion that he thought his father had caused himself some trouble." The elder Bush, by coincidence, was the third president in recent years, following Jimmy Carter and Gerald Ford, who both clashed with Israel and failed to win reelection.

George W. Bush jokes good-naturedly about his lackluster college grades. But he was a keen student of politics who made a special effort to understand what was important to various constituencies. Doug Wead, who acted as liaison to conservative Christians for the first President Bush and also befriended George W., recalled the son drifting to sleep one night when Wead read the Bible with him. But on another occasion, "When I did a twenty-page paper on evangelicals in Texas, he just lit up," Wead said. Bush devoured even the minute details of the polling data. "He said, 'This is the missing piece. All I needed for Texas,'" the former adviser said.

Bush took a similar approach in trying to understand how his father had lost support among Jews. "We spent lots of time talking about it. I've said to him over and over again—way before he was president—that his father got a very bad rap," Zeidman said in the 2006 interview. "President Bush 43 understood very well his issues in the Jewish community. And arguably, the Bush family relationship in the Mideast . . . I mean, that was the problem that 43 had when he was running. Everybody thought he was his father's son.

"Over and over and over again, the president said, 'What was the problem with my father?' I said, 'Wasn't the problem with your father, it was the problem of our community. Our community basically feels if you don't do everything that our community wants—and they don't even know what that is—that you're against us.'"

Brooks had similar conversations with the future president. "What was it about my dad's administration that hurt us in the Jewish community? What didn't resonate?" he recalled being asked by George W. The query stemmed "more from a political science–sociological point of view rather than a father-son point of view. He was particularly dispassionate about the subject, so far as there wasn't a lot of emotion. He was just trying to intellectually understand. It's not, 'Why are they beating up on my daddy?'"

Brooks's own assessment was that there had been "a tremendous failure of communication. They just never quite understood how they could communicate to the Jewish community. They had a tin ear on how to communicate to the Jewish community."

He says he explained to George W. Bush that "the Jewish community is a community which listens for every nuance, which listens for every code word, which listens to how elected leaders say things, to look for signals and hidden messages—more so probably than any other community and constituency in the country. You either know how to calibrate your language to communicate at that level or you don't. People who are particularly good at it are rewarded with great friendship, and people who don't. . . ." Brooks didn't complete the sentence.

The younger Bush made his own verbal misstep. In a 1993 interview in Dallas, Bush told of asking the Reverend Billy Graham to referee a discussion with his mother over a passage in the New Testament. Based on the text, Bush argued that only people who accept Jesus Christ as their personal savior could expect to go to heaven. Barbara Bush disagreed. Graham urged both of them not to attempt to play God.

Bush's view may have matched the beliefs of many evangelical Christians, but it offended Jews. Abraham Foxman, national director of the Anti-Defamation League of B'nai B'rith, later indicated that Bush had rebuffed his attempts to get him to correct the damaging impression. "We had exchanges a number of years ago which went nowhere," Foxman told the *Austin American-Statesman* in 1998.

Despite the younger Bush's expressed eagerness to visit Israel, four years would elapse from the time of his conversation with Zeidman before he found it politically convenient to make the trip. "There was a lot of pressure on him as governor of Texas not to leave the state. . . . We couldn't arrange the trip for a while because the state of Texas— everybody in your profession [journalism]—was watching his every move and felt like he ought to be at home running the state and not out running around the world," Zeidman said.

Improving ties with American Jewry was clearly on Bush's mind in January 1998, when Foxman met with him in Austin, the Texas capital, and mentioned the 1993 interview. "When I was in Texas and visited with him, he raised the issue. He said, 'Listen, I have this problem.' I said, 'You need to deal with it,'" according to the *Austin American-Statesman*.

The governor's political calculations coincided with a movement within the Republican Party away from the policies of Bush's father, which were aimed at forging a lasting peace between Israel and all its Arab neighbors and stressed a balanced attention to the needs of all parties. By late 1998, while the Clinton administration pursued much the same approach in hopes of a comprehensive settlement involving Israel, the Palestinians, and Syria, the return of a conservative Likud government to power in Israel had deepened a split in the American Jewish community.

American Jews who backed the peace process continued supporting Clinton, and Jews remained overwhelmingly Democratic. But those who shared the Likud's distrust of Arab intentions increasingly turned to the GOP. Zalman Shoval, still active in the Likud, made frequent visits to Washington and kept in touch with out-of-power Republicans. "People in the political desert appreciate it when diplomats don't neglect them," he said. A vocal and intellectually powerful group of Republican neo-conservatives, both Jews and gentiles, recoiled at attempts by the Clinton administration to humanize Yasser Arafat's image and the modest pressure he exerted on Israeli prime minister Benjamin Netanyahu. They viewed the Clinton policies as a tilt against Israel and toward appeasement of Palestinians.

Instead of Arab-Israeli peace talks, GOP hawks campaigned in the media and in Congress for a new Middle East strategy: completing the job left unfinished when the elder Bush went to war against Iraq—ousting the regime of Saddam Hussein. Meanwhile, ties deepened among right-wing Israelis, conservative American Jews, and the evangelical Christians who were exerting ever-greater influence within the GOP.

Three events in January 1998 crystallized the trend and provided an important backdrop to Bush's trip and his future campaign. In mid-January 1998, Aaron Miller, one of the State Department's most determined advocates of Israeli-Palestinian peace, sparked a furor with his suggestion that Washington's Holocaust Memorial Museum extend a VIP invitation to Arafat—both as a gesture of reconciliation and as a way of acquainting Arafat with the horrors of Jewish history. Miller had the clout to suggest the visit, not only as a prominent diplomat, but as a State Department representative to the museum's board. His family, prosperous Cleveland real estate developers, were also major donors to the museum. The idea produced a bitter split within the board, led to the firing of the museum's director, and caused the board chairman to flip-flop, first rejecting special treatment for Arafat and then issuing an invitation, by which point Arafat bowed out of the visit. Among those outraged at the invitation was prominent neoconservative columnist Charles Krauthammer, who called it an "act of desecration."

Arriving in Washington a few days later for meetings at the White House, Netanyahu moved immediately to highlight his own links with the Christian Right. To what the *New York Times* described as "thunderous applause," he joined a rally of Voices United for Israel, featuring the Reverend Jerry Falwell, one of Clinton's harshest critics, who compared the prime minister to conservative icon Ronald Reagan. On the dais sat Morton Klein, executive director of the Zionist Organization of America, a veteran lobbyist against concessions to Arafat and a strong supporter of Israeli settlement in the occupied territories.

Then, on January 26, advocates for a tougher policy against Iraq coalesced around a public call on Clinton to make regime change a top priority. In an open letter to the president sponsored by the Project for the New American Century, led by neoconservative guru William Kristol, the group urged Clinton to "enunciate a new strategy that would secure the interests of the United States and our friends and allies around the world. That strategy should aim, above all, at the removal of Saddam Hussein's regime from power." Signers included future advisers to the Bush campaign and key members of his administration.

More than an appeal to Clinton, the project's manifesto marked an early salvo in the struggle to shape the foreign policy of the next Republican administration.

Bush never shut out more moderate views. Early in the planning stages of his campaign he invited Rita Hauser, who would cochair his campaign in New York, to Austin for a meeting with other supporters. A wealthy international lawyer who was close to Scowcroft and leaders of the Israeli Labor Party, Hauser had been a pioneer among American Jews in promoting a dialogue between the United States and the Palestine Liberation Organization in the late 1980s.

"Maybe I wanted to hear, but I certainly heard it, as did others, at least when he was getting ready to run, he was going to pursue a realistic foreign policy, something like his father's," she recalled in a 2005 interview at her office off New York's Fifth Avenue. "Certainly I had very high hopes that he would be somewhat as his father and Baker were in trying to get a balanced approach to the Palestine-Israel problem, by pressing on both sides to do what was required and that was to resurrect in some measure the Oslo process, which was languishing, since neither side was respecting it, and move forward on a negotiated basis."

As the campaign progressed, it became clear Bush would approach the Middle East and the peace process differently from Clinton. Dov Zakheim, a campaign adviser and national-security expert who would later become Pentagon comptroller under Bush, said, "Most people thought Arafat was a problem."

The campaign itself avoided criticizing Clinton's last-ditch struggle to broker a peace agreement. "I personally had a lot of misgivings about it; many people did, thinking they were rushing something, that Arafat wasn't going to agree, but we didn't [criticize] because we felt we wanted to convey to both Arab Americans and Jewish Americans that our Middle East policy was bipartisan, in that all we're trying to do is get peace for the region, and if Clinton could pull it off, good luck." Still, Zakheim told Jewish groups he spoke with, " 'If you want to measure the difference, count how many times Bush is going to invite Arafat to the White House as opposed to how many times Clinton did.' I told that to Jewish groups . . . throughout the campaign."

Hauser would go on to become a member of the President's Foreign Intelligence Advisory Board, chaired by Scowcroft, during Bush's first presidential term. The prestigious post gave her the chance, on occasion, to press her views on the Middle East conflict in conversations with National Security Adviser Condoleezza Rice. It also allowed her to compare U.S. intelligence on Iraq with the way the threat from Saddam Hussein was being portrayed publicly by the Bush administration. She refused to support Bush's 2004 reelection.

2

FIRST IMPRESSIONS
■ 1998 ■

THE IDEA OF A Bush visit to Israel, broached in 1994 by the newly elected governor, resurfaced in June 1998, when Dore Gold, Israel's envoy to the United Nations, met with him for an hour on a visit to Texas and extended an invitation. Israeli media reported that Netanyahu's national security adviser, Uzi Arad, had also visited the governor as part of a government effort to get to know the likely future presidential hopeful.

Bush decided to make the trip once he was safely reelected as governor that November. The announcement did not make big news. Numerous ambitious American politicians avail themselves of similar opportunities to show an interest in and solidarity with the perpetually embattled Jewish state. It was the kind of trip that Israel's committed and energetic network of American supporters was adept at sponsoring, and that Israeli officials were eager to host with tours and briefings. Like Taiwan, another small and threatened country heavily dependent on U.S. goodwill and security assurances, Israel—with its American friends—courted supporters at all levels of American public life, from sheriffs to Senate leaders.

But the stakes were higher for Bush's visit, since it was immediately interpreted as a sign that he would run for president. If Bush wanted to improve on his father's relationship with Israel and the Jewish community, so did the Israeli government and Jewish Republicans. Brooks, of the National Jewish Coalition (which later became the Republican Jewish Coalition) took charge of the planning, together with Mel Sembler, a highly successful developer of shopping centers in the southeastern United States and Puerto Rico.

Like Zeidman, Sembler had remained loyal to the Bush family through the crisis with American Jewry. When the dispute between then President Bush and the pro-Israel lobby erupted in 1991, he was half a world away, enjoying a reward for raising $100,000 for GOP coffers by serving as ambassador to Australia. He helped Jeb Bush's unsuccessful 1994 campaign for the Florida governorship and subsequent establishment of a think tank to keep Jeb in the public eye. He supported Dick Cheney early in the 1996 presidential race and then, when Cheney dropped out, backed another former Bush cabinet member, Lamar Alexander. He became the GOP's national finance chairman in 1997 and was later appointed by George W. Bush as U.S. envoy to Italy.

Sembler, in turn, consulted about details of Bush's trip to Israel with Zalman Shoval, who was then on his second tour as Israel's ambassador to Washington.

"There were no Texans on the trip . . . so that there was never any issue about which Texas friends got to go and which didn't," Zeidman said. Three other governors were included: Paul Cellucci of Massachusetts, Mike Leavitt of Utah, and Marc Racicot of Montana. But it was clear among Republicans and Israelis that the purpose of the visit was to introduce a likely presidential candidate to Israel's leaders.

"It was built around the governor, and I can tell you that it was at his request that the whole thing started," Zeidman said. A Republican strategist described the trip to *U.S. News and World Report* as "a mutual courting between him and the Jewish community." The strategist, who was not identified, added, "He's doing it partly because of the Jewish community's problems with his father."

After he decided to go, Bush touched base with another friend in the Texas GOP, State Senator Florence Shapiro, whose paternal grandparents had been killed by the Nazis, along with many other members of their family. Shapiro became the second Jewish state senator in Texas following a campaign in which a swastika was painted on one of her campaign billboards. "His expectations were very high," she remembered of Bush's call, although he really did not know what the trip would bring.

Bush offered little public explanation for traveling to Israel. Beyond viewing the trip as politically driven, neither the Texas nor the national media showed much interest in exploring the itinerary in detail or in quizzing Bush about what policies he would adopt toward the Middle East. He said he had been interested in visiting Israel because "it is the Holy Land, and secondly because Israel is a longtime friend of the United States. Obviously it's an area of international focus, and I want to learn more about it." Besides high-tech trade, Bush said he was interested in learning about Israeli defense. "It'll help explain why Israel is so security conscious. . . . It'll broaden my perspective," he said. He also looked forward to "seeing firsthand the roots of my religion."

Bush didn't touch on the Arab-Israeli peace process, which a month before had been rescued from near collapse by President Clinton, who brokered a new agreement between Israeli prime minister Benjamin Netanyahu and Palestinian leader Yasser Arafat at the Wye Plantation on Maryland's Eastern Shore. The pact, pulled together after tense and exhausting negotiations, was aided by the pragmatic negotiating skills of retired General Ariel Sharon, who had recently been named foreign minister, and a dramatic intervention by King Hussein of Jordan, then just months away from dying of cancer. It called for an Israeli withdrawal from 13 percent of the West Bank and a new Palestinian crackdown on militants, to be overseen by the U.S. Central Intelligence Agency.

A wisecrack a few weeks before his trip revealed that Bush still had something to learn about others' religious sensitivities. He made it while chatting with reporters at the Republican governors conference in New Orleans in November. The *American-Statesman* recounted: "As he gazed out a hotel hallway at the Superdome and waited for an elevator, Bush—clearly going for a laugh at his own expense—said the first thing he was going to say to Israeli Jews was that they were all 'going to hell.'" Foxman, told of the remark a few weeks later, called it "inappropriate."

"Religion is serious. . . . Comedians can joke about it. I think serious people, people in leadership positions, people who set a role model for behavior and values—that's something not to joke about."

Bush has seldom, if ever, mentioned his father in connection with Israel and the Middle East conflict. While he clearly wanted to know how his father had lost support among American Jews, both men have been circumspect about what advice, if any, he sought on policymaking or diplomacy from the former president. But before traveling to Israel, he took a day out of a family vacation in Italy to fly to Cairo and join his father at a meeting with Egyptian president Hosni Mubarak, a loyal friend and ally from the Gulf War.

The elder Bush was quoted as saying, "He learned from that eighty minutes with President Mubarak more than he could possibly have learned from reading textbooks on the Middle East." At the time, Egyptians were becoming frustrated with what they called the "negative" approach toward the peace process by Israel's right-wing government. The elder Bush himself was worried about continued roadblocks in the process he had launched seven years earlier, according to a United Press International account. Speaking to a Cairo audience, he said, "I confess to you I'm concerned . . . about the peace process. There seems to be a lack of trust between the parties. And in many quarters the U.S. sometimes would seem to be less than fair." At the meeting with Mubarak, the younger Bush let the two elder statesmen do most of the talking, although it's unclear how much substance was discussed. A fellow guest was Daniel Kurtzer, the U.S. ambassador to Egypt, whom Bush would later greet with a reminder of their shared passion for baseball. In a 2006 e-mail, Kurtzer wrote: "The central character of the visit was Bush 41, and he and Mubarak spent much time reminiscing."

The Israel that welcomed Bush had just passed its half-century mark and faced a crisis of confidence. Historians were looking more critically at how the Israeli military had forced Palestinians to flee their towns and villages in 1948, exposing unpleasant truths that undercut the long-accepted national narrative of an infant state acting purely in self-defense. The peace process with Syria was moribund. Faith in the peace process with the Palestinians had been shaken by violent opposition in both populations. Prime Minister Yitzhak Rabin was shot to death in 1995 by a right-wing Israeli. A rash of Palestinian suicide bombings in 1996 killed and wounded Israelis and exposed the limits of Palestinian leader Yasser Arafat's ability or willingness to rein in dissidents.

Frightened and disillusioned, Israeli voters that year brought the Likud back into power in a government led by the glib but politically unsteady Benjamin Netanyahu. The weak trust that had developed between Israeli and Palestinian leaders began eroding further as Netanyahu tried to satisfy his right-wing supporters. Bloody riots erupted after he agreed to open a tourist tunnel in the Old City adjacent to a site holy to both Jews and Muslims, the Temple Mount/Haram al-Sharif. He not only allowed settlement expansion but encouraged a provocative new development between Jerusalem and Bethlehem called Har Homa that was viewed by Palestinians as a move to sever links between their hoped-for capital in East Jerusalem and the West Bank. Netanyahu was intent on showing Palestinians that their dream of a state on 22 percent of historic Palestine was a nonstarter. If Palestinians continued to demand a state that combined all the territory occupied by Israel, with half of Jerusalem as its capital, "that will not produce a solution. . . . It will produce, ultimately, a breakdown," Netanyahu told a Washington audience in 1997.

U.S. president Bill Clinton found himself repeatedly frustrated with Netanyahu, who kept resisting the phased withdrawals from occupied West Bank territory called for by the Oslo accords. But Clinton shrank from the kind of heavy-handed pressure the elder Bush had used against Yitzhak Shamir. He remained popular with many Israelis because of earlier dramatic gestures of support, like flying to the Middle East to organize a counterterrorism conference after the 1996 bombings. But his determination to push the peace process forward grated on the Israeli right wing, which has always preferred American policymakers who treat Israel simply as an ally and adopt a more hands-off stance on Israeli-Arab relations.

At one point, Clinton snubbed Netanyahu outright, refusing to see him at the White House when the prime minister traveled to the United States. For part of 1998, he refused to take the Israeli's calls. In turn, the

Israeli government and its conservative backers in the United States watched in fury and frustration as onetime terrorist pariah Arafat met regularly with Clinton in the White House and was received as a statesman around the world. Administration officials believed that by lavishing attention on Arafat and appealing to his vanity, they would win his continued cooperation. As long as Netanyahu obstructed U.S. plans, Arafat was happy to oblige.

In a political triumph for the Palestinians, Clinton agreed to come to Gaza to deliver a speech and to witness the fulfillment of an Israeli demand—ratification by the PLO's executive body of a change in the PLO charter. The change would remove parts inconsistent with the Oslo accords, particularly a Palestinian claim to all of Palestine. Clinton would land by helicopter at Gaza's new international airport, seen by Palestinians as an important symbol of their sovereignty and emerging statehood. His visit would take place ten days after Bush's.

As Arafat basked in his new stature, Israel continued to struggle for what, outside the United States, was an elusive goal: international acceptance, or, as the title of a 1993 book by Netanyahu put it, a "place among the nations." Isolated from much of the surrounding region, ordinary Israelis got a chilly reception even in the two Arab nations with which their country had a formal peace treaty, Egypt and Jordan. Nowhere was Israel reminded of its diplomatic challenge more often than in the General Assembly of the United Nations. There, PLO diplomats turned the tables on Israel in their zero-sum contest, deftly mobilizing Arab and developing-world allies to focus attention on Israel's alleged misdeeds. Israel continued to hold second-class status within the world body as a whole, frozen out of the regional groupings that would allow it an occasional seat alongside nonpermanent members of the Security Council and, with that, some leverage over UN decisions. A variety of UN offices and instruments served to highlight the Palestinian cause at Israel's expense. An annual day of solidarity with Palestinians amounted to ritualistic Israel-bashing.

That day, November 29, marked the anniversary of the 1947 General Assembly resolution partitioning Palestine into two states—one Arab and one Jewish—"the oldest unresolved issue on our organization's agenda," as the assembly's president put it in 1998. That year, it fell on a Sunday, which was also the first full day of Bush's visit in Israel with his fellow governors.

In a General Assembly debate the next day, Palestinian representative Farouk Kaddoumi, a hard-liner who never accepted the Oslo accords, delivered a slashing broadside against the "racist Netanyahu." Belittling the Jews' attachment to the ancient land of Israel, he claimed that the Likud government intended to keep permanent control over 60 percent of the Palestinian territories. Then he asked rhetorically, in an unmistakable allusion to the Nazis, "Is this the final solution from Israel's perspective?"

While Netanyahu continued to act in ways Americans viewed as both clumsy and slick, Sharon was making a remarkable comeback in Washington, where the elder Bush had shunned him a decade earlier. His appointment by Netanyahu as foreign minister in October 1998, just before the Wye Plantation peace talks, put Sharon prominently on the world stage for the first time since he was ousted as defense minister in 1983. Providing valuable right-wing political cover for Netanyahu, Sharon brought to the table his own pragmatic negotiating skills and a solid relationship with a Washington ally, King Hussein, both of which helped nail down the Wye accords. And he did this without betraying his own supporters; while negotiating across the table from Palestinians, he refused to shake Arafat's hand. He also kept the cabinet portfolio of "national infrastructure," which allowed him to continue planning and building roads and water and power lines for settlements in the occupied territories. Like Bush, he was a careful student of politics. He was learning how to bring his famed tactical prowess—which had served him so well in battle and his own public resurrection—to his relations with the United States.

Martin Indyk, who served as a top Middle East adviser to Clinton in three different posts and clashed publicly with Netanyahu, won over Sharon by helping to rehabilitate him in Washington. "I had an excellent relationship with him because I was the one who broke the taboo. You know, for ten years he was persona non grata in Washington, and when I was assistant secretary of state, I hosted him at the State Department. That was his first meeting since 1982."

Had Netanyahu's governing coalition not been fracturing in November, Sharon might have been absent from Israel for most of Bush's visit. To help shore up the government, Sharon canceled his participation at a Washington donors' conference set up to raise hundreds of millions of dollars for the Palestinians following the Wye accords. Sharon himself was expected to seek as much as $4 billion over ten years for a major regional desalination plant serving Israel, the Palestinians, Jordan, and possibly Syria. The mutual dependence generated by such a project would promote peace, he argued. At the time, Israel controlled major West Bank and Gaza aquifers. Remaining in Jerusalem let Sharon play an expansive and memorable role in Bush's trip.

Sharon's opportunity was Yasser Arafat's missed chance, and, as it turned out, his only chance to meet with Bush. By the late 1990s, it had become common for prominent American visitors to Israel to make a brief detour to Gaza or Ramallah to see Arafat or other Palestinian leaders. But Bush and his delegation didn't. Arafat was in Washington for the donors' conclave for much of the governors' visit. Organizers of the Bush trip were understandably most interested in fostering good relations between the governor and Israel. But one of them said, though not for quotation, that they had made repeated efforts to arrange a meeting, either with Arafat or a senior aide, without success, and that the Palestinian leadership never really made an effort to make a meeting happen.

Saeb Erekat, a longtime Arafat aide and interlocutor with Washington, remembers it differently. "I remember we were willing to meet with Governor Bush. They said to us, as I recall, that the schedule was very tight," he recounted in a 2006 telephone call to his home in Jericho. "President Arafat would have been very happy to meet with him . . . I think we called about a meeting and they apologized." Under Arafat's autocratic and disorganized governing style, subordinates may have been afraid to reach out to Bush on their own while their leader was out of town. Years later, Racicot speculated that Bush took this as an early sign that the Palestinian leader couldn't be relied upon. "The very first thing he ever did [in relation to Bush] was leave when he had the chance to meet. I've always felt that one of the reasons the president said we need a dependable partner [on the Palestinian side]—the genesis was that first encounter." When the two men both came to the United Nations at the same time three years later, Bush refused to meet with Arafat.

The governors' three-day visit mixed policy and tourism. In brief comments to the press while meeting with Israeli president Ezer Weizman, Bush said, "I came to learn not only about Israel, but also about the history of my religion." He easily dismissed questions about his possible presidential run ("I am not here for any political purpose"), but a member of his party saw the governor's jaw tighten in anger when he was asked about Palestinians. *Newsweek* reported that Bush was angered by Palestinian charges that he didn't want to meet with them and took this as an early sign of the Palestinian leader's mendacity. Other press accounts, however, indicate Bush was asked to respond to Palestinian complaints about his plan to visit Jewish settlements.

Bush and his wife, Laura, shared a hotel room that looked out on the walls of the Old City of Jerusalem, Jaffa Gate, and the dominant David's Citadel tower. He toured the Church of the Holy Sepulchre and the Western Wall, drawing crowds of American tourists, shopkeepers, and Israeli soldiers. The Associated Press's Laurie Copans reported, "As Bush walked through the Muslim quarter of the Old City, several Palestinians recognized him and bid him to stop and talk or have coffee. If the delegation heard the invitations, they did not respond."

Some religious pilgrims can be overwhelmed, even to the point of instability, by icons of Judeo-Christian heritage in the Holy City. Others can point to precise biblical references. But according to Doug Wead, Bush's own belief was more personal and mystical. "He was not impressed by the clutter of history," Wead said. The core of Bush's faith was belief in redemption: "He was a drinker. God turned his life around."

The "most moving moment," Bush later told Wead, came when the group stopped at the Mount of Beatitudes, the hillside with a sweeping command of the Sea of Galilee, where Christ is believed to have delivered the Sermon on the Mount. Members of the delegation took turns reading aloud from favorite religious passages. Wead was surprised to hear Bush tell him later that he had chosen "Amazing Grace," a hymn of redemption, rather than any lines from the Bible.

At a dinner in Jerusalem followed by dessert at the prime minister's house, Bush was said to get along well with the sharp-witted, Americanized Netanyahu, whose views on economics closely matched those of the future president. A meeting with new Labor leader Ehud Barak went less well; Shoval was told that he "talked down" to the governors. In a series of briefings by ministers, defense chief Yitzhak Mordechai reminded Bush of unfinished business from the Gulf War, according to the *Jerusalem Post*: "We in Israel very much admire your father President Bush for the brave stance he took in the Gulf War. But Saddam Hussein is still president and this symbolizes more than anything the absurdities of the region in which we live." He also warned of a threat from Iran.

Sharon presented a map of the latest partial withdrawal from the West Bank and "briefed the governors on Israel's security needs and the principles guiding its aspirations for peace agreements with the neighboring Arab states and the Palestinians," according to a statement, which however did not spell out those needs and principles. According to the *Jerusalem Post*, Bush asked Sharon during the briefing about the U.S. contribution to the peace process. Sharon's careful reply, paraphrased in his statement, suggested that Americans should rebuff Palestinian attempts to pull them into the crucial talks still to come on statehood, borders, Jerusalem, and refugees. "Sharon stressed the contribution of the U.S. over the years, without which it would not have been possible to conclude the various peace agreements. However, he added that the sides must try to reach agreement on their own before seeking American assistance."

Longtime Sharon aide Raanan Gissin said Sharon was content to hold a meeting with Bush in his office. "I said to him, 'Listen: You're at your best when you explain in the air, with a helicopter ride, so he can see the Land of Israel.' I said, 'Who knows? . . . The worst that could happen is that you gave a helicopter ride to one of the candidates. But the best that could happen [is] that one day this man could become president.' And that convinced him."

Sharon was indeed practiced at giving helicopter tours of Israel and the occupied territories. Two decades earlier, he conducted one for a newly arrived American ambassador, Samuel Lewis. "When I first went to Israel in '77 and met him, he was then agriculture minister and [Prime Minister Menachem] Begin had given him carte blanche to develop the settlement project. He launched a campaign which lasted until the Lebanon war, in which he tried very hard to convince me, to co-opt me to his concept of how to deal with the territories, thinking I might have some influence in Washington, I guess. And he invited me early on to let him show me the settlement problem. So I had the helicopter trip early on, and we landed on top of that high hilltop or low mountain right close to Tulkarem, where he got out *the map* and spread it out on the ground and showed me exactly what he intended to do. And that's the same map he carried around for the rest of his life."

Years after his 1998 visit to Israel, speaking before the Republican Jewish Coalition in Washington, Bush described Sharon's next move: "And after the briefing he introduced himself. He said, 'Would you like to go on a helicopter ride and take a look at the West Bank?' " Here Bush adopted a facial expression conveying skepticism. "I said, 'Are you flying?' 'No'—(laughter from the crowd). I said, 'You bet.' "

In fact, the Foreign Ministry had already released advance word of the tour to the press, drawing protests from the Palestinians about plans to stop at two Jewish settlements: Alfei Menashe, east of the armistice line near the Palestinian town of Qalqilya, and Kohav Hashahar, on a rise west of the Jordan Valley. From each, Bush could have seen vistas displaying Israel's vulnerability to attack: from one, the country's narrow midsection along the Mediterranean coast; from the other, the access that Arab armies could gain coming from Jordan across the West Bank.

Palestinians feared the tour would serve to legitimize the settlements, considered illegal by much of the world. The U.S. embassy in Tel Aviv weighed in to discourage setting the helicopter down in the West Bank as part of an official Israeli tour. Hasty negotiations ensued among the Israelis, Brooks, and Sembler, resulting in a clever move to sidestep the problem.

"I had a big argument about that because they didn't want the helicopters to land on occupied territory, so to speak," said Gissin, speaking in a 2005 interview. "So we came to a compromise. I said, 'They'll only hover. They'll be hovering over the ground. They won't touch the ground.' "

The solution still allowed Sharon to make his point as he sat in the lead helicopter with Bush and Montana governor Racicot.

"They really went very low to show the Jordan River, to show the strategic importance of the ridges overlooking the Jordan River which must be controlled and the narrow waist of the state of Israel," Gissin said. "And the president was very much impressed by the geographical dimensions." 'Gee,' he said, 'I never realized that Israel is so small.' " When Bush was told of Israel's width at its narrowest point (less than ten miles), he is said to have quipped that in Texas, there were driveways longer than that.

Wearing headphones with microphones to communicate over the helicopter noise, Bush and Racicot listened as Sharon identified important scenes from Israel's multiple wars.

"It was like living history through the eyes of a witness who was in a position to talk about what had occurred since the state of Israel came into existence," Racicot said in an interview in 2006. Sharon described Israeli-Syrian tank battles on the Golan Heights, which were captured by Israel in 1967, invaded by Syria in 1973, and then recovered by Israel in the October 1973 Yom Kippur war after a bloody fight. Racicot, interviewed by telephone eight years later, recalled with admiration how Sharon "knew every detail [of the landscape], the aquifers, settlements." And he pointed out where he had fought as a soldier in the wars of 1948 and 1967, and the Yom Kippur War. "The life experiences he had been through were remarkable," said Racicot, himself a veteran.

The three men conversed easily. Sharon, casually dressed, belied his headstrong "bulldozer" image. He was, Racicot said, "extraordinarily interesting, soft-spoken, understated," as well as patient. "There was so much to know—thousands of years of human history compressed into a small piece of the planet."

Racicot also came away with a relatively benign view of the settlement enterprise. "I don't think you could refute the fact that those who were willing to live in those settlements had immense courage. . . . [Sharon] believed in the possibility that people living side by side could develop a heightened level of understanding and tolerance. . . ." On the prospects for peace, Sharon indicated there would be adequate movement on Israel's part "if there was adequate security."

Bush, speaking to the Republican Jewish Coalition in 2005, reflected on the tour in a way certain to appeal to Sharon's admirers: "It's interesting how history works, isn't it? In 1998, fall of 1998, the future president of the United States and the future prime minister of Israel were flying across the—across that country, with him describing to me how to keep Israel secure. A couple of lessons I took away from there—is, one, you know, how tiny the country is. You know, a guy from Texas, we got a lot of space there—there's not a lot of space there [in Israel]. How vulnerable Israel can be. I also came away with the strong impression about how strong the people there—not only want to defend themselves, but how much they love democracy, that democracy is a critical part of their existence."

If Bush's three most important meetings in Israel were with Netanyahu, Barak, and Sharon, "the most successful from Bush's point of view was the one with Sharon," Shoval said he was told later. With his formidable military record, Sharon drew "a certain attitude of admiration and respect similar to Clinton and Rabin," Shoval said.

Racicot sensed that the visit made Bush grapple more seriously with what becoming president could mean. This was reinforced by the expectation among Israeli officials that he would run. The Texas governor became "profoundly aware that his political life was changing. . . . That's when he started to realize this is a serious enterprise" presenting "incredibly serious issues." Doug Wead said that, after Bush's return home, "He told me he said to Sharon, 'Someday you'll be the prime minister of Israel, and I'll be president of the United States, and we'll solve this thing.'"

Two men of roughly the same generation with vastly different perspectives were now positioned to exert a profound influence over Bush's approach to the Middle East, source of the most important of the world's remaining regional conflicts. One was his father, still active at seventy-four, who had moved forcefully seven years earlier to shatter the regional taboo against open dialogue between Arabs and Israelis, setting in motion a series of negotiations aimed not only at ending a century of conflict but at fostering long-term regional cooperation between the bitter adversaries over arms control, water and the environment, economic development, and refugees.

"I can think of no endeavor more worthy, or more necessary," the elder Bush told the 1991 Madrid peace conference he and James Baker had worked for a year and a half to assemble. "Our objective must be clear and straightforward. It is not simply to end the state of war in the Middle East and replace it with a state of non-belligerency. This is not enough. This would not last. Rather, we seek peace, real peace. And by real peace, I mean treaties, security, diplomatic relations, economic relations, trade, investment, cultural exchange, even tourism.

"What we seek is a Middle East where vast resources are no longer devoted to armaments; a Middle East where young people no longer have to dedicate and, all too often, give their lives to combat; a Middle East no longer victimized by fear and terror; a Middle East where normal men and women lead normal lives."

The father's direction had proved politically costly in antagonizing an important American constituency. And, from most signs available in 1998, it had by then lost traction and stalled. Immense effort would be required to restart it, with uncertain gain. Meanwhile, Iraq was a menace and Iran was a looming threat.

The other man was Ariel Sharon, then seventy, a warrior-politician who personified the determined Zionism that had turned a tiny haven for a decimated and threatened Jewry into "a country of genius," as the younger Bush described it.

Sharon's direction offered the path of least resistance for many American politicians, including a sizable majority in the U.S. Congress. It called for little more than bolstering Israel's defense until such time as the Arab world sued for peace. Yet, as the elder Bush's advisers could have told the Texas governor, this path was unlikely to bring lasting security.

Back in Texas, Bush placed another call to State Senator Florence Shapiro to tell her the trip had been "extremely meaningful to him and Laura Bush"; to dwell once again on Israel's small size and describe the air tour given by Sharon; and to say he was "humbled by the fact that such a noted military hero was giving him a history of the country."

"He said to me immediately he felt a connection when he was there," Shapiro recalled. Bush also did her a favor, filling in on short notice for an absent Rudy Giuliani at a speech to the Jewish Federation of Greater Dallas.

The week he returned, Bush sent a letter to Abraham Foxman, who, like Shapiro's parents, was a Holocaust survivor, to close the loop on his offensive 1993 remark:

Dear Abe:

I am troubled that some people were hurt by my remarks. I never intended to make judgments about the faith of others. Judgments about heaven do not belong in the realm of politics or this world; they belong to a Higher Authority. In discussing my own personal faith as a Christian, I in no way meant to imply any disrespect or to denigrate any other religion. During my four years as governor, I have set a positive tone that indicates my respect for individuals from all faiths, all backgrounds and all walks of life.

I regret the concern caused by my statement and reassure you and the Jewish community that you have my deepest respect. I am staunchly committed to the principles of religious freedom, tolerance and diversity that are embodied in the First Amendment.

Sincerely,
George W. Bush

3

PALESTINIANS

ONE CAN ONLY SPECULATE ON what kind of impression Arafat might have made on George W. Bush had a meeting been arranged. Invariably warm and hospitable with American visitors, Arafat kept his cards close to his chest; offered mumbled, baffling responses; referred to himself as a general; spouted theories and allegations with little factual basis; and made promises he couldn't keep. Many visitors came away frustrated after trying in vain to discern the man behind the image. Matthew Brooks, Bush's traveling companion and a key organizer of his trip, had his own well formed views, which were stated clearly in a letter he cosigned that was sent to Republican members of Congress the same week Bush was in Israel: "Yasser Arafat and the PA [Palestinian Authority] have proven to be reckless and criminal in practice when dealing with foreign financial assistance," the letter said, demanding that tough restrictions be imposed on any U.S. aid. It went on to warn of "Yasser Arafat's continuing threats to violate the Oslo accords and unilaterally declare an independent state in May 1999. Such an act would not only be a direct violation of the previous agreements, but would clearly bring down the entire peace process. . . ."

A Bush visit to Arafat's headquarters, however, might have given the Palestinians an early clue not to expect the future president to follow his father's Middle East policies. Many Arabs at the time cherished the fantasy that a second Bush administration would lean more toward their side in disputes with Israel. James Zogby, president of the Arab American Institute and ordinarily a realistic observer of the U.S. political scene, wrote in the Saudi-owned *Asharq al-Awsat* (subsequently translated and reported by *Mideast Mirror*) of Bush's tour, "If G. W. Bush is, like his father, an old-line pragmatic business-oriented Republican, this could be a positive development and his involvement in the party's internal policy debate would be welcomed by Arab American Republicans."

For Bush, his failure to witness what was happening inside the Palestinian territories except from his lofty perch in a helicopter would turn out to be a significant blind spot. A side trip by motorcade to Ramallah from his Hilton hotel in West Jerusalem, a modern structure faced with pale stone, would have transported Bush in minutes from an advanced industrial nation into the developing world. Past the timeless Old City, traditionally Arab neighborhoods of East Jerusalem lagged noticeably behind the Jewish sector in the upkeep of roads, uneven development, and aging storefronts. Depending on the hour, Bush might have seen a line of cars at a checkpoint that formally separated Jerusalem from the West Bank. The route would then have passed open spaces littered with uncollected trash and the impoverished Qalandia refugee camp, a congested collection of cement-block dwellings that arose haphazardly over the years on ground once intended for temporary shelter.

In Ramallah, beyond the grim walled compound that was Arafat's West Bank headquarters, Bush would have seen a well maintained small Levantine city with Ottoman-era buildings and a bustling market exuding the aromas of fresh produce and spices. But even here, the contrast was stark between what existed seven years after the dawn of peace and what might have been. Throughout the West Bank, Gaza, and East Jerusalem, the occasional new or refurbished hotel or office building, the showplace of an international airport, and the repaved streets stood out as exceptions to overall stagnation and decay.

With an economy struggling to recoup after a sharp decline in the mid-'90s, weak governing institutions, and degraded infrastructure, the Palestinian territories were becoming hotbeds of public discontent. Far from producing hoped-for peace and prosperity, the Palestinian self-rule launched with the Oslo accords in 1993 had instead been accompanied by periodic eruptions of violence: suicide bombings targeting Israeli civilians by Palestinian militants out to shatter the peace process; bloody gun battles between Palestinians and Israeli soldiers and between rival Palestinian gangs; assassinations of militants by Israel; and occasional rock-throwing riots by Palestinian youths reminiscent of the 1987–1991 intifada. A few days before Bush's arrival in Israel, Agence France Presse reported violent clashes across the West Bank as Palestinians held a number of demonstrations calling for the release of prisoners. Israel's most frequent response to having its civilians and soldiers targeted was to seal off entry points for Palestinian workers and goods, imposing a crushing collective economic punishment.

Restrictions on the movement of Palestinian workers and goods into Israel and between the West Bank and Gaza, coupled with continued Israeli control over much of the land and water, brought a steady decline in the Palestinian economy, according to the United Nations. Unemployment had climbed and wages were depressed. Close to one-fourth of Palestinians were impoverished, according to government figures.

Without ports or exit routes through Egypt or Jordan that they controlled, Palestinians had no choice but to import and export through or from Israel. This system resulted in higher prices and tethered Palestinians in a lopsided way to their neighbor's advancing economy. Palestinians relied on Israel as the source of sophisticated manufactured goods and sold Israelis the simpler crafts and fabricated items made in family-owned workshops. With their labor-intensive growing practices and frequent security-related delays in transferring goods into Israel, Palestinians were also unable to compete with the highly mechanized Israeli farms in selling the most profitable and perishable produce.

Worse, the economic impact among Palestinians was sharply uneven. While many suffered, a select few acquired luxury villas and drove big Mercedes and BMWs. The Arafat regime used its new power in the territories to perpetuate and expand into the economic sphere the same autocratic style the Palestinian leader had himself honed over thirty years to control the far-flung and fractious PLO. With state-controlled companies, monopoly imports of cement, fuel, and cigarettes, rights to develop telephone service won by a well connected firm without competition, and holding companies through which a trusted subordinate controlled various enterprises, Arafat was able to achieve two goals: First, he rewarded loyalty and punished potential or actual opponents through the awarding of contracts and dealerships. Second, he acquired a separate source of money outside the government revenue stream that his regime could rely on in case outside aid dried up.

Along with a stifling of market forces, the regime's deep involvement in the economy and its delays in creating a modern legal framework discouraged outside investment. Mounting outrage at corruption and cronyism soured the public on the Palestinian Authority, although Arafat himself continued to enjoy an almost iconic status. A June 1998 poll showed that 65 percent of Palestinians considered the authority to be corrupt.

More and more, the territories hung on with handouts from abroad, which in part ended up impeding necessary reforms. The European Union subsidized a bloated public payroll rife with patronage, nepotism, and inefficiency. Gaps in public health and safety were exposed in sharp relief in October 1999, when fire swept through an unregulated cigarette-lighter factory in a residential building in Hebron, killing sixteen young workers earning $150 to $200 a month. Strained sewage systems posed a health hazard.

The United States, bowing to a congressional aversion to Arafat, refused to send aid directly to the authority and instead funded a series of projects run by nongovernmental organizations, as did many other governments. Numerous international development agencies helped improve education, health care, water quality, and local roads while training and employing Palestinians. But their efforts suffered from an absence of central coordination. Arafat viewed foreign-funded civil society groups as a threat to his regime. Had the United States assumed a leading role in mobilizing all the outside organizations toward a common goal, it would have risked boosting Palestinian sovereignty and infuriating Israel.

One government function the United States was eager to support was the section of the sprawling, duplicative Palestinian security establishment devoted to preventing militant attacks against Israelis. While effective in restoring a measure of calm between the two populations in the late 1990s, the "preventive security" apparatus also drew criticism for serious human rights abuses. Many Palestinians viewed it as means of crushing opponents of the regime or, worse, as an arm of Israel's security apparatus.

While doling out large sums of foreign aid for specific projects, donor countries ended up squeezing the UN refugee agency that provided schools, health clinics, and other services for millions of refugees not only in Israel, the West Bank, and Gaza but also in Lebanon, Jordan, and Syria. Faulted by American and Israeli critics for helping perpetuate the refugees' longing to return to their farms and villages, the United Nations Relief Works Agency, as it was formally named, can claim a large share of the credit for one of the highest literacy rates in the Arab world. Peter Hansen, the agency's director, warned the United Nations in late 1998 that everything it had accomplished to date was in danger.

Despite a strong public desire for democracy and institution-building efforts by aid groups such as the Burlington, Vermont–headquartered ARD, Inc., funded by the U.S. Agency for International Development, the Palestinian parliament proved impotent under the shadow of Arafat's autocratic rule, meekly waiting while he avoided signing key legislation like a basic law, or a constitution. The press was largely either government-controlled or docile.

Unlike the political leadership of the two sides, the Palestinian criminal underworld had little trouble cooperating with its Israeli counterparts. Illicit collaborations took root as Israeli forces withdrew from Palestinian territories after the Oslo peace agreement in 1993, leaving a law-enforcement vacuum that the new Palestinian Authority was slow to fill. Car thieves were the first to draw attention. Israelis and Palestinians would steal cars in Israel and drive them to the West Bank. There, the vehicles would be sold or stripped for parts, which would then be sold back to Israelis. Drug traffickers smuggled marijuana and hashish into Gaza from Egypt, and from Egypt to Israel. Israeli criminals, in turn, sold tens of thousands of semiautomatic rifles to Palestinians. Such cooperation extended to economic crime, particularly the production of counterfeit goods. Small West Bank factories fed Israel's booming trade in pirated videocassettes, audio cassettes, compact discs, even state-of-the-art computer software. Gaza workshops turned out knockoff blue jeans with designer labels.

It took six years following the Oslo accords before Gaza's airport opened and another for a passage to open between Gaza and the West Bank, easing the movement of people and goods. A port giving Palestinians access to the outside world would never materialize. The absence of a peace agreement, periodic violence and the resulting closure of borders, and an ineffective Palestinian government kept the territories depressed and economically backward. A late-1990s World Bank study said the Palestinian economy was operating at one-third to one-half its potential.

The sad irony was that among peoples of the region, the Palestinians were among the best equipped to achieve democracy and export-driven prosperity. They had relatively high levels of education, a strong work ethic, resourcefulness, civil society organizations, plentiful outside help, a diaspora elite worth tens of billions of dollars, and a location close to Mediterranean trade routes—all in addition to the religious shrines and cultural heritage of the Holy Land. In short, they had all the necessary attributes for building a state. But this was a word that Washington dared not utter for fear of jumping the gun on negotiations.

Had Bush spent time in the territories, he might have become aware of this widening gulf between potential and current reality and sensed a growing frustration that would lead to violent upheavals against Israel and, years later, between Palestinians.

That something was deeply wrong weighed most heavily on members of the generation that had watched or participated in the late 1980s intifada as young teenagers or students, getting swept up in hurling rocks and gasoline bombs and subsequent arrests. Many Palestinians still had relatives in Israeli prisons from the four-year intifada that began in 1987. A number of freed men in their twenties or early thirties could describe harsh interrogations and torture that they had undergone as detainees. And now the Palestinian Authority, bound by agreement with Israel to crack down on militants and determined to crush its own opponents, was using similar or worse techniques on its own inmates.

Students were becoming champions and soldiers of resistance. Among the eleven Palestinian universities in the West Bank and the Gaza Strip, training grounds for skilled engineers, lawyers, and technocrats who were supposed to propel Palestine forward, were centers of protest against government mismanagement and corruption. Some were incubators of Islamic militancy.

"The more disillusioned the students are with the PA about issues like corruption, mismanagement, and lack of democratization, the more opposed to the peace process they become," wrote Khalil Shikaki, the widely respected analyst of Palestinian public opinion, in *Foreign Affairs*.

One school in particular stood out. An-Najah National University in Nablus, a proud, ten-thousand-student institution of stone buildings and graceful plazas, was deemed by Israeli security officials to be prime recruiting territory for Hamas, the militant Islamic Resistance Movement. It certainly was a wellspring of support for Hamas, whether or not this translated into terrorism. Just days before George W. Bush arrived in the Middle East in 1998, a Hamas-affiliated group won a student election there. A little more than seven years later, An-Najah faculty members would assume prominent posts in a Hamas-led Palestinian government whose election in January 2006 stunned Washington and triggered harsh U.S.-engineered sanctions felt by hundreds of thousands of Palestinians.

As the largest university in the territories, however, it was more than just a hotbed of militancy. It attracted academic partnerships from around the world, including U.S. universities. A major benefactor was Munib al-Masri, the Nablus notable. An-Najah was developing a cadre of trained academics and technocrats to run Palestine.

Little publicized at the time of Bush's 1998 visit to Israel was the role the United States played—and would continue to play well into his presidency—in building up An-Najah and other Palestinian universities, including Islamic University, where sympathy for Hamas is strong among students and faculty. Among them was a group of Western-educated economists and educators. Their affiliation with or sympathy for Hamas could not have been a secret from the international community, including the United States, which continued to provide them with scholarships, research funding, and invitations to international conferences. But it would be years before they could put their knowledge and skills to work. And then, when their opportunity struck, they found themselves blocked at every turn.

Three members of the An-Najah faculty—Omar Abdel-Razek, Aziz Dweik, and Samir Abu Eisheh—personified how advanced Western training could coexist with an ideology rooted in the Muslim Brotherhood, a regionwide movement formed in Egypt in the 1920s that seeks to fuse religion and government and rejects many Western mores.

In the final decade of the cold war, hundreds of Arab students enrolled in American universities with help from U.S. government–funded Agency for International Development (USAID) and Fulbright scholarships, the Saudi-funded Arab Student Aid International, and other programs. The influx dovetailed with American policy priorities of halting the export of Iran's Shiite revolution; driving the Soviets out of Afghanistan and undermining their influence elsewhere; and shoring up American allies in Egypt and the Persian Gulf by supplying Western-trained officials.

The attraction of studying in the United States was particularly keen for Palestinians, many of whom turned to education as a pathway to financial security after losing agricultural land in the 1948 war. The USAID program that Dweik joined was aimed at training Palestinian university teachers.

Omar Abdel-Razek applied to the Arab Student Aid International group, which steered him to Coe College, a small, well regarded liberal arts college in Cedar Rapids, Iowa. He arrived knowing little English and nothing about the college, Iowa, or the young man who would be his first-year roommate: Brooklyn-born Hank Orenstein.

"Quite a unique situation—a Jew and [a] Palestinian sharing a small dorm room!" Orenstein recalled in an e-mail.

The two developed a friendship that lasted even though their social circles diverged. Abdel-Razek met Orenstein's parents on visits to campus. "We really just made an effort to get along with each other," Orenstein said from Manhattan in a follow-up telephone interview.

Both were good students and members of the International Club.

Orenstein was struck by the importance of education in both Palestinian and Jewish cultures. He found his roommate to be brilliant and quietly devout, praying in his room and avoiding alcohol.

Abdel-Razek recalls, "My English was very bad, very slow, and he decided that he would help me with my English and I would help him with understanding the political situation in the Middle East. So we'd sit every night . . . talking about the Middle East and talking about the Palestinian cause and the Israeli aggressions against the Palestinians and so on and the Jewish belief in things and the issues of their education and their conditions and their political differences."

As his language skills improved, he branched out beyond the dorm room to write articles, speak in local churches, and help organize a campus discussion about the Middle East conflict. Steve Feller, a Coe physics professor, recalled a mutually respectful exchange but noted Abdel-Razek's uncompromising attitude toward Israel: "He certainly did not accept it as a legitimate entity."

In a series that appeared in the *Cosmos*, the Coe student newspaper, Abdel-Razek described the stages of the Israeli-Palestinian conflict in often bitter language. He wrote of the early Zionist leader, Theodor Herzl: "He informed the world that their policy was to slaughter the Palestinians." He portrayed the U.S. media as being "to some extent, controlled by influential Zionists" and took pains to explain, if not justify, certain terrorist acts as a way to draw attention to the Palestinian problem.

He made a distinction between the state of Israel and the Jewish people and wrote that Zionism initially grew out of persecution suffered by Jews "almost everywhere in the world."

After Coe, Orenstein and Abdel-Razek lost touch. Orenstein went on to graduate school and a social work career that included running a homeless shelter in the south Bronx. Now he is a New York City tour guide and landscape photographer.

After graduating magna cum laude, Abdel-Razek pursued a PhD in economics at Iowa State University, completing it in four years rather than the usual five. He went on to teach economics at An-Najah National University in Nablus, on the West Bank, and conduct research at the Ford Foundation–funded Palestine Economic Policy Research Institute in

Ramallah. Recently, Orenstein wrote in an e-mail, "I remember thinking that someday Omar would likely be a leader among the Palestinian people due to his intelligence, warmth, and ability to communicate and motivate others."

Abdel-Razek said of his time at Coe: "They were the best four years in my life, actually. I made so many friends. I think my personality was shaped and formulated at that time. It's very difficult to believe that I would have been the same person had I not been to Coe College for four years."

In Philadelphia, meanwhile, Aziz Dweik labored at the University of Pennsylvania for a PhD in regional science, a discipline that combined geography and economics. Instructors described him as hardworking and focused, eager to complete his degree and return to his wife and five children in the West Bank, where his oldest son risked getting caught up in the first intifada. His schedule appears to have limited his social interactions, but he belonged to the Muslim student association and sometimes preached at a local mosque.

Doug Buchholz, who worked alongside Dweik in a part-time job at the Van Pelt Library, recalled asking him at one point about his impression of life in the United States. Dweik hesitated at first, then responded that "Americans are very sad because of a lack of spirituality or spiritual foundation," Buchholz said.

Dweik paid attention to the unfolding Iran-contra affair triggered by the Reagan administration's sale of arms to Iran and diversion of the proceeds to anti-Communist rebels in Nicaragua. According to Kamel Ghozzi, a Tunisian-born student who also worked at the library, Dweik compared the congressional probe of the scandal to the relative lack of openness in Arab countries.

"No one is above the law—the Senate can question everybody," Ghozzi recalled Dweik saying. "He admired the transparency," said Ghozzi, who went on to teach at the University of Central Missouri.

According to the *Philadelphia Inquirer*'s correspondent Michael Matza, Dweik "returned to Hebron imbued with democratic values, including a deep respect for freedom of speech."

Like Abdel-Razek, he felt the Palestinian cause sharply and resented what he considered Arab leaders' "lip service," according to Ghozzi. But Dweik was also deeply influenced by a different struggle half a world away.

He attended a local meeting at which a visiting cleric from Afghanistan, Abdullah Azzam, was raising money for the jihad to drive out the Soviet occupiers. Originally from a village near Jenin, in the West Bank, Azzam was reputed to be a spellbinding preacher and a spiritual mentor to Osama bin Laden. He was killed by a car bomb in 1989.

Azzam and his cause made enough of an impression on Dweik that he later composed this dedication for his doctoral thesis: "To the best emigrant in the twentieth century, Dr. Abdullah Azzam and his companions, in the land of Khurasan. May Allah, the Almighty, guide your efforts." Khurasan is an ancient name for territory that includes parts of Afghanistan and Iran.

Dweik, in a spring 2006 telephone interview, said he knew nothing about bin Laden until the attacks of September 11, more than a decade later. He described Azzam as a cold war ally of the United States.

"I'll tell you," Dweik said, his voice rising: "During that time, the Muslims of Afghanistan with the alliance of the United States government, they were collecting money to fight against communism. So we had a common enemy. It was communism. They were invading our lands in Afghanistan, like what the United States is doing right now. You see? So Azzam came and collected money and we were very much impressed with that personality."

Dweik's return from the United States roughly coincided with the beginning of Hamas as a Palestinian offshoot of the regionwide Muslim Brotherhood, the movement launched in the 1920s that promotes Islam as the answer to society's ills. Speaking out in public against the Israeli occupation, he was arrested and spent four months in prison. There, he met members of Hamas, according to the *Inquirer*.

Dweik's fluency in English and familiarity with the West proved extremely useful to the resistance movement in late 1992, when Israel expelled more than four hundred Palestinian militants from the territory into Lebanon. The group, which included such prominent Hamas members as Ismail Haniyeh, now prime minister, and Atef Udwan, minister for refugee affairs, tapped Dweik as its spokesman with the Western media. Judging from the volume of articles that appeared, he performed well. The episode turned into a public relations debacle for Israel, which allowed the men to return before a year was over.

The expulsion provided valuable training in other respects. On that barren and cold Lebanese hillside, the exiles created a well-ordered Islamic society that Mohamed Nimer, a Palestinian American academic who studied the small community, called "a working model of the ideal societal infrastructure sought by Islamists."

As the decade wore on, Abdel-Razek was also arrested by the Israelis in 1997 and held without charge in administrative detention for four months, he says. He would later claim that he was not a Hamas member but an Islamist who believed Muslim teachings "can shape the political and economic and social life of Muslims" and provide life with "very good meaning." Speaking of the government as a whole, he said, "We believe that Islamic teachings are suitable for modern life and are suitable for political, economic, and social systems." He said he opposed the September 11 attacks and bombings in London and Madrid but refused to consider violence against Israeli occupiers as terrorism. "When you talk about resistance movements in Palestine it's different—it's totally different. We are fighting occupation," he said. Reminded of the commonly accepted definition of terrorism—deliberate violent attacks against innocent civilians—Abdel-Razek responded by questioning whether many Israelis could even be considered civilians, since so many retain a military status as reservists until they reach age sixty-five. Others are settlers, he added, suggesting that they are legitimate targets.

Arab student-exchange programs were supposed to have a moderating effect on participants, bridging cultural differences and getting students to view each other as human beings. But in the case of returning Palestinians, "The daily experience of living under occupation overrides any other factor" in shaping their political views, said Mohamed Nimer, research director at the Council on American-Islamic Relations in Washington, interviewed in 2006.

Reuven Erlich, director of the Intelligence and Terrorism Information Center at the Center for Special Studies in Israel, an institution created as a memorial to fallen members of the Israeli intelligence community, has gathered, translated, and published a number of Hamas documents seized in raids by Israeli forces. He saw no moderating effect from a Western education on Hamas leaders. Rather, he said, it made them more effective militants.

"In general they use the education and technology they [acquire] from the United States and the West to fight the West. Most radical Islamists got their education in the West," he said. "After they returned, they used what they learned in the U.S. and other Western countries against the West."

Yet in a region rife with crude anti-Semitism, aggravated by the Israeli-Palestinian conflict, it is significant that prominent members of the Hamas government had working relationships with American Jews, and, in Abdel-Razek's case at least, a friendship. It suggests that beyond the poisoned confines of the current conflict, the Western training shared by many Israelis and Palestinians could serve as a bridge to cooperative efforts.

In the territories, Palestinians most often encountered Jews in hostile settings: as soldiers, settlers, and guards at checkpoints or in prisons.

Abdel-Razek is remembered with admiration by his physics instructor at Coe, Steve Feller, who is also a former president of Temple Judah in Cedar Rapids, a Reform synagogue. After an uncomfortable start, Abdel-Razek says he came to appreciate his chief adviser at Iowa State, Harvey Lapan, who was Jewish.

As for Dweik, "It's inconceivable to me that someone from Palestine would not be aware of a Jewish presence at the university," said Thomas Reiner, a regional-science professor who had befriended him at Penn and one of three Jews in the small department that supervised Dweik's work.

But U.S. academic training certainly sharpened the intellectual tools Palestinians could wield against the Israeli occupation.

Dweik's dissertation, analyzing West Bank and Gaza labor flows using mathematical models, points out negative long-term consequences for Palestinians from the close integration between Palestinian labor and markets, on the one hand, and Israeli industry on the other. The movement of Palestinian labor into low-skilled Israeli jobs served to keep wages up in the West Bank and Gaza while limiting economic development and stunting agriculture in the territories, he wrote.

While at the economic research center, Abdel-Razek explored ways the Palestinians could reduce Israel's huge influence on the Palestinian economy and prevent the sharp dislocations that result when Israelis deny entry to Palestinian workers. "The World Bank research and every research in that regard has reached the conclusion that the very big and huge and single relationship of the Palestinian economy with the Israeli economy is not healthy, is not in the right direction. So there is a need to reduce the dependence on the Israeli economy and a need to increase ties and economic relations with not only the Arab world but also Europe and the States," he said in the 2006 interview.

Abu Eisheh, a transportation specialist, would later describe in a paper how Israeli-imposed travel restrictions had produced a severe decline in the movement of Palestinian freight, while increasing the costs.

These students' exposure to Americans didn't end with their return to the territories. Aziz Dweik met up with Reiner in Jerusalem's Old City in 1991. Together, they visited a shop owned by Dweik's uncle, a moment Reiner remembers as slightly awkward, since tourists in the Old City are invariably pressed to buy something.

Abdel-Razek took part in a 1992 conference at Harvard's Kennedy School. Until 2004, when he left the economic research center because travel from his home in Nablus had become so difficult, he met periodically with officials from the U.S. consulate in Jerusalem and USAID, he says. He was placed in administrative detention by Israel in October 1997, and freed the following February, ten months before Bush's trip to Israel.

Samir Abu Eisheh, who earned a doctorate in engineering at Pennsylvania State University, may have kept the closest ongoing ties with the United States, having taught as well as studied at Penn State and, in 1990, at Texas A&M University, where the first President Bush would establish his presidential library. He also got a research grant from AMIDEAST, the U.S.-funded institution that helps Arab students in the United States. He worked closely with Purdue University professor Fred Mannering, a widely published transportation expert.

Abu Eisheh may have come under Israeli suspicion while he was dean of engineering at An-Najah. In 1995, Israel barred him from traveling to Paris to deliver a paper on Palestinian utilities at a UNESCO conference

on Palestinian government reform. His paper circulated anyway, revealing a detailed knowledge of the poor condition of water, electricity, and
sewerage systems in the territories and a prescription for how to correct them.

The year after Bush's visit to Israel, Abu Eisheh headed to the University of Washington on a Fulbright scholarship.

Bush's trip coincided with a renewed debate in Washington over
whether the United States should provide money directly to the Palestinian Authority. Competently administered, these hundreds of millions
of dollars could have been used to rebuild the territories' degraded infrastructure and hire technocrats like Abu Eisheh to begin laying the building blocks for an economically successful Palestinian state. The
Republican Jewish Coalition warned against providing direct aid unless
strict political and financial conditions were imposed. Ultimately, Congress decided to furnish the aid only indirectly, through nonprofit organizations. The Palestinian Authority continued operating as before as a
haven for patronage, while the necessary investment in the future of the
territories proceeded in an uncoordinated fashion.

Abu Eisheh would spend the next seven years at An-Najah, along with
Aziz Dweik and Omar Abdel-Razek. Seven years later, they stood on the
threshold of turning their plans for Palestinian statehood into action. By
then, the Palestinian government barely functioned and much of the
infrastructure that existed had degraded or collapsed into rubble. Their
time to act was short.

4

Two Risk-Takers

RARELY HAS HISTORY paired leaders with such contrasting backgrounds as George W. Bush and Ariel Sharon. Yet as chief executives, the American and the Israeli shared important characteristics. Each displayed an unwavering faith in his own instincts. Each viewed the world in stark terms of black and white, friend and foe, good and evil.

Each was willing to risk political standing, soldiers' lives, and national treasure to serve a strategic vision with a questionable basis in reality.

Bush was born in 1946 into a Protestant elite at the peak of its influence on American economic and public life. Several generations of wealth and excellent schooling had lifted his family to social prominence and political leadership. He followed his father to Andover and his father and grandfather to Yale and its prestigious secret society, Skull and Bones. Later, he followed them into Republican politics. Investments from family associates cushioned him against reversals in the risky oil business. Bush's pedigree showed in his self-assurance as a decision-maker, an easy grace with guests and visitors, a gift for the appropriate comment, and a seemingly innate sense of the deference due a president.

Handsome, charismatic, and a cutup, he acquired a wide circle of friends and had little trouble finding dates. His acute political skills built on his early camaraderie, scrappy competitiveness, and rambunctious leadership qualities. At Andover, he led the school's cheerleaders in bawdy skits and formed a popular stickball team. At Yale, he became president of the Delta Kappa Epsilon fraternity.

"I think the qualities to me that were distinctive about George at Andover were qualities that he exhibited at Yale and qualities that I see him benefiting from today, which are energy, and interest in people, a facility with people," schoolmate Clay Johnson said in an interview on PBS. "A sense of humor. An upbeat, glass-is-half-full, let's get going, let's not reflect on what's not happening. Let's get upbeat. Let's get going. Very upbeat. Energetic. People-oriented person. George's interest in people is exceptional, and it's not a people skill, it's not a developed ability to remember names. I think it all comes from a real, live, deep-seated interest in people." Nicholas Kristof, who delved deeply into Bush's youth in a pair of *New York Times* articles, reported: "Ever since Andover, Mr. Bush has consistently demonstrated the same kind of leadership: not a powerful intellect or dazzling policy expertise but rather an exceptional ability to make friends, work a crowd, cheer people up, and take them all in his direction."

But inside the privileged patrician dwelt a boy whose childhood was shaken by the death of a little sister from leukemia, and who spent his formative early years in the distinctly middle-American setting of Midland, Texas, attending public school, before his family moved to Houston. A down-home manner and west Texas accent never left him. Nor did a feeling that he came from a different world from many prep school and college peers. When he married, he picked a hometown girl.

Years later, Bush would remember what he perceived to be an insult about his father from Yale's liberal chaplain, William Sloane Coffin Jr. By Bush's account, reported by Kristof, Coffin commented on the elder Bush's loss to Democrat Ralph Yarborough in the 1964 Senate race, saying, "Yeah, I know your father, and your father lost to a better man."

In an August 2000 op-ed in the *Times*, Coffin offered high praise for future Democratic Senator Joseph Lieberman as representing the idealistic activism of the 1960s but had a subtle barb for Bush: "I am sure Governor Bush is right in criticizing the self-righteousness of many of us in the antiwar movement at Yale. It is hard to fight national self-righteousness without personal self-righteousness. But it is also sad not to share in the action and passion of your time."

A Yale roommate of the future president, Terry Johnson, told CNN: "What George is—does not respond well to are people who are snobs, whether you're a social snob, an intellectual snob, or any other kind of snob."

Bush acquired self-discipline and ambition relatively late in life. While college classmates were caught up in protests against the Vietnam War, Bush spent his off-hours at fraternity parties and drank a lot, getting Cs. He appears to have stayed aloof from the youthful turbulence and angry debate of the 1960s. If he challenged his parents' generation with some of his conduct, he seems to have accepted its ideals and worldview. He took the route of other well connected sons to avoid Vietnam combat, joining the Texas National Guard.

Sharon, born in 1928, eighteen years earlier than Bush, was descended from middle-class Jews living on the fringes of the Russian empire, a minority clinging to an ancient religious and cultural heritage against the threat of pogroms and revolution. His early life was a hard-scrabble existence in British-ruled Palestine. His family lived in a three-room cabin built by his father on a moshav, a Jewish cooperative farm. Rats scampered in the rafters, but the home was steeped in appreciation for music and literature.

Sharon's parents were loners. His father, an irascible agronomist, was estranged from others in the moshav; he was better educated than they and a stubborn experimenter with new crops. "Like his neighbors, he was a passionate Zionist," Sharon later wrote in his autobiography, *Warrior*. "But unlike them, he was no socialist." And unlike many Israelis, who are warm and demonstrative, Sharon's parents rarely displayed affection, he recalled. Discipline came early. Sharon tended the livestock and performed other chores while also traveling an hour each way to high school in Tel Aviv.

Sharon joined the Haganah, forerunner of the Israel Defense Forces (IDF), as a young teenager, as civil unrest grew between Palestine's growing Arab and Jewish populations and the British proved unable to stop it. He came of age in a Jewish homeland struggling to absorb the trauma and the survivors of the Holocaust while carving out a new nation in a region bristling with hostility and resentment. Prestate Israel prized the bronzed warrior whom Sharon came to personify.

While Bush's leadership qualities evolved naturally from an outgoing personality and popularity, Sharon's emerged in a military career marked by daring, creativity, and a tendency to flout or go beyond orders. He was wounded twice. "I do not know a better field commander than Arik [Sharon]," wrote legendary Israeli chief of staff and defense minister Moshe Dayan. "We also had our quarrels. But even when I feel like murdering him, at least I know he is somebody worth murdering." Sharon inherited his father's contempt for others' capabilities; he often viewed his military and, later, political superiors as feckless.

Early on, Sharon learned about responding with force to Arab threats to Jewish settlement. "He knew how to deal with Arabs because he saw how his mother did it: with a baseball bat," said Samuel Lewis, who came to know Sharon much later while serving as U.S. ambassador to Israel from 1977 to 1984. "There were some marauding bands of young Arab toughs who would carry out minor vandalism on this moshav. The mother, who was a tough woman, kept a baseball bat, I mean a big stick. And whenever any of these Arab kids would come around she would just go out there and beat the bejesus out of them. And chase them off. And that's how she trained Sharon to deal with Arabs."

Guile and brutality characterized his treatment of adversaries. As a young soldier, he once lured Jordanian soldiers across the border with a ruse and then captured them. As commander of an elite antiterrorism unit dubbed "101," he led a reprisal raid in 1953 on the Palestinian village of Kibya that claimed sixty-nine lives, including many women and children. To stamp out terrorism in the occupied Gaza Strip after the 1967 war, Sharon's men found and raided underground bunkers, demolished houses, and widened alleyways. "Behind every commander's jeep, I wanted to see a bulldozer," he wrote in his autobiography. To Yitzhak Berman, a former cabinet colleague and critic, Sharon's lifetime of conflict made him "a hater of Arabs," as Berman put it in an interview. "Ridiculous," retorted Sharon's son Omri during a brief roadside conversation in early 2001, when he managed his father's campaign for prime minister. "In the house I grew up in, we always believed we were going to live with Arabs. . . . They're part of our lives, part of our society. My father always had Arab friends."

What Berman viewed as hatred, Samuel Lewis saw as distrust: "He is not a man who ever believed that you could negotiate peace with Arabs. In fact, he really had a tremendous distrust for Arabs, period, and saw the way to live with the Arabs [was] only by having Israel sit on them and them [to] accept the fact that they were going to be sat on, passive, subordinate to a double standard sort of role in Israel proper and in the surrounding territories. . . ." In Sharon's view, according to Lewis, "The only way to get the attention of the Arabs was to show them who's boss. And they respect that and they will respond to that."

Deprived of the job of army chief of staff, Sharon turned to the raw civilian combat of Israeli politics. He participated in founding the right-wing Likud Party just as the nation's voters were beginning to sour on the centrist Labor movement that had long dominated Israel's political scene. In Israel's small, intimate, yet fractious political class, a strong military background was usually a prerequisite for success, since national security dominated public debate. While military mistakes could bring the people's wrath down upon the most experienced leader, lack of experience produced scorn, particularly in a crisis.

Bush rose to political power from a similarly restricted circle—the top public officials and fund-raisers in the Republican Party. In the royalist upper precincts of the GOP, Bush was the dauphin, heir to the presidential mantle snatched unfairly from his admired father after only one term. The younger George Bush showed the toughness required to gain support of the party leadership by succeeding in business as the part owner of a Texas baseball team and in bare-knuckled behind-the-scenes management of the George H. W. Bush White House. After defeating a popular Democrat, Ann Richards, to become governor of Texas and winning a second term, he demonstrated enough political appeal to seek the presidency. In the primaries, he benefited from having courted the Christian Right since his father's 1988 campaign. His chief competitor for the nomination, Arizona senator John McCain, was knocked out of the race in the February 2000 Republican primary in South Carolina.

Bush's climb to national leadership was brief and effortless compared with Sharon's. The Israeli parlayed his military exploits and ties with religious Zionist settlers into the Knesset and the cabinet. As agriculture minister in Menachem Begin's government, formed in 1977, Sharon championed and aggressively planned and built a series of Jewish settlements in the occupied territories as a way to keep the high ground and other strategic locations in Israel's hands. Although the settlements defied the spirit of the 1978 Camp David accords and were viewed by most of the world as a violation of the Fourth Geneva Convention, they became an unstoppable force, their growth aided by special tax breaks for home buyers and new road networks.

Sharon's campaign to erect settlements reflected a drive to keep in Israel's hands the territory he thought was necessary to secure its defense. Later, as prime minister, he would attempt to put in place Israel's permanent borders, beginning with a dramatic, complicated, and politically wrenching pullout of Israeli settlers and forces from the Gaza Strip and northern West Bank. The withdrawal was launched in part to head off international pressure for a territorial compromise with the Palestinians that he would find unacceptable.

Zalman Shoval, who served twice as ambassador to Washington for Likud governments, said Sharon's determination to act unilaterally was rooted in the policies of David Ben-Gurion and others of Israel's founding generation. "If you examine the whole history of the Zionist movement in Israel and Palestine, most of it [involved] unilateral steps," Shoval said in a 2005 interview. In debates within the Zionist movement, Ze'ev (Vladimir) Jabotinsky and others placed priority on securing international agreements to establish a state. Ben-Gurion and his allies "said 'No. We have to establish facts; we have to establish settlements, we have to establish our own defense units . . . our own economy. We have to create a state within a state which will then develop into the really recognized state. If we wait for international agreements, we'll wait forever.'

". . . Sharon, coming not from the ideological right but from the practical Zionists, was imbued with that," Shoval said. "Because he was never basically ideological, he was much closer, with all the differences, to people like [prominent commanders and cabinet ministers] Yigal Allon, Moshe Dayan, and to a certain extent Yitzhak Rabin, who also saw things through the prism of security and not through the prism of being accepted by the Middle East, by the Arab states."

Many of the settlements took hold without official approval but came to be officially accepted after the fact, once houses were rising and infrastructure installed. Sharon took the same approach after the Israel-Egypt peace agreement. In his autobiography, he recounted how he opposed withdrawing from Sinai unless the border were changed to reflect what he considered to be the true line. According to Sharon, British members of a survey team in 1906 had put down border markers incorrectly so as to place strategic high ground in Egypt, which Britain ruled at the time. Sharon didn't mention that he bulldozed the British markers, something confirmed years later by mediator Abraham Sofaer, then State Department legal adviser.

As defense minister, Sharon overreached, launching an ill-fated invasion of neighboring Lebanon in 1982. The operation's stated intent was to destroy the Palestine Liberation Organization's stronghold in southern Lebanon, which the guerrilla group used as a base to attack northern Israel. "We spent eighteen months preparing until we said, 'OK, we're ready,' and then waited for the opportunity. And then they tried to kill the ambassador [Shlomo Argov in London] and we said, 'Gentlemen, we're invading Lebanon,'" Ami Ayalon, who headed a naval commando unit at the time, told the *Jerusalem Post* in a 2007 interview. The assault exceeded what the Israeli government, the Israeli public, and the United States had been led to expect. Billed publicly as a two-day operation, its actual aim was to turn Lebanon into a subservient client, free of terrorist strongholds and pressure from Arab nations hostile to Israel. Israeli forces moved along a path of bloody destruction well beyond the twenty-five-mile limit Sharon had led the government to expect, establishing themselves as a virtual colonial power in east Beirut. "I lived through that period and I watched him thumb his nose at the United States over and over again, persuade Begin over and over again up until very close to the end of the war that he was doing what he said he was doing. He was lying to us, he was lying to Begin. He had a game plan and he was sure he could carry it out," recalled Samuel Lewis.

Sharon underestimated the power of Lebanon's communal strife to suck even a powerful invasion force into a costly guerrilla war. "He didn't prepare his homework sufficiently," Berman said in an interview shortly before Sharon's 2001 election as prime minister. Careful preparation later became a Sharon hallmark. But in the case of Lebanon, Sharon overestimated the capability of his Christian allies in Beirut and underestimated the manipulative might of Syria, which sided first with one Lebanese faction and then with another to protect its influence in the country. The crisis exploded with disastrous consequences for Sharon after Israel had forced most of the PLO fighters from Beirut, including their leader, Yasser Arafat. Lebanon's newly elected president, Bashir Gemayel, from the Christian Phalangist Party, was assassinated. To keep the guerrillas from regrouping in the power vacuum, Sharon later said, he allowed Phalangist militias to enter the Palestinian refugee camps of Sabra and Shatila in suburban Beirut and expel PLO stragglers. Home in Israel on September 16, 1982, Sharon learned after the fact what happened next: a massacre of about eight hundred Palestinians in the two camps. An international outcry followed, leading to a major Israeli investigation that found that Sharon bore indirect responsibility for the disaster. The cabinet voted in early 1983 to accept the findings of the inquiry, ignoring Sharon's warning that to do so would brand Israel and the Jewish people with the "mark of Cain," the Bible's first murderer. He was the only member opposed and had little choice but to resign as defense minister. But in Israel's self-contained political world, even the worst setbacks are rarely permanent. Sharon remained in the government as minister without portfolio and soon began his ascent from pariah status. In 1984, two years after the Sabra and Shatila massacres, he had a new portfolio as minister of industry and trade and held senior posts in every Likud-led cabinet thereafter. Bringing to politics the same tactical creativity he had used so successfully as a young army commander, he built his own base of support on the right wing of the Likud Party. By 1986, according to biographers Nir Hefez and Gadi Bloom, "Sharon had spent the last three years attending forums and weddings, bar mitzvahs and brises. He knew thousands of Likud Central Committee members personally and was considered a friend by many." Party leaders evidently concluded it was safer to keep Sharon in a prominent position. "I always said this about Sharon: When he is in government, and responsible for the future of the Jewish people, he will act responsibly. When he's out of government, he will be a politician and a spoiler," said Abraham Sofaer, who came to know Sharon from the vantage point of a U.S. federal judge and a State Department official. "He sort of relishes being called upon to do the hard things that are needed, where he agrees that they're needed, whether it's a war or dismantling a settlement."

In his slow climb back to the upper reaches of power, Sharon honed the tactical skills and understanding of the Israeli public that would eventually give him an unmatched command of the Israeli political system.

The outside world, including official Washington, continued to shun him. When he visited AIPAC headquarters in Washington in the early 1990s, "a few people in the staff would meet with him," recalled Keith Weissman, then a newly hired analyst at the organization. "What I always loved about him was his sense of humor. He was the funniest of all Israeli politicians . . . very self-deprecating." An end to the U.S. freeze came in the mid-1990s, when he was invited to the State Department by Martin Indyk, then assistant secretary in charge of the Middle East. Gradually, Sharon moved back to the center of Israeli decisionmaking and made himself a force to be reckoned with in U.S.-Israeli relations. Under Prime Minister Benjamin Netanyahu in the late 1990s, he agitated against turning over territory to the Palestinians as part of the Oslo peace process even as Netanyahu drew countervailing pressure from Washington. Sharon became so influential that, as foreign minister in 1998, he was summoned to lend a hand in tough Israeli-Palestinian talks at Maryland's Wye Plantation brokered by President Clinton. A month later, no longer persona non grata, he met Texas governor George W. Bush.

Still, it would take seventeen years from the Lebanon war before Sharon became the Likud Party's standard-bearer.

The Lebanon debacle taught Sharon "that the Arab population wasn't as easily dominated by force as he thought they would be; would not be intimidated like he thought they could be. That ultimately led to the Gaza withdrawal decision," said Samuel Lewis. "[The] second thing he learned was not to undertake an operation in a way that would produce a very deep split in the public, as the Lebanon war did. And the third thing he learned was, 'Don't get on the wrong side of the American president. Don't thumb your nose at Washington. Co-opt Washington.' In the '82 period, in that era, he didn't believe you had to co-opt Washington."

But Sharon's obstinacy toward Washington never quite disappeared. In 1989, having mediated the Taba border dispute so as to complete the Israeli-Egyptian peace treaty, Abraham Sofaer sought out Sharon's support before the cabinet voted: "I was lobbying him and hoping our relationship would help me, and my country, in getting him to go along."

Sofaer, personally deeply supportive of Israel, had presided as a federal judge in the trial of a libel case Sharon filed against *Time* magazine in 1983. *Time*, citing a secret appendix to the Israeli inquiry into Sabra and Shatila, had written that Sharon "reportedly discussed . . . the need for the Phalangists to take revenge" on Palestinians. Sharon failed to meet the high burden for proving "actual malice," which would have entitled him to damages. But Sofaer's charge to the jury allowed the panel to isolate the question of "actual malice" and nevertheless find that *Time* had acted negligently and defamed Sharon. "Sharon felt that was fair. He lost the case but he won the war, morally speaking," Sofaer told me in 2005.

When Sofaer went to Sharon's office in 1989, the former general greeted him warmly. Nevertheless, Sharon turned down Sofaer's request to support the Taba agreement: "This is nothing personal, Judge Sofaer, but I'm going to vote against your settlement."

Overall, Sharon placed little faith in diplomacy and negotiated settlements—even when he had a hand in them. Pulled into Israeli-Palestinian talks at the Wye Plantation in Maryland, he told then Secretary of State Madeleine Albright that Yasser Arafat would never keep any agreement, according to Zalman Shoval. Throughout his term as prime minister, he resisted direct talks with the Palestinians, believing that peace was not possible in the current generation. Nor was he prepared to pay the widely understood price for peace with Syria: Israeli withdrawal from the Golan Heights.

His guide in dealing with the outside world was suspicion that in a crunch, Jews would once again be abandoned to their fate. "The allies knew of the annihilation of the Jews. They knew and did nothing," he told the Knesset in a 2003 speech marking the sixtieth anniversary of the liberation of Auschwitz. "On April 19, 1943, the Bermuda Conference gathered, with the participation of representatives from Britain and the United States, in order to discuss saving the Jews of Europe. In fact, the participants did everything in their power to avoid dealing with the problem. All the suggestions for rescue operations which the Jewish organizations presented were rejected."

Sharon, preoccupied by his own strife-ridden corner of the globe, found in George W. Bush a partner who, for different reasons, also had a somewhat restricted view of the world. Bush was skeptical of diplomacy and rejected advice that fell outside his own worldview. He didn't travel much and showed little interest in foreign policy before preparing for his presidential run. Whereas predecessor Bill Clinton sank his teeth into the details of negotiations, Bush tended to get impatient with complexity and diplomatic nuance.

Despite Bush's respect and appreciation for the courage shown by British prime minister Tony Blair in joining with the U.S. decision to invade Iraq, Bush rejected the Briton's strategy for dealing with the broader Middle East. Blair wanted, first, a strong Western intervention to solve the Israeli-Palestinian conflict, believing it to be central to the whole complex of Arab attitudes toward the West. And he tried desperately to achieve a broad international consensus on how to deal with Saddam Hussein, believing this would either make Iraq buckle or, failing that, give an invasion a greater chance of success. Likewise, Bush rejected cautious voices in his own administration and among his father's advisors who thought the Iraq War was either a mistake to begin with or required more diplomatic preparation.

Had Bush heeded Blair's advice, as well as that of numerous others, and pressed for negotiations between Israel and the Palestinians, he would have found Sharon a hard nut to crack—everything in Sharon's record suggested that. Sharon was of the belief that Israel couldn't compromise enough to satisfy the Palestinians. He wanted to press ahead with establishing Israel's borders unilaterally. Yet he wanted to avoid friction with the United States, and he was a pragmatist.

Shoval noted, "After the Oslo agreement, there was a meeting of the central committee of the Likud. Likud was set against the Oslo agreement, of course. Everybody spoke against it—these terms and those terms. And Sharon made a speech, and he even prepared a paper. He opposed Oslo without any doubt, underlining the deficiencies. But, he said, 'It's a fact. And in any future situation, arrangement, or whatever—formula—Israel must make sure that it keeps the security zones, security areas, in its control.' And the way I interpreted this was, if you say you have to keep certain areas, that means you don't have to keep other areas." And for all Sharon's distrust of Arabs and a lifetime of using blunt instruments against them, he told the Knesset in 1998, "Gentlemen, believe me, it is hard to be a Jew, as the saying goes, but being a Palestinian is equally hard." Former U.S. president Jimmy Carter, a harsh critic of Sharon's policies generally, wrote of him in his controversial book, *Palestine: Peace Not Apartheid*: "Having observed Sharon in action for three decades, I had no doubt that he would fulfill his promises." Miguel Moratinos, European Union envoy and later the Spanish foreign minister, recalled, in a 2005 interview, Sharon's saying he was the only one who could bring peace to the region. Moratinos was asked if he agreed with Sharon's claim. He paused: "I think so . . . we will see."

This was the Sharon whom Bush didn't try to probe, and didn't try to develop as a partner in seeking a settlement with the Palestinians and attempting to stabilize the Middle East. A leader as effective as Sharon appears on the Israeli political scene at most once a decade. Rarely is a strong Israeli prime minister matched with an Arab leader who is as eager to negotiate a settlement as was Palestinian prime minister, and later president, Mahmoud Abbas.

Both Bush and Sharon had grand schemes that ultimately were sacrificed to the wars each pursued. For Bush, it was the spread of democratic reform throughout the Middle East. This was and remains a necessary part of a lasting peace between Israel and the Arab world, but events during Bush's presidency showed that it required stability to get started. Bush's Iraq War triggered the opposite: chaos in Iraq, a scramble among regional leaders to position themselves for the sake of their regimes' survival, and suppression of dissent. Sharon dramatized his own grand scheme one afternoon in early 2001, standing atop the Halutza dunes in the Negev. He wanted to secure Israel's borders and bring a million more Jews to Israel, hoping that within two decades the majority of world Jewry would have made aliyah to the Jewish state. This desert high ground commanding the frontier with Egypt had been considered by Israel as part of a land swap with the Palestinians—to be exchanged for territory that would expand Israel's vulnerably narrow midsection. But Sharon opposed any such compromise. "This will not come to pass," Sharon declared as he waved his right arm majestically toward Egypt. The next four years of conflict, resulting in part from Sharon's inflexible attitude toward negotiating an exchange of land for peace with the Palestinians, saw immigration to Israel flatten. The number of new entrants in 2006, after Sharon's career had just ended, was the lowest since 1988.

5

UNITED STATES AND ISRAEL: A UNIQUE BOND

FROM ARIEL SHARON'S words that day, you might have thought he was issuing instructions to his staff or mobilizing party activists. "I am not going to address you today, I am going to tell you what I believe you have to do," he told the gathering at Jerusalem's Inbal Hotel on February 3, 2003. "I am sorry for using military terms as an order to the group. I would like to tell you exactly what we expect you to do." Then he spelled out his audience's responsibilities: combating a global rise in anti-Semitism; defending Israel's cause on college campuses; explaining the Jewish state's history and achievements; encouraging "Jewish continuity" through the teaching of Hebrew, traditions, and the Bible; boosting Jewish immigration to Israel; developing the Negev, in Israel's barren south, and the Galilee region, in the north, so that both would have Jewish majorities; preserving Jerusalem as the capital of world Jewry; and preventing a large-scale return of Palestinian refugees to Israel.

Sharon wasn't speaking to subordinates, party members, or even fellow Israelis, but to representatives of more than fifty American organizations led by distinguished and often wealthy business, civic, and philanthropic leaders. These were men and women as accustomed to command in the private sector as Sharon was on the battlefield or in government.

The occasion was one of frequent visits to Israel by the Conference of Presidents of Major American Jewish Organizations, the umbrella grouping of prominent supporters of Israel and leaders of Jewish charities and community groups in the United States. The conference spanned the political spectrum, from the hawkish, conservative Zionist Organization of America to the left-leaning Americans for Peace Now. Its chairman at the time was Mortimer Zuckerman, a real estate and media magnate listed by *Forbes* magazine among the four hundred richest Americans, who owned the *New York Daily News* and *U.S. News and World Report*. His successor was Harold Tanner, an investment banker and former executive at Salomon Brothers and Rothschild, Inc., who had also chaired Cornell University's board of trustees. Over the years, the conference had become an important bridge between Israel and American Jews and an influential force in lobbying the U.S. government on behalf of Israel and promoting the Jewish state in U.S. public opinion.

Together with the American Israel Public Affairs Committee, known by the acronym AIPAC, the conference represented a key part of the pro-Israel lobby, one of the most muscular and effective special-interest groups operating in Washington. The lobby's clout has helped maintain overwhelming support for Israel in the U.S. Congress and kept Israel as the biggest recipient of U.S. foreign aid. Privately, American Jews have historically been generous, as well. Israel gets an estimated $1 billion a year through philanthropy and another $1 billion in Israel bonds proceeds.

At the time Sharon spoke to the conference and for the rest of his tenure in office, until the end of 2005, both Israeli leaders and American Jews could count major gains in the U.S.-Israeli relationship. Not only was Bush shifting ground in Israel's favor on major issues at stake in the conflict, but he had given Israel much wider latitude than his predecessors in combating Palestinian terrorism. Moreover, Bush had changed the sequence of a land-for-peace trade: "In the past, the Arabs got territory, then they gave peace. Now the Arabs have to give peace before they get any territory," said Israeli historian Michael B. Oren, speaking in a 2005 interview. Oren said that "the Jewish domestic element in the United States," a powerful political force, was at least partly responsible.

Given these gains for Israel under the Bush administration, Sharon's authoritative, demanding manner toward the Conference of Presidents, some of Israel's most committed supporters and benefactors, stood out in sharp relief. It revealed an uneasy undercurrent in the complicated relationship among the Jewish state, the United States, and American Jews. It's a relationship where shared strategic interests, common democratic values, deep attachment, and religious, family, and cultural ties coexist alongside vulnerability, insecurity, and, at times, flashes of tension.

Before World War II, American Jews had been divided over the establishment of a Jewish state in the Biblical homeland, even as waves of Zionists from Europe were erecting the foundations of nationhood in Palestine. But as the world grasped the full extent of the mass slaughter that wiped out two-thirds of the Jews of Europe, more and more Americans, and not just Jews, came to see a Jewish state as necessary to protect the Jewish people. Although the United States had led the defeat of the Axis powers, it failed to rescue Jewish victims of the Nazis' industrial-scale extermination campaign. Nor did the United States—or the British authorities then ruling Palestine—welcome Jews who managed to escape. The birth of the state of Israel and its victory over Arab invading forces meant that Jews had a refuge, defended by fellow Jews, after centuries of recurrent and often murderous anti-Semitism.

Under a determined Harry Truman, the United States recognized the state of Israel within minutes of its founding in 1948, becoming the first nation to do so. Truman went against the advice of U.S. diplomats and his secretary of state, George C. Marshall, who complained that the decision would hurt the United States' position at the United Nations and be seen as a bid for Jewish votes. An incensed Marshall told Truman that if he went ahead and recognized Israel, he, Marshall, wouldn't vote for him in the next election.

In *Support Any Friend: Kennedy's Middle East and the Making of the U.S.-Israel Alliance*, historian Warren Bass wrote that "most of the elements of America's special relationship were laid by the time Truman left office in 1952. Even in those early days, the American attachment to Israel melded an affinity of regimes, the backdrop of the Holocaust, domestic politics, and cold war realpolitik." But the young state entered a rocky relationship with Truman's successor, Dwight Eisenhower, and counted France as its main ally and arms supplier through the 1950s. Frequently annoyed by Israel's reprisal attacks against Arab neighbors and worried that it harbored expansionist impulses, Eisenhower at various times cut off aid and arms. When Israel joined Britain and France in a war with Egypt over Suez, an angry Eisenhower came down hard on both Britain and Israel, while at the same time bluntly warning the Soviets to stay out.

As Israel established itself, the post–World War II period saw important improvement in the lives of American Jews, who for generations had faced nonviolent but widespread bigotry. Barriers to their advancement—admissions quotas at top private universities, restrictions on where they could live and acquire property, and what organizations and clubs they could join—began to crumble. Drawing on a powerful tradition of scholarship and an adaptability born of displacement and survival, many American Jews were able to reach the upper reaches of academia, professions, and commerce. For Americans, at least, the need for another safe haven diminished.

But to Sharon and a number of other Israelis, security and self-defense were only part of the Zionist narrative—and not the most important part. "In my view, [Israel] is not a refuge from anti-Semitism," Sharon said in a speech at Bar-Ilan University. "We are an ancient nation, with roots that run deep, united by a common memory and history and faith and hope, a nation that has returned home." Rather than a country that rose in response to the Holocaust, as many Americans think of Israel, Sharon stressed its biblical origins. "Throughout their years in exile, Jews turned here in prayer, and only here can the Jewish people realize its full potential—for its own benefit and for the benefit of the entire world," he told the Jewish Agency.

Sharon never fully accepted the fact that Jews would want to continue living outside Israel. He gently chided the Conference of Presidents: "Of course, you still live abroad, though of course we are expecting you here. But you are still there, and we have to carry most of this burden on our shoulders." Less gentle was the palpable sense of superiority that some Israelis could convey in such offhand comments as this from L. Marc

Zell, an American Orthodox Jew who moved with his family to a religious settlement in the West Bank. "[W]e don't have a problem with our identity. Most American Jews do have a big problem with their identity. We don't."

Nevertheless, Sharon and other Israelis sought to persuade foreign visitors that security for diaspora Jews was a fragile thing. To them, it depended heavily on preserving Israel's strength. Even as Israelis prospered and became more cosmopolitan, some drew invidious comparisons between the comfortable lives of diaspora Jews and Israel's proudly rugged, pioneering heritage.

Reminders of the Holocaust appeared frequently in Israeli media. On the day set aside each year for remembrance, a siren sounds, traffic halts, and, for a few moments, the entire nation stands still and silent. Sharon vividly recalled the world's abandonment of the Jews in their bleakest hour. During a 2003 commemoration of the Allied victory over the Nazis, he said, "The strong and prosperous state of Israel is the most concrete proof of the great Jewish triumph over the Nazi attempt to annihilate and destroy every remnant of Jewish existence."

Although Israel, in practice, has been unable to protect Jews abroad from attack—in Kenya or Argentina, for instance—Sharon nevertheless saw the country as responsible for the Jewish people as a whole, saying at one point: "We shall be strong, determined, and steadfast in defending ourselves and will cut off any hand raised against Jews anywhere."

Sharon opened his 2003 speech to the Conference of Presidents with a dark warning of where diaspora Jews would be without Israel. "When I speak about your responsibility, I would like to emphasize that if Israel, if God forbid, will be weakened, do not expect—for one day—that you will be able to live the lives that you have now. Therefore, it is your responsibility no less than ours. Most of you are very young, and maybe not all of you remember. I believe that some of you do remember and have been eyewitnesses to what happened to the Jews before we had an independent Jewish state. So that should be remembered. Therefore, I believe that you have [to] stand together with us."

Raanan Gissin, a Sharon adviser, drove the point home more sharply, speaking to a Jewish delegation from Baltimore in 2001: what was it like for Jews in the United States before the state of Israel existed? Gissin supplied his own answer: "Heads down, cowering."

Such warnings resonated even among Americans in positions of stature and influence. "Israelis—and Jews in general—have learned that you cannot willy-nilly trust the non-Jewish world with the lives of Jews," said Abraham Sofaer, a former New York federal judge who was the State Department's top lawyer under President Ronald Reagan and, later, a fellow at Stanford's Hoover Institution. "That's a tough thing to say, but I say it, clearly and explicitly: I do not trust the world with the lives of Jews."

Sofaer, who traced his ancestry to the Jewish scribes of Baghdad, said, "If I were an Israeli, I would think of the United States as my best friend, and certainly not the equivalent of the Europeans who have in fact collaborated or actually been part of the Axis. Nonetheless, I still wouldn't trust the United States with the future of the Jewish people. I wouldn't turn over to the United States the decisions that are critical to the security of Israel."

This lack of faith in non-Jews' commitment to Israel persisted despite repeated assurances by a succession of presidents that the United States would stand behind Israel—assurances backed by money and close military and intelligence consultation. Starting in 1959, military loans were added to annual economic aid packages. Aid levels shot up after the 1973 war, and grants replaced military loans. Since 1985, Israel has received more than $3 billion annually. It also gets certain benefits that are usually not available to other aid recipients, such as the ability to deal directly with American arms manufacturers rather than go through the Defense Department.

The implication of American commitment to Israeli security is that the United States would be the Jewish state's protector of last resort. In 1973, when Israel scrambled to recover from a surprise attack by Egypt and Syria, then President Richard M. Nixon ordered an emergency resupply of the weapons it lost on the battlefield. "The Israelis must not be allowed to lose," he said at the time, according to historian Abraham Rabinovich. To prevent Soviet intervention, he put U.S. forces on alert. Interviewed a decade later by Frank Gannon, a writer and former special assistant to the president, Nixon recalled that Israeli prime minister Golda Meir "told many people who interviewed her that without the decisions I had made . . . in the 1973 war . . . Israel could not have survived."

Neither the flow of aid nor the U.S. commitment to Israel's security was totally magnanimous. The American actions in 1973 fit into a larger strategy of checking Soviet influence and maintaining U.S. pre-eminence in the Middle East. While Israel was grateful for this support, its whole ethos recoiled at being—or even appearing—dependent on the United States. It welcomed the wherewithal to defend itself—but did not want the United States to fight its battles. To the extent that Israel was seen as a dependent and a supplicant, its leaders felt their psychologi-cal deterrence against their enemies would be undermined. Viewed by its neighbors as an overbearing superpower, Israel more often than not feels under siege by Palestinian and Hezbollah militants and their patrons in Syria and Iran—and facing threats to its survival from Iran's nuclear program. While independent-minded Zionists in Israel chafed at the leverage the United States exerted, Israel's supporters in Wash-ington were acutely sensitive to any sign of a weakening American commitment and the message this would send to Israel's adversaries.

"[S]ee, the biggest thing that AIPAC fears is pressure from America, because—mostly it's the money, the foreign aid money, but it's also symbolic," said Keith Weissman, a senior AIPAC analyst for more than a decade who was fired in 2004. "It's the knowledge in the Arab world and in the Middle East that if things get really bad for Israel, the United States will show up, like in '73. It's that knowledge, I think. When the Americans are in the position where they start pressuring Israel to make moves that the Israeli public is uncomfortable with, that's the thing that makes AIPAC the most scared that it gets—when it looks like there's going to be pressure."

During much of the cold war, Israel provided added value to the United States as a bulwark against Soviet inroads in the Middle East, along with Iran under the Shah and Saudi Arabia. But a common strategic vision and a joint U.S.-Israeli approach to the Middle East and the rest of the world were never realized. At times, the United States tended to differentiate support for Israel from broader U.S. interests in the Middle East. This made Israelis anxious. On the one hand, Washington backed Israel with weapons, money, and a U.S. veto in the UN Security Council. On the other hand, it maintained strong strategic ties with Saudi Arabia and other Gulf states that refused to recognize Israel, at least formally. The result was that Israel and the Arab states tended to view American policy in zero-sum terms. U.S. attempts to broker Israeli-Arab peace were regarded in Israel as attempts to appease the Arabs. Arabs, in turn, viewed the American proposals with suspicion as designed to benefit Israel.

A common approach would be hard to achieve even between nations of roughly equal size and strength. There is no way that a dominant global power can view the world the same way as does a nation of six million people, despite extremely close ties. In Israel's case, the relationship is also freighted by history and its sense of being, in the words of the biblical verse, "a nation that dwells alone."

Dov Zakheim understood the inherent tensions in the relationship perhaps better than anyone. As deputy undersecretary of defense for planning and resources during the Reagan administration, Zakheim engaged in a bruising battle with Israel's defense ministry and aircraft industries over the joint development of a fighter plane, the Lavi. He considered the project a waste of American tax money. The Pentagon ultimately succeeded in killing the project, but not before Zakheim, an Orthodox Jew, drew bitter complaints from the Lavi's backers in Israel and in Washington. He and several of his Israeli adversaries subsequently repaired their relations. "[A]fter I left the government, virtually every [Israeli] cabinet minister who was involved in that decision—except Mr. Arens [Moshe Arens, former Israeli ambassador to Washington and defense minister, and a strong champion of the Lavi project]—came up to me and told me that they really supported me, privately. And I thought to myself, 'Well, at least they supported me privately.' It was nice to know. They hadn't exactly supported me publicly."

At issue for Israel was more than just an American subsidy. Having its own fighter plane would give Israel a measure of strategic independence—as well as pride—that it wouldn't have if it continued to rely on U.S.-built warplanes.

While serving as a campaign foreign-policy adviser during George W. Bush's 2000 race for the White House, Zakheim disappointed the Israelis again—this time over technology sales to China. Israel's defense industry can't sustain itself without exports, which sometimes puts it in competition with U.S. arms manufacturers. But competition was not the problem here. American officials had long been wary of Israel's cultivation of China as an expanding market for weapons and technology. The United States could veto Israeli sales to China that relied in part on American technology. But since China is seen as a potential strategic rival to the United States across the Pacific region, any Israeli sale with a military application raises serious concern in Washington—whether it includes American technology or not. Opposition to such sales is particularly strong among the same hawks who are ordinarily among Israel's strongest supporters.

In 1999 and 2000, Zakheim and other Bush advisers backed the Clinton administration in opposing an Israeli sale of Phalcon airborne warning and surveillance technology to China. "I told them [the Israelis] not to get involved. They totally miscalculated the reaction on Capitol Hill. They seemed to think the Hill would support them because it was generally very supportive of Israel. I warned them that when it came to China and Taiwan and that whole balance and our role in the Far East that they were getting into circumstances that they really didn't need to initiate [and] things would not go well."

U.S. pressure again forced Israel to back down, but China exacted a price from Israel for not fulfilling its commitment. After Bush was elected and Zakheim joined the administration as Defense Department comptroller, Israeli officials approached him for U.S. help to compensate the Chinese. "I wasn't very sympathetic," Zakheim recalled dryly. "Their argument was they had to pay it back to the Chinese so they wouldn't have money for their own defense budget—which probably was true, but it was a hole they had dug for themselves."

After Zakheim left the Pentagon in 2004, a worse dispute flared, causing a bitter rift between the director general of Israel's defense ministry and the Pentagon. In this case, one of Israel's chief American antagonists was Douglas J. Feith, undersecretary for policy, one of the most pro-Israel officials in the Bush administration. (Retired Colonel Lawrence Wilkerson, chief of staff to Secretary of State Colin Powell, called Feith a "card-carrying member of the Likud Party." He claimed in an interview that Powell himself used the same language to describe Feith to President Bush during a farewell meeting at the White House in early 2005. Powell, through an aide, denied it.)

The dispute centered on Israel's plans to upgrade Harpy attack drones, or unmanned aerial vehicles, that it had previously sold to China. The Pentagon claimed Israel violated an understanding that it would coordinate its sales to China with the United States and suspected that the drone deal was part of a pattern of such violations. Prime Minister Ariel Sharon intervened and halted the Israeli-China deal, but the Israeli Defense Ministry's director general, Amos Yaron, became persona non grata at the Pentagon and subsequently retired. Eventually, tempers died down with an Israeli commitment to set up strict export controls, but close American scrutiny continued. "I think the Israelis, watching them over the years, certainly push the envelope," Zakheim said. "Sometimes they do improve our technology—no question about it. I remember, I think this was during the Lavi time, they briefed us on the F-16; they improved the F-16 and wouldn't tell us about the systems they had put into our aircraft."

In addition to restrictions on what Israel could sell and to whom, the aid relationship also gave the United States leverage over how U.S.-supplied weapons could be used. In 1982, Washington suspended delivery of cluster bombs to Israel after concluding that they may have been used in civilian areas of Lebanon. Later, when a congressional probe confirmed the suspicions, the United States imposed a six-year ban on further cluster bomb sales to Israel. The United States opened a new probe into cluster bomb use in Lebanon during the 2006 war.

Outside the military sphere, Israel's drive to advance economically has generated competitive friction with the United States. A constant irritant is copyright and patent infringement by Israeli firms on American pharmaceuticals, software, and recordings. Israel is one of thirteen countries, including China, Russia, Ukraine, and Egypt, on the U.S. Trade Representative's (USTR) Priority Watch List of nations that have failed to protect U.S. intellectual property rights. Despite American pressure, Israel actually weakened its laws on protecting foreign drug patents, according to a 2006 USTR report.

Expansion of the American war on terrorism after the attacks of September 11, 2001, brought back some of the attributes of an alliance that had fallen into disuse after the cold war. Israel was happy to share intelligence, terrorism-fighting innovations, and counterinsurgency tactics, not only with the U.S. military and spy agencies, but with a host of law-enforcement agencies, in the process deepening the U.S.-Israeli relationship at various levels of government.

But the two countries' priorities were not in sync. Israel was less troubled by the global al-Qaida threat, the United States' initial target, than by Hamas and the al-Aqsa Martyrs' Brigades in the Palestinian territories and Hezbollah, menacing Israel's northern border from Lebanon. Israel supported President Bush's plan to invade Iraq and topple Saddam Hussein, a longtime enemy of both countries, but did not press for it, senior American officials said. Like most Western spy agencies, Israeli intelligence accepted as an article of faith that Saddam had exploited the absence of UN inspectors since 1998 to rebuild his arsenal of weapons of mass destruction. Saddam was also encouraging anti-Israeli terrorism by paying large sums to families of suicide bombers and other "martyrs."

"What you had in our government was an anti-Iraq lobby, which was highly successful because we went to war against Iraq," said a senior American official at the time. "I don't think this goes, 'Pro-Israel lobby equals war on Iraq.' You had 'Anti-Iraq lobby equals war in Iraq.'" Israelis were highly skeptical of Bush's notion that regime change in Iraq would spur democratic change in the region.

U.S. special envoy Anthony Zinni, the retired Marine general who in 2002 tried and failed to generate security cooperation between Israel and the Palestinians, recalled sitting in on a discussion of Iraq between Ariel Sharon and Vice President Dick Cheney. "Sharon brought it up. Sharon wanted to be clear that they weren't pushing for this military action. . . . I think the only point Sharon wanted to make clear on all this—you bring

up the Scuds—is they're not going to sit out if they start taking Scuds,"
Zinni said in an interview. Iraq terrorized Israel with Scud missile attacks
during the 1991 Gulf War, but Israel did not respond, bowing to Washington's request that it stay out of the conflict. "If Saddam decides to start
shooting Scuds, or provoke them, they have to defend themselves. They
didn't want any assumption [made] about their role. . . . [A]s a matter
of fact, most of the IDF generals and others I talked to, leaders up there,
just were nervous about something like that."

Israeli military leaders were worried about timing, Zinni recalled.
"They had this view of them being pushed into an incursion into the
West Bank and everything, the same time we were fighting." It was telling
that Sharon's 2003 speech to the Conference of Presidents fell a month
before the U.S.-led invasion of Iraq—and yet he made no mention of
the coming war.

Zakheim, who was involved in soliciting assistance from other countries for the invasion, said the Israelis "offered to be supportive, although,
unlike a lot of other countries, they weren't ready to give stuff. They were
prepared to manufacture and sell it; they weren't ready to give it. One
of my jobs was to try to get equipment from different countries. Paying
money wasn't the idea. We were paying enough money."

Yossi Alpher, a respected Israeli analyst who copublishes the Web
site bitterlemons.org, reported in an essay that "sometime prior to
March 2003, Sharon told Bush privately in no uncertain terms what
he thought about the Iraq plan. Sharon's words . . . constituted a
friendly but pointed warning to Bush. Sharon acknowledged that
Saddam Hussein was an 'acute threat' to the Middle East and that he
believed Saddam possessed weapons of mass destruction. Yet according to one knowledgeable source, Sharon nevertheless advised Bush
not to occupy Iraq. According to another source—Danny Ayalon, who
was Israel's ambassador to the United States at the time of the Iraq
invasion, and who sat in on the Bush-Sharon meetings—Sharon told
Bush that Israel would not 'push one way or another' regarding the
Iraq scheme.

"According to both sources, Sharon warned Bush that if he insisted on occupying Iraq, he should at least abandon his plan to implant democracy in this part of the world."

Richard Armitage, deputy secretary of state in George W. Bush's first term, said of Israel's attitude toward the Iraq War: "Oh, they were all for it. But they wanted to be sure, and we wanted them to be sure—the last thing we needed was Israel coming into the fray. That would have caused us trouble, so one of the things we were attempting to do was get all their ideas—is there something we were missing? Is there something we didn't see? Because we wanted to make sure we had, to the extent possible, alleviated all their concerns, so they wouldn't enter the fray. Their chief concern was that they were going to get hit. [Second to that,] reaction of the Arab world. Syria. How are you going to handle Syria? . . . We discussed it and came to a common point of view and diplomatic messages were sent [to Damascus] . . . which were classified."

The Iraq War did provide strategic benefits to Israel. "Israel's greatest strategic nightmare—conventional strategic nightmare—was what is called the eastern front. It was the convergence of Syrian, Jordanian, and Iraqi armies on our narrowest border [between Israel and the West Bank]," said historian Oren, author of a book on the 1967 war. "What the Iraq War did was eliminate the nightmare, because there was no more Iraqi Army, at least one that was going to come at us." At the time Oren was interviewed, in late spring 2005, Iraq had not yet become the bloody quagmire that would produce widespread disillusionment in the United States and wreck Bush's once-high approval rating. To Oren, the United States had struck fear into the region and that, in his view, was a good thing. "Syrians are scared to death of Bush. Everybody in the Mideast is scared to death of Bush. The image of America in the Arabs' imagination prior to 2003 . . . [was] one of a cowardly, decadent country that just needed one more push and it was going to fall over. That's gone. Arabs no longer think of the United States as cowardly and weak. They think of it as crazy and dangerous. . . . That again works to Israel's benefit. Everyone's afraid of him. Every Arab leader wants to talk to us because they're afraid of Bush."

An unstated benefit for Sharon was that the war diverted American attention from the Israeli-Palestinian conflict. Even had President Bush wanted to broker negotiations between the two sides, the invasion and occupation of Iraq would have made it hard, if not impossible, for U.S. officials to devote the necessary time and effort.

From his position at AIPAC, Keith Weissman saw an improved relationship between his organization and the executive branch during the George W. Bush administration: "Something really changed with Bush . . . maybe it was 9/11. Something changed that made the relationship between the administration and AIPAC—to what I considered to be much closer than I had seen it at any time." The absence of pressure from the administration on Israel to negotiate peace with the Palestinians suited AIPAC, which traditionally advocates positions advanced by Israel's elected leadership. Ariel Sharon wasn't interested in negotiations.

The improved relationship between the pro-Israel lobby and the administration eased anxieties on another front: while many American Jews are perfectly comfortable lobbying and protesting against U.S. government policies they disagree with, others remain highly sensitive to the appearance of dual loyalty. In a democracy comprising a multi-hued quilt of national origins, religions, and ethnicities, with an assortment of overseas attachments, the whole question of dual loyalty is an anachronism. Indeed, if citizenship connotes loyalty, then dual loyalty is entirely legal, since U.S. law allows Americans to hold dual citizenship and even to serve in another nation's armed forces.

An example of just how explosive this issue remains in part of the American Jewish community was the intense reaction that greeted a 2006 study of the pro-Israel lobby's impact on U.S. foreign policy. The response began almost as soon as the paper, by political scientists Stephen Walt of Harvard and John Mearsheimer of the University of Chicago, was posted on the Web site of Harvard's Kennedy School. Their thesis was that the lobby's influence had steered the United States away from foreign policies that would more clearly reflect its own interests. They also charged that the lobby was a driving force behind Bush's invasion of Iraq.

Whatever the merits of their argument, the paper was a legitimate exercise in academic debate in a free society. Had Walt and Mearsheimer described the influence of, say, oil or weapons manufacturers, or even of Greece or Taiwan, all of which have powerful Washington lobbies, it's hard to imagine the fallout would have been nearly as harsh.

While Israel enjoyed considerable sway in Washington through AIPAC and other advocacy organizations and think tanks with a pro-Israel orientation, and while Jewish leaders developed strong connections with the Republican leadership and the White House, they had a close rival for influence behind the scenes. The Saudi royal family maintained close ties with the Bush family and with Vice President Cheney even when many Americans and more than a few members of Congress grew hostile toward the kingdom after September 11.

The United States, Israel, and the Saudis shared a strategic worry: a nuclear-armed Iran. The Iraq War may have convinced the Islamic Republic that it needed its own nuclear deterrent against becoming the United States' next target. At the same time, Iran made the most of its other opportunities in the region, forging ties with Shia militias in Iraq, strengthening an alliance with Syria, arming Hezbollah in Lebanon, and funding Hamas in the West Bank and Gaza. By early 2006, Iran and its allies and proxies were in a position to inflict serious harm on both the United States and Israel, even without nuclear weapons.

Since the mid-1990s, Israeli leaders had watched in frustration as the United States did little to prevent Tehran from progressing with its nuclear program, which the Iranians claimed was solely for civil purposes. In 1994, Weissman recalled, then Prime Minister Yitzhak Rabin sought AIPAC's help in getting the United States to take the threat more seriously. One reason Rabin wanted to press ahead in seeking peace with Israel's immediate neighbors, Syria, Jordan, and the Palestinians was to put Israel in a stronger position in case it had to confront Iran. U.S. officials recognized a long-term threat from Iran but didn't share Israel's alarm. They didn't think Tehran could develop a nuclear weapon as rapidly as the Israelis feared. They also saw Iran as wanting chiefly to dominate the Persian Gulf—an age-old Persian ambition—rather than to destroy Israel.

In supporting Bush's decision to invade Iraq, Israelis repeatedly stressed, "Don't forget Iran," a senior U.S. official said.

"They were always raising Iran," added Zakheim, speaking of the Israelis. "I think Iran is a problem for the Israelis not just because of the inherent threat from the ayatollahs, but because for the first thirty years of Israel's existence Iran was part of their security policy. Ben-Gurion had this formulation of the inner circle of enemies and outer circle of friends. There was Ethiopia [under] Haile Selassie, there was Turkey, there was Iran—the Shah.

"And the Israelis have never gotten over that shock" of the 1979 Iranian revolution that led to a hard-line clerical regime under the Ayatollah Ruhollah Khomeini, Zakheim said. "Nor have the Israeli Iranians who live in Israel. So it's not surprising that they are exceedingly sensitive to Iran in a way that they are to almost [no one] else, including Syria. And [then Defense Minister Shaul] Mofaz would raise concerns about Iran and he certainly wasn't the first. If you look back at Israeli predictions, the Israelis have been predicting at least for the last eight or nine years that Iran would have nuclear weapons. . . . They wanted us to do whatever we could possibly do to restrain the Iranians. If you go back and look at various reports coming out of Israel, at least into the 1990s, you'd see, 'The Iranians are going to have a bomb in two years.' It comes two years and 'They're going to have a bomb in two years.'"

By early 2006, the threat posed by Iran was shaping up as the most serious crisis in the U.S.-Israeli relationship since the Yom Kippur War, or even since the birth of the Jewish state in 1948. At stake for Israel, in the minds of much of its security establishment, was nothing less than survival. They saw a nuclear-armed Iran married to the desire repeatedly and publicly expressed by Iran's president, Mahmoud Ahmadinejad, to see Israel wiped off the map. Retired Israeli chief of staff Moshe Yaalon told the Hudson Institute in Washington in March 2006: "Understanding that it cannot defeat Israel in one aggressive step—such as in a conventional war against Israel—Iran has adopted a strategy of constant attrition, aimed at both weakening Israel militarily and under-mining its international legitimacy. It has thus sought nuclear capabilities—the superconventional capability—as a means of achiev-ing strategic supremacy, further serving as an umbrella for subconven-tional aggression, including terror attacks and aggression against Israel and moderate regimes in the region." For the United States, the stakes were equally high: protection of its vital interests in the Middle East, including the oil-producing Arab nations of the Persian Gulf and a Jew-ish state in Israel.

The moment called for a cool assessment of intelligence, strong American leadership, and steady nerves. By early 2006, all three were in short supply, raising the risk of a miscalculation with colos-sal consequences for the world. Iran's intentions, ambitions, and fears, and the question of who called the shots in Tehran, were sub-ject to a variety of interpretations in Washington. Assessments seemed prone to the same sorts of biases and distortion that had plagued intel-ligence on Iraq. The danger of error was compounded by the Bush administration's refusal to open a dialogue with the Islamic regime. Intelligence-gathering on Iran degenerated almost into farce in 2003, when a frustrated midlevel Pentagon analyst, Lawrence Franklin, allegedly sought to enlist Keith Weissman and Weissman's supervisor at AIPAC, Steven Rosen, to alert the White House and Israeli gov-ernment to the danger he saw emerging from Tehran. He pleaded guilty in October 2005 to passing government secrets to the two AIPAC representatives.

Widely disliked throughout the Arab world, the United States by early 2006 had seen its influence in the Middle East sink to its lowest point in decades as a result of mismanagement of the war in Iraq, the Abu Ghraib torture scandal, and President Bush's neglect of the Middle East peace process. As for nerves, political control over Israel's national secu-rity was now in the hands of relative amateurs, Prime Minister Ehud Olmert and Amir Peretz, who would plunge Israel into an ill-prepared and ill-considered war in Lebanon in the summer of 2006.

A tiny nation embraced and nurtured by Americans from its infancy was imperiled. The commitments to Israel's security, repeated over four decades by U.S. presidents, faced a supreme test. If these American pledges to Israel and to the Jewish people were to mean anything, the United States had to be prepared to act if the Iranian threat proved genuine and serious. But whom could Israelis and Americans trust to act wisely?

6

New Administration

EDWARD S. "NED" WALKER JR. had a low expectation
of President George W. Bush when the new chief executive opened the
first National Security Council meeting of his administration, a session
devoted to the region Walker knew best: the Middle East. A career diplomat entering his thirty-fifth year in the foreign service, Walker had
thrived under Bill Clinton, winning two of the most prestigious U.S.
postings in the region, as ambassador to Egypt and then to Israel.
Walker had also been No. 2 at the United Nations mission under
Madeleine Albright. He knew most of the top leaders of the Arab
world. Neither a media star nor dynamic nor even especially articulate,
he nevertheless brought a direct, low-key style to working with such
diverse and difficult leaders as Ariel Sharon and Hafiz al-Assad of
Syria. Now he was assistant secretary of state for the Near East, a significant job even if its authority over the peace process had been swal-
lowed up in the 1990s by special envoy Dennis Ross.

Among many of Walker's foreign-policy peers, Bush was considered untutored and little interested in world affairs. So the Middle East
veteran was pleasantly surprised by Bush's grasp and preparation. "It
was actually a pretty impressive performance. All this stuff about the
president not being engaged—he certainly was engaged in that meeting.

I was impressed particularly since I had not been expecting to be impressed. . . . He ran a good meeting. He asked the right questions," Walker recalled in a 2004 interview.

Much of the world had misjudged Bush, who made little effort during the 2000 election campaign to display any foreign policy competence. Europeans had trouble seeing the leader behind the Texas twang, the garbled syntax, the frat-boy swagger, and the mediocre college record. They didn't anticipate Bush's quick grasp of issues and deep faith in his own instincts or, after the attacks of September 11, his immersion in the role of warrior-president. Nor did they anticipate how the traditional bureaucratic and cultural rivalry between the State and Defense departments would be compounded by powerful, continuing tension among Bush's top advisers, with Cheney and Rumsfeld forging a common front to block Powell.

In the Middle East, the Bush family ties to the oil business led many Arabs to expect—and Israelis to worry—that the new administration would reprise George H. W. Bush's prickly relationship with Israel, draw the United States closer to Egypt and Persian Gulf Arabs, and adopt a balanced role in the peace process.

Walker knew that in the Arab world, Vice President Cheney's ties to Persian Gulf oil monarchies through his leadership of Halliburton were taken more seriously than the foreign policy advice Bush got during the campaign from neoconservatives like Richard Perle, who opposed an American role in Israeli-Palestinian peacemaking. "Every Arab in the world wanted Bush to win," Walker believed.

In September 2000, with the outcome of the presidential race unknown, several leading Palestinians had expressed disillusionment with the Clinton team and hoped for better treatment from his successor. "We are waiting for the end of the Clinton-Albright administration," Hani al-Hassan, a longtime political adviser to Arafat, said as Arafat and his entourage alighted in Gaza City after an acrimonious meeting with the Americans and Barak at the United Nations. "We will see. Maybe a better president will come." Mohammad Nashashibi, the Palestinian finance minister, added, "We have faith in President Clinton but not in others," a pointed reference to the Clinton "peace team."

The fact that several members of the Clinton team were Jews, and therefore assumed to be predisposed to side with Israel, had been a fixture of Arab officials' private conversations and back-channel contact for years. But what upset Palestinian negotiators, Walker believed, was their impression that U.S. peace proposals were cooked up with Israelis before the Palestinians saw them. This impression often was correct, but the reason was benign, he said: "Because so many times we had come out with positions that the Israelis had simply deep-sixed, there was a tendency to check with the Israelis first." Aaron Miller, the State Department's most experienced hand in the Arab-Israeli arena before he left in early 2003, said, "They [the Palestinians] engaged in this fantasy, 'We'll wait for the Republicans.'"

Not all Palestinians looked forward to the new administration. Four years later, negotiator Saeb Erekat claimed to have worried about the change. "We did not have neon [signs] saying 'stupid' on our foreheads. We knew we were going to miss President Clinton. This man devoted much of his time in the White House to peace between Palestinians and Israelis. And we knew that Governor Bush was not particularly an expert [about] the Palestinian-Israeli affair," he said. "It was a matter of, how much time would it take him to grasp the situation? Secondly, and this was before he became president, our assessment was, 'If this man looks at what President Clinton devoted, how much time he spent and how much effort he put, and how many times he received Arafat in the White House and how many times he received all the Israeli prime ministers, will he touch us? Will he dare touch us?' So we did not have any illusion about the new administration."

As Bush took office, a few Arab commentators echoed Erekat's worry. In the London-based Arab newspaper *al-Hayat*, Hazem Saghiyeh wrote that Bush "can be expected to care less about what the Europeans think than former president Bill Clinton did. . . . As the European position has always served to offset America's bias toward Israel, this is cause for concern." He added that "the isolationism of the Bush administration could leave Israel with a free hand, or relieve it of any pressure. . . ."

In Israel, L. Marc Zell sought to soothe fears that Bush would adopt his father's approach to the region. He headed an organization of

Republicans—U.S. citizens or dual nationals—living in Israel. On election day 2000, he wrote on the op-ed page in the *Jerusalem Post*: "After eight years of unprecedented interference in Israel's domestic politics, Bush will be a welcome change. We can expect a more 'hands off' approach. Israel has had about as much American intervention as it can handle." Zell, a hard-liner who lived in a Jewish settlement in the West Bank, knew this from conversations with his Washington-based law partner, Douglas Feith, who would become the third-ranking official in Bush's Pentagon and a powerful force against the State Department's interest in renewing the Middle East peace process. Feith "was my principal eye on the administration-in-formation," Zell said in a 2005 interview.

The day he was sworn in, Bush got an earful from his predecessor on the failure of the Israeli-Palestinian peace effort that had dominated the final months of the Clinton presidency. The deeply disappointed Clinton placed heavy blame on Palestinian leader Yasser Arafat. The political lesson the new administration took from Clinton's experience was that the outgoing president had been personally screwed by Arafat, and they would not allow this to happen to Bush.

Vice President Cheney told the Los Angeles World Affairs Council in 2004, "I'm always struck by the memory that I'll always carry of January 20, 2001, when President Bush and I were sworn in. We went to— as is traditional that day, you go to church service, and then you go over to the White House and have coffee with the outgoing administration— in this case, President Clinton, Vice President Gore, and their families. And you spend several hours together by the time you go through the ceremony, the swearing in and so forth. And Bill Clinton talked repeatedly all day long about his disappointment in Yasser Arafat, how Arafat had, in effect, torpedoed the peace process." Edward Abington, a former U.S. consul general in Jerusalem who became the Washington lobbyist for the Palestinian Authority, was told later by someone in the room that "Clinton basically said this is a guy that is very untrustworthy and very, very difficult to deal with."

For all his criticism of Arafat, Clinton expected Bush to continue the peace process. He called Powell on inauguration day and delivered a detailed up-to-date briefing on what he had learned about Israeli-Palestinian talks then under way in Egypt. A Powell aide paraphrased what he told the former chairman of the joint chiefs: "Now, here's where we are and here's what you can do, and here's so-and-so's position—and [Clinton] went on and on, and Powell said it was all very interesting but somehow it seemed a little too late." The Bush team didn't send an envoy to participate in the talks.

The following day, George Mitchell visited Powell. A former law-maker from Maine, who had risen to become Democratic leader before quitting politics for a lucrative law practice, Mitchell went on to distinguish himself as a creative and determined diplomatic troubleshooter for the Clinton administration. After lengthy mediation between bitter nationalist and Unionist adversaries in Northern Ireland, under the skeptical eye of the British government, he succeeded in crafting a durable agreement—the Good Friday accord—that guided the Irish Republican Army away from violence and terrorism and into a new, accepted role in the country's political life.

The previous October, Israeli prime minister Barak and Yasser Arafat had agreed to let Clinton launch an independent outside inquiry into the causes of the intifada, then in its early, violent spasm. In November, Clinton tapped Mitchell to head a prominent panel that also included the European foreign policy chief, Javier Solana, and retired Republican senator Warren Rudman of New Hampshire. By the time of Bush's inauguration, its probe was still at an early stage. Israeli officials—always suspicious of international investigations—were, at a minimum, leery of the panel.

A shrewd lawyer-politician, Mitchell wanted to make certain of where he stood with the new Republican administration. In his meeting with Powell, "I told him I was prepared to resign as chairman of the committee if he and the president felt that they wanted to appoint someone of their own choice. In addition, I told him that the committee was prepared to terminate its activities without any further action and without making any report if the president and the secretary of state determined that they did not want the committee to proceed.

"Secretary Powell told [me] that the president wanted me to proceed and wanted me to continue to serve as chairman."

The January 30 NSC meeting, Bush's first such session, fell a week before the Israeli elections, but Ariel Sharon held a virtually insurmountable double-digit lead in Israeli polls over incumbent prime minister Ehud Barak and was widely expected to win.

Veteran Washington policymakers were wary of Sharon. Bush didn't consult Brent Scowcroft, his father's national-security adviser, but if he had, he probably would have heard something like what Scowcroft said in a 2005 interview, drawing partly on experience in the Ford White House in 1973: "From the Yom Kippur War on, he's been a millstone around our neck," Scowcroft said of Sharon. "When we had a truce in the Yom Kippur War, the Third Egyptian Army was almost surrounded. We didn't want them to be destroyed because we wanted an armistice, a peace settlement, which left Egypt with its self-pride. Sharon broke the cease-fire to complete the surrounding of the Egyptian Third Army. Then the Soviets said we need to send, both of us, send troops in. That was a crisis. That was Sharon.

"The second time was the Shatila camps in Lebanon. And the third time was up on the Temple of the Mount visiting the shrines, which were not the cause but the precipitation of the second intifada. Bad news."

Israel's ambassador to the United States, David Ivry, knew Sharon faced trouble in Washington and went to work to head it off. One of his first visits was with Richard Armitage, who would become deputy secretary of state. A veteran of the Reagan administration who had watched the 1982 Lebanon invasion unfold, Armitage thought the title of one of Sharon's less-flattering biographies captured him exactly: a man who wouldn't stop at red lights. "[H]e was very hardheaded and didn't give up."

Still, Armitage listened attentively to Ivry's requests: congratulate Sharon on his election; send a message that he would be judged according to his actions; fend off anti-Israel votes at the United Nations; and arrange an early visit by Sharon to Washington. Ivry also asked for a joint U.S.-Israeli military exercise. In the end, he later recalled, all of his requests but the last were met. He also met with the late Senator Paul Wellstone, the Minnesota Democrat, whom he expected would be a sharp critic of Sharon, urging the outspoken liberal to give the new Israeli prime minister a chance.

The eleventh-hour negotiations in Taba, Egypt, broke off three days before Bush's first NSC meeting, with both sides announcing they had never before come closer to agreement. Months later, Israeli negotiator Gilad Sher told the Washington Institute for Near East Policy, in summary: "The Barak government came within inches of achieving a package deal for permanent settlement. The issues and the spectrum of possible solutions will not change in the future, and when the two sides finally conclude a permanent agreement, it will be almost identical to the one that was formulated recently. There will be no letup in the violence unless there is some movement in the political process. Therefore, any Israeli government should work with the PA on two tracks: to stabilize the situation with a measurable reduction in violence and incitement, and to return to the political negotiations with a final-status deal in mind. Israel should continue to seek a final-status agreement with the Palestinians."

If Sharon had his way, the talks would not be renewed.

For Bush, this reality buttressed his decision to set U.S. Middle East policy in a new direction, pulling back from a central American role as a mediator between Arabs and Israelis and focusing instead on what he viewed as more serious threats to U.S. interests in the region, starting with Iraq and Saddam Hussein's ambition to rebuild his armed might.

"Iraq was a priority, and regime change was one of the objectives," recalled Edward Walker in a 2003 interview. Getting rid of Saddam had been official U.S. policy under Clinton. But now there was a "fundamental difference," Walker said: whereas Clinton hoped covert U.S. backing for a coup or insurrection would accomplish the task, Bush was open—even as early as that January meeting—to the idea of using American ground troops. The new president instructed aides to craft two sets of options, Walker said: a tightening of sanctions, and both clandestine and military action to topple the regime.

On the Israeli-Palestinian conflict, "He indicated that it was questionable whether these parties wanted to make peace, but that we would give them a chance and then send the secretary of state out for the first round of meetings," Walker said. But the president also signaled that Ivry's message had gotten through. He would not be guided by the views of outsiders about either Sharon or Arafat but would let each man build his own record with the new administration.

At one point, he asked if anyone in the room besides him knew Sharon. Walker, who had worked with the Israeli on and off since the 1980s, gave a bland response. "I said I had known Sharon for many years, that he was a man who was deeply concerned about security, that he was not an ideological 'Land of Israel' supporter, but that his approach to the West Bank is based on his concerns about security."

Bush was clear about what he *didn't* want to do. "He did not want to repeat the same mistakes that he felt Clinton had made by engaging too deeply with Barak, in the process itself. He wanted to stand back," Walker recalled. "The primary thing was that he . . . did not want to be the desk officer for the peace process." In addition, Cheney, Defense Secretary Rumsfeld, and Rice didn't want the president to invest much of his prestige, time, and energy on the problem.

His decision to "stand back" provided an opening for the Likud in Israel. Zalman Shoval, a Sharon political ally and adviser, developed foreign-policy ideas for the new prime minister's first one hundred days. "My recommendations were very clear: the focus of whatever Sharon would do and plan must be the United States." Not only was it necessary for Sharon to forge a bond with Israel's patron and ally, but the new administration provided Israel with an opportunity, Shoval thought. A visit to Washington, where he met with Cheney, Powell, and NSC officials, convinced Shoval that the new U.S. team and Sharon were "like-minded." They shared the view that "our predecessors made the mistake of thinking that this conflict [between Israelis and Palestinians] was the most important reason for all the ills of the Mideast, and that if only it were laid to rest, all the problems would go away." Sharon and his staff planned to capitalize on the new administration's lack of enthusiasm for a new spurt of Mideast diplomacy, according to Israel Radio: "Sharon's adviser said he will urge that Israel and the United States end what was termed their 'obsession' with the Palestinian problem and instead concentrate on wider regional problems."

Bush's perception that the two sides weren't ready for peace wasn't the only reason for shrinking the United States' diplomatic role. According to

Aaron Miller, the new administration had a "determination to define its own policy separate from the one the previous administration has followed.

"I worked for five administrations. Rarely have I seen an administration more determined to define its approach on this issue in a way that was so different from its predecessor's." One upshot was a refusal to appoint a Middle East envoy to replace Ross. A second was a decision to jettison the "Clinton parameters" for a division of territory between Israel and the Palestinians. "The ideas and parameters that were discussed in the last few months were President Clinton's parameters and therefore, when he left office, they were no longer a U.S. proposal or a presidential proposal," State Department spokesman Richard Boucher said on February 8, 2001.

Introduced in December 2000, the Clinton parameters had been accepted by both the Barak and Arafat teams as the basis for the Taba talks. Abandoning them left the U.S. government with no clear outline for ending the conflict. In keeping with the zero-sum nature of the conflict, Sharon's opportunity meant Arafat's loss. If the Israeli prime minister had his work cut out for him to gain Washington's confidence, the Palestinian leader had a worse problem, thanks to Clinton and, subsequently, Dennis Ross. Ending eight years as Middle East envoy to join the right-leaning Washington Institute for Near East Policy, Ross began a prominent role as commentator. In print and public remarks, he repeatedly pinned the greatest responsibility for the failure of the peace process on Yasser Arafat, describing him as "unable to conclude a permanent agreement. . . ." He also didn't think Sharon would make a deal, writing, "Indeed, both leaders are unable to take the steps that would make it possible to end the conflict now."

Bush took three weeks to telephone Arafat, who proceeded to sink further in U.S. esteem. His government in financial disarray, Arafat did nothing to control violence against Israelis, perhaps hoping that Sharon would live up to his image, overreach, and allow Palestinians to play the role of victim in regaining world support. While U.S. officials were divided on whether he had a role in precipitating the intifada, all blamed Arafat for not stopping it, by failing to assert a monopoly over the use of force among Palestinians.

Reflecting in 2004 on Arafat's attitude, Walker said: "I think it was after the fact, as this thing developed, that Arafat made several conclusions coming out of Camp David. One was that he couldn't rely on the United States because he felt the U.S. team had tilted heavily towards Israel, that the president had fundamentally lied to him when he said you can leave without being criticized by me [and] he was criticized. And he generally does one or two things when he gets to feeling he has no backing from the U.S. He either goes on a worldwide tour to try and get all his friends to treat him like a head of state in European capitals, and so on . . . or he goes back and he sulks and starts creating problems. He was trying to get our attention. So the will was there to create problems. The immediate cause, I don't think he really had that in mind. This was fortuitous."

When Powell made a brief visit to Jerusalem and Ramallah, Arafat wasted the chance to get on a better footing with the new administration. Amjad Atallah, then a member of the Palestinian negotiation support group made up of savvy, Western-educated lawyers, suspected that even by then Arafat was losing his mental acuity. At the time, Arafat was carrying around with him a press release from U.S.-based antiwar group Voices in the Wilderness, reporting that the group had been barred by Israel from taking samples of weaponry out of the country so they could be tested for depleted uranium. To Arafat, the press release represented an "official American study" proving that Israel was using depleted uranium in the territories.

Atallah described efforts to prepare Arafat for his first meeting with Powell: "We said, 'You can't use the depleted-uranium argument with Powell.'" "But no," Arafat insisted. "It's an official American study." His advisers countered: "That's a left-wing group in America that said they didn't find evidence that this was being used." Arafat: "No, no, no, I have it here. You're not reading it right." The advisers changed tack, telling Arafat: "OK, nobody has used depleted uranium more than General Powell. There is nobody on earth more responsible for depleted uranium than Secretary of State Powell. So, using this argument with him would be a waste of your time."

Arafat was not to be deterred. He proceeded to complain to Powell that Israel was using depleted uranium. Powell, who says he has never seen satisfactory evidence that the material poses a health risk, brushed him off: "I've been around it—most of my career we've had depleted rounds."

At their joint press conference, Arafat performed almost a self-parody by saying, "Of course, the two of us are generals together." (In private meetings, he styled himself "the only undefeated Arab general.") He repeated the charge of Israel's using "prohibited" types of ammunition. He raised a point few in the Bush administration liked to be reminded of: the strained relations between the first President Bush and Israel: "Also, we call for the stopping of settlement activities. President Bush the father stood against that issue and he used the ten billion dollars' loan guarantee to make his point." When it came to actions he could take to halt violence, he replied helplessly: "If they [the Israelis] allow me to use my own car to enable me to move from one Palestinian town to another, that would help. They are preventing me from using my own helicopter. If it wasn't for King Abdullah of Jordan who gave me his helicopter, I would not have been able to come here and meet with Secretary Powell."

Powell emerged from his first meeting with the Palestinian leader "not very pleased," said Walker, who recalled that Arafat seemed to be in poor physical shape. "So that was the first black mark on Arafat. He played that meeting totally wrong." Sharon, by contrast, showed his pragmatic side to the top U.S. diplomat, leaving the impression among Powell's team that "there might be something we can work with Sharon."

A few weeks earlier, the newly elected prime minister had revealed some of the same pragmatism to Terje Roed-Larsen, the United Nations' Middle East envoy. Among the right wing in Israel, Roed-Larsen had two strikes against him: he played a key, early role in framing the Oslo peace accords, which the Right considered a major strategic error for Israel. And he belonged to an international institution they considered anti-Israel. Nevertheless, Roed-Larsen was summoned to meet with Sharon at the hotel suite where the Likud leader was savoring his victory and weighing his next moves.

"If you were me, what would you do?" the prime-minister-to-be asked the Norwegian diplomat. "I would pull out of Gaza immediately," said Roed-Larsen. "Why?" Sharon asked. "I've just reread your autobiography and you're a man of dash and dare," Roed-Larsen said. "If you do that, it will change the whole equation. It will be impossible for Palestinians to continue the terror and you would immediately get international legitimacy and support for whatever you do."

Sharon didn't dismiss the idea. "But I can't leave Netzarim," he said, referring to a small but strategically situated hilltop settlement overlooking the Mediterranean outside Gaza City. "I need it to secure the harbor" that the Palestinians planned to build on the nearby shore. Israelis feared the harbor could be used to import military equipment and wanted a post nearby to be able to respond quickly.

The exchange signaled to Roed-Larsen that Sharon was prepared even then to relinquish occupied territory and dismantle Jewish settlements, provided they didn't have strategic importance, and that ideologically "he didn't have any illusions at all."

Arafat remained a problem, but one that the new administration might have neutralized had it wanted to. While the White House didn't trust him, State Department Middle East experts were wedded to the idea that there was no alternative to dealing with him directly, a high-level official said in 2006. There were those who believed they knew how to get him to cooperate. One was Miguel Moratinos, the European Union envoy who later became foreign minister of Spain. "I knew how to deal with him—when to be tough, when to be soft," he said in 2005. "I used to say, he was the problem, he was the solution." Arafat was surrounded by knowledgeable negotiators who were well acquainted with Americans and Europeans. "[Mahmoud Abbas], [Mohammed] Dahlan, all the others who met separately with me, they were quite open to a flexible approach," Walker said.

According to Abington, his Washington lobbyist, Arafat would cut off at the knees any subordinate who attempted to intrude on his authority, requiring U.S. officials to be subtle in shifting power away from him. These aides lacked Arafat's acute sense of the public mood—one reason he failed to control the intifada. To the extent that he could, Arafat tried to avoid taking any action until he achieved a consensus among all or most Palestinian factions. For that to happen, Americans and their allies on Arafat's team needed to work on shaping Palestinian public opinion and winning support for moderation from factional and community leaders. If the public saw a payoff for compromising, Arafat might have bent. There are few signs that such moves were attempted.

The streets of Ramallah offered indications of an already hostile Palestinian mood at the time of Powell's first visit. His mission was either denounced because of his expressed determination to make containing Iraq a priority for the United States in the region, or dismissed as pointless. Waving Palestinian and Iraqi flags and carrying pictures of Saddam Hussein, a group of demonstrators gathered outside the gates of the authority's headquarters, chanting pro-Iraq and anti-American slogans. One demonstrator hoisted a sign, apparently produced by the militant Islamic group Hamas, featuring a picture of terrorism financier Osama bin Laden. A sign on a nearby wall said in English: "Oreo go home."

Yet for all the noise and public hostility toward Israel and its patron, the intifada was still in a relatively mild early stage. Hamas was still holding fire, unwilling to plunge in alongside the less-disciplined Fatah Tanzim group, led by the eloquent firebrand Marwan Barghouti. Melissa Boyle Mahle, a CIA operative in Jerusalem who tracked Palestinian militants, recalled: "Hamas and Palestinian Islamic Jihad sat it out because frankly they thought it was a trap. And they thought that what Arafat intended to do was to permit, to fan the flames a little bit, of street reaction and then to have Hamas and Palestinian Jihad come in and pick up the mantle and then he would sell them out to the Israelis, and say, 'You see, this is the problem,' and there would be a mass crackdown à la 1996, a crackdown against the militants."

President Bush's decision to back away from the Israeli-Palestinian conflict made it Powell's problem, since the Middle East was too explosive to be ignored. He had his work cut out for him, since historically, Arabs and Israelis have demanded strong U.S. presidential involvement before they will make serious concessions. Sharon's refusal to resume peace talks where they left off at Taba, and the Bush team's rejection of the Clinton parameters, posed another obstacle. And Arafat's evident physical and mental deterioration further dimmed the prospect of a renewed peace process.

More important, Powell shared the general administration view that getting deeply involved in Middle East diplomacy was unlikely to yield results, and he didn't have a clear strategy to achieve them. When he did plunge into the thicket later in 2001 and subsequently, he did so most often in response to pleas and pressure from the United States' Arab-world allies to demonstrate U.S. involvement, not to advance the peace process significantly.

As a result of this attitude, he and his top aides may have missed an opportunity that emerged during the new secretary's tour d'horizon with Sharon. The prime minister, like the whole Israeli security establishment, saw Iran's unchecked nuclear program and development of long-range missiles as the No. 1 strategic threat facing the Jewish state.

Here was a chance to follow James Baker's successful playbook from 1991: seize on something Israel desperately wants; make a strenuous effort to deliver it, thereby demonstrating a commitment to an ally's needs; and then use it as leverage to get concessions from Israel on the Palestinian front. Baker had worked on two challenges: repealing the UN General Assembly resolution equating Zionism with racism, and persuading Syria to enter direct face-to-face negotiations with Israel, something it had resisted up until then. Israeli prime minister Yitzhak Shamir, in turn, for the first time recognized the stateless and previously marginalized Palestinians as a legitimate negotiating partner, provided they sat in a delegation together with the Jordanians.

Whether an early international campaign against Iran's nuclear program would have been effective—either in curbing the threat or in making Sharon more flexible—is impossible to judge. But it wasn't tried until it was too late to make an impact on the Israeli-Palestinian arena.

"I never could understand why we could never focus on Iran," Walker told me in 2004, as he recalled the first months of the Bush administration over several cups of coffee. "We never got to it. It was supposed to be No. 2 on the hit parade and we never got beyond Iraq . . . in the first five months. The whole idea was to have a serious review of the Iraq policy, of the Palestinian policy, of the Iran policy—those principally, and some of the others. We got to Iraq and we stopped there."

While Washington left Israel and the Palestinians to their own devices, it also began a benign neglect of the peace process between Israel and Syria, which had collapsed shortly before the death of longtime dictator

Hafiz al-Assad the previous June. Whereas Barak had been willing to give up most of the Golan Heights for peace with Israel's most powerful close neighbor, Sharon—at least in his rhetoric—wanted to keep all of it. And there was little indication from Damascus that Assad's son and successor, Bashar, was politically strong enough to be more flexible than his father.

Signs emerged early on of the huge cost this neglect of the peace process would eventually exact—in blood, treasure, and hatred—but they didn't raise an alarm in Washington.

One issue was Lebanon. Israeli military leaders desperately wanted Barak's planned withdrawal from Lebanon to occur in the framework of an agreement with Syria and Lebanon that would prevent Hezbollah from being able to threaten northern Israel at even closer range. Experts warned that the UN monitoring force, the United Nations Interim Force in Lebanon (UNIFIL), was not up to the job of policing the border. "If the IDF withdrawal takes place under conditions that leave southern Lebanon in disarray, it is unlikely that UNIFIL will attempt to fulfill its mandate to help restore peace and security to the region," wrote John Hillen, a member of the U.S. Commission on National Security/21st Century.

Instead, the border was kept tense but mostly quiet through a balance of terrorism. Hezbollah, backed by Iran and Syria, cemented its hold on territory Israel had just vacated and gained domestic and regional hero status for having driven the Israelis out of a swath of south Lebanon, dubbed a security zone, after an eighteen-year occupation. Six years later, it would have a fearsome arsenal of short- and long-range missiles to fire deep into Israel and an array of launching platforms.

Palestinians in the Gaza Strip heard a repeated siren call from Beirut on al-Manar TV, Hezbollah's satellite broadcast station. Just days before Americans went to the polls in November 2000, as funeral marchers carried the body of a Palestinian killed in the intifada through Gaza's streets, a yellow flag bearing a black Kalashnikov rifle—the Hezbollah symbol—stood out in a sea of bright-hued banners of various Palestinian political factions.

Hezbollah claimed credit for wearing down the Israeli public's endurance and causing mothers to oppose keeping young occupation troops in a "security zone" in southern Lebanon, where two or three troops a month fell to guerrilla ambushes and roadside bombs. Bunkers of reinforced concrete, roads sheared of brush and trees failed to keep them safe. The guerrillas' triumph served as a pointed reminder to Palestinians of what their own leaders had failed to accomplish over a decade of negotiating with Israel. Sheik Hassan Nasrallah, Hezbollah's charismatic and ambitious leader, made sure to drive the message home: "It is unacceptable for Palestinians to continue fighting with stones," he said in one broadcast. "They should be able to use real weapons to defeat the enemy."

Youssef Ahmed, forty-seven, who ran a tire-repair shop close to the Karni junction, the border post that was also a frequent flash point between Israeli troops and young Palestinians, gave a thumbs-up sign when asked about Hezbollah. "What you have to do is flatten the Israelis like Hezbollah has done," he says. "I want Hezbollah to open [fire] now," said Shifa Homade, fifty-four, a schoolteacher and mother of four who lived outside Gaza City. "Hassan Nasrallah is a big headache for them [the Israelis]. Not one country is standing by us."

Al-Manar also celebrated Palestinian "martyrs," not just its own, and exhorted Palestinians to follow Hezbollah's example. It inspired, among others, a fourteen-year-old Gazan named Faris Odeh, whose family had lost ten men in fighting against the Israelis over the years. Watching film of Hezbollah guerrillas training in southern Lebanon, he wanted to be like them. Skilled with a rubber slingshot, he slipped out of his house or school at every opportunity to join the rock-throwing mob at nearby Karni crossing, for weeks a flash point between Palestinians and Israeli soldiers. One day a cameraman caught him hurling a rock at an Israeli tank. The picture conveyed a David versus Goliath image much like the similar scene more than a decade earlier of a young Chinese demonstrator facing a tank at Tiananmen.

Eight days later, Faris headed to Karni again. Slipping out of school, he climbed a wall, shouting to a friend who refused to join him, "Go tell the headmaster: Faris is martyred." That afternoon, his mother, Anam, got a call from the gas station near Karni, announcing that he had been shot. Later she heard from his friends that the bullet had struck him as he stooped to reach for a sandal that had fallen off his foot as he ran from Israeli gunfire. The wound proved fatal.

In early January 2001, about two weeks before the new Bush administration took office, Faris Odeh's family kept its television tuned to al-Manar. Periodically, the station broadcast the video showing him confronting the tank. A caption appeared in Arabic and Hebrew: "He's stronger than you." Anam Odeh must have seen the same clip scores of times, but she gave out a momentary sob at the sight once again of her son on the screen. After watching the video with a visiting journalist, she pulled her two-and-a-half-year-old nephew close and asked him who shot Faris. "A Jew," the child replied. Where? "In his throat. I'm going to shoot the guy who shot him." Where is Faris now? "In paradise."

7

BELFAST TO JERUSALEM

■ SPRING 2001 ■

ONE OF PRESIDENT BUSH'S earliest actions on the Middle East was to ease Democrat George Mitchell out of the picture. But the poker-faced former U.S. senator from Maine, known as a tough partisan when he led the majority, was not the type to disappear quietly. He had a proven method for ending stubborn conflicts and wanted to see it applied in the Israeli-Palestinian arena.

An immigrant's son who rose from working-class beginnings to become a U.S. attorney, federal judge, U.S. senator, and ultimately Senate Democratic leader, upon leaving Capitol Hill Mitchell built a record as a diplomatic troubleshooter that was hard to beat. After twenty-two months of dogged mediation, he brokered a 1998 power-sharing deal between Northern Ireland's majority Protestants and minority Catholics called the Good Friday accord. The agreement, approved by eight political parties and blessed by Whitehall and Dublin, ended a bloody thirty-year conflict that had grown out of centuries of religious hatred and discrimination. Mitchell was rewarded with the Presidential Medal of Freedom by Clinton and an honorary knighthood from the British government, which at one time had recoiled at American interference in the "troubles." The following year, Mitchell was summoned to Belfast again to prevent the accord from collapsing. He clocked several more months before the two sides returned to the politically painful job of implementing the pact.

On November 7, 2000, then President Clinton enlisted Mitchell to head a five-person commission that would explore the causes of spiraling Israeli-Palestinian bloodshed and recommend ways of getting the two sides back to the peace table. Appointment of a fact-finding panel had been agreed on the previous month at Sharm el-Sheikh, Egypt, where Clinton and Egyptian president Hosni Mubarak tried to get Yasser Arafat and Ehud Barak to agree to a cease-fire.

Based on his success in Ulster, Mitchell had developed a formula for easing the distrust that keeps bitter adversaries from making peace. In an early 2005 interview, he described getting Unionists and Nationalists to negotiate "a very detailed series of steps that they would take—statements, actions, very precise as to their timing down to the hour and minute that the statements would be made." Even the substance of public statements was negotiated.

"And so when that agreed-upon process began, every one of the participants knew exactly what would occur over the next several weeks. They had in their possession copies of statements that everyone was going to make. They knew exactly when it was going to be made, they knew what actions were going to be taken. That was necessary because there was a complete absence of trust. . . . Nobody would take an action unilaterally based on trust because they didn't believe what the other side said or what they would do."

The bloodshed was worse in the Middle East than in Northern Ireland, but the two conflicts were similar in that there was "a complete absence of trust," Mitchell believed.

As a former congressional leader, Mitchell could be trusted with an assignment fraught with political sensitivity. Like the Middle East, the Northern Ireland conflict resonated among a key American constituency. By championing a peace process that would give a new measure of political power to minority Catholics, Clinton stood to earn the gratitude of powerful Irish American politicians, particularly the Massachusetts-based Kennedy family, and win back some of the Catholic vote lost to Republicans as Irish Americans became more prosperous.

With Israelis and Palestinians, the U.S. political tables were reversed, since an overwhelming majority in Congress and the public tended to support the stronger of the two adversaries: Israel. But the implications for Mitchell were the same. He had entered a minefield and had to tread carefully. As if to underscore the political delicacy, Clinton announced formation of the fact-finding panel on election day, too late to distract in any way from the presidential race of Al Gore or the New York Senate race of the president's wife, Hillary.

The son of a Lebanese mother and an Irish father, Mitchell had avoided being pigeonholed on one side or the other of the Arab-Israeli divide while leading the largely pro-Israel Senate Democrats. In 1992, in fact, he publicly disagreed with President George H. W. Bush's effort the previous fall to face down the pro-Israel lobby, telling an annual meeting of the American Jewish Committee, "Contrary to President Bush's remarks at a press conference on September 12, I support 100 percent your constitutional right to come to Washington to ask your elected leaders to support programs you favor." Nevertheless, the fact-finding panel also included retired New Hampshire Republican senator and fellow lawyer Warren Rudman, who was Jewish, along with European Foreign Policy Chief Javier Solana; former Turkish president Suleyman Demirel and Norwegian foreign minister Thorbjoern Jagland.

Mitchell, whose monotonous, bland speaking style matches his opaque, owlish expression, began work in a typically low-key fashion, seeking clarification from Clinton on how the panel should operate. The president urged them to avoid anything that would make a bad situation worse. If the panel wanted to hire professionals to help, "they should conduct their work quietly outside the glare of publicity," he wrote Mitchell, and the committee should avoid "any step that will intensify mutual blame and finger-pointing between the two parties." Finally, he urged them to collect the views of each side in writing and to comment on the others' presentations.

"This should not be a tribunal whose purpose is to determine the guilt or innocence of individuals or of the parties; rather, it should be a fact-finding committee whose purpose is to determine what happened and how to avoid it recurring in the future."

The panel also sought to lock in cooperation from the two sides. Palestinians were eager for the Mitchell team to hear their case, hoping this would lead to the introduction of an outside protection force that would keep Israeli troops from launching military operations inside the West Bank and Gaza. Israelis were anxious, even though Barak had agreed to the panel. Sharon, the opposition leader when the panel was formed, said later that he had repeatedly warned Barak that it was a bad idea. He refused to accept the panel's assurances that its job was not to pin blame. Interviewed by Israel Radio on March 26, Sharon let loose what appeared to be a lifetime's worth of built-up suspicion about world attitudes toward the Jewish state and international investigators:

"I told [Barak] that by agreeing to the formation of such a committee, Israel would be making a historic mistake because no one has the right to put Israel in front of an international tribunal. . . . No one in the world has the right to put Israel on trial. No one! On the contrary, Israel may have the right to put others on trial, but certainly no one has the right to put the Jewish people and the state of Israel on trial. . . ." He also complained to Mitchell, who was prepared to stop work if Israel refused to cooperate. However, since the incoming Bush administration had urged Mitchell to continue, Sharon faced international isolation if he failed to support the panel.

Israelis were alert for signs of committee bias, even demanding to have one of their own officers present during meetings with Palestinians, a request that Larry Pope, a seasoned diplomat who headed the staff, said was "obviously a nonstarter for an independent international commission." The panel made one move that inadvertently violated Clinton's injunction against actions that could add fuel to the conflict. Members of the committee staff visited the original and most sensitive intifada flash point, Jerusalem's Temple Mount/Haram al-Sharif, in mid-January 2001, in the company only of the shrine's Muslim custodians. The visit went off quietly but was subsequently picked up by the Israeli press. Furious that it hadn't been coordinated with them, Israeli officials cut off cooperation with the panel. Pope, who happened to be in New York to meet with Mitchell at the time, "decided that my resignation would help defuse the flap, and convinced a reluctant Senator

Mitchell that it would be in the best interest of the effort for me to turn the staff over to Fred Hof—who did a brilliant job and produced a fine report, as I knew he would."

The intifada was still at a relatively amateurish stage when the mission got under way, with a lopsided advantage in favor of the better-armed and -protected Israelis and a four-to-one ratio of Palestinian to Israeli dead. Pope, in a 2006 e-mail, later recalled visiting Beit Jala, where Palestinian gunmen bearing light arms fired across a valley at the Jewish settlement of Gilo, on the edge of Jerusalem. The Palestinian gunfire terrified Gilo residents while causing few casualties. Israeli retaliation produced heavy damage in Beit Jala, causing some of the Christian town's residents to turn against the militants, who came from elsewhere in the West Bank.

"I took one of the Palestinians there aside and suggested to him in Arabic that this was a foolish business," Pope related. "The small arms fire had no effect on the Israelis at that range, but the return fire was devastating—so why didn't they cut it out? 'You're absolutely right,' he said—'what we need are heavy weapons.'"

Frederic Hof, who led the panel staff after Pope left, visited checkpoints and other active zones of confrontation between rioting young Palestinians and almost equally young Israeli soldiers. A former army officer, he was deeply familiar with the ugly turns that Middle East conflicts can take. He was one of the authors of the report of a probe led by retired Admiral Robert L. J. Long into the 1983 terrorist attack in Beirut that killed 241 U.S. Marines. A few years later, working in the office of the secretary of defense, he was part of a team that tried to secure the release of an American colonel, Richard Higgins, who had been kidnapped by Hezbollah while serving as a UN observer. "I am one of a small handful of Americans who knows the exact manner of Rich's death," he recalled while giving a talk in 2006. "If I were to describe it to you now—which I will not—I can guarantee that a significant number of people in this room would become physically ill."

The confrontations Hof witnessed in the Palestinian territories may have lacked the sheer viciousness of the violence perpetrated against Colonel Higgins, but they were nonetheless disturbing.

"One of the really disquieting things we found on both sides was that in many respects, the intifada and the counter-intifada was a war of children," he said in a 2005 interview. "On the Israeli side, I was really struck in the visits I made to checkpoints and various places by seeing young people, teenagers—I did not witness personally anything I would characterize as trigger-happy behavior, perhaps because I was there in plain sight. But what I was struck by on the Israeli side was the age of the kids and the absence of supervision, the absence of an officer.

"As a former army officer I found this professionally unforgivable. . . . This was the confrontation point. This was the point at which an eighteen-year-old kid could be stampeded into unloading a clip into a crowd of people and creating political ramifications that go way beyond the authority of a private or a corporal. Therefore, [the] presence of an officer, in my view, was absolutely required. And not only an officer— an officer could also be a twenty-year-old—but somebody with some experience."

"And of course on the Palestinian side, there was not even the pretense of supervision. You had uniformed police hanging in back as thirteen-, fourteen-year-old kids advanced toward Israeli positions with slingshots. In my view that was disgraceful."

As the weeks passed, the conflict became less and less a child's war and more one fought for high stakes with brutal force. Palestinians became intent on destabilizing Israeli society with terror; Israelis on crushing any organized Palestinian militant force or potential force, including the buildings that housed Palestinian institutions—security services, too—suspected of backing them. After waiting on the sidelines, worried that Arafat would betray them to Israel, Hamas operatives entered the fray in late December and stepped up their attacks in the early months of 2001, a period roughly coinciding with Sharon's assumption of power. The first deadly suicide bombing occurred March 3 in the coastal city of Netanya, killing three and injuring dozens more. If Arafat didn't explicitly sanction these attacks, an Islam Online Internet conversation April 1 with Hamas spiritual leader Ahmed Yassin indicated that the Palestinian Authority was doing nothing to stop them: "Today, after we have entered the al-Aqsa Intifada, the situation is much improved. The resistance is legitimate and the authority shuts its eyes and does not pursue the fighters."

To crush the ever-bloodier uprising, the Israeli military gained a freer hand from Sharon to increase its firepower and broaden its array of tactics. Using rockets fired from helicopter gunships, the army continued its use of targeted assassinations of men it accused of participating in or planning acts of terrorism. A number of innocent bystanders also died. Rockets damaged the headquarters of the Palestinian Authority's security services, built up over the previous decade, including members of Force 17, Arafat's bodyguard service. In a further blow to Palestinian autonomy in the spring, Israel sent tanks into Palestinian areas.

Israel's actions battered its international reputation and put the United States in an uncomfortable spot in its relations with its allies in the Arab world, which Washington was trying to enlist once again in squeezing Saddam Hussein. Reporting on the calendar year 2000, covering the early and mildest period of the intifada, before Sharon was elected, the State Department's global human rights survey, released in February 2001, said Israel's security forces had committed "numerous serious human rights abuses," often used excessive force, sometimes exceeded their rules of engagement, and abused detained Palestinians.

But as pressure grew for Washington to intervene, the period in mid- to late March brought a series of diplomatic events that helped create a bond between Bush and Sharon and deepen Bush's disdain for Arafat.

In mid-March, the aggressive Palestinian observer at the United Nations, Nasser al-Qidwa, renewed his lobbying effort for an international observer force that would serve to protect Palestinian civilians from harsh Israeli retaliatory measures. A committed and sometimes emotional nationalist and a nephew of Arafat, al-Qidwa carried a stature and influence that far exceeded his formal title; he was able to rally as many as 130 nations from the Arab world, Islamic Conference, and the Non-Aligned Movement to the Palestinian cause. (His Israeli counterpart bantered with him that the UN was "Palestinian-occupied territory," to which he retorted, "We have a small space on the East River; you have the whole United States.")

Al-Qidwa enlisted Arab and nonaligned colleagues with the aim of getting a Security Council vote on the resolution in time for the Arab leaders' summit in Amman opening March 27. They wanted to send the secretary general to the summit with a mandate to carry out the terms. As the draft gained support, Europeans and, eventually, the United States entered the negotiations. They viewed the observer force as a non-starter, knowing Israel would reject it. So they set to work on a substitute resolution that would push both sides away from violence and back into negotiations.

On March 20, just as the Mitchell panel arrived in the Middle East to resume its probe of the violence, Sharon met Bush for the first time in the Oval Office. The presidential setting brought out a different—more subdued and formal—side of the genial warrior who had hosted then Governor Bush on a helicopter trip in 1998. The prime minister came across as straightforward but stiff. While Bush tried to engage him in a direct conversation, Sharon methodically worked his way through the "talking points" prepared beforehand.

An official who was present at the meeting recalled: "Sharon pitches to Bush that the greatest threat that the West faces is terrorism, and the president of the United States is the only one to lead the coalition against the world of terror. . . . Israel of course would be with him, involved in this war, but he's the one who has to lead us." Six months before the attacks of September 11, this message "fell completely on deaf ears," the official said. Yet Bush gave Sharon an important signal when it came to waging war against Palestinian terrorists, according to the American official. When he told Bush, "We are going to remove them from our society," the president replied: "Mr. Prime Minister, I understand, say no more." The official, experienced in the winks and nods of U.S.-Israeli relations, interpreted this as a way of saying, "Just do what you have to do, but don't implicate me." Later, the message to Sharon was clarified, cautioning Sharon against actions that could destabilize the region or threaten American interests. The two leaders also settled on a method of operating—no surprises—that both would strive to uphold in coming years.

Sharon said later that he also warned that inviting Arafat to the White House would amount to rewarding terrorism. "I told the Americans in a very clear way I don't intervene in their decision of who to invite. I said, 'It's your decision. But know that the thing will look, as long as he does- n't take the necessary steps, as if terror pays off and it could definitely [have an] influence on a worsening of terror activities in the future,'" Sharon told Israel's Channel 1 television station.

At the UN, negotiations intensified in the last week of March, with Europeans and Arabs nearing agreement on a resolution that would also gain the support of the United States, or at least its acquiescence. But they failed to reach consensus by the time the Arab summit opened.

Then al-Qidwa overplayed his hand: he pushed for a vote on the original nonaligned movement resolution, which the United States opposed. It aimed solely at protecting Palestinians and said nothing about Israelis victimized by terrorism. In Amman for the Arab sum- mit, Kofi Annan and a second high-ranking UN official, Kieran Pren- dergast, went to Arafat's suite late at night on March 27 to get him to head off a collision and instead back a resolution the United States could live with.

"I asked [Arafat] whether he was aware that they were heading for an American veto," Prendergast said in 2005. "I said to him it was a very strong [consensus] resolution—they were only talking about a few words. 'Now if you were an Israeli, what would you prefer: a strong res- olution which has fourteen positive votes and an American abstention, which is then carried, or one with a few stronger words which is vetoed by the United States, which pushes the new administration into the arms of Israel, and which irritates the hell out of them as far as the Palestin- ian Authority and you are concerned?'

"And he looked rather alarmed, and he asked Nabil Shaath [a top adviser] to phone up Nasser al-Qidwa and ask him what the hell was going on, and there was a kind of conversation at the end of the room, and he said, 'Don't worry, we've now sent instructions.'"

But whatever instructions were sent didn't steer al-Qidwa off his course. At 11 PM in New York, the Security Council convened in a grim atmosphere, with envoys from the United States, Europe, and Ukraine seething at being pushed to vote on a resolution none of them wanted. It gained the nine votes necessary for passage, with Europeans abstaining. U.S. envoy James Cunningham cast a veto, calling the resolution "unbalanced and unworkable."

The Palestinians, with few diplomatic cards to play, had used the most important one they held—their sway at the UN—to push the new administration into an early, public clash with the Arab world. If Arafat imagined that a veto by the United States would help him generate support and money from Arab leaders in Amman, he was making a fatal choice in terms of repairing his own relations with Washington. David Welch, then the State Department's assistant secretary for international organization affairs, called Edward Abington, the retired diplomat who was the chief Washington lobbyist for the Palestinians, to convey the deep anger felt at the National Security Council and the State Department. Tell the Palestinian leadership, he instructed Abington, that Arafat has angered President Bush and "done irreparable damage to himself over this issue."

In Amman, the Arab leaders friendly to the United States found themselves adrift on a wave of public fury over the Israeli siege and the rising death toll among Palestinians. The summit became an anti-Israel hate fest. Even Kuwait, the tiny, oil-rich emirate that the United States and its allies had rescued from Iraqi occupation in 1991, joined in. In his speech to the summit, Foreign Minister Sheikh Sabah Al-Ahmad Al-Sabah didn't mention his country's decade-long grievances against Iraq, but he had a lot to say about Israel, accusing it of "the most savage forms of extermination, blockade, and starvation" against the Palestinians.

The leaders' communiqué expressed "extreme indignation" at the U.S. veto of al-Qidwa's resolution calling for an international protection force. Far from isolating Saddam, they praised him for pledging one billion euros in oil-sales proceeds to benefit the Palestinians, including "the families of the intifada martyrs." The Iraqi regime would soon be shelling out grants of $10,000 and more to the families of suicide bombers. Saddam himself, in a speech read by a representative, offered to mount a large army to fight the Israelis and ended his speech saying, "May God damn the Jews." Syria, meanwhile, sought to reclaim its role as pan-Arab champion. President Bashar al-Assad, in office less than a year, used his summit speech to compare Israelis with Nazis and got the summit to back a revival of the Arab economic boycott of Israel.

Arafat's triumph proved to be momentary. A wave of stepped-up Palestinian terror undercut his claims to victimhood outside the Arab world. After months of seeing scores of Palestinian teens and youngsters killed or maimed by Israeli forces, militant groups targeted young Jews, in what some Israelis suspected was a move to goad Israel into a harsh retaliation that would, in turn, galvanize Arab leaders. The escalating attacks began the day before the summit, when a Palestinian sniper fired from a hill into the militant Jewish settlement in the West Bank city of Hebron. A bullet killed a ten-month-old girl, Shalhevet Pass, in the arms of her father, who was wounded. On March 27, a suicide attacker blew himself up on a bus in East Jerusalem's French Hill, one of the earliest Jewish settlements beyond the Green Line (the 1948 borders, so-called because they were drawn in with a green pencil) in the city, injuring twenty-seven people. An earlier bombing in the city injured several bystanders. The same day, an Israeli soldier shot and killed an eleven-year-old Palestinian boy, according to Agence France Presse.

At a gas station on the edge of the West Bank the following morning, a young Palestinian in a leather jacket approached a small group of Israeli teenagers, spoke some words of Hebrew, then detonated a bomb, killing himself and two Israelis, Eliran Rosenberg, sixteen, and Naftali Lanzkorn, fourteen, and wounding several others. The bomb was packed with nails, which hit the heart, liver, lungs, and other organs of one of the boys who survived. The teens were headed for a religious school in the West Bank Jewish settlement of Kedumim that offered special instruction and small classes for students with attention deficit disorder. Because of recent violence, they had regularly been driven to the gas station and picked up by an armored vehicle that took them to the settlement. Hamas claimed responsibility for the attack and released a videotape showing a twenty-year-old man it said was the suicide bomber. On the tape, the man said he was prepared to turn his body and bones into shrapnel.

At Rabin Medical Center near Tel Aviv, doctors were unable to prevent Tani Herskovitz, sixteen, one of the injured boys, from losing sight in one eye. His mother, Pearl, an American émigré, showed the resilience Israelis expect of one another during a crisis. "It's just an eye. Two other kids were killed," she said. Harder for her would be visiting the mother of one of the dead boys. She appeared in the hospital waiting room wearing the simple, modest costume of an Orthodox Jew with understated elegance—a perfect fit on her trim figure, with the pale colors of her long-sleeved blouse, ankle-length skirt, and shoes all in harmony. A physician herself, she matter-of-factly assessed her son's condition and arranged for his care acting as both a parent and a medical professional. She had spoken with Tani about pulling out of the school because of the danger of violence in the West Bank. "He said, 'Without this school, I don't have a life.'"

At a cemetery nearby, the family of Eliran Rosenberg laid the boy to rest just before dusk, in keeping with Jewish rules for rapid burial. As mourners paused for a final prayer before leaving, Benny Streissfeld, a friend of Eliran's father, expressed the bewilderment and fear spreading throughout the country as a result of the surge in violence: "This situation comes once a day, twice a day. Where is it going? It's looking bad. I don't think we can go on like this. Something has to happen." Within a few hours, something did.

Three weeks had passed since Ariel Sharon had presented his government to the Knesset, formally becoming prime minister. The old general had moved cautiously against the Palestinians, determined not to upset the Bush administration as it attempted to gain support in the Arab world and Europe for tougher sanctions against Iraq. He refrained from a harsh crackdown, while failing to act on American appeals for direct talks with the Palestinians and taking only partial measures to lift the economic siege on the territories and remove checkpoints. When Powell called Sharon just after the Shalhevet Pass killing, the prime minister complained that because of rising Palestinian violence, it was difficult to carry out his promised steps. Still, he resisted domestic pressure for retaliation. "I know how to deal with this issue and I will deal with it," he told reporters after consulting with security officials, according to a dispatch by Dan Ephron carried by the *Boston Globe* and *Washington Times.* "I suggest we all exercise patience and we'll see the results."

The next day, both Bush and Powell called the prime minister amid tense last-minute bargaining over the UN resolution and the opening of the Arab summit. In an account of the Powell-Sharon conversation put out in Jerusalem, Sharon charged that Arafat's troops were directly involved in the attacks and were cooperating with Hezbollah and other terrorist organizations. Arafat and the Palestinian Authority would bear the consequences, he warned Powell.

Sharon held his fire during the Arab summit. Any serious attack on Palestinians then would have been viewed in the region and beyond as deliberately provocative and would have embarrassed U.S. allies, particularly King Abdullah of Jordan, the host, whose close ties with Israel put him at odds with much of the region and even his own population. But once Arab leaders ended their meeting, helicopter gunships launched the first major military assault by the Sharon government, striking four posts of the elite Palestinian Force 17, Arafat's personal guard service—one in Ramallah and three in the Gaza Strip—as well as a presidential guard-training camp and an armored vehicle. Palestinians said two people were killed and more than sixty wounded.

Arafat's home in Gaza was also damaged in the attack, although he was absent. One member of Force 17 and a Palestinian woman were killed during the raids on Ramallah, hospital sources said. More than sixty Palestinians, most of them members of Force 17, were also wounded in the strikes on Ramallah and several areas of the Gaza Strip, especially Gaza City.

With careful timing and by limiting civilian casualties, Sharon avoided criticism from Washington. Reading a statement the next day, Bush said he was "deeply concerned about the escalating violence in the Middle East" but put primary emphasis on urging the Palestinian Authority to "speak out publicly and forcibly" in condemning violence and to arrest terrorists. Addressing Israel, he said it "should exercise restraint in its military response. It should take steps to restore normalcy to the lives of the Palestinian people by easing closures and removing checkpoints."

Sharon had passed his first test in managing ties with the new American administration. While not gaining a blank check to cripple the Palestinian Authority and punish Arafat, he avoided being accused of brutal excess and of blindsiding Washington, as had happened nineteen years earlier in Lebanon. Equally important, he blunted growing pressure from two leading U.S. allies who were due to arrive shortly in Washington, Egypt's President Mubarak and Jordan's King Abdullah, for the United States to resume a powerful mediating role between Israelis and Palestinians.

For Arafat, the die was cast. By forcing the United States to cast an embarrassing Security Council veto that coincided with the Arab summit, he allowed Washington to blame him—and not Sharon—for straining U.S. ties with—and its image in—the Arab world. He thus alienated the shrinking number of U.S. officials who wanted to cooperate with him and bolstered the argument of his enemies in the administration and Congress that he was an unreliable leader with one foot in the terrorists' camp. Worse for his relations with Bush, he undercut what was already the administration's top priority: building regional pressure against Saddam Hussein.

"I don't think that Arafat ever recovered from that," said Prendergast of the UN, referring to American anger at being maneuvered into a situation where officials felt they had no alternative but to veto a resolution. Far from learning from this mistake, Arafat and some of his inner circle proceeded to dig a deeper hole for themselves.

The shrewd maneuvering by Sharon and maladroit moves by Arafat obscured the larger regional trend that would come into sharp relief in coming months: after a decade of halting steps toward coexistence and peace, both Israel and the United States were becoming increasingly alienated from the Arab world and straining ties with countries elsewhere that had interests in the Middle East. In the years leading up to the end of the Barak government, Israel had begun to crack the wide circle of ostracism and hatred that for decades had forced it to rely on the United States as its sole protector, benefactor, and friend. It had commercial ties with two Persian Gulf emirates, Oman and Qatar. Europeans showed increasing interest in business and investment links. The Clinton administration's global free-trade push and the explosion of Internet technology had encouraged an emerging generation of leaders and technocrats in the Arab world to look beyond the ideological barriers of the past.

"I remember in July 2000 during the [UN] General Assembly of the millennium when 165 heads of state came to the United States, Barak was greeted like a hero," recalled Yehuda Lancry, Israel's ambassador to the United Nations at the time. "He got congratulations from people that you would never imagine—President Musharraf of Pakistan. . . . Even Fidel Castro came and congratulated Barak for his courage, for his audacity and his peace vision."

Now, this tentative opening was rapidly being reversed as the Middle East slid backward into the hardened attitudes of the pre-Madrid, pre-Oslo period. Rather than softening prejudices, the booming satellite TV networks and Internet sites spread images of bloodshed and destruction across the region, stimulating rage at Israel and the United States, putting moderate leaders on the defensive, and boosting support for violent extremists.

George Mitchell, who left the region just before the major flare-up of violence that erupted March 26, felt a "pervasive sense of gloom," the *New York Times* reported. He knew the rising bloodshed would make any peacemaking effort harder. "It obviously became more difficult," he said in 2005. "The history of warfare is that the longer it goes on, the more intense and brutal it becomes. . . . The longer it goes on, the greater the extent of demonization of the other side."

But his panel remained intent on producing a report that the Bush administration could use as a guide. Preparing it over the next month, they discarded the blame that each side heaped on the other and took pains to avoid recommendations that would be rejected out of hand. They did not urge an international protection force that would interpose itself between Israelis and Palestinians. And after lengthy discussion, they stopped short of calling for the dismantlement of any settlements.

It took, as Mitchell put it, "a good bit of skill" to follow Clinton's instructions and produce a factual report on how the intifada had erupted without assigning blame. Israel claimed it had evidence that Arafat's regime planned the intifada but failed to provide it. Similarly, the Palestinians failed to substantiate their claim that Sharon's visit to the Temple Mount/Haram al-Sharif was the cause.

"During all of our discussions with Israeli and Palestinian officials alike, they disagreed on almost everything," Mitchell said. There was one striking exception: both felt that the security cooperation that existed before the start of the intifada had been effective. "[T]hey both wanted it resumed and felt that it would be helpful in the effort now under way to rebuild confidence. Further, that it was greatly facilitated by the presence of American officials, and specifically Mr. [George] Tenet."

So practical and balanced was the final document that it put all sides on the spot, including the White House. Indeed, the report endures as one of the most sober and insightful documents of the Israeli-Palestinian conflict. It included a factual account of how the conflict evolved from rock-throwing riots quelled by lethal and nonlethal force to a guerrilla war of suicide bombs, helicopter gunships, and targeted killings. A detailed series of recommendations required both sides to take politically difficult but commonsense, parallel, and sequential steps to reduce the bloodshed. But the panel stressed that no cease-fire would endure without a resumption of peace talks: "[I]f the cycle of violence is to be broken and the search for peace resumed, there needs to be a new bilateral relationship incorporating both security cooperation and negotiations."

Before the report was published, Martin Indyk told the Israelis the Bush administration would likely accept its recommendations, including one calling for a freeze on settlements "including natural growth." For years, Israel had taken the position that it would not build new settlements but reserved the right to expand existing ones to accommodate growing families and their daily needs. This loophole allowed for rapid construction and elastic boundaries. As the champion of settlements who had exhorted Jews to seize the hilltops of the West Bank, Sharon could be expected to react defiantly. Instead, he was pragmatic.

"I told Shimon [Peres], who was the foreign minister at the time, that you need to get him to accept this," Indyk said. "Shimon never thought he could sell it to Sharon, so he started to negotiate with Powell. This is the famous Powell-Peres understandings. Well, there were no understandings. Peres did his typical call-up—'Go on—you have to agree to some natural growth. You'll have just growth within the settlements.'"

When Powell failed to contradict him forcefully, Peres went ahead and said publicly that he and the secretary were in agreement.

Indyk continued: "So I was instructed to go in to Sharon and tell him there were no understandings. The language meant what it said, the president wanted him to accept a settlements freeze [that] included natural growth. He said, 'Well, I want you to go talk to [Natan] Sharansky, who was minister of housing, and tell him this, and let's see what it in fact meant in terms of what was in the pipeline and what we have to stop.' So I went and talked to Sharansky and then I asked for another meeting with Sharon and, lo and behold, Sharansky's there at that meeting. And Sharon said, 'Well, we can accept that.' He said, 'But, there's a condition. The terrorism has to stop.' And I said that's part of the Mitchell recommendations as well. Palestinians have to act against the terrorists. So he said, 'Well, I can do that. Maybe it'll have to be for a time, let's say six months, settlements freeze.' . . . Sharansky says, 'Wait a minute, Prime Minister, what are you talking about? We've got this and we've got that and how can we do that?' And he said, 'Menachem Begin did it. If the terror stops, I can do it.'"

Sharon may have counted on Arafat to let him off the hook by failing to curb terrorism. But his willingness to commit to a total settlements freeze meant he was agreeing to what for any Israeli prime minister at the time was, politically, the most difficult requirement of the Mitchell report. Even his Labor predecessor, Barak, had been unwilling to face the wrath of the settlers for much of his term. It was also a major concession to Washington. If the administration were serious, it could have used the pledge as leverage to pressure the Palestinians into halting violence.

Sharon didn't say this publicly, and neither did the Israeli government in its official response to the committee's findings, which were given privately to the Israelis, Palestinians, and the Bush administration several weeks before their public release. (Mitchell was told to deliver it to the State Department—and not even to Powell, but to a staffer who received it on the secretary's behalf.)

In fact, both sides added enough qualifications to their formal acceptance of the report to make Hof, for one, sure the report would be discarded. Mitchell himself believed Israel opposed a settlements freeze.

"My personal view is that both sides rejected the report," Hof said. "They covered their rejections with some very nice rhetoric, with a lot of polite language and with what I think was a sincere compliment to Senator Mitchell in terms of the basic fairness and integrity of the report. . . . But if you look at the objections of both parties, what they're saying, in essence, is, 'We accept every last word in terms of what the other side needs to do. And we accept little or nothing in terms of what is required of us.'"

Hof conveyed his pessimism to Mitchell. But the former majority leader followed one of the rules of pragmatic diplomacy: make the most of whatever tools are at hand and work around the obstacles. Hof recalls: "And he said, 'I understand your point of view, but I think as a practical matter we should characterize the responses as acceptance of our report in the hope that the administration will now move to implement the recommendations.'"

Mitchell followed up privately with Powell, speaking with him by phone several times in the week before the report was publicly released. Hof recounts: "I understand that during the period between our submission of the report and the public release of the report, the senator had a couple of conversations with the secretary of state in which the senator said something to the effect [of], 'You understand, Mr. Secretary, this report will not implement itself. We have not, in the body of our report, said anything prescriptive about implementation. It's not part of our charter, and we don't feel that we have the right to try to bind the administration to a certain course of action. But understand, Mr. Secretary, that as is the case with Northern Ireland and other places, recommendations do not implement themselves.' The secretary indicated that he understood."

Mitchell didn't stop there. He offered himself and other members of the panel as special envoys in the model of his own work in Northern Ireland. When Bush called to thank him for the panel's efforts, Mitchell sensed an opening.

As Mitchell remembered the call later, the president "said something like, 'Stay ready; we may call upon you at some time,' or a colloquial phrase, 'Keep your uniforms handy.'" Hof interpreted Bush's words as "at most, a signal of the president's interest in using Senator Mitchell in some way in the future."

But Mitchell wasn't about to let the opportunity pass, telling Bush: "We anticipated this matter arising, we discussed it, and the members of the committee authorized me to say that we would be prepared to continue to participate if you so choose, but we all felt that the decision should be that of the president and the administration."

The report might not have gained widespread attention had it not emerged in a diplomatic vacuum. But neither the United States nor any other power up until then had mounted a serious effort to subdue the escalating Israeli-Palestinian conflict. As a result, interest in the report, and in how the United States and the two warring sides would react, was intense. Contents of the report were widely reported before its official release. It was prominently mentioned in news stories. Meanwhile, mounting bloodshed continued to spread alarm through the region and heightened world speculation about Washington's response. Five Israelis were killed in a suicide attack in Netanya three days before the official release of the report. Israel responded for the first time with attacks from U.S.-supplied F-16s, drawing a rebuke from Vice President Cheney. The Arab League urged member states to sever contact with Israel.

As politicians, Mitchell and other members of the panel were not shy about promoting their handiwork. Two days before the report was officially released, Mitchell gave an interview to National Public Radio: "I think it's a very dangerous escalation that's gone on throughout the six-month period, and that's why we stress with such great urgency the importance of an immediate and unconditional cessation of violence and an immediate return to security cooperation which existed during the Oslo period, was ended last fall, and which I think is necessary; and then a cooling-off period and several steps to try to rebuild the confidence that's been shattered."

He added: "I think the administration is well aware that, while the United States cannot impose a peace process on the parties in the Middle East, there can't be a process unless the United States is fully engaged and active and plays a leadership role." And he said both sides in the conflict had told him that "life for the people in their societies has become unbearable."

The next day, panel member Javier Solana embarked on a four-day Middle East trip to press both sides to pull back from the abyss. Heavy press coverage attended the formal unveiling of the report at a New York press conference, where Warren Rudman, the Republican former senator from New Hampshire, issued an eloquent plea for Israeli and Palestinian leaders to "put aside old beliefs and old canards" and "get ahead of their own constituencies and take substantial political risks." Rudman warned, "If they do not, and they're not willing to take those risks, to reach out to one another and follow the outline of these recommendations or similar recommendations, then I fear that we will see this deteriorate into a conflagration that could be far worse than anyone has imagined."

In 1991 and 2000, the United States had exerted strong pressure on Arab and Israeli leaders to take these risks. The Clinton administration made it a policy to hold out substantial rewards for those willing to assume them. As a result, decades-old political barriers to negotiations and to peace between a Jewish and a Palestinian state had been widely accepted by the two populations. The most serious obstacles to a complete agreement—a solution to the refugee problem, division of Jerusalem, borders, and settlements—had at least been seriously discussed at various stages. A top negotiator for the Barak government, Gilad Sher, believed the two sides had come "within inches" of a deal by early 2001.

Israeli and Palestinian leaders had taken bold risks in the past. Sharon's audacity, toughness, tactical shrewdness, and survival skills had brought him unmatched mastery of the Israeli political scene. To keep American trust and friendship, he was prepared to throw this formidable power behind additional bold steps, provided Israeli security was not compromised. As he indicated to Terje Roed-Larsen and Martin Indyk, he was no ideologue and could be broadly pragmatic. Arafat, for his part, had defied Arab radicals in 1988 in accepting the partition of Palestine, and in 1993, when he agreed to pursue peace with Yitzhak Rabin despite continued Israeli occupation of part of Gaza, much of the

West Bank, and East Jerusalem. Two-faced, autocratic yet incompetent at running a modern government, indulgent of corrupt subordinates and erratic, Arafat was nonetheless the Palestinians' preeminent political figure.

Mutual loathing and mistrust meant direct discussions between these two leaders would probably get nowhere. Yet each was surrounded by skilled and knowledgeable negotiators accustomed to dealing with each other. Several Arafat advisers considered the ongoing violence counterproductive. Anthony Zinni, the retired Marine general and Central Command chief who tried for months to foster security cooperation between the two sides, said later, "As a matter of fact, I would tell you my discussions with [Arafat advisers] Abu Mazen [Mahmoud Abbas], with Abu Alaa [Ahmed Qurei], with Mohammed Dahlan, with Jibril Rajoub and several others in the Palestinian leadership, I felt—even though they didn't say this in so many words—I felt they felt Arafat was on the wrong path in trying to continue to promote, push, support the intifada, and to—at best—allow the terrorism to go on without interfering in any way."

In Mitchell's view, the key was "swift and decisive action to get the parties together to try to gain implementation of the recommendations," starting with a cease-fire and a cooling-off period. He knew, from his Senate days, how to use incentives. "The Senate majority leader has a few carrots and no sticks."

Had Bush asked him, "We would have immediately returned and sought to convene the parties, understanding that our role would have been different from what it had previously been," Mitchell said. He had no illusions that quelling violence and getting the two sides back into negotiations would be easy, particularly given the number of people who were ready to use indiscriminate violence to obstruct the process.

"The whole history of the region is that there are negative voices on both sides and that unless one moves very quickly and decisively in these situations, the negative voices gain traction and it gets more difficult rather than easier over time."

Also required, Mitchell believed, "is perseverance." Recalling his twenty-two months chairing negotiations in Northern Ireland, he said he was confronted daily with questions about whether the process had been a failure. "There were bombings in Northern Ireland, there were assassinations . . . there were cease-fires made and cease-fires broken, parties were accepted into the talks, evicted from the talks, returned to the talks. . . . I was at times very discouraged. But we stayed with it. . . . I think in these conflict situations there is no easy, simple, quick way to resolve them. It requires tremendous patience, perseverance, and endurance. It requires great discipline in the face of high levels of violence and emotion, charges and countercharges."

As powerful as the emotions were on both sides, Mitchell believed there were powerful desires that could be harnessed to a peace effort. "I believe that the Israelis have a state, and what they want is security. The people of Israel live in unbearable fear and anxiety. . . . The Palestinians don't have a state, and they want one: a sovereign, geographically contiguous, economically viable state in which they can decide their own futures and live with some degree of dignity. I believe that neither can attain its objective by denying to the other side its objective."

Bush left it to Powell to deliver the administration's response, a signal that the Mitchell report would not form the basis of a major presidential initiative. As Powell put it in an interview in 2005, the Middle East conflict was "my problem." Another senior official said the president "didn't care . . . I don't think he cared that much. . . . I think that he wasn't engaged in this process fully. He was episodically engaged in it."

Vice President Cheney, for one, was skeptical that the time was ripe for restarting negotiations and offered low expectations of what the report could accomplish. Appearing on NBC's *Meet the Press* March 20, the day before the report's release, he said, "The circumstances, in terms of the possibility of getting the parties together across the table, are pretty remote at this point. . . . We hope that the Mitchell report, which will be released this next week, may provide some basis to begin to provide for a reduction in violence and get some kind of confidence-building measure started."

Powell reached for the resources available in the State Department: he announced he was instructing Indyk, in Tel Aviv, and Ron Schlicher, consul general in Jerusalem, to "begin working immediately with the

parties to facilitate the implementation of the report's recommendations" and tapped Bill Burns, a career foreign service officer and Middle East expert who was then ambassador to Jordan, to join the effort
and serve as "a special assistant to me for this purpose."

As a sign to the region of American involvement, this lineup represented little more than the status quo. These men were skilled and
committed diplomats, but they lacked the clout and stature of the
Mitchell panel. Worse, Indyk, a Clinton holdover, would soon be leaving, and Burns would be moving to Washington as assistant secretary for
the Near East, responsible for the entire region and especially the confrontation with Iraq. Experience over several administrations had shown
that without active effort by the president or someone acting expressly
for him, Middle East leaders would not respond.

Just then, the stakes in the conflict were rising, though in a way that
would not become clear to the public until early the following year. Late
on May 29, 2001, Yasser Arafat arrived in Moscow for meetings the following day with Russian president Vladimir Putin, foreign minister
Igor Ivanov, and the Russian Orthodox patriarch. His stated intent was
to draw the international community more deeply into ending the conflict. He warned on his arrival, "A delay will spark an explosion both in
Palestine and all over the region." On his next stop, Copenhagen, he
appealed for international observers.

But Arafat was apparently working on a backup plan in case the outside world failed to heed his call. During the Moscow visit, one of his
aides, Fathi al Razem, whose title was deputy chief of the Palestinian
naval forces, met with Iranian officials. The meeting set in motion a major
arms deal, aimed at providing Palestinians with much more sophisticated
weapons than any used by them to date. The middleman in the trans-
action was Imad Mugniyah, one of the most-wanted Hezbollah terrorists, suspected of involvement in deadly attacks on Americans and other
Westerners in Lebanon and on Israeli and Jewish targets in Argentina.

Burns, Indyk, and Schlicher worked on a timeline for implementing
Mitchell's recommendations, starting with a cease-fire. But they had not
yet gotten a deal on a cease-fire when a twenty-two-year-old Hamas
recruit, Saeed Hotary, pushed the conflict back onto Washington's front

burner. Raised in Jordan among a poor family, Hotary had moved to the West Bank about two years before and found work as an electrician in an Israeli-Arab village. In recent months, work had become scarce, and he complained to a cousin that he was having trouble buying medicine for his sick father.

On Friday, June 1, with a bomb packed with shrapnel, Hotary ventured along the Tel Aviv beachfront, where throngs of young people enjoy summer evenings with carefree abandon whether there is war or peace. He pressed among a crowd of teenagers and twentysomethings waiting to get into the Dolphinarium Discoteque, a disco particularly popular with recent immigrants from the former Soviet Union. Triggering the device, he blew himself up and killed twenty others, leaving scores more wounded in a scene of gore and panic. It was the worst single incident of the intifada and the deadliest suicide bombing in five years.

German foreign minister Joschka Fischer happened to be staying at a Tel Aviv hotel close to the carnage. He was quoted later as saying he thought of his own two children, seventeen and twenty, the same age as the victims. Immediately, he became the leading point man for an international response. With UN envoy Terje Roed-Larsen, he met the next day with Arafat and pressured him into denouncing the bombing publicly and pledging "to do all that is needed" for an effective cease-fire and return to negotiations.

As they worked, the anguish of the Israeli public was palpable. Tearful and exhausted friends and family members of the scores of wounded from the blast filled hospital waiting rooms awaiting word on the patients' survival chances and extent of injuries. The crowd at Tel Aviv's Ichilov Hospital included three generations of the family of Itzik Alazraky, twenty-four, who had gone to the club with his wife and several friends to celebrate a birthday. He survived with injuries to his legs, hands, and face. His grandmother, Frieda Keret, said there was only one way Israel could combat terrorists: "The truth is, you must do as they do. But we don't do it because we are human beings. They are beasts." Hundreds of young Israelis, shouting "Death to the Arabs," hurled rocks and bottles at a landmark mosque across the street from the wreckage of the Dolphinarium, trapping eleven worshipers, who responded in kind. Seventeen people were injured before police brought the riot under control.

Israel tightened closure of the border between Israel and the West Bank as Hamas claimed responsibility for Hotary's suicide blast. Following its usual practice, the militant group helped erect a mourning tent, where friends could pay respects to the family of the *shaheed*, or martyr. A Hamas banner hung near the tent's entrance. It depicted a bus engulfed in a fireball.

Israeli media carried expectations of a violent military response to the bombing. Yet to the surprise of many, Sharon held back. On Saturday afternoon, Martin Indyk met with Peres and Defense Minister Benjamin Ben-Eliezer. "They both said to me, 'We've just had a cabinet meeting. The prime minister and we have decided that we will exercise restraint. We want you, the United States, to come in and get Arafat to stop this."

This was a propitious moment for American action: diplomatic spadework had been done by U.S. envoys; a senior European official friendly to both Israel and the Palestinians was in the region; Turkish and Russian envoys would soon come, followed by Kofi Annan. Arafat was cornered and under pressure from all sides, and Sharon was holding his fire.

But Washington met the moment halfway. President Bush reversed himself and dispatched CIA director George Tenet to develop a package of steps to cement a cease-fire. Tenet enjoyed the confidence of Palestinian and Israeli security services, but the administration had previously canceled his involvement, begun under Clinton, in trying to halt the conflict. By June 12, he had a deal for security cooperation. This was a start to implementing the Mitchell plan, but the timing of further steps, starting with a cooling-off period, had yet to be nailed down.

Over the next two weeks, scattered violence interrupted the cease-fire, and the economic effects of the closure deepened. Kofi Annan, after six days in the region, told a Paris conference the cease-fire could only be consolidated by "embedding it in a wider political process—one which offers the Palestinians hope of an end to the occupation, and of an independent state." Mitchell himself weighed in with a gentle warning during an appearance June 25 at the National Press Club: "The level of violence is down, but the cease-fire must be strengthened with a full effort

by both sides. Then there must be prompt movement to the next steps,"
he said, referring to a cooling-off period and confidence-building measures by both sides. "As we said in our report, a cessation of violence cannot be sustained for long without movement on the further steps we
recommended." Commission member Warren Rudman warned that
the Palestinians' huge proportion of young people and high unemployment threatened a worse crisis: "It is literally a ticking time bomb."

Sharon made his second visit to the Bush White House just hours
before a trip to the region by Powell to work on implementing the
Mitchell plan. The Powell trip marked a significant ratcheting up of
American involvement, and Bush seemed eager to show that the time
was ripe. At a boisterous photo session with U.S. and Israeli journalists,
the president and prime minister talked past each other.

"I know there's a level of frustration, but there is progress being made.
And for that progress, we are grateful," Bush said. "The prime minister has shown a lot of patience in the midst of a lot of—in the midst of
casualty. But progress is being made. Is it as fast as we'd like? No, it's not.
But the fundamental question my administration makes is, are we making progress; is peace closer today than it was yesterday. We believe the
answer is yes. And, therefore, the secretary of state leaves tonight to try
to advance the process, to make peace more real."

Sharon put a damper on the optimism: "One must understand that if
last week we had 5 dead, it's like the United States, Mr. President, having
250 killed, or maybe even 300 people killed by terror. And that is saying
that one should not compromise with terror. And, therefore, I believe that
if we stick to what we have been saying for so many times, such a long time,
that it should be full cessation of terror before we move to the other phase,
then our neighbors will understand that they have to do it.

"Yesterday," he said at another point, "we had sixteen terror attacks,
and that included multifire, it included side bombs, it included shooting
and sniping. We had ten wounded. So altogether, generally speaking,
maybe there are less, but still terror is going on."

Their meeting, however, was not testy, according to Indyk. Sharon
was still prepared to be pragmatic and cooperative while he felt out the
administration. He had avoided launching the fierce retaliation for the

Dolphinarium attack that many had expected and had told Indyk he would agree to a six-month settlement freeze after the terror stopped. Speaking to reporters outside the White House, Sharon laid out his terms: "Once it will be quiet, then we'll start [to] count ten days. When we'll see the ten days is completely quiet and nothing really happened, and that Chairman Arafat did not manipulate us and did not maneuver us, and it's really quiet, then we will start the meaningful cooling-off period. Our demand was eight weeks. It will not be in any case less than six weeks. We hope it will be completely quiet then, no terror, no violence, no incitement. And if that will happen, we will start the confidence-building measures phase."

Pressure from Arab states had as much to do with the timing of Powell's trip and the relative calm prevailing at the time. The trip didn't go according to the script devised by Indyk, Burns, and Schlicher. Their intent was to have Powell nail down with Israel and the Palestinians a timed sequence of steps both sides would take in pursuing the Mitchell plan. Emerging from a meeting with Arafat and other Palestinian officials, he endorsed an idea regularly pushed by Palestinians but viewed negatively by Israel: an independent monitoring group to watch "what's happening on the ground" after a cease-fire took hold between Israel and the Palestinians. U.S. officials knew Israel wouldn't accept monitors unless they were American or led by Americans, and even then only in a limited role. Israelis feared monitors would be able to witness cease-fire violations by Israeli troops but not by Palestinians in civilian garb firing from hideouts. But Powell didn't make this point clear. His statement was quickly picked up by wire services and the traveling American press corps as a potential source of friction with Sharon. At the White House, reporters questioned Ari Fleischer, who denied that Powell was endorsing a Palestinian demand, according to wire services. "There is no change in the United States position. . . . Both parties would have to agree to what that monitoring function would be," he was quoted as saying. Fleischer's rapid clarification gave the impression that Powell's every move was being scrutinized and second-guessed by the White House, a pattern that would repeat itself on future trips. The press coverage startled Powell, according to a senior U.S. official.

After meeting with Sharon, Powell backpedaled, stressing that he didn't mean "some outside group of forces coming in," and echoed Fleischer that the idea would have to win consent from both sides. "Arafat was very upset," Abington later recalled. "Arafat said that he had discussed monitors with Powell; he thought he had agreement on it."

Powell got Sharon to scale back his demand for "ten days of quiet" to seven days, at the end of which a six-week cooling-off period could begin. Arafat agreed. "I'm telling you, general to general, seven days of quiet, I can do that," he insisted, according to a Powell aide. But the Palestinian record didn't inspire confidence.

In fact, Sharon would have withdrawn his "days of quiet" demand altogether if pressed by Powell, Indyk believed.

"I flew back with Powell and said, 'We didn't need to do that. Start the timeline. If there's no quiet, then it's not going to work—it just won't go ahead. But, seven days of quiet before we start? We're never going to get anywhere.'" Powell also didn't elaborate much on the timeline or moving in sequence to the next stages of the Mitchell recommendations. At trip's end, a diplomat said: "He left there with everybody in total confusion about what we were doing."

Signs of a resumption of violence were already evident while Powell was closeted at separate meetings with Israeli and Palestinian leaders: Katya Weintraub, a twenty-eight-year-old West Bank settler, was killed in a drive-by shooting near the Palestinian city of Jenin. Israeli authorities also reported a number of Palestinian mortar, shooting, and firebomb attacks in the occupied territories. By July 2, with Powell back in Washington meeting with Israeli defense minister Shaul Mofaz, the U.S.-brokered cease-fire had frayed to the point of collapse after a bloody twenty-four hours that saw the assassination of three Palestinian militants in Jenin by an Israeli helicopter strike, the shooting death of an Israeli in the West Bank, and a pair of car bombings outside Tel Aviv.

Powell's second trip to the region had done nothing to enhance his stature as a statesman. Instead, it offered new signs of what would be the dominant story of his tenure, that of a secretary out of sync with the White House, engaged in running policy battles that he would frequently lose.

Others now tried to pick up the slack. In Tel Aviv, Indyk met over a meal with envoys from the UN, European Union, and Russia; together they agreed to coordinate their approach to the conflict. Powell endorsed the idea. At the UN, Annan dubbed the new grouping the Quartet and urged, successfully, that it be elevated to the foreign ministers' level, plus himself and the EU foreign policy chief, Javier Solana. At the State Department, the Bureau of Near Eastern Affairs, headed by Bill Burns, devised a new plan to keep the Mitchell process alive. Toward the end of the summer, Burns reached out to retired Marine General Anthony Zinni to act as a mediator in building a cease-fire. The department also planned a public announcement of the administration's support for a Palestinian state. But the attacks of September 11 put the plan on hold for months.

Meanwhile, political pressure mounted in Israel for new measures to block suicide bombers like Hotary from entering Israel. A national consensus eventually settled on a measure that would add a new irritant to Bush's relations with Israel and divide the United States from its allies: an elaborate separation barrier of walls, sensors, and fences. Israel would dub it a security fence; Palestinians would call it an "apartheid wall." Visually, it loomed as a new, ugly obstacle to peace.

Daniel Kurtzer, who succeeded Indyk that summer as ambassador to Israel, believed the Mitchell report should have triggered a stronger U.S. diplomatic effort.

"What was interesting about the Mitchell report was that it had an essential trade-off in it, which it was striking that the two sides would accept. On the one hand, Palestinians understood from that they would have to dismantle terrorism—not just stop the terrorism, but dismantle the so-called infrastructure. And Israel had to stop settlement activity. Now, everybody's always walked around this very gingerly because there's not a moral equivalency between terrorism and settlement activity. But they are both activities that drive the other side away from making peace. So here, Mitchell put it down into one document, along with a lot of other stuff, and the two sides accepted it. And—nobody did anything. . . . It was early enough in the administration that I think the president was not yet persuaded a kind of robust diplomacy was in order.

"That was a moment that I think we should have exploited," Kurtzer said.

The Bush administration needn't have chosen the Mitchell team, Hof pointed out; what mattered was the approach: "It could have been us, or it could have been another body entirely. But the idea is that there had to be a team in the region very quickly to sit down with the parties and orchestrate, using very specific timelines, an exchange of very tightly choreographed confidence-building measures, one building on another—at such and such a time you will do this . . . a cascading effect of confidence-building measures focusing first and foremost on a suppression of violence. Very detailed, very precise timeline."

Mitchell, during a 2005 interview in his New York law office, kept a poker face when asked his own view. "We regretted that there was not swift and decisive action. . . ."

What Hof called a war of children was creating an enduring legacy, even as adults increasingly took charge with deadly effect. At Al Wafa Rehabilitation Hospital in Gaza, Hussein Naizi, seventeen, wheeled himself into a waiting room wearing rolled-up trousers that exposed withered calf muscles. He had been shot in the neck while throwing rocks and Molotov cocktails at Israeli forces stationed at the Karni crossing, one of the key flash points at the time. The incident occurred in November 2000, the same month Mitchell was appointed, and left him a paraplegic. He said he had no regrets.

Dr. Pearl Herskovitz, mother of sixteen-year-old Tani, who was blinded in one eye by a suicide bomb, said in a July 2001 interview, four months after the attack, that her son had recovered enough to return to school and complete his year-end exams. But his attitude had changed: "Now he really hates all Arabs."

8

"Israel Will Not Be Czechoslovakia"

■ FALL–WINTER 2001–2002 ■

THE TERRORIST ATTACKS of September 11, 2001, transformed the Republican administration on many fronts. Overnight, they created a new political framework for the George W. Bush presidency. The uncertain leader with an opaque but in no way distinguished Vietnam-era National Guard record suddenly assumed the role of war president with surprising sure-footedness and resolve. Tax cuts, reform of public education, faith-based initiatives, and other domestic policies got lower billing as Bush rallied the nation against a demonstrated "evil" threat to the homeland. Strategic challenges were reshuffled. Terrorism, which both Israeli prime minister Ariel Sharon and White House aide Richard Clarke had sought unsuccessfully to make Bush view with alarm, suddenly became all-important, eclipsing other preoccupations, such as the North Korean nuclear threat and the shadow cast over the Pacific by a more muscular China. Antiballistic-missile defense yielded top-priority status to offensive military readiness. For the first time in a decade, the United States had an enemy in the form of an individual—Osama bin Laden—at least until the hunt for him went cold. And for the first time in a generation, it also had an enemy movement, an "ism," seen as bent on killing Americans and hobbling U.S. power and prestige. Loosely labeled terrorism, it encompassed in various descriptions all the vengeful, violent, and doctrinaire impulses of the Near East and South Asia, from the drive to reimpose an Islamic caliphate to suicide martyrdom and hatred of the West and its freedoms.

The language and logic of war quickly came to dominate political discourse, spending, and foreign policy, making the Pentagon–National Security Council axis the administration's center of gravity. A threshold was crossed in media commentary and public opinion that made large-scale military action widely acceptable. So amorphous was the threat the United States was fighting and so powerful the military momentum unleashed that it became possible for the Bush administration to segue from a war against al-Qaida in Afghanistan to completing the unfinished business of 1991 and toppling Saddam Hussein in Iraq. Diplomacy, ordinarily a means to securing national interests without war, was now pressed into the service of making war possible: recruiting allies or tacit supporters and reducing opposition abroad.

One thing didn't change, and that was confusion about where the Israeli-Palestinian conflict fit into the United States' national security strategy. Bush had made clear early in 2001 that he didn't share Bill Clinton's ambition to be peacemaker. He was prepared to prod the two sides toward cooperation, but only to assist as a mediator when they were ready. He showed little inclination either to pressure Sharon, whom he respected, or to cooperate with Arafat, whom he had been given reason to distrust.

In his administration and in the larger Washington policy community of former officials and Middle East experts, the attacks of 9/11 created a new prism through which the conflict was viewed. But depending on an individual's job and where his or her sympathies and expertise lay along the Arab-Israeli spectrum of opinion, the pictures that emerged from that prism were starkly different.

To many who valued Israel as an ally or felt attached to the Jewish state out of long friendship or shared heritage, Palestinian rage at Israel and the suicide attacks it produced were a symptom of an Arab-world pathology that had continually threatened Israel's survival since Arab armies invaded in 1948. That pathology had brought forth al-Qaida, bin

Laden, and Palestinian terrorists and now threatened not just Israel and Jews but Western civilization itself. It was a force that couldn't be reasoned with and had to be fought and contained, if not destroyed. Others, including many who sympathized with Israel, put forward a different diagnosis: the prolonged Arab-Israeli conflict inflamed popular opinion in the Arab world, which violent extremists could then exploit in their campaigns against Israel and the United States. Negotiations and the prospect of peace would help push extremists back to the margins of society.

Based on his actions, Bush never accepted either analysis. He didn't side totally with Israel against the Palestinians, although criticism of Israeli military tactics, particularly targeted killings, subsided over time.

"They understood it's a war of prevention," said David Ivry, then Israel's ambassador to Washington. If before 9/11 the frequent message from Washington would be criticism of a military operation, afterward it became, "Be careful."

Israel labored to be seen as a full-fledged ally in the war on terrorism in a way that would deepen its relationship with Washington and reciprocate American friendship. Intelligence officials provided briefings on everything from hardware to interrogation techniques. "We don't have secrets on counterterrorism with allies," said Avi Dichter, head of the Israeli domestic security agency Shin Bet. Israel opened its facilities "like a supermarket—whatever you need, you can take it. They've been to our supermarket. They know everything about our interrogation strategy, tactics, capability, restrictions, tricks," he said.

At the Pentagon, Defense Secretary Donald Rumsfeld saw the Israeli-Palestinian conflict as a side issue that he summed up succinctly in a 2003 BBC interview: "That is a problem that's a tough one, and it's been a tough one my entire adult lifetime, and that it has not been solved in the last twenty months ought not to be a surprise to anybody. . . . Obviously Israel has offered to give back a major portion of the occupied territories. We know that. The agreement was there. It could have been solved if Arafat had accepted it. He didn't." Officials beneath him, lumped together by critics under the label neoconservative, were in fact divided. Deputy Secretary Paul Wolfowitz backed a two-state solution and spoke of Palestinians sympathetically, while the Pentagon's No. 3, Douglas Feith, came into office with views similar to those of Likud Party hard-liners who opposed the internationally accepted land-for-peace formula. He was also a founding member of an organization created in opposition to plans by the former Labor government to grant Palestinian sovereignty over Arab neighborhoods in Jerusalem.

State Department officials viewed the conflict mostly in terms of how it affected American goals and interests in the wider region. Repeatedly, in interviews, U.S. diplomats stressed the importance to the administration of being "seen" as caring about the Palestinians and engaged in trying to end the conflict. Few stressed the urgency of peace as a way of securing Israel or winning justice for Palestinians.

"The fact is, the Israel-Palestinian issue, even more than Iraq, is at the center of so many competing regional issues for us," a senior official said in a 2005 interview. "[T]o be seen as actively engaged, as the government, in moving this forward concretely toward resolution, would have a tremendously powerful impact on the other things we're trying to do: world terror, regional transformation, reform of Iraq."

Immediately following the attacks on New York and Washington, some Israelis and their supporters in the United States imagined that the bond between the two countries would tighten as a result of their common traumatic encounters with Arab terrorism. One of Ariel Sharon's favorites in the Israeli press corps, *Jerusalem Post* columnist Uri Dan, predicted that "the United States will join Israel in a totally new approach to the war against terrorism. A unique situation has arisen in which the dictatorial terrorist threat against both the American democracy and the sole democracy in the Middle East has become crystal clear. This situation will obligate special, more drastic steps to be taken by both countries, both individually and with greater coordination than ever before." Bush, he wrote, had already shown understanding of Israel by refusing to meet with Arafat and accepting Sharon's refusal to negotiate under fire. A prominent American supporter of Israel, Abraham Foxman, head of the Anti-Defamation League, was quoted in the *Baltimore Jewish Times* as saying, "It will bring home to people the reality of what Israel has been living with on a day-to-day basis—at a very high price. . . . It will produce a new understanding of what Israeli leaders are facing."

Instead, the moment produced a crisis in the relationship, fraught with mistrust and miscommunication, that included one of the worst public flare-ups between Sharon and the Bush White House. The incident revealed an American blind spot about Israelis' sense of isolation and vulnerability, and its suspicion about being used.

An immediate U.S. priority was to gain support in the Arab and Muslim world for a war to cripple al-Qaida's worldwide network and destroy its sanctuary in Afghanistan. The United States badly needed reliable intelligence on al-Qaida and its followers from security agencies in the Middle East and Asia. While the Pentagon took the lead in preparing for war in Afghanistan, the State Department laid the diplomatic groundwork. Secretary Colin Powell set out to create a "great coalition," as he put it. To prevent a regional backlash from an invasion of Afghanistan, a Muslim country, the United States needed to persuade Muslims there and elsewhere that it was not engaged in a crusade against Islam.

Powell, though now the nation's top diplomat, sounded like the military strategist of old as he approached the problem: "You're dealing with a very, very skilled, knowledgeable, thinking enemy. And we just have to think better than them, think faster than them and be cleverer than them in order to respond in a sensible way with all of the weapons at our disposal, and one of those weapons is military force used in an appropriate way."

Resentment had mounted over the humanitarian plight of ordinary Iraqis suffering under UN sanctions and over a widespread perception that the United States ignored Israeli shelling and siege of Palestinian towns. In the age of satellite television, pro-American autocrats no longer had the power to control public opinion and were forced to compete for the hearts and minds of their poor and uneducated with the anti-American clarion calls of militant Islamists. Behind the public declarations of support for the United States lay lingering resentment. A diplomat from a Muslim nation, who refused to be identified by name or country, told the *Baltimore Sun* that while many in the region sympathized with the United States, there was a feeling that "when you bully around other countries, this is what happens to you." Jordan's King Abdullah bluntly told CNN on September 12: "If the United States had resolved the problems in the Middle East, notably the Israeli-Palestinian question, I seriously doubt that they [the attacks] would have taken place." A month earlier, Saudi crown prince Abdullah bin Abdul Aziz, a longtime U.S. ally and personal friend of the Bushes, had expressed alarm in a letter to Bush about the American failure to address the Middle East conflict seriously, warning that the Saudi kingdom might have to reassess its ties to the United States.

Suddenly, Arab allies of the United States, who for months had stood by in helpless frustration as popular anger grew against Israel with little response from Washington, were in a position to influence American policy toward Sharon. Their price for joining Powell's coalition was a greater effort by Washington to rein in Israel and bring an end to the conflict. "Unless the United States does something visibly" to ease the Palestinians' plight, "not a single Arab government can join this coalition in a serious way," remarked Mohammed Wahby, then the Washington columnist for the influential Egyptian magazine *Al-Mussawar*.

In future years, George Bush would come to view some of these same autocratic regimes as contributing to the resentment and economic backwardness that fed popular support for Islamic militants. Rather than pressure Israel, he would promote democratic reform in Arab lands. But for now, he was willing to at least make a down payment on their demand.

In the Office of Policy, Planning, and Resources, the State Department's in-house think tank, director Richard Haass and his staff saw an opportunity to use the coalition being assembled as leverage for larger strategic gains. Ten days after the attacks, he told the National War College, "We must use such cooperation against the threat of international terrorism to find common ground on how to respond to a host of other bilateral and transnational challenges. We also now have real prospects for making meaningful progress in ameliorating tensions between regional rivals in South Asia and the Middle East. We have opportunities, therefore, to create enduring and positive memorials out of the wreckage of the recent tragedies."

The United States would seek cooperation even from nations that heretofore had sponsored or tolerated terrorism, such as Syria and Iran. "Countries' and organizations' willingness to work with us in the future—not the animosities of the past—will guide our efforts," Haass told the Council on Foreign Relations several weeks later. His Middle East analyst, Flynt Leverett, proposed using with Iran and Syria the same approach already being applied to Libya in an effort to change the behavior of its mercurial dictator, Muammar Gadhafi: persuading them to end their ties with terrorism "in exchange for a positive strategic relationship with the United States." Leverett also believed that, more than ever, the United States needed "a credible plan for ending the Israeli-Palestinian conflict."

In Jerusalem, Ariel Sharon reacted with alarm to what he learned about Washington's coalition strategy. More was demanded of Israel than the help it was willing—even eager—to provide: skills and knowledge derived from decades of experience in tracking and killing terrorists. It was being asked to stand by while the United States cut quiet deals for cooperation from Arab states that remained at least formally hostile to the Jewish state. Worse, the United States was seeking cooperation from Syria, Israel's most hostile immediate neighbor.

For six months, Sharon had been able to evade U.S. pressure and avoid making significant concessions to the Palestinians. Now, in repeated phone calls, Powell pressed him to reach agreement on a cease-fire with Arafat. U.S. officials believed Arafat might be more cooperative now that the whole world was reacting with shock and outrage against terrorism and wouldn't want to antagonize an angry superpower. On September 14, Bush called Sharon with the same demand. Sharon said the two had "an exceptionally warm and long conversation" in which "President Bush told me that this may present an opportunity to try and change the situation." But an Israeli Channel 1 reporter, citing unnamed U.S. sources, claimed the exchange was "difficult and unpleasant."

Publicly, Powell played down the images of Palestinians cheering the 9/11 attacks, telling *NewsHour with Jim Lehrer*, "I got a message in from our consul general in Jerusalem saying that his switchboard is swamped with calls from Palestinians—Palestinian officials, Palestinian people—expressing their distaste for that kind of display, and letting us know that they were expressing their condolences and sympathy to us, as well."

Powell urged Sharon to agree to a meeting between Arafat and Israel's foreign minister, Shimon Peres, to work out terms of a cease-fire that would lead the two sides back into peace talks according to the Mitchell plan. An early stage of that plan would require Israel to pull back its military forces from populated Palestinian areas, freeze settlement construction, lift closures and other restrictions on Palestinian civilian life—and then resume peace talks. Meanwhile, U.S. policy called for confronting terrorist groups "of global reach," a term that relegated to a lower priority the groups that were attacking Israeli civilians.

To Sharon, Washington was making a distinction between al-Qaida and the perpetrators of terrorist attacks against Israel who had spilled the blood of thousands of Jews over decades. In fact, a double standard was at work, though it wasn't quite what Sharon imagined. Unlike the war against al-Qaida, with whom negotiation was deemed to be impossible, U.S. officials continued to believe that the Israeli-Palestinian conflict was a political and territorial dispute that was amenable to diplomacy and compromise.

Complicating the picture for Sharon, Powell found an ally in the seventy-eight-year-old Peres, a longtime dove who had a reputation in Israel for diplomatic freelancing. Unlike Sharon, who viewed Arafat purely and simply as a mass murderer of Jews, Peres argued that he had successfully secured the Palestinian leader's compliance with agreements in the past and could again. Resisting the U.S. request would cause Israel to be blamed for undermining the U.S.-led coalition, he said, whereas meeting Arafat would place the burden on Palestinians. Uri Dan, the *Jerusalem Post* columnist, believed a plan was being hatched between Peres and "State Department guys who always kiss the ass of Arafat" to "whitewash Arafat through their laundry."

Sharon also felt pressure from elsewhere. "There were some calls, European, others, to look into the matter of why is the Arab world so angry and all this. The Europeans tried to connect it to the Palestinian-Israeli issue," recalled Danny Ayalon, then a top aide to Sharon in Jerusalem.

Sharon began to fear betrayal by the only nation whose friendship he valued. In a conference call with a group of American Jewish leaders on September 14, Sharon vented his anxiety. "The coalition against terror should fight against all terrorist organizations. There is no good terror and no bad terror," he said. According to a detailed *Jerusalem Post* account of the conversation, he told them: "I feel that there is an attempt to draw distinctions between terror in Israel and terror against the rest of the world," said Sharon. He urged the Jewish leaders to "make it very clear that one cannot draw any distinctions between terror against Israeli citizens and terror against American citizens. There is not good terror and bad terror. Terror is terror, murder is murder," he told the leaders, according to the *Post.* He said states that the coalition should be targeting because of their role in sponsoring and sheltering terrorists included Syria, Iran, and "the terrorist organization that is led by Arafat," whom he compared to bin Laden. He added that certain leaders were pressuring Bush to lean on Israel and demand concessions to the Palestinians. "One thing is clear—that Israel cannot pay for this coalition. We cannot pay for this with our blood," he said.

Malcolm Hoenlein, executive vice president of the Conference of Presidents of Major American Jewish Organizations, recalled that conversation during a telephone interview five years later. Sharon, he said, sensed a familiar pattern: "Whenever there is a trauma and people look to find solace, there's pressure for an Israeli concession." The prime minister felt the U.S. administration was "rushing into something that was not thought-out, not prepared."

Gauging how to respond to U.S. pressure, Sharon paid attention to the president's poll numbers, which soared in the days following 9/11, bolstering Bush's political strength. Two days after the two leaders spoke, Sharon announced he would allow a Peres-Arafat meeting if it were preceded by forty-eight hours with no violence. He also offered to halt the army's "initiated activities," a reference to incursions, arrests, and assassinations, if Arafat declared a halt to Palestinian violence. But in a Knesset speech, with U.S. ambassador Daniel Kurtzer and his wife in attendance, the prime minister reminded Americans they weren't the only victims of terrorism and brought his resentment and fears about American strategy into the open.

"We are all too familiar with the pain of bereavement now suffered by the American people," he said, launching bitterly into a litany of Arafat's terrorist crimes: Arafat, he said, "was the one who legitimized the hijacking of planes already dozens of years ago; and Palestinian terrorist organizations were those which started to send out suicide terrorists. All the extremist movements were given powerful legitimization by Arafat since the murder of the Israeli athletes in the Munich Olympics, the murder of the children in Avivim, and the murder of the children in Ma'alot."

Arab states, he went on, "are demanding, as a price for their entering the coalition, a political-security price on Israel's part, and we cannot accept this." Perhaps, he said, Arafat himself would be brought into the coalition, "just as it is possible that Syria will become part of the coalition. This is a very dangerous thing because it will allow Arafat to continue with terrorism without our being able to operate against him."

Peres and Arafat did indeed agree on a cease-fire ten days later. But despite Powell's strenuous effort to manage the truce from Washington, neither side appeared determined to implement its responsibilities unless it was persuaded the other side was serious. Arafat began saying the right things publicly but failed to control the militants, and continued violence was encouraged by groups based in Damascus. Israel, in turn, pulled its forces back only partially and kept ready for renewed incursions into the territories. Sharon, meanwhile, continued to find reason to view the U.S.-led antiterror coalition with suspicion.

In an article timed to coincide with a visit to Iran, British foreign secretary Jack Straw wrote, "One of the factors that helps breed terrorism is the anger which many people in this region feel at events over the years in Palestine." Furious, Sharon refused to meet with Straw when the Briton subsequently arrived in Israel, changing his mind only after Tony Blair intervened by telephone.

The Bush administration, feeling the need to provide Palestinians a "political horizon," disclosed that before the 9/11 attacks, it had been developing a peace proposal that included a Palestinian state. The president told reporters, "The idea of a Palestinian state has always been part of a vision, so long as the right [of] Israel to exist is respected." Israeli officials thought Bush's remark gave Arafat an undeserved windfall.

As it turned out, Palestinian statehood was about all that had been fleshed out in the American initiative. But according to David Ivry, Sharon began to get alarming reports from American Jewish leaders of an administration plan being hatched behind his back. "They didn't have a kind of open door like they'd had with the Clinton administration—at that time. And they didn't like it and they came up with a kind of an assumption that the Bush administration is hiding from them a . . . plan to force Israel into a kind of peace process (to which Israel couldn't agree), and they're planning it with Arab countries, and so on. And they put the case to Sharon."

Although Ivry's own administration contacts told him the United States would continue to follow the sequential Tenet and Mitchell plans, "Sharon was very nervous."

Weeks of dark brooding exploded in a statement Sharon delivered aloud on October 4. "I call on the Western democracies, and primarily the leader of the free world—the United States: do not repeat the dreadful mistake of 1938, when enlightened European democracies decided to sacrifice Czechoslovakia for a 'convenient temporary solution.' Do not try to appease the Arabs at our expense—this is unacceptable to us. Israel will not be Czechoslovakia." He went on, signaling that he was through with the cease-fire and American efforts to make it work: "All our attempts to achieve a cease-fire have been foiled by the Palestinians. The gunfire did not stop for a single day. The inner cabinet therefore instructed the defense establishment to take every necessary step to achieve full security for the citizens of Israel."

"We have only ourselves to rely on, and as of today, we will only rely on ourselves."

It was hard to imagine harsher criticism of an ally than to compare its policy with Neville Chamberlain's abandonment of Czechoslovakia to Hitler, perhaps the most shameful—and futile—moment in twentieth-century diplomacy. Bush couldn't let it pass. Danny Ayalon got calls that night from the White House demanding a retraction. Sharon refused.

He "was not going to retract it until he was assured that Israel was not going to be sold out," Ayalon said in 2005. The next day, Powell called Sharon to relay a response that White House spokesman Ari Fleischer delivered publicly: "The president believes that these remarks are unacceptable," he said. "Israel can have no better or stronger friend than the United States and better friend than President Bush."

The flare-up died down when Sharon, in interviews with American newspapers, expressed regret for the way his remark had been interpreted and praised Bush's conduct against terrorism. U.S. officials also offered reassurance, Ayalon said: "We were told, you know, 'You shouldn't worry.'" By the following week, the incident was buried by the start of the war in Afghanistan.

But Sharon had laid down a marker in his dealings with Bush. Although he could be pragmatic and flexible when he thought Bush was serious, as when Indyk approached him in the spring on a settlement freeze, he had a recurring fear that Israel's interests would lose out on the chessboard of the big powers. As a U.S. official noted, Sharon's sense of responsibility for the fate of the Jewish people and Israel mixed with a suspicion of foreign powers—it was us versus them. Sharon would not be pressed into peace talks just to make life easier for the United States in the Arab world. If Bush wanted his cooperation, the United States would have to consult him closely. Sharon's outburst also revealed the tight-lipped administration's need to maintain better communication with Jewish leaders who had their own direct lines into the Israeli political establishment. At the National Security Council, that would eventually become part of Elliott Abrams's job.

In coming weeks, the White House tried to make the case to Israel that it would benefit from American success in the war against terrorism and simultaneously pressed both sides to renew the shattered cease-fire. At a White House meeting with Peres October 23, Bush drew a direct connection between Israeli-Palestinian violence and the difficulty of holding together the antiterrorism coalition, Peres said later. This didn't stop Israeli forces from braving U.S. criticism by occupying six Palestinian towns and inflicting numerous casualties, following the assassination of a right-wing Israeli minister,

Rehavam Ze'evi, by militants from the Popular Front for the Liberation of Palestine.

In Tel Aviv, Daniel Kurtzer, the U.S. ambassador, didn't want the United States to miss a chance to advance Israeli-Palestinian negotiations. A veteran of Middle East negotiations since 1979 and an active participant in Israeli-Palestinian affairs since 1990, he had seen too many opportunities slip for lack of a well-timed, powerful American response. He worried that the conflict was evolving from a political-territorial dispute to an ideological-religious one that would be much harder to solve.

He had no illusions about the obstacles. Eleven years earlier, he had noted in an interview that Israelis and Palestinians could both be "tough bastards" in negotiations. Since his arrival the previous summer after a successful tour as ambassador to Egypt, he had received occasionally rough treatment from the Sharon government in leaks to the Israeli press and suspicion from the Israeli right wing, which accused him of pro-Palestinian bias. He had endured worse: early in his Cairo tenure, Egyptian newspapers played up his Orthodox Jewish faith with anti-Semitic caricatures.

Kurtzer knew, and told Washington, that the prime minister would be tough to enlist in a peace process leading to negotiations with the Palestinians. "He was not at all open to the ideas of others, especially if they came from the United States. He would have resisted mightily," he said in late 2005. This wasn't Sharon's idea of the way Israel's relationship with the United States should work; he wanted the two countries to pursue shared strategic interests. Kurtzer offered these observations so his superiors would know what they were up against but repeatedly urged them to try anyway to overcome the inevitable hurdles. "That's what diplomacy is all about," he said.

But eager as it was to tamp down the fires of the Israeli-Palestinian conflict, the administration was slow to mount a serious on-the-ground effort to halt what had become a war of attrition. In fact, the administration was reluctant even to issue a comprehensive policy statement. Powell responded awkwardly to a question about the administration's "vision" for the Middle East during a congressional hearing on October 24, 2001: "We had been looking at putting down a comprehensive statement of

American policy, and events interceded, and we don't yet have a date set where we might lay down such a statement. It is not going to be as revolutionary a statement as some suggest. I think it will be just a clear, comprehensive statement of American views that have been held over a long period of time, to make sure everybody knows what this administration stands for with respect to the Middle East peace process—the Mitchell plan, getting into the Mitchell plan; confidence-building measures—all leading to negotiations on the basis of [UN Resolutions] 242 and 338."

November offered a period of relative calm. Israel pulled its troops from several cities it had occupied several weeks earlier. In mid- and late October, Peres had met repeatedly with Arafat and other top Palestinians. Tony Blair held his eleventh meeting with Arafat and toured the Middle East, proclaiming at each stop a straightforward formula for a renewed peace process: "Security for Israel, and justice and equality of treatment for Palestinians and the Palestinian state." After briefing Bush on his trip November 7, he told reporters, "It is in everybody's interest that we make progress in the Middle East, and we will strain every sinew we possibly can to do so." Nearly five years later in Los Angeles, he would make the same pitch, stressing the need to "bend every sinew of our will to making peace between Israel and Palestine."

But the White House moved reluctantly, in fits and starts. Bush included a short but resonant passage in his address to the United Nations November 10, picking up Blair's theme: "We are working toward a day when two states, Israel and Palestine, live peacefully together within secure and recognized borders, as called for by the Security Council resolutions. We will do all in our power to bring both parties back into negotiations." For the first time, an American president referred to a future state by the name that was used by Palestinians and accepted by much of the United Nations.

This time, the administration took care to ensure Sharon wouldn't be surprised. Israelis knew Bush was planning to call for a two-state solution. In fact, David Ivry worked to have some of Israel's views included in the Bush speech, which was mostly devoted to terrorism. He wanted Bush to stress Sharon's view that "there is no good or bad terror," and that political reasons don't justify killing innocents. He was gratified to hear Bush say, "There is no such thing as a good terrorist. No national aspiration, no remembered wrong can ever justify the deliberate murder of the innocent."

Bush's pledge to "do all in our power" reopened the prospect of a new peace effort, but only by a crack. It was accompanied by a continued refusal to meet with Arafat—even in one of the choreographed "spontaneous" UN corridor encounters that sometimes break the diplomatic ice at the annual General Assembly. Sir Kieran Prendergast later recalled how Bush reacted during Kofi Annan's lunch for world leaders when the idea of meeting Arafat was broached:

"Solana came over to me and said, 'Why don't you ask the secretary general to ask the president to shake hands with Arafat. It would make a very good photo opportunity and it would repair this breach.' And I said, 'I don't want to do it. Ask him yourself—because I don't think he's going to do it.' So Solana went over and hung his arms around the secretary general from behind and chatted to him and the president. And then after a couple of minutes he went home. So I asked the secretary general what had happened. And he said, 'Well, Solana came over and he was kind of hugging me and he said to the president, 'Wouldn't it be nice if we had a nice handshake afterwards? Wouldn't it be nice if there was a handshake with Arafat?' And the president said, 'Shake your own hand.'"

State Department officials struggled to put some flesh on the bones of their promised peace effort, as both Israel and the Palestinians each took further steps away from violence. Palestinian security forces arrested Mahmoud Nurasi Tawalbi, an Islamic Jihad militant accused of recruiting suicide bombers. Israeli forces pulled out of Tulkarem, another West Bank city it had invaded in October.

But inside and outside the administration, advocates of robust Middle East diplomacy faced mounting opposition. With the early success of the Afghanistan invasion, the Israeli-Palestinian conflict was increasingly sidelined and overtaken by the broadening horizon of the war on terrorism. Against the emerging U.S. doctrine that saw terrorism on a par with such evils as genocide, slavery, and piracy, continued dialogue with a Palestinian leadership that condoned or failed to control it began to seem counterintuitive. Many conservatives saw Bush's actions on the Israeli-Palestinian front as a contradiction of his message on October 7, 2001, when he said: "Today we focus on Afghanistan, but the battle is broader. Every nation has a choice to make. In this conflict, there is no neutral ground. If any government sponsors the outlaws and killers of innocents, they have become outlaws and murderers themselves."

Israel's supporters on Capitol Hill accused the administration of hypocrisy and of holding Israel to a double standard. At a hearing October 24, California representative Tom Lantos demanded of Powell, "Is the state of Israel, a democratic ally and friend—a country which has been the target of more terrorism than any other country in modern history—entitled to pursue the terrorists who act against them exactly the same way we are entitled to pursue Osama bin Laden and his ilk?"

"Very difficult question, and one we struggle with in the department," Powell replied. "For a long period of time, we have been trying to get the peace process under way in the region. . . . And what I found is that in the daily response to provocation, rather than things getting better as a result of the responses, things are getting worse. And all you have to do is look at the events of the past several days to see that things get worse. And so the department for a long time, before this administration, has always viewed that kind of activity of targeted assassination as not being a useful strategy to pursue, and has spoken out against it." Powell's reference to "the department," rather than the administration, was apt. Vice President Cheney, for one, had expressed sympathetic understanding of Israel's assassination policy even before 9/11.

Rather than try to heal the long-festering sore of the Arab-Israeli conflict, the administration became increasingly absorbed by enlarging the war begun in Afghanistan. Influential White House advisers argued that Afghanistan, while the headquarters of al-Qaida, was far removed from the real source of the terrorism directed against the United States. That source was the Arab Middle East and the "desert Islam" that demonized the United States. Over the decade since the first Gulf War, these advisers felt the United States had shown weakness and impotence. A new demonstration of American power was needed. Iraq was the most tempting target because of an accumulation of problems it was causing, not least of which was the severe fraying of UN-imposed sanctions. The prospect of toppling Saddam Hussein had long preoccupied Republican hard-liners. September 11 and the early success in Afghanistan made continued war politically digestible to the American public. Hard-liners were split between those who were persuaded that Saddam was a long-term threat and idealists, like the Pentagon's Paul Wolfowitz, who viewed a transformed Iraq as a model for democratic reforms throughout the backward, corrupt region. To Bush, championing the spread of democracy held more appeal and offered better return for risk-taking than a highly uncertain peace process. In the top ranks of the State Department and the NSC, no one tried to persuade him to be a peacemaker.

"In the mind and conviction of the president, was the sense that there had to be . . . changes in the region if we were ever going to deal with the problem of violent extremism, and that you had to expand political space as well as economic space for people and that leaders who were not prepared to move in that direction were in a sense obstacles, and that's where Arafat began to appear," a senior official said.

A sharp break was occurring with policies pursued with remarkable continuity by six presidents of both parties and with particular urgency by Clinton. Not only had Clinton welcomed Arafat to the White House repeatedly and sent his secretary of state shuttling between Jerusalem and Damascus, but for at least part of his presidency he was in monthly contact—by letter or forty-five-minute phone calls—with Syrian president Hafiz al-Assad—all with the aim of securing a comprehensive peace between Israel and its neighbors.

"After 9/11, we became much less risk-tolerant with bad actors," said an official who was a veteran of the Bush 1 and Clinton administrations and, disillusioned, joined in framing the emerging policy. "There was a sense of the region beginning to spiral out of control. . . . Oslo was structurally misconceived. There were broken promises. Arabs had driven us to be part of their process, but took no responsibility. They were pumping out hatred . . . 99 percent of Egyptians hate us. This just confirmed what I knew—something was fundamentally wrong with the way the United States was pursuing its interests in the Middle East. There was an escalating pace of significant terror acts against the United States—and all this while Clinton was seeing Arafat and Assad. There was a hollowness at the core of American strategy."

Powell, having promised to spell out U.S. Middle East policy, scheduled a speech for November 19 in Louisville. In it, he would announce the dispatch of Burns and retired General Anthony Zinni to the Middle East to work on securing an Israeli-Palestinian cease-fire. He got assurance from Israel and the Palestinians that security talks could be conducted at a higher level than in the past. But getting the speech "cleared" by the White House was a problem. "Powell had to work like a dog to get it out because the vice president and the secretary of defense hated it," Richard Armitage, Powell's deputy and close friend, told me. "It was too balanced."

The secretary, in a 2005 interview, described how 9/11 had colored the administration's view of the Middle East. "[T]he Israelis were able to use the terrorism card to say, 'We're with you. We're fighting terrorism. . . .' So it strengthened the Israeli position and the Israeli arguments with respect to how we have to have a firm response to terror coming out of the occupied territories with Arafat, who the Israelis felt . . . was supporting it, perhaps even financing it. And so it made it a lot harder to deal with him, and it also, in the post-9/11 environment, made it that much harder to find anyone in Washington, in the administration, who really wanted to do much for Arafat. And that in turn meant, 'How could we really help the Palestinians?'"

As the date for the Louisville speech approached, "[T]here were strong reservations about whether the president should stick his neck out on this. . . . And everybody knew I was giving the speech, for a couple of weeks. And as the draft started circulating, as is the case with drafts, everybody got nervous. And the nervousness was that I was pushing the president out on a limb again with this speech. And there he would be with the secretary of state giving this speech and if people criticized it then the president would get sucked into this one way or the other. . . . I said, 'Look, I can't not now give the speech. It's out there. Everybody knows it's coming.' I think they were catching hell from the Israelis. I know they were catching hell from the Israelis. . . .

"I said, 'I got to give it. It's too late. And by the way, it's the right thing to do. We've got to make a statement. We've been in this administration now for ten months. We've got to say something about the most pressing issue of the day—among other issues, I mean—it still is; notwithstanding Iraq, it's the most pressing issue. And so they essentially stopped bugging me about it. But they also said [and here Powell drew a finger along the front of his throat]: 'You're on your own.'"

Again, the Israelis weighed in with suggestions. Powell made what Ivry later said gratefully was a crucial point, demanding that the Arab world accept Israel as a Jewish state. This was the first time the United States had stressed that Israel's Jewish character, not just its existence, had to be recognized by the region. To Ivry, this meant "in some way, denying the right of return" by Palestinians who had fled or been expelled in 1948. Israel had long maintained that a right of return would in time overwhelm Israel demographically and grant Arabs a majority.

Besides announcing the dispatch of Burns and Zinni, Powell spelled out in the most comprehensive way to date how the Bush administration envisioned a peace agreement taking shape in the Middle East, saying both sides need to face "some fundamental truths." Jewish settlements in the territories "cripple" chances for peace, he said; there needed to be a "viable" Palestinian state; he implicitly rejected Israel's claim to all of Jerusalem and said a resolution of the refugee issue had to be both "just," meaning a recognition of some Palestinian rights, and "realistic." The speech went as far as his staff could to spell out for Palestinians what they could expect if they cooperated in halting terrorism.

Powell told reporters on his return to Washington that "there are a lot of other things waiting there to happen, once we get started," but stressed that a cease-fire and confidence-building measures had to be tackled first. "My ultimate interests are the negotiations, not just a process of getting there. We've got to go through this process, and there is no deep pass that takes you over this." He emphasized Zinni's toughness, as he would with another special envoy nearly two years later: "You'll see what 'pushing and prodding' is when Tony Zinni gets on the ground."

Besides being tough, Zinni was also personable and fair-minded and a serious, sensitive student of the region, where he had come to know many of the key players as chief of the U.S. Central Command. He commanded respect within the Israeli military, who tended to view Western peace envoys as naive. But those qualities mattered less than the clout he carried with him. When Zinni and Powell met with Bush in the Oval Office at the time his appointment was announced, "The president made it very clear that I was the secretary of state's emissary," Zinni said later. "[I]t was clear to me this was his [Powell's] baby. That was it. The fingerprints would stay there."

This was bound to make an important difference to the Israelis and particularly to Sharon. Kurtzer, reflecting on his own experience, said in 2005: "The thing that's critical with him, he has to be persuaded whoever is delivering the message is speaking with the authority of the White House. . . . They do check; they call; they have their lines of communication."

Zinni believed he had another problem—with the Pentagon. Three years earlier, he had given congressional testimony against a plan then popular among a group of Republican activists to arm the Iraqi National Congress in a bid to depose Saddam Hussein. Recalling the Bay of Pigs fiasco, he quotably dubbed the Iraqi gambit a "Bay of Goats." Some of those activists were now in senior Pentagon positions.

"It was clear to me, right from the beginning, in our first talks at the State Department, with Rich Armitage, Secretary Powell, and others, that nobody was under any illusions that this was something [where] the odds were with us," Zinni said later.

The odds turned against him three days before his arrival in the region and quickly got worse. On November 23, Israel assassinated a senior Hamas leader in the West Bank, Mahmoud Abu Hanoud, firing a missile from a helicopter. Sharon's office said he'd helped plan two of the year's most stunning suicide bombings: at the Dolphinarium Discoteque in Tel Aviv in June, which killed more than a score of teenagers, many from the former Soviet Union; and at the Sbarro pizza restaurant in Jerusalem in August. His continued freedom to operate was also an embarrassment both to Israelis, who botched an attempt to capture him in 2000, and to Palestinian security forces, who freed him after Israel bombed the Nablus prison, where they had incarcerated him.

The next day, a Palestinian mortar attack killed an Israeli soldier in

Gaza. Israel retaliated with air strikes against Palestinian security services and Fatah offices and demolished the homes from which the mortars had been fired. Then a bus bomber killed three Israelis in Hadera.

Sharon was in New York December 1, two days before a scheduled White House visit, when a pair of coordinated Hamas bombings at a Jerusalem shopping mall killed ten people—retaliation, the militants said, for Abu Hanoud's death. The brutality of the attack was of the kind that can tip the balance of the Israeli body politic and produce a harsh retaliation. Uri Dan, at the Park Lane Hotel as part of Sharon's press entourage, urged the prime minister to ask Bush to move the meeting forward so he could return to Israel early. "After less than an hour he calls me: 'The meeting is tomorrow at the White House. Thank you, Uri,'" Dan recalled in a 2005 interview.

By the time they met, a third bomb—in the northern city of Haifa— killed fifteen more. As Bush faced the microphones on the south lawn flying home early from Camp David for the meeting, he betrayed growing impatience with Arab and other world leaders who had repeatedly demanded a stronger American role in renewing the peace process: "Now is the time for leaders throughout the world who urge there to be a peace to do something about the terror that prevents peace from happening in the first place."

Sharon blamed Arafat and let Bush know the crackdown would be severe. "Israel must act to defend the lives of its citizens," an Israeli official quoted him as saying. "We are at war. On one side is Israel; on the other side is Arafat." There is no indication that Bush appealed for restraint—apart, possibly, from extracting a promise from Sharon not to harm Arafat physically and not to reoccupy areas still under full Palestinian Authority control. In his public statements, the president placed full responsibility on Arafat to track down and arrest those responsible. Separately, Defense Secretary Donald H. Rumsfeld gave a bluntly critical assessment of Arafat. "He is not a particularly strong leader, and I don't know that he has good control over the Palestinian situation," he said in a television interview. "He has not ever delivered anything for the Palestinian people throughout history. . . . So his record is not a particularly impressive one."

A White House spokesman said Arafat would have to take "decisive action" against Hamas and Islamic Jihad, meaning dismantling their ability to commit further acts of terror. "I didn't feel any pressure," Sharon told *New York Times* columnist William Safire, an avowed fan. "On the contrary, he understands the situation in the area and the need to put pressure on Arafat."

Two days later, ABC's Barbara Walters asked Bush if he supported what Sharon was doing. "I support the fact that we must root out terror in order for us to get back to a peace process," he said. "Listen, I was so sympathetic . . . to Ariel Sharon. When he's standing in my office, obviously agonizing over the loss of innocent life, the clear attempt of murdering innocent people and a successful attempt of murdering innocent people. And this is a man who is the only elected official in the region, democratically elected official in the region who has got the responsibility to defend his people. And he will do so." Walters turned to the president's wife: "Mrs. Bush, do you discuss these things at night?"

"We do discuss some of them, certainly," replied Laura Bush. "We talked about Ariel Sharon, we talked about the situation that he faces as a leader when his people are terrorized. Just essentially the same situation we're facing in our country now."

Dramatically, the First Couple had fused the American and Israeli struggle against terrorism, bolstering Sharon, and without mentioning Powell's special envoy, Zinni.

Sharon, likewise, made no mention of Zinni when he addressed the nation on Tuesday, December 3. His speech made the prospect of a U.S.-brokered cease-fire almost irrelevant: "The president told me that the United States is a true partner and friend of the state of Israel. In times of peace as well as today, in times of war against the terror, the United States and Israel stand together. . . . Whoever rises to kill us, his blood will be upon his head! Just as the United States, under the courageous leadership of President Bush, has been acting in its war against world terrorism, using all its might against terror, so will we act: with full force and determination, with all the means we used to date and with new means at our disposal. Don't be taken in by false prophecies and don't be deluded by promises of immediate results. This struggle will not be easy, this struggle will not be short, but we will win.

". . . For a long time the world didn't catch on to Arafat's nature, but a significant change has occurred in recent times. There is more understanding towards our position, and the true Arafat is being discovered by all. Arafat is the biggest obstacle to peace and to stability in the Middle East. That was the case in the past, and we also see it today, at present, and I am sorry to say it, probably in the future as well. However, Arafat won't succeed to fool the government I head. This time Arafat won't manage to fool us."

Sharon's cabinet the next day adopted "a wider scope of activity against Palestinian terrorism." While rejecting the outright demolition of the Palestinian Authority, the army over the next two weeks bombarded a series of security facilities and symbols of the Palestinian Authority over a wide area, demolished Arafat's helicopters, damaged his compound in Gaza, and fired missiles close to his office in Ramallah. On December 13, the cabinet declared Arafat "irrelevant," cutting off all contact with him. Under heavy international pressure to crack down on militant groups, Arafat called for a halt to all attacks on Israelis, and his authority declared Hamas and Islamic Jihad outlaw organizations. Arafat pledged to make arrests of militants demanded by Zinni, with only partial results. Whatever crackdown he conducted failed to prevent an attack on a bus on December 12, 2001, near the settlement of Emmanuel that killed ten Israelis.

Zinni would later say that Mohammed Dahlan and Ahmad Jibril, who headed the preventive-security agencies responsible for combating terror groups, were fed up with the intifada and ready to cooperate with the United States and Israel—but they never got a clear order from Arafat. "I felt strongly they felt it was time to move on. I felt that had Arafat issued them the order to crack down, they would have and could have."

Yet three weeks after Powell said he wanted Zinni to "to stick in the region for a while and get this thing started," the envoy's arrival and presence had only seemed to increase the level of violence, and he was summoned back to Washington.

The U.S. cease-fire effort looked like a failure. In fact, Zinni had persuaded Sharon to back off from "seven days of quiet" before engaging in confidence-building steps to forty-eight hours, and to drop his demand for "100 percent success" from Arafat. As Zinni watched from the United States, the next few weeks saw the violence subside. Palestinians were desperate, he later wrote, and "the Israelis were also in a bind" over what else they could do. "I think that for different reasons they were both desperate to get this thing [cease-fire talks] restarted."

In Tel Aviv, Dan Kurtzer watched, perplexed, as another chance for active American diplomacy presented itself, only to be overtaken by renewed conflict. He later recalled: "There was a period of about three weeks when it was very quiet. The Palestinians had almost stopped everything. We knew we were never going to get absolute quiet. . . . We didn't move fast enough."

This was typical of the administration's whole approach to the conflict, he reflected. It wasn't enough that the president and Powell had presented a forward-looking vision and dispatched a special envoy. For a conflict that presents so many difficulties, "You need a lot of engine power to keep cutting through." This power needs to be exhibited in big ways and small, down to the "day-in, day-out stuff," like press statements issued by the embassy spokesman. Rather than rapidly and forcefully responding to events in a way that would show U.S. determination, Kurtzer said, "press guidance would get watered down" by Washington. Typical was the all-purpose response to heavy-handed military action: "Israel has the right to defend itself, but needs to keep in mind the consequences of its actions."

The U.S. initiative, he concluded, "didn't have legs. . . ." Diplomacy was something that "parts of Washington affirmatively didn't want."

By the time Zinni arrived back in the region on January 3, a new chapter had opened that would finally wreck just about any chance for Arafat to redeem himself in the president's eyes.

For some time, U.S. and Israeli intelligence, working cooperatively, had been tracking a Palestinian purchase of tons of weapons from Iran. The arms were more sophisticated than anything so far used in the intifada, which had involved mostly AK-47s, suicide-bomb belts, and improvised roadside bombs. The shipment included millions of dollars' worth of rockets, plastic explosives, armor-piercing weapons, and ammunition. If used against Israelis, these arms could put major Israeli cities within range of the Palestinians, drastically escalating the conflict. To evade the Israeli blockade of the Gaza shoreline, the weapons were to be transported through the Suez Canal—with Egyptian officials being bribed, if necessary—and off-loaded in submersible containers that would float just below the surface, with only a small buoy visible from above, according to Israeli security officials. Some of the weapons might also have been sent in through tunnels between Gaza and Egypt, a frequent smuggling route.

On its own, the United States had evidence pointing to Arafat's involvement. "It would be hard to imagine that Arafat or people close to him had no knowledge of this shipment," a U.S. official told the *Baltimore Sun*. Israel would quickly supply more. The operation may have begun as early as the spring, when Arafat went to Moscow and one of his aides is believed to have stopped in at the Iranian embassy, according to information obtained by Edward Abington, the Palestinian lobbyist in Washington. It was reportedly brokered by Imad Mugniyah, one of the world's most-wanted terrorists, a man who, Abington said, was "number one on our shit list, along with Osama bin Laden."

The implications were twofold, and devastating for Arafat: here was evidence that the Palestinian Authority was playing a double game— talking peace while arming for a prolonged conflict. "It seems, at a minimum, that some Palestinian officials wanted the option of continued, heightened violence over the long term," Deputy Secretary of State Richard Armitage said in an interview at the time. Perhaps worse was the tie to Iran, a sworn enemy of both the United States and Israel. The Islamic Republic had worked to undermine the peace process. It was a longtime patron of and weapons supplier to Hezbollah and a financial backer of Hamas and Islamic Jihad. But until now, the secular Palestinian Authority had steered clear of Iran's mullahs. Israelis said the deal, brokered by Hezbollah, offered Iran a foothold in the Palestinian areas.

Ivry said the agreement gave Iranians "access to hospitals and assisting some of the communities by Iranian money." This meant, he said, "when they are in, you cannot get them out. It means the Iranians are going to get some kind of control in the territories."

Israel seized the ship January 4, just as Arafat was meeting with Zinni in Ramallah. Israelis had briefed Zinni shortly beforehand.

"Mr. Chairman, we have a big ordeal on our hands called the *Karine A*," Zinni told Arafat, according to Saeb Erekat, a top Palestinian negotiator, who was present. Arafat denied having "anything personally to do with it," Erekat said. Zinni later wrote that he told Arafat's top subordinates, "We and the Israelis know that Arafat made payments to the Iranians, bought the weapons, and chartered the ship; we know that the captain of the ship is a Palestinian Authority guy; and he is now spilling his guts."

Arafat's first response was to send a letter to Bush denying any knowledge. U.S. officials suspected this was an outright lie. "I was told that was the final stroke for George Bush," Abington recounted. American suspicions deepened as a result of compelling briefings by a high-level Israeli intelligence team dispatched to Washington.

In the zero-sum contest for world credibility, this was such an intelligence and propaganda windfall for Israel that Sharon didn't have to respond militarily, but only let the facts spill out. "For a change they had cleverly handled a potentially messy event," Zinni wrote. Badly shaken, Arafat's team tried to regroup. Abington flew to the region and told Arafat that Bush "felt you personally lied to him." He and Saeb Erekat, a leading Palestinian negotiator, drafted another letter for Arafat, this time to Powell, pledging to find and punish those responsible for the arms deal. A few weeks later, Arafat fired Fuad al-Shubaki, who handled finances for the Palestinian security services, and issued warrants against two officers who were abroad.

Zinni later wrote that "the *Karine A* just may have had a sobering effect on everybody. My hopes were up." He noted a new level of cooperation at the security meetings he chaired. When he left the region January 7, he wrote: "I couldn't wait for the next trip."

If this was the point where Bush concluded that Arafat was irredeemable, he didn't show it. In fact, when he spoke with reporters January 10, Bush said, "I think it's very important for our administration to remain engaged with both parties," even though he was "beginning to suspect that those arms were headed to promote terror."

Asked if Arafat had been less than truthful in saying he had nothing to do with the shipment and denying knowledge, Bush replied, "We will find out the facts, John. But he is—you asked a question, should we basically disengage? And the answer is no, we won't disengage from the Middle East. We will stay involved in the Middle East peace process—or trying to get to the peace process. And it starts with making the region more secure. Mr. Arafat must renounce terror, and must reject those in the region that would disrupt the peace process by the use of terrorist means." Significantly, he also assumed responsibility for Zinni's mission, saying, "I intend to ask Zinni to go back to the region at the appropriate time, to keep pushing for a dialogue, to keep pushing for the process to go forward."

In truth, many U.S. officials involved in the Middle East didn't believe Arafat had ever given up the terror option. The question for them was how to respond. Bush, at this point, was still leaving the field open for diplomatic heavy lifting. With a deeper, more energetic involvement, *Karine A* could have provided an opportunity. Arafat had a reputation for never taking a decisive step unless he had no other choice. Now he was cornered. Discovery of the arms shipment could have been used to bludgeon him into more effective action against militant groups, beginning the process of restoring shattered trust.

Karine A should also have served as a danger sign for both the United States and Israel. Iran, which already had ties to at least two of the militant groups, was now stepping up its involvement in the conflict. Neither the United States nor Israel could depend completely on intelligence services to provide early warning of Iran's next move. To Tehran, this was a cost-effective investment in keeping the West off-balance. To counter it, the United States had to help engineer a shift in the Palestinians' political center of gravity, persuading a majority that violence was counterproductive and that they had a genuine alternate route to a Palestinian state.

But it would be several months before Zinni returned. He would be dispatched amid a renewed explosion of violence that, once again, was complicating an American strategic objective—in this case, to line up regional support for, or at least acquiescence in—a war against Iraq. Ultimately, terrorists would succeed in aborting the mission.

In a lengthy interview for this book, Zinni said, "I walked away with the belief that Arafat would never come to the table willing to make a compromise of some sort; that he couldn't, for whatever reason. I also came away [with the feeling] that, for the Palestinians, they can't take a step with a major risk without an assurance there is a second step."

But the administration didn't keep him on the scene long enough to test this proposition or, alternatively, to find a way around the Arafat impasse.

Two vignettes from Zinni's doomed mediation effort reinforce the point made by George Mitchell about the necessity of perseverance in a peace mission. Zinni described how, like George Bush before him, he had been taken on one of Sharon's famous helicopter trips over the West Bank. "I think he had the sense of, 'Ah, I got a soldier here . . . somebody who I can relate to . . . no diplomats.' So 70 percent of the discussion was tactical level—the tactical importance of the terrain, the security aspects of what needed to be done." Significantly, Sharon did not press the case that the settlements covering many West Bank hillsides and in the Jordan Valley needed to stay in Israel's hands. Instead, he spoke of Israel's vulnerability to attack. "For example, in two-and-a-half minutes, an incoming jet, you'd have to respond to it. . . . There were certain avenues of approach and other things that could make them vulnerable, if they didn't have some way of—he didn't use the term *controlling*, but he wanted me, I think, more to see the value of these things in the security sense, in their own right . . . he never came on as saying, 'We must control this, we must have this, you have to see what we must have.' Not anything like that. I think in his own mind he felt that the security situation would speak for itself, that as a military man I could get an appreciation for the terrain and the military aspects of the terrain, and that sort of thing. And that's what he was highlighting."

As Ned Walker and Terje Roed-Larsen had already noted, Sharon did not have an unmovable ideological attachment to the settlements. His overriding concern was security. Over time, working with a fellow general like Zinni, he might have come to trust the American mediator—"someone I can relate to"—to the point where he could be persuaded that his needs—and the Palestinians'—could each be met in a final agreement. Zinni, at the time, was also gaining the Palestinians' trust. Erekat recalled, "Zinni is one of the most decent, precise, direct persons I've ever met in my life. And he's a straight shooter."

Like Mitchell in Northern Ireland, Zinni had encounters outside officialdom: "Especially when you're on the ground, you start meeting Israelis and Palestinians. I mean the day-to-day people in the streets somewhere, people grabbing my coat and saying, 'Don't quit on us, don't give up on us.' As a matter of fact, it was almost like it had been staged. I had a couple pushing a baby in—I think it was Tel Aviv—come up to me, an Israeli couple, saying, 'General Zinni'—They spotted me. I almost had the same thing happen in Ramallah with a Palestinian couple. 'Don't give up on us, whatever you do . . . seek the peace.'"

9

PASSOVER HORROR

■ MARCH 2002 ■

SIGALIT SHIMLA WOULD have preferred to join her
mother and siblings around a family table on that first night of Passover,
the eight-day Jewish holiday that celebrates a universal theme of liberation. Sigalit cherished Pesach, as the holiday is called in Hebrew. She
loved the ritual feast that uses symbolic foods and simple readings to
depict the Israelites' escape from slavery in ancient Egypt under God's
protection. She even welcomed the preparations, which, for an observant
Jew, could be exhausting. "You have to clean the house, you have to do
all the shopping, the food, the dishes—everything is supposed to be new
for Pesach, supposed to be new and kosher for Pesach," says Sigalit, a
pretty, colorfully dressed English instructor in her late thirties who lives
in Netanya, Israel, with her husband, Eli, and their four children. "Even
the dishes are supposed to be very delicate. And the clothes: you buy
everyone new clothes. Everything is so new—it's spring, and happy and
cheerful. And although you work very hard before this holiday, you feel
the freedom in the holiday. You feel gratefulness. You feel so blessed to
have this holiday."

But Sigalit didn't get her preference. Holidays often bring a difficult
choice for couples over which side of the family to celebrate with. For
this year's Passover—starting March 27, 2002—Sigalit's husband, Eli,

implored her to bow to the wishes of her in-laws and join them for the ritual Seder meal at the Park Hotel on the Netanya seafront. She reluctantly agreed. The decision would pull Sigalit—together with more than two hundred other unwitting Israelis—into a cruel national trauma that mocked Passover's joyous message of freedom. That trauma would place Netanya on the lips of newscasters around the world, send political shock waves from the Middle East to Washington, and bring about a lasting change in the relationship between Israeli prime minister Ariel Sharon and U.S. president George W. Bush.

At 5 PM, Sigalit entered the hotel lobby with her four young children, including two-year-old twins. She and her husband, Eli, who describe themselves simply as "religious," made sure to arrive in plenty of time to be present for the lighting of candles that would mark the beginning of the holiday. In summer, Netanya almost achieves the ambience of a semitropical resort, with surfers descending its sandy cliffs to the sun-dappled Mediterranean and an occasional nude sunbather lying a discreet distance from the beach crowd. But this wet, chilly afternoon before Passover showed a different Netanya: a gritty, care-worn, mostly working-class town of Russian immigrants and Jews of North African descent, a town seemingly a world away from the office towers, luxury hotels, world-class restaurants, and lush suburban gardens of Tel Aviv, just twenty miles away.

Netanya, and places like it all over the country—including parts of the biblical jewel Israelis call Yerushalayim—are what most Israelis call home in a small, isolated country showing its age after six decades of war interrupted by fleeting periods of calm and prosperity. Culturally, they fall midway between the youthful, hedonistic secularism of Tel Aviv and the self-absorbed ultra-Orthodox enclaves of Jerusalem.

Despite its American-sounding name, the Park Hotel fits neatly into this middle Israel, a place where English is spoken infrequently, where life is hectic, rewards are few, holidays like Passover are conscientiously observed, and word of disaster spreads rapidly. A modest seafront hotel catering to the elderly and to middle-income visitors, it featured, on Passover 2002, a kosher Seder, with a rabbi presiding, that to many families offered the best combination of festivity, tradition, and value.

Venturing into a crowded public place like the Park Hotel posed a danger all Israelis had come to recognize by then, a year and a half into a guerrilla war in which pedestrian malls, cafés, and bus stops became frequent suicide-bomber targets. This was particularly true for residents of Netanya. A half-hour drive from the West Bank town of Tulkarem, home to a large, angry population of Palestinian refugees, Netanya had witnessed a series of bombings and gun attacks that provided stark evidence of Israel's vulnerability to terror in its narrow "waist."

On March 9, two hours before the café bombing in Jerusalem, two Palestinian gunmen tossed grenades and opened fire at a different seafront hotel, killing a nine-month-old baby, wounding about thirty other people, and covering the hotel lobby and sidewalk with blood. On March 4, three Israelis were killed in Netanya when a Palestinian set off explosives strapped to his body.

But Israelis often show a defiant urge to go about their lives in the face of danger. Describing her wait in the Park Hotel lobby during a 2005 interview, Sigalit recalled most vividly her efforts to entertain and distract her twins, who remained with her while Eli took the two oldest children to a nearby synagogue for pre-Passover prayers. At twenty-four months, twins David and Eden were then at the stage of being totally dependent on their mother, who had to minister to the needs of both at once: "This is the year, until they are three years old, it's very hard with them. . . . And with twins, everything is twice."

While Sigalit waited, a twenty-five-year-old Palestinian—Abdel Basset Odeh—scouted the seaside area in a car driven by a man who carried a fake Israeli ID. He'd taken a precaution against getting caught, donning a wig and lipstick to look like a woman. Beneath his clothes, he wore a belt containing twenty pounds of explosives and shrapnel. According to Avi Dichter, then chief of the Israeli domestic security service Shin Bet, Abdel Basset Odeh was looking for a crowded place to kill as many Jews as possible. He went first to a large shopping mall near the entrance to Netanya but found it already closed for the coming Passover holiday. Another mall in the coastal suburb of Herzliya Pituach, home to diplomats and many of Israel's wealthy elite, was also closed. Before giving up, he decided to explore the hotel district close to the Netanya beach.

Abdel Basset Odeh grew up as one of eight children in a family of refugees in Tulkarem, exposing him to the bitter longing of families that had lost homes and livelihoods in war but also to the promise and peril of life in a town smack on the Green Line, the de facto border between Israel and the West Bank, created in 1948.

During tranquil times, Tulkarem's bustling central square and markets drew crowds of Israelis who drove the short route from their heavily populated coast on weekends. In the late 1990s, its technical college—part of a network founded by a member of the wealthy Jewish Kadoorie family of Hong Kong and Shanghai—was viewed by Israelis, Palestinians, and Americans as a potential crucible of economic growth, turning out technicians who could be employed at an industrial park planned nearby.

Since the intifada had started, this struggling town and its neighboring refugee camps had become, in a dark, twisted way, almost a sister city to Netanya, a mere ten miles away by road. A frequent source of suicide bombers and gunmen who preyed on civilians of Netanya and nearby communities, Tulkarem regularly felt the full force of Israeli retaliation and preemptive strikes, drawing tank incursions, bombardments, and assassinations, along with border closures that cut off Palestinian day laborers from their livelihoods at jobs in Israel. Tulkarem offered repeated examples of the kinds of Israeli military tactics that drew harsh criticism from human rights groups for excessive force and a disregard for likely civilian casualties.

As the intifada worsened, Tulkarem's refugee camps, home to some of the most desperate Palestinians, became cauldrons of hatred. The entire town was reoccupied for thirty hours in January, drawing a UN warning. In early March, troops again took over the area in an operation that left at least fourteen dead, rounding up and arresting hundreds of young men and stoking demands for vengeance.

Majdi Jayusi, twenty-eight, chairman of the technology education department at Kadoorie Technical College, had witnessed the change. Before the intifada, the college was the centerpiece of plans for an industrial park that would be developed in cooperation with Israel and draw foreign investment. After the uprising, it became a shooting gallery at night, drawing Israeli fire that left its buildings badly damaged.

When he was growing up, he told me, it was a rare thing for a Palestinian child ever to see a human corpse. After the intifada, he said, the dead became a familiar sight to all.

In young adulthood, Abdel Basset Odeh profited from Tulkarem's proximity to Israel, earning a good living selling vegetables and cars and installing tiles, according to his father, Mohammed Qassim Saed Odeh. At a time when access to Israel was relatively easy for West Bankers, he imported fruits and vegetables from across the Green Line, ventured to Tel Aviv and for a time worked at a hotel in Netanya, possibly the Park Hotel, site of the Passover Seder. "He spoke, wrote, and read Hebrew," the older Odeh said proudly. The family was stricken by tragedy in 1999 when Abdel Basset Odeh's ten-year-old sister died of a lung ailment. According to the father, Abdel Basset became so distraught he knocked his head against the wall. Later, he became engaged to a girl who lived in Iraq. He traveled there seven or eight times to meet her because she was unable to get permission to come to the West Bank.

Acquaintances from Tulkarem said Abdel Basset appeared to become more religious after the intifada began. It was while he was staying with a group of Muslim proselytizers that his father learned that Israelis suspected him of being part of a terrorist ring. In July 2001, Abdel Basset Odeh and his older brother, Assam, were blocked at a border crossing into Jordan en route to Iraq and what was supposed to be a party to celebrate his marriage. Summoned for interrogation, Assam was told of a letter the Israelis had obtained that revealed plans for Abdel Basset to commit a bombing that would cause numerous casualties. Agents tried to enlist the father to help locate Abdel Basset but were told he had left home three or four days before—the last time the elder Odeh remembered seeing him.

The chill rain that fell on Netanya the afternoon before Passover seemed more appropriate to the bleak mood of the country than a festive holiday that would usher in the spring. A year and a half after the outbreak of pent-up Palestinian rage called the al-Aqsa Intifada, the conflict over Israel's control of territory it won in 1967 had broken free of most restraints. From its early clashes, mostly exchanges of rocks and rubber-coated bullets, with limited live fire from both sides, the uprising had by early 2002 become a vengeful and destructive guerrilla war.

The worsening situation sent angry tremors of rage from the West Bank throughout the Middle East, strained Israel's relationship with its patron and chief supporter, the United States, and put Washington at odds with longtime allies in the Arab world.

What Palestinians saw as their own struggle for freedom, Israelis viewed as a campaign to kill Jews.

Secular and Islamist Palestinian militant groups competed with each other to commit the bloodiest suicide-bomb, gun, and grenade attacks on civilian targets—nightclubs, cafés, crowded shopping areas, and buses—afterward trumpeting claims of responsibility in videos and student-government election pamphlets. Israeli preemptive raids and counterattacks—in the form of bloody incursions into Palestinian towns, villages, and refugee camps, assassinations of known militant leaders, air strikes, and building demolitions—claimed an even greater number of civilians on the Palestinian side, although the gap was shrinking.

Warnings by world leaders of a slide into full-fledged war made no impact on either side. "Truly, we are nearing the edge of the abyss," Secretary General Kofi Annan told the UN Security Council on February 21, 2002. Three weeks later he was back, saying the toll of dead and wounded had reached appalling levels, tensions were at a boiling point—the worst in ten years—and the scale of carnage was horrifying.

B'Tselem, an Israeli organization that documents human rights abuses in the occupied territories, released a report in March criticizing the army for unclear rules of engagement. Entitled "Trigger Happy," the report said live ammunition was at times being used when there was no clear threat to life, and that extensive injury had been caused to Palestinians who were not involved in attacks against Israel. The army, it said, conducted only superficial probes into the shootings. An army spokesman rejected the allegations.

The month leading up to the start of Passover at sundown on March 27 was the worst since the intifada began, over the weekend of September 29, 2000, when Israeli forces in Jerusalem fired on Palestinian youths who were hurling rocks from the stone plateau of the Muslim shrine of Haram al-Sharif toward Jews worshipping at the adjacent Western Wall, Judaism's holiest site.

Now, Israelis were trapped in a new kind of bondage, a seemingly endless struggle with neighbors who hated them enough to die killing them. By the afternoon before Passover, more than one hundred Israelis had died in March alone.

With their country's international standing eroding, Israelis felt more and more cut off from the rest of the world, living a recurring nightmare that they were a nation alone. Tourism had collapsed, hard on the heels of a sharp downturn in the high-tech industry, which in the late 1990s offered Israel the promise of unprecedented economic growth. International opinion tended to equate Palestinian terrorism with heavy-handed Israeli military tactics. Worse, Israel's response to the intifada seemed to stimulate anti-Semitism in the Arab world and Europe, reinforcing Israeli fears that the world was basically hostile.

Even the United States, the only other nation in whom Israeli leaders placed any faith, viewed the raging conflict as a serious impediment to its own plans for the Middle East, posing a tough dilemma for Israel's prime minister, who counted support from Washington as a crucial political asset. Since terrorists struck the World Trade Center towers and the Pentagon on September 11, 2001, Israel had struggled to be accepted by Americans as a fellow victim and one of its closest, if not the closest, ally in President George W. Bush's war on terrorism. Now it was being made to appear part of the problem.

Following the rapid U.S. military success in getting rid of the Taliban regime in Afghanistan, Bush had trained his sights on Saddam Hussein's regime in Iraq, which he feared would, in a matter of years, break free of UN-imposed sanctions, rebuild its arsenal of chemical and biological weapons, jump-start its stalled quest for nuclear weapons and, at a minimum, gain much greater leverage over the future of the region, endangering Western oil supplies and stoking anti-American extremism.

Ever since Sharon and Bush came to power within a few months of each other in 2001, an understanding had been maintained whereby Israeli actions should not endanger American interests in the broader Middle East. Now, in the weeks before Passover, a line was being crossed by Israel, in the U.S. view. Arab-world outrage at Israeli military actions fueled hostility toward the United States, whose $3 billion a year in military and economic aid to Israel was widely seen as enabling Sharon's harsh measures. Popular pressure from the Arab "street" on Washington's main Arab allies, Egyptian president Hosni Mubarak, the Saudi royal family, and Jordan's King Abdullah, made them all the more skittish about acquiescing in any American scheme to oust Saddam Hussein.

With the region in an uproar, senior U.S. officials felt compelled to speak out about Israeli tactics. Staffers at the American consulate in Jerusalem and the State Department routinely documented and reached harsh judgments about Israel's use of excessive force against Palestinians, producing a catalogue of serious human rights abuses for the department's annual human rights report. The volume for 2002 would be particularly damning toward both sides in the conflict. But senior officials rarely criticized Israel in public, and, when they did so, they usually minced their words.

Now, in March 2002, the Americans found Israeli actions hard to justify from either a humanitarian or a tactical standpoint. The impact of the Israeli measures was felt particularly in West Bank and Gaza refugee camps, where Israeli assaults during the month left more than one hundred dead and five hundred injured, according to the UN Relief Works Administration, which provided aid to the camps. On March 6, for instance, the UN's refugee agency for the Palestinians complained about damage from air strikes to a school for the blind in Gaza. "At least fifteen classrooms have been put out of action, dozens of windows have been ripped from their frames, and a children's playground and garden has been turned from an oasis of calm into a wasteland of twisted metal and rubble," the agency said in a statement.

Private conversations with Israeli leaders didn't sway them. Indeed, Israel's ambassador to Washington David Ivry noticed a pattern of Secretary of State Colin Powell and other U.S. officials thinking they had made a forceful point over the phone, only to have it fail to register in Jerusalem. So Powell sounded off.

"If you declare war on the Palestinians and think you can solve the problem by seeing how many Palestinians can be killed—I don't know if that leads you anywhere," Secretary of State Colin Powell said in congressional testimony March 6, challenging Sharon "to take a hard look at his policies to see whether they will work."

In a tour of Arab capitals to sound out potential support for attacking Iraq, Vice President Dick Cheney heard a chorus of demands that the United States assert itself in trying to end the Israeli-Palestinian conflict. You Americans, Arab leaders said, "have got to do something about these pictures we're seeing daily on every satellite TV channel if you want to get a hearing on Saddam or anything else in the region."

Before Cheney set out on his trip, Bush acted to blunt complaints from the vice president's Arab hosts by announcing that Anthony Zinni would be dispatched to Israel and the Palestinian territories in a renewed attempt to broker a cease-fire between Israel and the Palestinians. Two previous Zinni trips had failed amid an explosion of violence that brought tentative moves toward cooperation between the two sides to a halt. "Nobody was under any illusion that the odds were with us," Zinni recalled later. In the U.S. State Department, his chances of success were rated in the "single-digit percents."

In the days before Zinni arrived on March 14, 2002, less than two weeks before Passover, Sharon moved on two tracks to strengthen his own bargaining position. For Zinni's benefit, he made two diplomatic concessions: he backed off on his insistence on seven days of calm before cease-fire negotiations could start, and he declared that he would let Arafat out of his compound in the West Bank city of Ramallah, for the first time in three months, letting him move through the West Bank and to Gaza.

At the same time, Sharon intensified a military assault on Palestinian territories that included incursions by soldiers and tanks into towns and refugee camps, arrests of some two thousand young Palestinian men, and bombardment of Palestinian Authority structures. Palestinian militants stepped up their own waves of suicide and gunfire attacks. Both sides, it appeared to observers, needed to make a show of strength and land a final blow before their fight was halted.

Sharon and Palestinian fighters weren't the only ones seeking to increase their leverage in the late winter of 2002. Hoping to pull Washington into more active mediation, Saudi Arabia's Crown Prince

Abdullah used an interview with a prominent American columnist, the *New York Times*'s Thomas L. Friedman, to float a peace proposal calling for peace between Israel and all Arab states, provided Israel withdrew from lands occupied since the 1967 war. Since the attacks of September 11, the Saudi royal family had come under relentless scrutiny and criticism from numerous members of the U.S. Congress for tolerating a stream of anti-U.S. hatred emanating from Saudi mosques and schools. Critics called into question the close ties between the Bush and al-Saud families, which deepened during the first U.S. war with Iraq. Abdullah felt the need to break out of the Saudis' usual quiet, behind-the-scenes style of diplomacy. The peace proposal served to position him as one of the Arab world's leading moderates.

Bill Burns, the State Department's assistant secretary for the Near East, worked with Jordanian foreign minister Marwan Muasher and the Saudis to reshape Abdullah's plan from a trial balloon into a formal proposal that could be adopted at the Arab summit in Beirut, due to open the week of March 25. To its land-for-peace offer, diplomats added the requirement of a "just-"agreed-on solution to the problem of Palestinian refugees. The careful wording avoided posing a "right of return" for the refugees to their original homes in Israel—a right viewed by Israelis as a demographic threat to their nation's existence as a Jewish state.

Even so worded, the proposal was unacceptable to Sharon, who had devoted years of his public career to expanding settlements to the point where Israel would find it next to impossible to surrender all the land it had gained in 1967. Indeed, Arab leaders appeared to see it as a chance to isolate the hard-line Israeli prime minister—even from other Israelis. "The importance of it is it sends a signal to the Israeli public by telling them that peace with the broader Arab world is possible should they make peace with their neighbors," Adel al-Jubeir, an adviser to the crown prince, said in a television interview.

Efraim Halevy, then head of the Mossad, the Israeli foreign intelligence service, urged Sharon not to dismiss the Saudi proposal. "The Saudi initiative was a very important initiative, because for the first time ever the Saudis took an initiative . . . which was an initiative in the service of peace," Halevy told me in August 2006. He sensed a growing impatience among Arab leaders with Yasser Arafat's efforts to inflame their populations. They wanted, he felt, some kind of constructive move that would "extricate everybody out of the mess." In quiet conversations with senior contacts—"very serious people"—in the Arab world, Halevy broached the possibility of Sharon's making an appearance at the upcoming Beirut summit to meet with Arab leaders. At first they responded with shock to the idea, Halevy recalled. Then they were curious as to what Sharon might say.

Two Labor ministers in Sharon's cabinet, Shimon Peres and Benjamin Ben-Eliezer, also welcomed the Saudi proposal. The proposal threatened to put Sharon into the position of spoiler, as the one ignoring an outstretched hand for peace, and to put him at odds with Bush, who called Crown Prince Abdullah to praise his initiative. A White House spokesman called the proposal "a gleam of light, a ray of hope in a Mideast that has too much violence and not enough of a focus by people on how to stop the violence."

As Cheney traveled through the Arab world and Zinni departed for Tel Aviv, Bush added to the pressure on Sharon during a press conference, criticizing the bloody Israeli incursions into West Bank and Gaza refugee camps. "Frankly, it's not helpful what the Israelis have recently done in order to create conditions for peace. I understand someone trying to defend themselves and to fight terror. But the recent actions aren't helpful." Then Bush appeared to question whether Israel was actually trying to avoid killing civilians. "I certainly hope that Prime Minister Sharon is concerned about the loss of innocent life. We certainly—I certainly am. It breaks my heart and I know it breaks the heart of a lot of people around the world to see young children lose their life as a result of violence—young children on both sides of this issue."

By the time Zinni arrived, Sharon had bowed to the public pressure from Washington and pulled Israel's forces back from Palestinian-controlled areas, shifting the burden for compromise to Arafat and the Palestinians.

From Washington's standpoint, the Zinni mission was at least in part an exercise in damage control, undertaken because, as a senior official later recalled, "we were sinking like a stone elsewhere in the region." But the character of Zinni himself, and that of his subordinate, Aaron Miller, meant that it would not be just a charade. Theirs was an odd but complementary pairing: Zinni, a short, crew-cut, powerfully muscled Italian American Catholic from a mill town outside Philadelphia, had climbed the ranks from serving as a junior Marine officer in the Vietnam War to become chief of the U.S. Central Command, in charge of all U.S. forces from Kenya to Kazakhstan, before retiring as a four-star general. Miller was tall and angular, a long-haired Jewish intellectual from a wealthy Cleveland suburb who had spent most of his career as a behind-the-scenes State Department civil servant wrestling with just one issue—the Arab-Israeli conflict. Where Zinni could be bluntly outspoken, Miller was cautiously circumspect, saving his judgments for later articles and speeches. But both men were problem solvers, fascinated by the Middle East and undaunted by the hatreds and fears that tear at the region. And they shared a vision for the region that went well beyond the nuts and bolts of a cease-fire. As Centcom chief from 1997 to 2000, Zinni had immersed himself in the cultures of Africa, the Arab world, and Central Asia as a way of gaining the confidence of leaders he dealt with. He dined and fished with Persian Gulf princes and kept in touch with General Pervez Musharraf even as Washington put its relationship with Pakistan on ice in the late 1990s. As president, Musharraf later became a crucial Washington ally during the Afghan war. As a result, Zinni became well-known and respected in the Arab and Muslim worlds. Even in a region where "the enemy of my enemy is my friend," and where an ally of one side becomes automatically suspect by the opposite side, Zinni drew automatic respect from the Israelis as a straightforward career military officer.

"Don't make enemies, but if you do, don't treat them gently," was a favorite Zinni motto. Zinni had powerful backers in Washington, chief among them the deputy secretary of state, Richard Armitage, a longtime friend and weight lifting partner. Zinni had tried studiously to come to grips with the personality of and pressures on Saddam Hussein, against whom he ran a four-day air campaign (Desert Fox) in 1998. His attempt to understand what drives allies and adversaries alike dated from his time in Vietnam, where he advised South Vietnamese Marines.

And as he assumed ever-higher commands, this son of immigrants kept the common touch. "He was the kind of leader who could tell his troops, 'I eat the same thing you do, get just as wet and go into just as much danger,'" said his friend John Sheehan, another retired four-star Marine general. Zinni's first Vietnam tour ended when he fell ill with malaria, hepatitis, and mononucleosis. In his second, he was wounded. He remained a stoic, according to Armitage, who described to me a weight lifting session with Zinni while the two were on a trip to Moscow in the early 1990s. "Tony is a very strong guy," he said, "but he struggled through the workout." Zinni kept silent on the reason—a broken elbow.

Miller, fifty-three, had labored in the pressure cooker of Middle East policymaking under six secretaries of state over two decades. His three books and numerous articles tapped a storehouse of knowledge accumulated over years of study and negotiating, knowledge that made him the department's near-indispensable institutional memory on the Arab-Israeli peace process. He had shuttled among Mideast capitals and gone back and forth between the prime minister's office in Jerusalem and Arafat's redoubt in Ramallah, in the process getting to know all the players personally. When his mother died in 1997, he got a condolence call from the Palestinian leader. The son of prominent Cleveland real estate developers, Miller grew up in a proudly pro-Zionist household and later lived on a kibbutz in Israel.

After earning a doctorate from the University of Michigan, he joined a think tank in Washington before joining the State Department and spending a year at the U.S. embassy in Amman, Jordan. He then went back to Washington to work at State Department headquarters. Holding various titles in different offices, he kept the Middle East as his specialty, winning department awards for service while operating discreetly in the background.

Miller was wedded to the peace process, which was for him both a professional and personal calling, but his experience had led him to be patient. He said the Arab-Israeli conflict had evolved over time and would only be resolved over time, when history and geography would force the two sides to find a way out of their predicament. While at the State Department, he actively supported Seeds of Peace, a program that sends Israeli and Arab youths to summer camp in Maine. The organization created an award in memory of his mother, Ruth Ratner Miller, and named him president after he left the government. Miller rarely yielded to pessimism, even during periods when the grief and bitterness consuming the region appeared overwhelming. At the same time, "He is always refusing to get intoxicated by overly optimistic views," said Joel Singer, an Israeli negotiator who played a key role during the Oslo talks between 1993 and 1996 and now practices international law in Washington. Miller's the one "who concentrates on the what-can-go-wrong scenarios," Singer said.

He was also, according to a colleague, a "spark plug of ideas." Not all his ideas worked out. Preparing for a Washington visit by Arafat during the Clinton years, Miller triggered an angry dispute when he suggested to officials of the U.S. Holocaust Memorial Museum, of which he was a board member, that they let Arafat visit the museum with VIP treatment. The proposed visit never took place. In Washington, where an early impression of Arafat as a terrorist and Jew-hater had never quite disappeared, grim jokes circulated over what lessons he would actually draw from exposure to the mechanics of genocide.

That episode reinforced a suspicion of Miller among conservative supporters of Israel as a Palestinian sympathizer. But as his 2002 mission opened, Palestinians who had sat across the table from him had no illusions that he would reflexively take their side. Hanan Ashrawi, a veteran Palestinian spokeswoman and former negotiator, described him as someone who would adopt a pro-Israel tilt when his superiors wanted that. "He's—let's put it nicely—he's adaptable," she said.

Zinni and Miller faced a huge obstacle in the deep distrust and animosity between Sharon and Arafat. Miller would later recall: "One Israeli said to me, that to understand the relationship you had to understand the story about the shark . . . when you're swimming away from the shark, you don't have to swim faster than the shark, you just have to swim faster than your friend." For both men, as Miller saw it, the peace process was a zero-sum game. "Each was trying to create circumstances that would gobble up the other; with every man for himself in the water with sharks."

But the team had some tools to work with. One was their sense of Arafat's desire to get back into the United States' good graces. A frequent visitor to the White House during much of Bill Clinton's presidency, Arafat had never even been allowed a meeting with George W. Bush, who entered office with grave misgivings about the Palestinian leader that Clinton personally reinforced in conversations with both Bush and incoming Secretary of State Colin Powell on inauguration day, 2001. Bush's doubts hardened into deep distrust when he turned his attention to fighting terrorism after September 11, 2001. Then, in late December 2001, when Israelis intercepted the *Karine A*, a ship loaded in Iran with mortars and rockets paid for by the Palestinians, Arafat was all but written off by Washington as duplicitous and a failed leader.

Another Zinni lever was Arafat's desire to travel. Up through late 2000, the Palestinian leader had crisscrossed the globe with the trappings of a head of state, even though no state existed and Israel exercised ultimate authority over Palestinian territories. These Potemkin journeys came complete with a lockstep color guard of uniformed Palestinian security officers that greeted Arafat on his return to his seaside compound in Gaza. Israeli leaders went along with this show and let Palestinian dignitaries pass easily through checkpoints while ordinary Palestinians suffered prolonged delays and humiliation. Even on Christmas Eve 2000, three months after the start of the intifada, Israeli officers whisked Arafat's motorcade through the darkened streets of Jerusalem after he attended the annual service at the Church of the Nativity in Bethlehem. But the rise of Sharon was accompanied by a series of moves that showed Israel was boss. Now Arafat was confined to the West Bank city of Ramallah with the threat that if he left the territories, he wouldn't be allowed to return. Arafat's Gaza headquarters was repeatedly bombarded and his helicopters and plane grounded.

Playing on Arafat's wish to reclaim his former stature, the Americans dangled before him the opportunity to get out from under this humiliating siege and attend the Arab summit in Beirut, set for the week of March 25.

In sum, the U.S. tactic was to offer to rehabilitate Arafat, an implicit rejection of the Israeli moves to render him powerless and irrelevant.

Cheney and a small clutch of aides, flying on Air Force Two, debated whether the vice president should meet with the Palestinian leader after they landed in Israel at the end of their Middle East trip. This would be Arafat's highest-level American contact since Bush took office.

Cheney said little as the two sides squared off inside his plane. No one aboard trusted the Palestinian leader to keep his word or to reject, completely, the use of violence as a tool to pressure the Israelis. Some argued that it would be crazy to meet with him, effectively rewarding terrorism. Burns argued that it would be a mistake not to at least offer a meeting, even if it were conditional. Arab leaders Cheney had just met with, Crown Prince Abdullah, President Hosni Mubarak of Egypt, and King Abdullah II of Jordan had agreed: "You can't come to the region and not meet the elected leader of the Palestinians. The issue is too central; it's going to cost you if you don't," they told the vice president.

Cheney explored a third possibility: using the prospect of a meeting to exert new pressure on Arafat and present him with a situation he couldn't wriggle out of. He also checked with Zinni, who told him, "I can't recommend that you meet with him. He's done nothing." Cheney then decided to demand that Arafat denounce terrorism publicly and take active steps to control it. When Arafat failed to act immediately, Zinni's mood darkened. Even though a cease-fire plan seemed to be coming together, he felt a growing sense that, in the end, Arafat would not do his part to carry it out.

Cheney, eager to show some progress with Zinni's mission, said he was prepared to return to the region and meet with Arafat in Cairo. Arafat brightened at the prospect of being able to travel to a foreign capital to see Cheney. "Sharon wasn't too shot-in-the-ass with that idea," Zinni said.

Although the vice president left without meeting Arafat, he joined in the administration's call for Israel to let the Palestinian leader travel to Beirut. Three days before Passover, as Israel reeled from a suicide bomb that had killed eleven people at a popular Jerusalem café, Cheney appeared on the Sunday *Meet the Press* program with a message of determination to back up Zinni and push for an end to the bloodshed.

"The fact of the matter is that there isn't anybody but us. I think what we've seen is that left to their own devices, the Israelis and Palestinians have been unable to resolve those issues," Cheney told NBC's *Meet the Press* host, Tim Russert. "[T]he parties appear to be unable to make any progress or even to be able to see their way out of it."

"Left to their own devices. . . ." In one dismissive phrase, Cheney diminished Israel from its prized stature as strategic partner and foremost regional ally of the United States in the war on terrorism to one of two troublesome "parties" whose conflict was getting in the way of American strategy and needed a firm guiding hand. The words could not have been reassuring to Sharon. After months of rejecting any comparison between Palestinian attacks on civilians and Israel's response, the Bush administration was putting Sharon on notice that its patience was wearing thin.

Along with this continuing pressure from Washington, Zinni's mission coincided with growing despair among the Israeli public and disillusionment with the leader whom they had elected eleven months before to crush the Palestinian intifada. As Passover approached, the national solidarity Israelis felt when they first came under attack was crumbling. For a vocal minority, the continued occupation and humiliation of the Palestinians flouted the standards of justice demanded by Zionism and Judaism.

A leaked military intelligence report surfaced in the mass-circulation *Yediot Ahronoth* a week before Passover, suggesting that Sharon's military tactics in the occupied territories had backfired, making the conflict worse. A poll reported in another large daily, *Maariv*, showed 67 percent dissatisfaction with Sharon's handling of the nation's security. Israel's ever-expanding settlement enterprise, the primary reason for its military grip on the West Bank and Gaza Strip, drew increasing domestic criticism. In January, more than fifty reserve officers broke ranks and refused to protect the settlements and participate in military operations they said were intended "to rule, expel, destroy, blockade, assassinate, starve, and humiliate an entire people." As the nation's gloom deepened, new ideas circulated on ways to end the conflict that ran counter to the prime minister's determined military campaign. A growing number of Israelis called for a barrier of fences, trenches, and electronic devices that would separate them from the Palestinians.

In the weeks before Passover, Sharon's coalition government betrayed signs of fracturing. His junior partners, Foreign Minister Shimon Peres and Defense Minister Benjamin Ben-Eliezer, backed his tough military actions, but both were eager to move into a cease-fire and, from there, to negotiate with the Palestinians.

On the defensive, Sharon moved to shore up his base of support and reassure the country. In a televised speech to Likud Party faithful aired two days before Passover, he vowed that Israel's military and security services—superior to any in the Middle East—would not be overcome: "I would like to say that although this is a difficult campaign, they will not be able to defeat the security forces, the IDF, the Israel police, the border police, the Shin Bet Israeli security service, and Mossad—all these people who are fighting this tough war today."

Then he paid tribute to the Jewish settlers in the West Bank and Gaza, whose ever-growing numbers had been a source of exasperation to American administrations for three decades and whose expanding communities—on land that Palestinians claimed for a state—were seen by most nations of the world—though not by the U.S. government— as a violation of the Fourth Geneva Convention.

"I would also like to send my greetings to those people who are standing on the front lines today together with the security forces, the residents of Judaea, Samaria, and the Gaza Strip, who for the past eighteen months have been engaged in this difficult struggle."

Sharon concluded by portraying the Palestinian Authority as an enemy: The Palestinian National Authority, he said, "is trying to break the strength of Israeli society, to undermine our endurance. They are making an effort to disrupt our unity. We have to stand united against the dangers. The Likud, as the ruling party, must provide an example to the Israeli people. Here in our own camp, we have to serve as an example of unity and cohesion. From Likud headquarters in Tel Aviv, I—together with all of you—am calling on the Israeli people to unite and close ranks at this time. We have to face the dangers together. Only together. This is the only way."

Sharon did not mention the United States. But as the broadcast aired, Zinni, the U.S. envoy, was presenting a cease-fire plan drawn up after lengthy meetings with Israeli and Palestinian security officials. He gave it to the two sides as a take-it-or-leave-it offer. He was in a hurry. He hoped for an agreement while the Arab summit, then getting started in Beirut, was still under way. He believed Sharon would let Arafat attend if there was a cease-fire, and the summit's focus would shift from the question of Arafat's attendance to the Saudi peace plan.

While Zinni sought acceptance of his plan, Arafat and his aides were preoccupied with the Beirut summit. Egyptian president Hosni Mubarak, in an interview published March 26, publicly urged Arafat to stay away, warning that Israel might not let him return to the territories. Later that day, speaking on an Israeli Arab-language television channel, monitored by Agence France Presse, Sharon set conditions: "In my opinion, the conditions are not ripe for Arafat to go to Beirut," he said. "President Arafat must declare a cease-fire in his language to his people and seek an end to the violence." Even if Arafat were to attend, he said, a decision on allowing him to return to the territories would depend on "whether there are any terrorist attacks in his absence."

Rather than comply, Arafat decided to address the gathering by video link instead of going to Beirut. Aides also reacted with fury to published excerpts of Passover holiday interviews that Sharon gave to two newspapers in which he voiced regret for having promised Bush not to harm Arafat.

On the evening of March 26, twenty-four hours before the start of Passover, Giora Eiland, then chief of planning for the IDF, worked late with a colleague, poring over Zinni's paper. "We read it carefully, and were quite content that it was the best we could achieve. Our recommendation was to say yes, but we had to get approval from the political echelon." With approval from Ben-Eliezer and Chief of Staff Shaul Mofaz, Eiland asked for a meeting with the prime minister.

"Come tonight" was the reply. At midnight, they joined Sharon in Jerusalem. Cautious and suspicious, Sharon went over the Zinni plan for the next two hours, asking specific questions. Other advisers weighed in. "We said there are some things that don't look good for us," recalled his national security adviser, Danny Ayalon.

Finally, Sharon said, "I can accept it. You can tell the American general that Israel accepts." Avi Dichter, head of Shin Bet, and Eiland called Zinni at 2 AM to tell him.

Zinni was surprised at Sharon's quick acceptance, but theorized that the Israelis didn't want to be the ones accused of holding back peace. He told the Israelis that he was sure the Palestinians would also give a positive response the next morning. "I hope that we are going to start a new era," he said, according to Dichter.

"I told him, 'Don't wake up too early, General Zinni, because I'm afraid you're going to be disappointed,'" Dichter said. "You know that they're going to give me a negative answer?" Zinni asked. "I'm afraid that you're not going to get any answer," Dichter replied.

Later that morning, Miller called Danny Ayalon, Sharon's national security adviser: "How late can the prime minister do a press conference?" he asked, exploring the idea of simultaneous Sharon and Arafat announcements of a cease-fire.

By then, Sharon was at his ranch north of the Negev for the holiday. "I told him the prime minister is ready almost any time to do it. Of course, before Passover comes, before evening. He told me, 'OK, I'm going to see Arafat now and I will call you back,'" Ayalon recalled.

Miller never called back. The Palestinians stalled. "The Americans continue work as if nothing has happened regarding the issue of the summit. They also continue work as if nothing has happened on the level of the statements made by the lunatic Sharon yesterday," Arafat aide Yasser Abed Rabbo complained in a radio broadcast.

Zinni sensed that Arafat couldn't bring himself to accept terms that meant he would have to confront Hamas and Islamic Jihad. The American envoy had tried at one point to do an end run around the Palestinian leader and persuade his top security officials, particularly Mohammed Dahlan and Jibril Rajoub, to carry out the tasks required of them by the cease-fire plan. He argued that they could be guided by what Arafat pledged to the United States in his repeated promises of cooperation. But the officials turned him down, saying they needed a direct order from the boss.

As sundown neared, Israel officially shut down for the Passover holiday. Sharon's aides left for their homes or family gatherings. The U.S. ambassador to Israel, Daniel Kurtzer, had already left the country to spend Passover with his family in Boston. Zinni and Miller were invited to the Jerusalem home of Ayalon's assistant, Toronto-born Shalom Lipner, to join his extended family for a traditional Seder.

The most propitious moment to announce a cease-fire was slipping away, but President Bush, making a campaign appearance for Republican Senate candidate Lindsey Graham in Greenville, South Carolina, was publicly upbeat in an encounter with reporters, despite Sharon's rejection of the United States' request that he free Arafat to travel to Beirut.

Asked if he had any plans to talk to Prime Minister Sharon, he said, "I don't today. I'm sure the secretary of state is in touch in the area, with the leaders of the area. But let me say this—and I think the important thing about the Middle East is that we're making very good progress on the Tenet accord." This was a reference to the security plan drawn up by CIA Director George Tenet that Zinni was working to turn into a more detailed cease-fire agreement. "In other words, there's a chance we'll have an agreement on the security arrangements necessary. . . . General Zinni is still in the area. Let me put it this way: I'm optimistic that progress is being made and I've asked General Zinni to continue to work with both parties, regardless of whether or not they're headed to Beirut. . . . The most important thing is getting into Tenet, getting into a security arrangement. And we're optimistic, and we'll see."

Bush also released statements commemorating both Easter, four days hence, and Passover, which was to begin at sundown. "In celebrating the Israelites' liberation from enslavement and their exodus from Egypt, Passover reminds Jews of their sacred tradition. It is a time for Jewish families to share together in long-established rituals and to offer prayers that celebrate the renewal of hope in the blessings of freedom.

"The story of the Exodus speaks across the millennia. By God's power and blessing, the children of Abraham overcame Pharaoh's tyranny forty centuries ago and found freedom in the Promised Land."

Toward 7 PM the lobby of the Park Hotel filled with people ready for the prayers, readings, and symbolic feast of Passover. More members of Sigalit's family arrived: Eli's sister, Korin Ben-Aroya, and her husband, Shimon, with their three children, and Eli's parents. Eli returned with the two older children.

Outside, "It was dark and stormy and rainy, which was very unusual for this date," Sigalit recalled. Many in the crowd wore coats. At 7:10, the crowd was summoned to the banquet room and moved slowly through the lobby. Eli and Sigalit lingered to strap the twins into a carriage "because they were such troublemakers.

"We were, like, the last ones to get into the dining room. Then I saw someone very, very strange," Sigalit recalls. The person who drew her attention was wearing a long wig, but his clean-shaven face was clearly that of a man. "He was wearing very modern and fashionable sunglasses, which also was very strange because it wasn't sunny. He was wearing a long coat, but this wasn't strange, because everybody was wearing long coats. His trousers were jeans, but they were like women's jeans and not a man's jeans," very wide at the ankles. "When I looked at this man, I thought he was going through something sexually, maybe he's doing a change, maybe he's homosexual . . . maybe he had psychological problems. And I felt pity for him.

"When we were walking, he was, like, pushing a woman. I thought to myself, 'A holiday, and someone is pushing. Why are you hurrying, for what? The dinner won't start until everybody sits.' I remember we were staring at each other, ten seconds, staring at each other. And I said to myself, 'Stop staring—it's rude to stare.'" He was three feet from her.

Inside the dining room, they moved farther apart. Sigalit went to a long table to join the other members of her family and sat down. The crowd of about 230 people in the dining room included numerous families containing several generations. With Sigalit and Eli were their four children, Eli's parents, Eli's sister and her husband, and their three children.

Minutes later, Sigalit saw the man again in an open space in the middle of the hall. "I thought to myself, 'He didn't find his family.' . . . Again I felt pity for him. He was, like, lost in the square. No one talked to him . . . I saw him looking at me and I turned my head or something.

"And then it happened," Sigalit said.

In addition to being a celebration of freedom, the Seder is also a family occasion centered on children, playing to their eager curiosity and delight in trying new things. Special tastes introduce them gently to the tragedy and triumph of Jewish history. Four ritual questions are reserved for the youngest to ask, beginning, "Why is this night different from all other nights?"

At Netanya's Park Hotel that night, the first question was never uttered. Before the service began, the man in the middle of the room with the long wig, strange sunglasses, and lipstick provided his own answer.

"I just remember a very, very big explosion," Sigalit recalled later. News accounts described the damage. The Associated Press version said: "The explosion tore through the ground floor of the hotel, blowing out walls and overturning tables and chairs. Bits of rubble and wires dangled from the ceiling. Some of the wounded were seen staggering out of the lobby, which was plunged into darkness by the explosion." As wind blew in from the ocean, the hotel's sprinkler system opened, producing a pool of water on the floor. Fifteen people were reported killed that evening, but the death toll would climb to twenty-nine. A number of the victims were in their seventies and eighties.

Thrown backward by the blast, Sigalit pulled a tablecloth off her face and began making out shapes in the darkness. She recognized her son Gavriel, four, unconscious, being held by another diner. She noticed a bloody wound in his elegant white Pesach shirt. A piece of shrapnel had pierced his neck, torn his windpipe, and broken one of his vertebrae. She called for her husband, who was clutching the twins' carriage: "Eli, come here immediately." She recounted, "And he came, and he saw Gavriel and he took him and said, 'I'm taking him out.'

"But we didn't speak. We were so in shock that we didn't say anything, just 'Take care of my kids.'"

Elsewhere in the hall, a combination of instincts—those of parent, ex-soldier, and medic—seemed to grab hold of Eitan Frankfurter, forty-two, who had come to the Park Hotel with his wife, five children, and eleven other members of his extended family. Immediately after the bomb exploded, Eitan heard a noise that sounded like shooting. "Get down under the table," he told his children. He took out his gun, which he carries everywhere, tried to see through the darkness for the source of the noise, and then realized it was caused by the sprinklers.

His wife, Aliza, pregnant with their sixth child, lost consciousness briefly and fell down. She came to in a panic. Looking around for her children, she noticed that her middle son was missing. "Find my boy," she shouted. Eitan later remembered a bizarre moment of disorientation. "I told her, 'I'm your husband.' She didn't recognize me."

Eitan told his other children, "Take the shortest route out," and looked for his missing son. The boy, it turned out, had pulled an injured friend onto his back and crawled through a window to escape. Eitan later found him covered in his friend's blood. He stripped off the boy's shirt looking for a wound before realizing the blood wasn't his. In a period of minutes that seemed at the time like hours, Eitan found all the members of his family and established that none of them had been physically injured. He sent his wife to the hospital as a precaution because of her pregnancy and dispatched his children to his father's home. Then he switched from being husband and father to medic, drawing on two years of army service in Lebanon and a year in the Golan Heights. Enlisting his brother to help, he went to work on the bomb's victims, grabbing pieces of clothing to use as bandages before emergency crews arrived with more supplies.

In the Park Hotel lobby, Sigalit Shimla held her distraught twins, one in each arm. "I remember I told them, 'Stop crying. Please, stop crying,' because it was so hard for me that they were crying." Gavriel lay next to her on a sofa, still unconscious. "I saw that he was in very bad condition, something that a mother can see. . . . And then I heard some ambulances coming, and someone came in and said, 'Give me your son. I'll take him to the ambulance,' and I said, 'Take him.'"

Any major attack triggered a practiced response from the town's emergency teams. Students from the ultra-Orthodox Sanz Yeshiva would pull aprons over their black coats and begin working as orderlies at the Laniado Hospital next door, pushing stretchers. Laniado's medical director, Avinoam Skolnik, who once served in a paratrooper unit, would preside calmly: "I'm like an old mechanic who raises the hood, looks inside, and knows what to do," he said during the early months of the intifada.

Two doctors would take up positions at the ambulance entrance to perform triage, steering patients to different sections of the hospital, depending on the severity of injury.

As four-year-old Gavriel was wheeled into Laniado, the triage team decided quickly that he belonged at Schneider Children's Medical Center in Petach Tikvah and returned him to an ambulance. During the fifteen-mile drive, the ambulance stopped twice so its crew could revive Gavriel's breathing. Despite three operations, the boy hovered between life and death for five days and remained hospitalized for five weeks.

Gavriel, one of whose vocal chords remained paralyzed, was comparatively lucky. His uncle Shimon Ben-Aroya, a forty-two-year-old Netanya garbage collector who was standing less than ten feet from the bomber, died instantly. Shimon's daughter Shery, twenty, an air force officer who worked with secret codes, was paralyzed on her right side. In addition, a piece of shrapnel pierced her right eye and went through her brain before exiting the left side of her skull. Three years later, she was still struggling to speak smoothly in Hebrew and had completely lost the command of Arabic and English that were key to her sensitive job.

Shimon's wife, Korin, thirty-nine, suffered a broken rib that punctured one lung during the bombing and fell unconscious. She awoke in a hospital trauma ward and didn't learn until the next day that her husband had been killed. She learned that he had been buried still covered in blood. Ordinarily, Jewish custom requires cleaning a body before burial. But in the case of a murder, Korin was told, the ritual is dispensed with "so the blood can shout to God."

Korin remained hospitalized for eleven days with her two youngest children, who were told by others of their father's death. But it was left to Korin to inform her badly injured oldest daughter. Shery became suspicious when she was visited just by her mother and her two siblings, noticing that the family was incomplete, but couldn't express herself. She instead used sign language, holding up her thumb to indicate the number five, as if to ask, "Where is the fifth?"

"I tried to make myself not understand, because I couldn't tell her alone," her mother recounted later. But she realized she had no choice and finally said, "You know what happened, and Daddy . . ." and opened her hands in a gesture of helplessness.

Wire-service bulletins quickly alerted the world to an explosion with dozens of casualties at the start of Passover in northern Israel, based in part on information supplied by paramedics. Within minutes, the blast had been confirmed as a suicide bombing at a hotel Seder. The import of a gruesome attack on a peaceful religious feast registered widely, but Gil Kleiman, the New York–raised foreign-press spokesman for Israel's national police, distilled what for him and others who rushed to the scene was the main point: "Innocent people killed while eating dinner."

Arriving at the Park Hotel half an hour after the blast, Kleiman immediately sensed the bombing would have "repercussions," as he put it later, and set about making sure the world got as vivid a look as possible. He appealed to the police commissioner to allow TV crews to film the scene immediately, instead of waiting until all the dead and their exploded body parts had been concealed in body bags. "We knew the foreign press would not put mutilated bodies" on the air, "but we wanted to give them the access."

"Let them in," responded the chief, Shlomo Aharonisky. An Israeli foreign ministry spokesman, Gideon Meir, assigned a name that wire services transmitted worldwide and that some American broadcasters quickly adopted without attribution: the Passover massacre.

Danny Ayalon, Sharon's national security adviser, learned of the bombing from a television report. But the news was slower to reach strictly observant households, which shun both TV and telephone during religious holidays.

At the Jerusalem home of Shalom Lipner, the Seder was proceeding according to custom when one of the American guests, Aaron Miller, excused himself from the table. "I'm very sorry," Miller said to his host and explained that he had just received a call from the Operations Center, the State Department's twenty-four-hour command post. The voice on the line told him of a bombing with casualties at the Park Hotel.

"I went back, grabbed Zinni, and took him to the vestibule," Miller recounted. "I said, 'This is the most serious threat since our mission started. The chances of the whole enterprise succeeding are probably nil.'" Zinni agreed. They informed the gathering of what had happened, alerted their drivers, and left for their hotel.

Meanwhile, Israel's top security officials received calls summoning them to a meeting with Chief of Staff Mofaz, the first of what would be a series of meetings that ran until Friday morning. Giora Eiland halted his family's Seder and left his home in Pardesiya, thirty kilometers from Tel Aviv. Ayalon traveled from Hod Hasharon.

In Ramallah, United Nations envoy Terje Roed-Larsen alternated phone calls with Israeli foreign minister Shimon Peres and meetings with Arafat. He tried to impress upon Arafat the enormity of what had occurred.

"What I told Arafat was, 'This is like blowing up a Christmas party on Christmas eve, and you have to understand that this is a total change in the situation [for Israelis]. This is like 9/11. . . . This will make a complete change in their attitude. This has got to come to a stop or else there will be no end to what the Israelis [will do]," he recounted in a 2005 interview.

Danny Ayalon recalled a meeting in the aftermath of the bombing: "I remember Shimon Peres was there and he was trying to talk to Terje [Roed-]Larsen. [Roed-]Larsen was with Arafat, trying to promise again, 'Give us time, give us a chance,' but there was no way."

For Israel, the die was already cast. Aaron Miller's assessment was right. "The event was beyond our capability to tolerate. It was the climax of a terrible month—there were 135 killed, hundreds injured. People were afraid to go out. It was clear we had to take much [stronger action]," Giora Eiland recounted later. That evening, he said later, he got Zinni on the phone. "I said, 'As far as our relationship with Yasser Arafat, we crossed the point of no return.'"

President Bush learned of the bombing while flying on Air Force One from South Carolina to Georgia. Aides grafted a statement into a prepared speech that put the burden on Arafat. It suggested that the United States and Israel were engaged in the same war, and that winning it would promote peace. This time, there was no mention of Zinni or a cease-fire. The bombing had overtaken and frustrated a two-week effort by two dedicated and skillful envoys, who appeared to have won a large measure of trust on both sides of the conflict.

"For those innocent lives that are lost on a daily basis, and today there was another suicide bomber who murdered innocent Israelis. This callous, this cold-blooded killing, it must stop. I condemn it in the most strongest of terms. I call upon Mr. Arafat and the Palestinian Authority to do everything in their power to stop the terrorist killing, because there are people in the Middle East who would rather kill than have peace.

"If the United States is firm and strong in routing out terror, if the United States stays steady in our quest for peace, I believe we can achieve peace in places where people think we'll never have peace.

"The road is going to be hard, there's no question about it. It'll test our will; it'll test our determination. But the enemy that struck us is going to find out what we're made out of. They've already found out a small taste about what we're made out of. You know, when they hit us they must have thought we were so self-absorbed and so materialistic that we would sue them."

Once again, the United States would stand back and let Sharon wield a blunt instrument. This time it meant, not only reinvading most of the major Palestinian cities, something the White House was prepared to accept, but occupying them for a period of up to eight weeks to gain intelligence on Palestinian militant groups. The United States opposed such a long occupation, but intervened too late to stop it and ended up looking weak and uncertain.

For Israel, the results of what would be its lengthiest and bloodiest military operation since its 1982 invasion of Lebanon were mixed. Giora Eiland, a principal architect of what was dubbed Operation Defensive Shield, would later argue that it brought an overall diminution of terrorism against Israelis:

"In both military and political dimensions, the results have been very significant. Since March 2002, there has been a steady decline in terrorism, both as a result of the fence and Israeli presence in Palestinian cities.

"If you decide to occupy a hostile city, with refugee camps, it could be to your advantage or it could be a huge disadvantage. The one

variable is the value of intelligence you gather. If you know how to operate and take advantage of the situation to improve intelligence, you can
control the city. If you fail. . . . We knew how to take advantage."

From a political standpoint, the Passover bombing marked a turning
point for Sharon, for Arafat, and for the United States' whole approach
to the Israeli-Palestinian conflict. For Sharon, it changed the way he
waged his military campaign. Even President Bush couldn't force him
to interrupt Operation Defensive Shield until he was ready. And the
bombing represented the beginning of the end of Yasser Arafat. By the
following June, the United States would cut off all contact with him,
drawing little protest from Europe or other Arab leaders. Bush would
demand that the Palestinians choose new leadership. But Israel's storm-
ing of Arafat's headquarters, reducing much of it to rubble, would
once again elevate Arafat to hero status among his own people and in
much of the region, giving him the political strength the following year
to undercut a new leader acceptable to Bush, Mahmoud Abbas.

Over the next few months, Bush's policy toward the conflict would
move ever closer to Israel, his Middle East ally and client, all but burying the Saudi-inspired Arab peace initiative and pushing a negotiated
peace even further into the future. Bush would fend off European,
Arab, UN, and even some of his own advisors' demands for a more
active American mediation role in the conflict until after the U.S. invasion of Iraq set the region on what Bush hoped would be the path of
democratic reform.

In Tulkarem on the night of March 27, Abdel Basset Odeh's father
heard news of the bombing on television and waited anxiously, as he had
after every announcement of a Palestinian attack on Israelis since his son
had disappeared eight months before. Mohammed Qassim Saed Odeh
hadn't at first believed the officer who said the young man was planning
a major bombing but had changed his mind after his son's disappearance.

"We had the feeling any time there was any operation," that his son
might be involved, the father said in a 2005 interview, speaking through
a translator. Usually, news of an attack would make the family happy
that Palestinians had exacted revenge for Israeli actions, but "even if we
were happy, we were worried. In every bombing during his eight-month

disappearance we were worried. This time we were more worried." After Hamas took responsibility for the Park Hotel attack and claimed Abdel Basset as one of their own, Mohammed's wife "fell down on the ground and lost consciousness," he said. Before Israeli forces demolished his house, the family drew comfort from a stream of visitors from Tulkarem and beyond, offering support and, in some cases, congratulations. "People were most happy for this bombing because it came after the killing of sixteen people at Tulkarem refugee camp," he said.

A young Palestinian professional in Tulkarem confirmed that this reaction was not limited to supporters of Islamic militant groups. Majdi Jayusi twenty-eight, chairman of the technology education department at Khedourie Technical College, said he and others he knew greeted news of the bombing with happiness, recalling the number of young people in their teens and twenties who had been killed by Israeli forces. "Because of what happened after the killing of Palestinians, Palestinians who had lost family, everyone was happy. I was happy to have families know someone is avenging their loss," he said.

More than three years after the bombing, children who narrowly escaped death that night continued to suffer in different ways. Teachers told Sigalit Shimla that her son Gavriel mostly seemed sad at school. At art-therapy classes, his drawings and stories told of death and destruction. He drew one picture of an exploding birthday cake. Eitan Frankfurter reported that his children were having problems concentrating in school. "All the children have problems," he said. One forgot how to read. Frankfurter's oldest son, formerly a quiet boy, developed such a quick temper that teachers routinely complained about his outbursts of shouting. "If someone hits one of his brothers, he can kill him," Frankfurter said.

Perhaps the final word on the Park Hotel attack came from Korin Ben-Aroya, whose simple eloquence managed to conquer her difficulty with English. "We lost our freedom. One terrorist came and bombed himself in a place full of people who are trying to celebrate their freedom. He took it away from all the people."

Sitting in her spare, pleasant Netanya apartment on a brilliant summer afternoon, wearing a simple blouse and slacks and a stylishly short haircut, Korin offered one more observation after an hour spent recounting that fateful Passover, the loss of her husband, her eldest daughter's difficult and slow recuperation, and her own struggle to be caregiver, father, mother, and psychiatrist to her three children—all while holding a job as a bookkeeper and rebuilding her own life with new hobbies, including ceramic sculpture, swimming, horseback riding, and theater.

"I think with enough patience, we are going to achieve the peace. It must come. There is no other way. You know, some people ask me, 'Don't you hate the Arabs?' I told them, 'How can I hate them, when the person who saved my life was an Arab doctor.'" She referred to the presiding physician at the trauma unit at Hillel Yaffe Medical Center in Hadera on the evening of Passover 2002, who performed emergency surgery to drain her collapsed lung of fluid. Then, speaking of Abdel Basset Odeh, she went on, "I can't hate someone that I don't know. I know it's wrong what he did, but I don't know him. I can't hate him. And it's not going to bring me back my life before. I can't spend all my life for revenge and hating."

10

TIME OF TESTING

■ APRIL 2002 ■

"**THIS ISN'T SUICIDE.** But you're going to lose some butt over this one," President Bush told his secretary of state in the spring of 2002. "But you've got to do it for me. And you've got enough butt to cover whatever you lose."

By "butt," Bush meant Powell's lofty standing with the American people and still-lustrous worldwide reputation. As much as Bush's popularity soared after the terror attacks of September 11 and the successful U.S.-led invasion of Afghanistan, Powell's approval ratings stood consistently higher. Among senior European diplomats and U.S. allies in the Arab world, he was widely viewed as the only top official in the Bush administration willing to cooperate with them.

Now Bush was sending Powell on a mission to help salvage the United States' sinking reputation in the Arab world. Before the trip was over, it would expose the limits of the soldier-statesman's influence over his president and over American policy in the Middle East. Powell's goals would be stymied by Israeli prime minister Ariel Sharon and Palestinian leader Yasser Arafat. Sharon would later salvage and even enhance his relationship with the president; Arafat would be punished and forever shunned. Although Powell later claimed the mission didn't cause him serious damage, the weight of the evidence shows that Powell emerged with his stature diminished. Powell would indeed "lose some butt," and so would the United States.

Powell's commitment to achieving any success in the Middle East was a question mark throughout his tenure. His chief of staff, retired Colonel Lawrence Wilkerson, recalled later, "We had had a number of conversations, starting when he was chairman [of the Joint Chiefs of Staff] when I first joined him in 1989. . . . He had said, over and over again, 'It's not going to work.' These people are intractable. They're recalcitrant. They're intransigent. You pick your adjective. They're hardheaded, they're stubborn, and any time you make any progress, the terrorists are going to strike and derail your progress. Because the terrorists are a third rail. They're not on anybody's side."

After the twenty-five-year-old Palestinian suicide bomber Abdel Basset Odeh killed himself and twenty-eight Passover celebrants at the Park Hotel in the Israeli coastal city of Netanya on March 27, Israel launched its biggest military offensive against the Palestinian territories in decades, throwing the region into turmoil and seriously straining the Jewish state's peaceful relationships with Jordan and Egypt.

Dubbed Operation Defensive Shield, the assault didn't take long to begin in the hours after Israelis saw their joyous holiday brutally desecrated. A national consensus emerged with lightning speed: "the Passover massacre," as it was widely called within hours, was the last straw for an Israeli population that had just been through its bloodiest month since the intifada began.

Convening what turned out to be an all-night cabinet session on March 28, Prime Minister Ariel Sharon at first proposed capturing Yasser Arafat and sending him into exile, a step that threatened to violate his early pledge to President Bush not to harm the Palestinian leader. Chief of Staff Shaul Mofaz had previously advocated such a step after Israelis discovered a boatload of weapons from Iran destined for the Palestinian territories. This time, Sharon was dissuaded by intelligence and security chiefs, according to Michael Herzog, a brigadier general who was a top adviser to the defense minister. Giora Eiland, then planning chief of the IDF, believed that it would be impossible to force Arafat into exile, and that the only choices were either to ignore him or "begin the operation with a one-ton bomb on the Muqata," Arafat's Ramallah headquarters.

There was another objection against trying to expel the Palestinian leader. "Arafat would be directing all this from the outside and also score all kinds of diplomatic points by traveling the world over," said Danny Ayalon, then Sharon's national security adviser. "Secondly, of course, even more important, the prime minister promised the president not to expel Arafat. It was very important for him to keep his word." Instead, Sharon and his cabinet settled on a compromise of isolating Arafat at his Ramallah headquarters while rooting out sources of terror in Palestinian militant groups and within security services employed by the Palestinian Authority.

In anonymous press briefings during the violent weeks before the Passover bombing in Netanya, Israeli officials had threatened to reoccupy the West Bank and finally demolish one of the last remaining structures of the Oslo peace accords—Palestinian autonomy in the main population centers.

Planning for such a major operation had actually begun five and a half years earlier, in late 1996, during a particularly fragile period for the Israeli-Palestinian peace process begun in Oslo in the early 1990s. When riots erupted in September 1996 following the decision by then Prime Minister Benjamin Netanyahu to open a tunnel entrance near to the Temple Mount/Haram al-Sharif in Jerusalem, gun battles broke out between the Israeli Army and Palestinian security forces, raising fears in Israel's military establishment that the Palestinian domestic police forces were in fact becoming a hostile national army. Preparing for the possible collapse of the entire Oslo process and a renewal of large-scale violence, the IDF began developing what Eiland called the "generic capabilities"—training, weapons, equipment, and intelligence— needed to "reconquer the Palestinian state."

In Sharon's first year as prime minister, and particularly after 9/11, Americans had come to tolerate Israel's repeated brief incursions into territory supposedly under Palestinian control, the so-called Area A. But Operation Defensive Shield was no mere incursion. It called for occupying Palestinian population centers, including cities and refugee camps, for up to eight weeks, using the time to bolster Israel's intelligence capabilities. "The goal was to regain control of the area so that Palestinian activities against us would be unable to reemerge. If you don't control the city in an effective way, you won't have intelligence and there is very little you can do to use it," Eiland explained in a 2005 interview.

Operation Defensive Shield put the plan into operation. For Shin Bet, the domestic security service, the invasion was a boon, according to its then director, Avi Dichter. First, it forced the terrorists to concentrate on their own survival, giving them less time to plan new attacks. Second, the reoccupation provided a vantage point for the arrest and interrogation of terror suspects. Without the presence of large numbers of troops in the territories, arrests required special operations that were at times too risky. In his view, an arrest, and the opportunity to obtain information from a suspect, were far preferable to targeted killings. "Whenever it's possible to arrest people, it has a huge advantage compared to other things." Among those arrested during Defensive Shield was the Hamas member who planned the Park Hotel bombing, Abbas al-Sayyid. While it occupied West Bank cities, Israel was able to halt targeted killings of terror suspects and arrest them instead, according to Dichter. "Whenever you are determined to stop someone from continuing to carry out terror attacks, and the only way to stop him is by targeted killing, you use this system of targeted killing. . . . If there was a possibility to arrest all the arch-terrorists . . . and not to target them down, that would be excellent, from my point of view," Dichter told me. "We know how to question with live people; we don't know how to do it with dead people."

Despite Sharon's pledge to Bush not to harm Arafat, top U.S. officials were nervous as the IDF stormed the Muqata with tanks and bulldozers, reducing part of it to rubble and setting up sandbag positions and wire fences. Israeli tanks and troops ringed the compound in proximity to Palestinian gunmen holed up with Arafat's presidential guard. But the Americans' more immediate concern was the boiling outrage throughout the Arab world over what was widely seen as an Israeli campaign to destroy the institutions of the Palestinian Authority. Such a threat was taken seriously at the United Nations, where Secretary General Kofi Annan warned in a statement March 29, "[D]estroying the Palestinian Authority will not bring peace; it will bring the region even closer to war."

Washington's initial reaction to Israel's new invasion was disjointed, revealing anew the Bush administration's internal divisions over the Middle East, uncertainty about Sharon's intentions, and a reluctance either to endorse Israeli actions or impede them. In his initial response to the Passover bombing—during a press stakeout at the State Department and an interview on National Public Radio—Powell gave no sign that he expected a major Israeli retaliation or that the bombing had doomed the effort by his envoy, Anthony Zinni, to broker a cease-fire. He stressed that Zinni would stay and keep working, although Zinni and his partner, Aaron Miller, both realized their mission was effectively over. Powell also said he would try to build on Crown Prince Abdullah's peace initiative at the ragged Arab League summit in Beirut, seeming not to realize that violence had overtaken it.

After a conference call with Bush and Rice Thursday evening, Powell spoke by phone with Sharon and extracted a new pledge from him not to harm Arafat. But he gained little insight into the magnitude of what Sharon planned to do or the problems it would pose for the United States. The next morning, Good Friday, after Israeli tanks rolled toward Arafat's compound on the outskirts of Ramallah through heavy rain and fog, Powell joined Cheney, Defense Secretary Donald Rumsfeld, White House Chief of Staff Andrew Card, and National Security Adviser Condoleezza Rice in a national security meeting via video hookup with Bush, who was in Texas for the Easter weekend. By that afternoon, amid reports of civilian casualties in Ramallah and Israel's call-up of twenty thousand reservists, Powell spoke for Bush in delivering the administration's standard words of caution to Israelis:

"The president and I are gravely concerned at the situation today in Ramallah. We deplore the killing and wounding of innocent Palestinians there. While we understand the Israeli government need to respond to these acts of terror and the right of the Israeli government to decide what actions best serve the interests of the Israeli people, we call on Prime Minister Sharon and his government to carefully consider the consequences of those actions."

But Powell, responding to reporters' questions, suggested that Israel's military actions would be limited. "The Israelis have said to me that it is not their intention to occupy any of these areas—and the only one that they are in at the moment is Ramallah—for some extended period. They are going in to find terrorists, to pick up weapons, and it is not their intention to occupy these places on any long-term basis. We ask the Israelis to show the necessary restraint with respect to that activity, so that they do not put Chairman Arafat's life in danger, and they minimize loss of life with respect to civilians."

Arafat's failure either to speak out forcefully against terrorism or to direct what remained of his security agencies to crack down on Hamas, Islamic Jihad, and militants in his own Fatah Party had by then soured much of the international community toward him—not just Israel and the United States. Secretary General Kofi Annan later wrote in a report to the UN General Assembly: "[T]he Palestinian Authority seemed to believe that failing to act against terrorism, and inducing turmoil, chaos, and instability, would cause the government and people of Israel to buckle—which I believed they would not."

But the siege of Arafat's headquarters turned the diplomatic tables on Israel and, as senior officials came to recognize, became a major public relations fiasco for the Sharon government, reinforcing the prime minister's bulldozer image. "It was not a very smart decision. From the very beginning, it was clear to us that it couldn't bring results," Eiland acknowledged in 2005.

Surrounded by tanks, with much of his compound destroyed, the Palestinian leader still had a phone and used it deftly. He spoke to world leaders, including Powell, Egyptian president Hosni Mubarak, and Spanish prime minister José Maria Aznar, a key Bush ally whose country held the European Union presidency. And he gave electrifying interviews and running commentary to Arab media. Indeed, the "old man" sounded almost intoxicated by the chance to revive his mythical stature among the masses.

"Thus far, I have seven martyrs and over forty wounded persons. However, morale is high because we are all potential martyrs. To Jerusalem we are marching, martyrs in the millions," he told Abu Dhabi

TV. To a sympathetic Lebanese interviewer, he said, "[W]e are like a mountain that cannot be moved by the wind."

In New York, Jordan and Qatar, both valued U.S. allies, called for an urgent Security Council meeting. It convened late Friday night, with the nimble Palestinian representative, Nasser al-Qidwa, speaking immediately after an opening statement by Secretary General Annan. With a blistering attack on Israel's "insane" military move, al-Qidwa declared, "Mr. Sharon wants to return to the pre-Oslo status and to attempt to create isolated Palestinian entities under local proxy leaders. . . ."

For the United States, the crisis risked alienating not only moderate Arab governments but also Europeans whose acquiescence the Bush administration hoped to gain for a confrontation with Iraq. Faced with diplomatic isolation, U.S. officials opted to water down what would otherwise be a harsh resolution condemning Israel and joined thirteen other council members in calling "for the withdrawal of Israeli troops from Palestinian cities, including Ramallah." Israeli envoy Yehuda Lancry complained bitterly that the council was "rewarding the Palestinian terrorists." In an example of how so many Israelis had been or would be touched by terrorism during this period, Lancry's eighteen-year-old niece, Noa Shlomo, would be among eight passengers killed two weeks later by a Palestinian suicide bomber on a bus near Haifa.

If the American "yes" vote demanding withdrawal seemed like a rare betrayal of Israel by its closest friend, Sharon could interpret it as little more than background noise. So far, he had heard nothing from Bush himself. This made a big difference. Sharon and his aides viewed the White House as more sympathetic to Israel than the State Department, where the need to maintain relationships with the Arab world historically tended to color attitudes toward the Jewish state. In delivering messages to Sharon, U.S. ambassador Daniel Kurtzer routinely made a point of stating which of his "instructions" came from the president, because he knew the Israelis would check. When neither Bush nor Rice would mention certain policies Powell was promoting, they would lose importance.

Equally important, the resolution didn't call for an "immediate withdrawal," giving Israel at least a brief grace period. Interviewed by

Israel's Army Radio, Lancry said, "The Americans explained to us in corridor discussions during those very tense moments before the vote that although Israel is being urged to withdraw its forces, the date for this has not yet been determined and we still have a blinking yellow light, which we have to observe carefully before it switches to red."

When the president appeared before the cameras on Saturday, he noticeably failed even to mention the Security Council's demand for an Israeli withdrawal. Instead, Bush told reporters, "Last night the administration supported a UN Security Council resolution that urges there to be a cease-fire, start a process that will end this cycle of violence." Most of the president's emphasis was on fighting terror. "[W]e're in constant touch with these governments and the next step is to continue our call and our efforts and our push to fight off terror.

"It appears to me these aren't just isolated incidents. I mean, there's a pattern, a routine, and a constancy. And so we will continue to lead, to talk and urge world leaders, particularly those in the region, to do everything they can to shut off the capacity of people to come and bomb."

"The feeling we got was, 'The U.S. really understands this,'" Brigadier General Michael Herzog recalled in 2005.

Earlier that week, the Arab League, meeting in Beirut, had offered "normal relations" with Israel in exchange for its withdrawal from the occupied territories. Unlike Sharon's government, which viewed the offer as a new form of pressure to give up the West Bank and East Jerusalem, officials in Washington praised it. At the same time, they were annoyed that none of the Arab leaders gathered in Beirut condemned the Passover bombing. Secretary of State Powell underscored this in a telephone conversation with Egyptian foreign minister Ahmed Maher, saying the Passover attack was "fundamental." Bush, who spent part of that Saturday before Easter on the phone with the leaders of Egypt and Jordan, Kofi Annan, Prime Minister José Maria Aznar of Spain, and Saudi Crown Prince Abdullah, said, "And every phone call I make, I remind people that if you're interested in peace—and the leaders I've talked to are interested in peace—we have all got to come together to stop terror. Our role is very visible and our role is very active. And I firmly believe that we can achieve a peace in the region, but not until—not until—there is a concerted, united effort to rout terror out."

"Israel is a democratically elected government, and the government is responding to the will of the people for there to be more security. And Israel will make the decisions necessary to defend herself. My point to the Israeli government is, as you do so, keep in mind there must be an avenue toward a peaceful settlement. As you defend yourself—and you have the right to do so—please keep in mind and work with the region to develop a strategy that will end up with a peaceful settlement."

The Israeli operation moved forward, with Sharon telling his countrymen March 31 of a "wide-scale operation" that would deal "a thorough blow" to terrorist organizations. From his standpoint, the only avenue to peace was victory: "The situation is not easy, but we have experienced tougher situations, and we have always prevailed. As always before, we will again prevail this time. We will again triumph, and when it happens, we will be able to live here together in peace."

It wasn't until the following Thursday—nearly a full week after Israel's decision to invade the territories—that Bush called on Sharon publicly to begin withdrawing. By then, Israel had laid siege to the Church of the Nativity in Bethlehem, where Palestinian gunmen had barricaded themselves inside along with priests, monks, nuns, and Italian journalists, and sent scores of tanks into Nablus, the largest city in the West Bank.

There was more to come. In the early hours of April 3, Israeli forces entered the city of Jenin and the refugee camp adjacent to it, declared them a closed military area, preventing all access, and imposed a round-the-clock curfew. By the time of the IDF withdrawal from Jenin and the lifting of the curfew on April 18, at least fifty-two Palestinians, of whom up to half may have been civilians, and twenty-three Israeli soldiers were dead. Many more were injured; approximately 150 buildings had been destroyed and 450 families were homeless.

Despite Sharon's earlier pledge not to harm Arafat, a microphone for Israeli television picked up a brief private conversation between Sharon and Mofaz in which both appeared to agree on the necessity of exiling the Palestinian leader, according to the *Baltimore Sun*'s Peter Hermann.

A UN agency, the Relief Works Administration, reported April 2 that thousands of refugees throughout the area of operations remained trapped with dwindling supplies of water, food, and medicine. "There are reports that twenty-five thousand people in the Ramallah area are without water. Bodies are piling up in hospitals, and medicines are in short supply," agency director Peter Hansen said in a press release.

By then, the Israeli invasion "had become a major problem for the president, whether we liked it or not," Powell recalled in 2005. "And the whole Arab world and the Palestinian world and the European, Arafat-loving world [said], 'What are you going to do? This old man's trapped in this building, no heat, no light, sitting by candlelight, leaning on his AK-47, and something's got to be done.' And the president came under enormous pressure to show some action."

U.S. officials feared that the war could spill over the borders of Israel and the territories, inviting greater involvement by Iran and Syria. Already, Iran-backed Hezbollah militants in southern Lebanon had fired missiles across the so-called Blue Line separating Israel and Lebanon for five days running. Angry mobs were pouring into the streets of Arab cities, demanding that governments in the region take tougher action against Israel. Egypt, the first Arab nation to make peace with Israel, responded by sharply reducing diplomatic contact with the Jewish state, and Jordan threatened similar action. European leaders and members of Congress stepped up demands that Bush assume a stronger role.

Both Powell and the president by then saw the Israeli invasion as counterproductive, a senior administration official said. The siege of Arafat's Muqata, they felt, served only to rehabilitate Arafat by making him a martyr at a time when his standing among Palestinians was sinking because the population was fed up with violence and corruption. Powell feared that Israeli military actions would generate new anger that could produce more suicide bombers.

Bush could no longer avoid making a clear demand that Israel cut short its military operation, and he did so in a statement delivered in the White House Rose Garden April 4. But the statement attempted to do more: Bush strived to deliver a harsh warning to Arafat; convey a deep understanding for Israel's predicament; spell out the responsibilities of all parties in the region; and sketch out a path toward renewed peace negotiations.

"At Oslo and elsewhere, Chairman Arafat renounced terror as an instrument of his cause, and he agreed to control it. He's not done so. The situation in which he finds himself today is largely of his own making. He's missed his opportunities, and thereby betrayed the hopes of the people he's supposed to lead. Given his failure, the Israeli government feels it must strike at terrorist networks that are killing its citizens."

Bush spelled out a series of obligations that would have to be met by Israel, the Palestinians, and the Arab world. With Powell at his side, Bush announced that Powell would go to the Middle East to broker a cease-fire and try to move both sides into peace negotiations.

After Bush spoke, the Security Council, with American assent, sought to increase pressure on Israel by unanimously demanding withdrawal from Palestinian cities "without delay." But again the Israelis got a mixed message. In his statement, Bush had asked Sharon to begin withdrawing. It wasn't until the next day, meeting reporters in Crawford with visiting British prime minister Tony Blair at his side, that Bush adopted the stronger UN language. In response to a reporter's question, he called on Israel to "withdraw without delay" and said, "I think they will heed the call." He also telephoned Sharon to reinforce the message but refrained from demanding a complete pullout by any specific date.

Sharon argued that he needed more time. "We tried to convince him that, you know, now we are in the middle, it would be counterproductive, but now we are winding out. And we kept going like twenty-four, forty-eight hours after this demand," Danny Ayalon said in 2005.

"It was very difficult," Ayalon recalled. Sharon tried to persuade Bush that "this is a matter of life and death. If it was stopped ahead of time, then all of the achievements will just be null and void. And I talked to Condoleezza and explained to her, 'We need a few more hours and in any case we are going to leave very soon.'" He recalled her reply: "Well, the sooner the better. The sooner the better."

The episode recalled an earlier crisis between an American president and an Israeli prime minister, one that would still be vivid in the memories of Sharon and Powell, though not of Bush. On August 12, 1982, the United States communicated President Ronald Reagan's outrage at a fierce Israeli bombardment of Beirut just as an American envoy was nailing down terms of the evacuation of thousands of Palestinian guerrilla fighters. Reagan followed the message with a blunt phone call to then Prime Minister Menachem Begin, details of which were quickly made public by the White House. The bombing stopped, and Sharon, who had ordered the attack as Israel's defense minister at the time, saw his freedom of action circumscribed by the cabinet.

Two and a half decades later, another test of wills took hold between the U.S. and Israeli governments. After Bush spoke, two days passed without signs of an Israeli pullback. On Monday, Bush adopted a tougher stand. Turning to the cameras during a visit to Knoxville, Tennessee, he said in a stern voice, "I meant what I said to the prime minister of Israel. I expect there to be a withdrawal without delay."

This time, the message got through. By the next morning, Israeli forces had begun to withdraw from the West Bank towns of Tulkarem and Qalqilya. But Sharon in fact was continuing to defy Bush's stated demand. Both towns were close to the Green Line, meaning they could quickly be reoccupied if the need arose. Otherwise, Operation Defensive Shield continued, without any further warning or public pressure from Bush.

In hindsight, it seems clear that in a standoff with the determined Israeli leader, Bush blinked. If this was "very difficult" for Sharon, as Ayalon said, it was a burden he was ready and able to assume.

This difficult and embarrassing moment passed, but the episode hovered like a cloud over Powell's mission. In public, the secretary projected optimism and determination. A senior State Department official billed the trip as "a defining moment" for Powell. It would be his most prolonged and intense involvement with the Israeli-Palestinian conflict.

Based on Bush's statement in the Rose Garden, Powell's marching orders appeared to be clear: nail down a cease-fire and then quickly build on that to set the stage for negotiations between Israelis and Palestinians that would ultimately lead to the creation of a Palestinian state.

In television interviews, Powell cast his mandate in expansive terms. "I would be absolutely delighted and very pleased if we were able to get a cease-fire in place in the not-too-distant future," he told Fox News's Tony Snow the morning before his departure. He went on to describe what would come next. "So once we get that cease-fire, it is important that the political process be moved up. We have to quickly get to negotiations because the Palestinian people are looking to those negotiations for the creation of a state. And we have to look for a way to get that state created as quickly as possible so both sides then have a vested interest in negotiating the permanent boundaries of the state, deciding how the two sides will live in peace with each other, restoring their economies."

Raising such expectations proved to be a mistake, and not only because they put Powell's credibility on the line with Palestinians and Arab leaders. They also added another incentive for Sharon not to cooperate with him. Since taking office, Sharon had resisted all efforts to pull him into peace talks so as not to appear to be making concessions under fire. Cutting short Operation Defensive Shield and then moving quickly to peace talks meant capitulation.

Worse for Powell, staking out an ambitious agenda carried the implication that the administration at that point was serious in seeking an end to the conflict, and he had reason to know that wasn't true. As he acknowledged in an interview three years later, "I was over there to relieve Arab pressure." Bush, as he said, needed to "show some action."

Indeed, "relieving Arab pressure" is an apt description of Powell's whole involvement in the Middle East conflict. In several interviews, senior officials stressed the need for the United States to be "seen" to be actively engaged in trying to end it. The motivation had much to do with improving the United States' image in the Arab world, in preparation for military action against Iraq, and shoring up longtime allies—and little to do with trying to restart a peace process that would lead to an Israeli-Palestinian agreement.

One reason was Bush. "My general impression, and I would never put my name to this, my general impression was that he was very reluctant to criticize or be critical of Sharon, even privately," a former senior official said. On the overall conflict, this official said of the president, "He didn't care. . . I don't think he cared that much . . . I think that he wasn't engaged in this process fully. He was episodically engaged in it.

. . . I don't think Mr. Clinton got it quite right when he locked himself up for two whole weeks with these characters, because there's other wheels of government that need to be greased, but the president would be in and then out, and in and out, and wasn't fully—wasn't always saying, 'Where are we on the peace process, what's happening?' " As a result, the official said, Powell was "always pushing a big rock up a big hill."

Another reason was distrust of Arafat and a growing conviction among a range of administration officials—not just pro-Israel hard-liners—that he was unable or unwilling to carry out commitments. Powell came to share this view, although he never developed the animosity toward the Palestinian leader felt by many in the administration and Congress.

"I had no illusions about Arafat. He lived in his own little world. He used facts as he saw fit. He was not known as somebody who would nec-essarily be beholden to the truth," Powell said. "[A]nd I don't use the word *liar*. He lived in his own little world where things that we would call falsehoods, to him were not. Things he would say which were blatantly false, to him they were not false. So when I say to him, 'You've got to get control of this terrorism—you've got to do something, we can't keep this up, and I must have days of quiet where it looks like you're speaking out and taking action against terrorism. Maybe you can't stop it all. But you've got to give us something to work with.' He leaps up: 'You are a general and I am a general and I obey you!' And well, you know, he meant it. But he didn't mean it. And even if he meant it he didn't intend to act on it, or he didn't know how to act on it. So with him you never knew what you were dealing with."

Early in the administration, Powell assumed the burden of the Middle East knowing that the White House had little interest in it. But the White House attitude circumscribed his freedom of action, since none of Bush's other key advisers wanted the president to spend pre-cious political capital on resolving a conflict when chances of success were slim.

"The White House did, politically and diplomatically, do everything they could to support Israel and support Sharon. And . . . politically and diplomatically they are not going to expend any capital pushing Sharon if, first and foremost, violence and, especially after September 11, terrorism was not stopped. So they did give Sharon a lot of slack in areas that we could have cared about, but there wasn't anything to be gained by it," a senior State Department official said.

Highly respected in Israel—by Sharon, among others—because of his military leadership in the first Gulf War, Powell also took pride in a connection to the Jewish people from his childhood growing up in a mixed Bronx neighborhood that included Yiddish-speaking Jews. From the early days of the Bush administration, an aide said, Powell maintained a discreet private "back channel" of communication with Sharon. Arye Genger, a wealthy American Israeli businessman who was a close friend of Sharon, was one of the first to act as the channel; later, Dov Weisglass and Sharon's son Omri were used.

"Powell was, frankly, the only one who would tell Sharon the truth," said the aide. "The basic message was, 'Don't cross the president on this. Don't do anything that puts the president out on a limb and then cuts him off.' "

But Powell's advantages proved to be inadequate to the challenge.

Israel's invasion of the West Bank had lasted nine days by the time Powell left the United States. The secretary's meandering itinerary gave Sharon plenty of time to wind it down before Powell got to Jerusalem—if he wanted to. Powell hoped to gain support from Arab and other leaders for heavy pressure on Arafat to denounce terrorism and maintain a cease-fire, while reassuring them of the U.S. commitment. He went first to Morocco to meet with Saudi Crown Prince Abdullah, who was vacationing there, and Morocco's young king, Mohammed VI. He quickly learned that Arab leaders were impatient to see pressure brought to bear on Sharon to carry out Bush's demand. Mohammed breached diplomatic etiquette by asking Powell in public, "Don't you think it would be more important to go to Jerusalem first?" Powell then went to Cairo and on to Madrid, for a meeting of the Quartet, the body he had helped create to encourage a renewed Middle East peace process. It included the United States, the European Union, Russia, and the United Nations. From Madrid he traveled to Jordan.

Meanwhile, the human toll from the invasion—and from a rash of new Palestinian attacks—continued to mount. According to the United

Nations, much of the fighting occurred in heavily populated areas, "in large part because the armed Palestinian groups sought by IDF placed their combatants and installations among civilians." Figures compiled by the UN showed that, all told, 497 Palestinians were killed and 1,447 were wounded from March 1 to May 7, a period that included Operation Defensive Shield, and Israeli forces arrested more than 6,000 Palestinians. Cities, villages, and refugee camps became closed military zones subject to round-the-clock curfews with periodic interruptions. Movement of international personnel, including medical workers, was restricted, and the incursions brought substantial destruction, including of buildings used by Palestinian security services.

Human Rights Watch reported: "During the operation, Israeli soldiers repeatedly used indiscriminate and excessive force, killed civilians willfully and unlawfully, and used Palestinian civilians as human shields. IDF troops also inflicted damage to homes, businesses, and government offices; looted and stole in the course of searches; coerced civilians to assist military operations; and detained at least 4,500 Palestinian men and boys, many of whom reported ill treatment during arrest and interrogation. From March 29 to April 19, the Israeli authorities impeded the entrance of outside observers, including journalists, human rights activists, United Nations representatives, and the International Committee of the Red Cross (ICRC). These violations reflected patterns of abuse that—partly reflecting the effective impunity enjoyed by Israeli soldiers—had progressively worsened since September 2000."

In one of his press releases, UNWRA chief Peter Hansen abandoned diplomatic euphemism in an urgent complaint: "The Israeli Defense Force has made a hellish battleground among the civilians in the Balata [Nablus] and Jenin refugee camps. We are getting reports of pure horror—that helicopters are strafing civilian residential areas; that systematic shelling by tanks has created hundreds of wounded; that bulldozers are razing refugee homes to the ground and that food and medicine will soon run out."

With the destruction and bloodshed came fear, as recounted by Tulkarem dentist Siham Thabet. Her husband, Thabet Thabet, also a dentist, was among the first Fatah leaders killed in one of Israel's targeted assassinations. The killing stunned many in the Israeli peace camp, since Thabet, fifty, had long been considered a strong advocate of coexistence. Israeli intelligence officials, however, described him as an impresario of violence.

Siham Thabet spent much of the period of the invasion in an interior room of her apartment with her teenage son to avoid being hit by a bullet flying through the window. At one point, an Israeli tank was parked menacingly close to their home. They lived on stores of rice, bread, lentils, cheese, and olives and kept the apartment dark at night to avoid being seen, moving about with a flashlight beamed at the floor.

The invasion of Jenin's refugee camp drew Israel deep into a guerrilla war, with house-to-house battles, a flight of residents, booby-trapped buildings, and a world waiting in suspense for an accurate casualty count. With a bravado that would damage their credibility, Palestinian officials claimed, without evidence, that a "massacre" was occurring, with five hundred dead. Israel rejected the claim but kept humanitarian workers and journalists from getting a more accurate assessment. Subsequently, Israel at first welcomed an international probe sponsored by the United Nations, then withdrew cooperation, claiming the investigation was biased.

Two days before Powell arrived in Jerusalem, Sharon declared that it would be a "tragic mistake" for the secretary to meet with Arafat, since it would only encourage more terrorism. Powell reacted strongly the next day during a brief press conference in Spain, insisting, "I believe it is important to meet with Chairman Arafat. He is the leader of the Palestinian people and I think the Palestinian people and the Arab leaders with whom I've met over the last several days believe he is the partner that Israel will have to deal with at some point. He and the other leaders of the Palestinian Authority. The reality is that no other Palestinian leader or for that matter, Arab leader, is prepared to engage as a partner until Mr. Arafat has had a chance to express his views to me and to others."

But at the White House, spokesman Ari Fleischer adopted a different tone: "We anticipate that the meeting will take place. Having said that, no one can predict what the results will be. There have been a series of events in the Middle East that depended in good part on Chairman

Arafat, and the results were not favorable. And so the president is look-ing at this as a chance to see what Yasser Arafat can or cannot do."

This would be one of a series of statements in which Fleischer's mes-sage veered from Powell's, deepening the impression that the White House was not fully behind Powell's efforts. A senior Powell aide speculated later that Fleischer was inserting his own views, or reflecting the views of White House staffers who may have been out of sync with the president: "We had our doubts sometimes when Ari was pronouncing on the Middle East in the name of the president. Powell sometimes knew that those in fact were not the president's views, and he personally had talked to the president about what he was doing, and the president was supportive."

The disconnect between Powell and the White House was not lost on astute observers of the Middle East, whether pro-Israel or pro-Palestinian.

"I detected that there were various occasions where the State Depart-ment was conducting its own foreign policy, independent of the White House," said Malcolm Hoenlein, executive director of the Conference of Presidents of Major American Jewish Organizations. "In fact, one sen-ior State Department person said to me at a meeting, 'Well, we have our own policy here that differs from people across town.' . . . I said to him, 'Are you saying to me there are two foreign policies?' And he said 'Yes.' . . . The White House knew it also. You would often see that the presi-dent would rectify something that came out of the State Department that was not consistent with positions he'd taken, positions he'd expressed."

POWELL'S FIRST MEETING with Sharon produced an impasse over the U.S. demand for an end to the Israeli operation. Neither man took much trou-ble to hide the disagreement. "Israel is waging a war against the infra-structure of Palestinian terrorism, and Israel hopes to conclude this war very soon," Sharon said at their first joint press conference on April 12. Powell responded: "The prime minister and I had good discussions on the nature of the operations that are under way. He understands President Bush's position. We had a chance to exchange those positions."

"Sharon was single-minded, bloody-minded . . . stubborn—always. So you kind of got used to that," a senior Powell aide said later. But the

obstacles facing Powell only grew. Soon after the meeting, a female suicide bomber blew herself up outside the Mahane Yehuda market in the
center of West Jerusalem, crowded with shoppers—many of them
Sephardic Jews—getting provisions for Sabbath meals. At the time,
Giora Eiland was standing just two hundred meters away. Powell flew
over the scene in a helicopter en route to getting an army briefing on rising tensions along the Lebanon border.

Powell postponed a planned meeting with Arafat the next day to pressure him into condemning the latest bombing. Arafat fulfilled the
requirement with a statement in Arabic that said, "We strongly condemn
the violent operations that target Israeli civilians, especially the recent
operation in Jerusalem." But the statement went on to "strongly condemn the massacres the Israeli occupation forces have been committing
for the past two weeks against the Palestinian civilians and refugees in
the city of Nablus and Jenin camp, against the Church of the Nativity
in Bethlehem and other areas."

In a sign of a balanced U.S. approach, Powell took the occasion of a
meeting with humanitarian workers to issue a warning to the Israeli military: "The United States is deeply concerned about the serious humanitarian situation of the Palestinian people. Israeli forces must exercise the
utmost restraint and discipline, and refrain from the excessive use of
force in the conduct of military operations, in order to ensure that
civilians are protected and to avoid worsening the already grave conditions inside Palestinian areas. We call upon Israel to respect international
humanitarian principles and to allow full and unimpeded access to
humanitarian organizations and services to provide basic humanitarian
services, including evacuation of the wounded and deceased. In this
regard, we are particularly concerned at the humanitarian situation in
Jenin." This was a polite version of a stronger message relayed to
Israelis behind closed doors, according to a senior official who was
with Powell. "What are you buying yourself? You're not solving your
problem. You're just making it worse, creating more terrorists . . . putting yourself in an occupation it's hard to get out of."

On Sunday, Powell set out for his showdown with Arafat at the Palestinian leader's battered compound. Staffers accompanying the secretary

made up a jingle, "Hakuna Muqata," playing on the name of Arafat's headquarters, based on a song from the musical *The Lion King* ("Hakuna Matata! What a wonderful phrase . . . Hakuna Matata! Ain't no passing craze").

The senior Powell aide later set the scene: "We drove to the Muqata and took a right turn at an Israeli tank, went across the burnt-out shells, pulled up into the space in front, including the beautiful press conference center—it was half-destroyed and occupied by the Israelis—went across the walkway to the main building and then there was about a ten-foot space between the Israeli guys with guns and the Palestinian guys with guns that our security—our guys with guns—took us across. I remember that as probably one of the most dangerous moments of my life.

"And then the Palestinian guys with guns took us up a little staircase and then down the hall . . . everybody warned us to go to the bathroom before we went down there because the plumbing was not functioning very well."

Powell proceeded to unload on Arafat: "We're going to help get you out of here, but you've got to do some stuff that shows you're serious, otherwise you're not getting out," the senior aide related. Bush, he told him, cared about the suffering of ordinary Palestinians but was unwilling to spend political capital pressuring Sharon unless Palestinians produced results in halting violence.

Powell recalled, "I'm inside the building in the dark with Arafat and all of his guards. And none of mine. And I made it clear to him. . . . 'You know what? I'm the only guy left who will talk to you. There's no one [else] in my administration. And the reason is, the terror has to stop. I will do everything I can to get you some freedom of movement. But this is not something I can keep doing. I can't keep coming over here and getting you to make promises and getting you to respond, and then nothing happens. So, Mr. Chairman, this may be the last time we see each other. I really wish you all the best, but unless you give me something to work with, I can't do anything for you.' "

A refrain in Powell's message to Palestinians, there and elsewhere, was, "You've got to trap Sharon. You guys stop these groups, do this on violence, and then Sharon has to deliver. We'll make sure."

The proposition never got a chance to be tested—at least not with Arafat. Unlike previous sessions when Arafat would make a show of cooperation and then not act, this time Palestinian officials demanded publicly that Israel withdraw its forces first. They also wanted international peacekeeping forces sent in. This was a nonstarter, as Powell explained to the press; Israel would only accept an American-led monitoring team.

The hurdles confronting Powell accumulated. Besides insisting on Palestinian action against terrorism, Sharon also demanded that the Palestinians turn over five men connected with the assassination of ultranationalist Israeli cabinet minister Rehavam Ze'evi. And the same day that Powell met with Arafat, Israeli forces captured Marwan Barghouti, one of the most popular Fatah leaders in the West Bank and a key figure in the uprising. An Israeli court would later sentence Barghouti to five life terms for the murder of Israelis. More significant, Sharon's national-security cabinet approved a plan for buffer zones, reinforced with fences and electronic surveillance equipment, along the West Bank to prevent Palestinians from entering Israel. This marked an early step in creating the separation barrier that would further inflame much of the world's attitude toward Israel.

That night, while dining at the seafront home of U.S. ambassador Daniel Kurtzer in Herzliya Pituach, outside Tel Aviv, Powell had a long telephone conversation with Bush and Rice.

The White House was showing nervousness. Interviewed on *Meet the Press*, Condoleezza Rice subtly shifted expectations for Powell's trip. "Secretary Powell is in the region to call to account all of the parties that have a role to play here to play a responsible role. And the secretary is— he has a difficult mission, but he has considerable authority and considerable flexibility from the president to do what he needs to do to call the parties to account." She said nothing about a cease-fire or renewed negotiations.

Pointedly, Rice refused to endorse an idea floated by Powell for renewing political talks: an international conference including Israel, the Palestinians, and Arab states. A Powell aide recalled: "The White House was not willing to commit to anything until they checked with Sharon first, basically, and were not willing to put their prestige on the line until they [saw] some chance of success."

Asked about the conference, Rice said, "We don't want to act prematurely here. We'd like to get Secretary Powell back here after his mission is complete. A lot has happened in the last week or so, and we need to assess where we are. But we're looking at a number of ideas that might help move this forward. But any conference, any meeting has to proceed from a set of principles, and the president laid those principles out in a stark reality, saying that peace in the Middle East is not going to come easily. It comes only when parties are willing to take hard steps."

The next day, Powell left subordinates to attempt to mediate renewed security cooperation between Israeli and Palestinian authorities while he traveled to Damascus and Beirut to persuade Syrian president Bashar al-Assad to calm the Israeli-Lebanon border, scene of increasing tension between Israel and Hezbollah. His intervention produced at least a temporary calm, easing fears of a spreading conflict.

While Powell traveled to Damascus, tens of thousands of demonstrators, mobilized by the Conference of Presidents and United Jewish Communities, arrived in Washington by bus, aircraft, train, and car to gather outside the Capitol in a show of support for Sharon's war on terrorism. Sponsors said it was the biggest pro-Israel demonstration ever held in the United States. If the size of the gathering was notable, so was the speed with which it had been assembled and the anger at any sign of sympathy for the Palestinians. While not front-page news in most papers, it was widely reported on television and in newspapers across the country. The trigger was the Passover bombing, which Malcolm Hoenlein, longtime top executive of the Conference of Presidents and one of the Jewish community's most effective players behind the scenes, called a "watershed."

"I would say it was a real turning point. It culminated all the frustration, all of the anger, all of the pain that people have felt—seven hundred, eight hundred , nine hundred people at that point having been killed—and this one-sided slam about whether Israel has the right to build the fence or Israel has the right to take the necessary steps to secure itself."

But an important subtext was anxiety among Israel's supporters that worldwide outrage over Israel's invasion would prompt the United States to put undue pressure on Sharon.

"We decided to do the event in Washington. Literally in less than a week we turned out at least 200,000 people," recounted Hoenlein. "And, by the way, many, many non-Jews. We didn't underwrite the buses for them, we didn't have to do anything. It was just, the word got out, and the response was immediate. People had reached the limit.

"And we did it on a Monday, not on a Sunday, to show that it wasn't just people who were taking a vacation day—it was right before taxes, everything, finals in schools, and the response was so overwhelming. In fact it was the White House that said to me, 'We don't think you're preparing sufficiently for this event.' We were so much involved in trying to do this in five or six days—five, actually. Five working days. It came from one of the security people, because we were trying to work on location and participation. Washington police, FBI started saying to us, we had to change location then because it wasn't big enough. We could not even get all the buses into the city in the end. We could not get a bus from Virginia to Maine that day. People flew from Hawaii, from England, they came from Los Angeles. Kids who left their campus drove for eighteen hours to get there. Hindus. We have a book and you can see the pictures of the blacks who came out, Hispanics who came out, people from every walk of life. And then on the podium was everything that represented America, from the head of the AFL-CIO to members of Congress of every persuasion. We tried to make it as broadly representative as possible; it was not just a Jewish outpouring. Because of that, I think people who had really reached their limits understood that, if you don't stand up against terrorism, terrorists perceive that as weakness and as cowardice."

Among the speakers was the glib and telegenic former prime minister Benjamin Netanyahu, Sharon's rival for support from Israel's right wing, who was visiting Washington. He stressed what the demonstration's organizers hoped would register as its main message.

"Israel and the United States are today fighting the same battle, waging the same war, confronting the same evil," he said. "Like the United States, Israel did not seek this war. It was forced on us by a savage enemy that glorifies in a culture of death, a culture where murderers are called martyrs and suicide is sanctified."

"We will stand with Israel, we will stand for freedom," said House Democratic leader Dick Gephardt of Missouri, speaking before an array of U.S. and Israeli flags on the steps of the Capitol Building. "We can't expect Israel to stand idle while its citizens are being slaughtered," said Senator Harry Reid of Nevada, then the Senate's No. 2 Democrat.

In a tribute to Hoenlein's influence in Washington, the White House opted to send a high-level representative, Deputy Defense Secretary Paul Wolfowitz, an unquestioned supporter of Israel and one of Washington's foremost hawks. By sending him, the White House positioned itself alongside the demonstrators—not as a neutral broker.

"Since September 11, we Americans have one thing more in common with Israelis: on that day, America was attacked by suicide bombers. At that moment, every American understood what it is like to live in Jerusalem or Netanya or Haifa," Wolfowitz said. But Wolfowitz drew boos from many in the crowd when he said, "Israelis are not the only victims of the violence in the Middle East. Innocent Palestinians are suffering and dying in great numbers as well. It is critical that we recognize and acknowledge that fact." According to the *Jerusalem Post*'s Janine Zacharia, "When he started a sentence, 'The people of Israel and Palestine . . .' some in the crowd started screaming 'What Palestine?'"

The Israeli government's official representative at the rally, Natan Sharansky, stopped in to the White House to see Condoleezza Rice. She praised him for spotting something in Bush's April 4 speech that most people had missed: the president had said Palestinians "deserve a government that respects human rights and a government that focuses on their needs—education and health care—rather than feeding their resentments."

The day of the Washington rally, Sharon sat down at his Jerusalem residence with Arye Golan and Yoni Ben-Menahem of Israel Radio. "First of all, I would like to clarify that we are not under any pressure. The United States has problems and I am aware of them. I knew from the outset that I had no intention of remaining there for long. The intention was to do the job and get out. Now, there is no pressure on Israel.

I know that the United States has problems which bother it; however, we carried out our activities and will continue to do so."

Late that afternoon, as the demonstrators were leaving Washington, Bush, who was in Cedar Rapids, Iowa, promoting tax cuts, placed a call to Sharon. According to White House spokesman Ari Fleischer, he "affirmed the importance of the Powell mission" and the secretary's efforts to bring peace to the region and underlined his concern about the standoff at the Church of the Nativity in Bethlehem.

But what the White House chose to highlight from the call was Sharon's response: "The prime minister confirmed to the president that Israel will withdraw from Jenin and Nablus within a week—Jenin will be sooner. The president expressed his belief that this will increase prospects to bring peace to the region."

Asked if this wasn't still far short of what Bush had demanded of Sharon, Fleischer called it a "positive development" and suggested Israel was carrying out the president's wishes.

"This is a region where each party is waiting for the other to go first. And the president believes what's important is for each party to say to themselves, what do they need to do to bring peace to the region. And if each party focuses on what they need to do, it'll make it easier for peace to be brought to the region. Israel has taken this action today."

Exactly two weeks after insisting that Sharon "withdraw without delay," Bush was accepting a promise of a partial pullout that would leave Arafat trapped in the Muqata and Israeli troops occupying Ramallah and remaining on the outskirts of other major towns. Bush also accepted that the standoff at the Church of the Nativity would have to be resolved before Israeli troops withdrew from Bethlehem.

Within a few hours of Fleischer's briefing, Israel Radio reported several new military operations in and around Nablus and Ramallah, and Israeli troops moved back into Tulkarem. The next day, Sharon told an interviewer that withdrawal would "be done gradually, in accordance with the rate at which we achieve our missions." Palestinians, for their part, failed to make any new commitments to a cease-fire or to act against terrorism until Israel withdrew. If a cease-fire were possible, it would not happen quickly. Even the special U.S. envoy, Anthony Zinni, was leaving to attend his daughter's wedding.

Powell was not prepared to stay for open-ended mediation. Neither did the White House want him to stay. Fleischer, speaking to reporters on Tuesday, April 16, again rolled back what Powell was supposed to accomplish. "The whole purpose of his trip was to try to bring about a diminution in the violence so that the chances of having meaningful political talks that can begin can be enhanced. And that's the goal of his mission."

The only thing left for Powell was to attempt to extricate himself without too much embarrassment. He made a final visit to Arafat, warning him that he was confirming the prevailing impression in Washington that he was not a partner. "I don't know if this now is the last time I will see you."

He also held a press conference at the David Citadel Hotel in Jerusalem, putting the finest gloss possible on failure. He acknowledged that he had been unable to put a cease-fire in place, saying, "Only with the end of the incursion and with the engagement in security talks can a cease-fire be achieved in reality, as well as rhetoric." In an exchange with reporters, he laid discreet blame on Israel for the failure. "So, I think there is now movement and I am anxious to see that movement because it is the operation at the moment that keeps us from moving into the strategic framework I described."

At one point, Powell reached over the heads of Israeli and Palestinian leaders to give their respective peoples some "questions to ponder."

"As I depart, I also leave behind fundamental questions for the people and the leaders of the region, and for the international community as well. Questions to ponder. For the people and leaders of Israel, the question is whether the time has come for a strong, vibrant state of Israel to look beyond the destructive impact of settlements and occupation, both of which must end, consistent with the clear positions taken by President Bush in his April 4 speech. Israelis should look ahead to the promise held out by the region and the world of a comprehensive, lasting peace.

"For the people and leaders of the Palestinian Authority, the question is whether violence and terrorism can be renounced forever and whether your sights can be set squarely on peace through negotiations. Terrorists and purveyors of violence must not hold the Palestinian dream of independence hostage, and prevent the emergence of a Palestinian state. For the Arab peoples and their leaders, the question is whether the promise and vision of Crown Prince Abdullah's initiative can be transformed into a living reality. It is important the ties between Israelis and Arabs, artificial barriers between states fall away, and distorted and racist images disappear from the media and from public discourse.

"For the people and leaders of the international community, the question is how we can help both sides solve the deep problems they face. The efforts being made by the Madrid Quartet deserve to be emulated and expanded. And all of us must exert greater efforts against terror as we pursue peace."

Two weeks earlier, the secretary had spoken of a cease-fire and then quickly progressing to peace talks. Now he was leaving with no cease-fire, no prospect of negotiations, a continued threat of terrorism against Israel, and still-rampant anger toward the United States throughout the Arab world. If the purpose of Powell's trip was to relieve Arab pressure, it failed.

For Powell, the ordeal left him even more reluctant than before to tackle the Middle East. "For President Bush and Cheney to leave him out there a couple of times, hanging in the wind, to leave Zinni out there hanging in the wind, was enough to get Powell to realize that, 'Hey, the predisposition is not only with me, and it's not even a predisposition with them—it's an iron-clad rule with them, they're not going to deal with Arafat. So . . . I've got lots of energies in other places, and the Middle East is just not going to be one of them.' . . . It wasn't something he was going to spend a lot of energy on—because he knew the administration wouldn't be behind him. In fact, they'd undercut him at every step of the way," said his chief of staff, Lawrence Wilkerson.

The Israeli military took some satisfaction from Operation Defensive Shield, even though it didn't last as long as officers had originally planned, drew widespread international condemnation, and failed to halt suicide bombings. Three years later, Giora Eiland would claim that the operation marked the beginning of a steady decline in anti-Israel terrorism that was later reinforced by the controversial separation barrier on the West Bank.

In an interview, Eiland offered an example of the way intelligence had been improved: "A year after this operation, our headquarters received information that two Palestinians carrying explosives were going from Nablus to Ramallah to meet someone who would bring them to Jerusalem for a double attack. We didn't know their identities, but we knew the identity of the person who would lead them [to Jerusalem] and we did know the location [of the meeting]. Twenty minutes was enough to send a special force. They were captured. If we didn't control Ramallah, there would have been little we could do."

As a measure to end terrorism, however, the operation was a failure, and steered Sharon and his government toward a major new policy— the erection of a separation barrier in the West Bank.

"These terrorist acts committed by the Palestinian side have led Israel to take security steps of various levels of severity," said Israel's chief justice, Aharon Barak, in an opinion that substantially endorsed the barrier. "Thus, the government, for example, decided upon various military operations, such as operation 'Defensive Wall' [March 2002] and operation 'Determined Path' [June 2002]. The objective of these military actions was to defeat the Palestinian terrorist infrastructure and to prevent reoccurrence of terror attacks. . . . These combat operations— which are not regular police operations, rather bear all the characteristics of armed conflict—did not provide a sufficient answer to the immediate need to stop the severe acts of terrorism. The Committee of Ministers on National Security considered a series of steps intended to prevent additional acts of terrorism and to deter potential terrorists from committing such acts. . . . Despite all these measures, the terror did not come to an end. The attacks did not cease. Innocent people paid with both life and limb. This is the background behind the decision to construct the separation fence."

Together with Powell's trip, the operation shifted ground in the relationship between Bush and Sharon. The Israeli prime minister tested Bush's determination and found that it did not match his own. One reason was the lack of an American strategy for ending the Israeli-Palestinian conflict, or even a strong desire to see it end. For the top policymakers in the White House and the Pentagon, the Israeli-Palestinian conflict was a distracting side issue in the overall war on terrorism and the looming showdown with Iraq. It needed to be addressed to quiet the Arab masses and calm the nerves of Arab leaders whose tacit support Bush needed for the larger war. But there was no desire to embark on a peace process for its own sake. Therefore, when Bush demanded that Sharon halt Operation Defensive Shield prematurely, his demand lacked moral authority. The president was in no position to take on Israel's supporters in the United States, demonstrating by the tens of thousands.

If there was a strong message to Israel during 2002, it was built around the administration's preparations for the Iraq War. "As we got farther and farther into Iraq, more and more we wanted the Israelis not to make themselves the focus. We had enough diplomatic baggage to haul without having to spend a lot of energy defending them or assuaging people who were getting pissed off at the Israelis and therefore might be less willing to cooperate."

The prime minister drew the obvious lesson: when Bush later demanded that Sharon "stop" settlement activity on the West Bank, his demand was ignored.

11

COMPETING FOR BUSH'S EAR

■ MAY–JUNE 2002 ■

EFRAIM HALEVY, urbane chief of the Mossad spy agency, didn't want Israel to stand still after Operation Defensive Shield. As a general rule, he believed his country needed "a political-strategic game plan at every point in time. Every action it takes, any decision on its part to refrain from action, must be somehow wedded to a plan." He had one in mind as he arrived at the White House in May 2002, accompanied by Giora Eiland, Danny Ayalon, and Moshe Kaplinsky, military aide to Prime Minister Sharon.

Their visit was well-timed. U.S.-Israeli relations were strained and tense as a result of Israel's offensive in the West Bank, Colin Powell's failure to secure a complete Israeli troop pullback, and the lengthy siege of Ramallah and Bethlehem. Tension increased over Israel's incursion to root out terrorists in the Jenin refugee camp. Palestinians noisily alleged that Israeli soldiers had massacred hundreds in close house-to-house combat. The charge proved to be a wild exaggeration and another blow to Palestinian credibility. But American and UN officials who went to the camp nevertheless encountered a grim scene that left one of them with a vivid memory of the stench of bodies and of people digging through rubble by hand to look for family members.

Persuaded by Foreign Minister Shimon Peres, Sharon reluctantly agreed to a UN fact-finding mission on the Jenin operation, expecting it to knock down the Palestinian claims of a massacre. The United States sponsored a Security Council resolution launching the inquiry. Then Sharon and his cabinet learned of the high-powered team picked by Secretary General Kofi Annan and its broad mandate. They feared a trap; Chief of Staff Shaul Mofaz threatened to resign. Israel decided to refuse cooperation. According to Yehuda Lancry, Israel's ambassador to the UN at the time, Bush agreed to scuttle the inquiry but exacted a price from Sharon: lifting the military siege on the Muqata compound in Ramallah, where Yasser Arafat had been trapped for thirty-five days. (A U.S. official corroborated his account.)

The Arab world was increasingly bitter toward Israel and its chief patron—the United States. "From Egypt to the Gulf, anger at Israel's treatment of the Palestinian people, seeming U.S. complicity, and Arab impotence is threatening to destabilize the region as a whole," the International Crisis Group warned in the summary of an April 10 report. Israel, in stretching the boundaries of self-defense, was coming dangerously close to President Bush's red line against precipitating a regional crisis.

THE RULERS OF Saudi Arabia, Israel's chief competitor for influence in Washington and with the Bush White House, believed the president didn't understand the pressure felt by the United States' friends in the region. On a visit to the president's Crawford, Texas, ranch in late April, Saudi crown prince Abdullah, the kingdom's de facto ruler, showed the president a video of footage aired by Arab television picturing the destruction wrought by Israel's offensive, as well as a collection of articles and pictures from Arab newspapers. "This is what we're up against," was his message. A Saudi official said Bush was described by participants as taken aback by the images. Abdullah demanded that Bush restrain the Israeli prime minister. "If Sharon is left to his own devices, he will drag the region over a cliff," Adel al-Jubeir, an adviser to the prince, told reporters.

Countervailing pressure on the administration was equally intense. Washington's leading pro-Israel lobby group mobilized its members to back Sharon. A crowd of five thousand attended an American Israel Public Affairs Committee convention in Washington, begun just before Bush met with Abdullah, in what the *Forward* described as "a massive show of Jewish political force." The mood was "undeniably militant," the newspaper reported; stony silence greeted White House Chief of Staff Andrew Card when he spoke hopefully of "a normal life for Palestinians trying to provide for their families," and of a two-state solution. Former Israeli prime minister Benjamin Netanyahu told the group of a conversation with Sharon: "I said, 'Arik, get rid of Arafat. Get rid of him. Get rid of that regime. And America will understand, and many in America will support you.'"

Prominent supporters of Israel sought to dispel negative accounts of Israel's conduct in Jenin. The Conference of Presidents set to work on its own extensive report, even as the UN General Assembly demanded that Annan revive an international inquiry. For Malcolm Hoenlein, the umbrella group's executive vice president, world reaction to the incursion still rankled three years later. "I was there in Jenin. I saw it myself. I was there during the fighting . . . I smelled the smells." He recalled footage, captured by an Israeli drone aircraft, of a Palestinian funeral procession "that was staged for the benefit of the UN and others." A figure wrapped in a shroud fell off the vehicle and was hoisted back up. "And then it fell off a second time and they put it back on. And it fell off a third time. This time the shroud came off, so the body put the shroud on and got back on himself," Hoenlein told me. "They put dead cats and dogs around to create the smell."

Amid signs that Crown Prince Abdullah's message was getting through to Bush, Israel took on the Saudis directly. At an embassy press conference in Washington May 6, visiting Israeli officials released eighty-five pages of documents—seized during the recent offensive in the West Bank—that they claimed showed a flow of Saudi money to Palestinian terrorists and their families. Saudis called the charges "baseless." At the time of Halevy's visit, the Bush administration was wrestling with its next move in the Middle East. Powell, the administration's main go-to

guy for Arab and European leaders, wanted to call an international conference in the summer to prepare the ground for a renewed peace
process. The notion evoked the Madrid peace conference of 1991, a
major breakthrough that opened direct negotiations between Israel
and its Arab neighbors. But White House officials diminished its importance, calling it a "meeting."

The London-born Halevy, then in his late sixties, knew the worlds of
intelligence and diplomacy, having risen through the Mossad ranks,
undertaking quiet missions for Israeli prime ministers and serving as
Israel's ambassador to the European Union. He had been brought
home from Brussels to lead the spy agency in 1998, after a botched
Mossad assassination attempt on Khaled Mashaal, head of the Hamas
political bureau. The mishap in Amman infuriated Jordan's king and
punctured Mossad's aura of stealthy lethality.

Halevy advocated creative diplomacy outside the Washington-
Jerusalem channel, which was Sharon's comfort zone. Under certain
conditions, he thought Israel should take political risks and "sup with the
devil," even breaking its long taboo and speaking directly with Hezbollah and Hamas. "There's no merit in simply saying all the time, 'All the
world is against us; Iran is Hitler; Hamas is part of Iran; Lebanon is
under Hezbollah; Hezbollah is Iran,'" he said in a 2006 interview. "So
what are we going to do? Are we going to sit and wait until the Messiah
comes, until out of the bowels of the earth will emerge a benign, right-
eous, pious leader who will sit down with Israel and shake our hand . . . ?"
Instead, "Let's look at what's happening around us. What pieces of the
jigsaw do you have? What cards do you have? See what you can do with
these cards."

One card Israel could play was the growing international frustration
with Yasser Arafat. Europeans were fed up with his empty promises and
uneasy with his handling of their aid money. Americans had turned hostile as a result of the *Karine A* episode and Arafat's refusal or inability to prevent terrorism. To these black marks was added alarm in the Egyptian
government over violent demonstrations that followed Arafat's public
exhortation of Arab masses to rise up and defend the Palestinians. Halevy
himself never trusted Arafat and believed his aim was to destroy Israel in

stages. He accepted as proof a speech that Arafat gave in 1994 at a Johannesburg mosque likening the Oslo accords to Mohammed's agreement with the Quraish, which the Prophet later abrogated.

On a previous visit to Washington, Halevy had raised with Rice and Tenet the idea of engineering a change in the Palestinian leadership. At the time, he got no response. Now, with Sharon's approval, he had received positive reactions from Egypt, Jordan, Russia, and Britain, and from Javier Solana, the European Union foreign policy chief, he said in a 2006 interview.

Inside the West Wing, the Israelis were shown into the windowless, yellow-walled Roosevelt Room. They were joined by Rice, Tenet, Deputy Secretary of Defense Paul Wolfowitz, and Bill Burns, assistant secretary of state for the Near East. Halevy, speaking English in the accent of the British upper-middle class, spelled out his ideas. The scheme was more subtle than assassination of Arafat, which Sharon had promised Bush he would avoid, or forced exile, which Israeli security officials had dissuaded Sharon from attempting several weeks earlier. As Halevy recounted his presentation, "A process should evolve whereby the Palestinians create the office of either a chief executive officer or a prime minister, and all executive authority should be invested in him, that the president should remain a figurehead, but we should negotiate with this new empowered leader—the term of which was 'empowerment.' We should empower a prime minister. . . . Thereby we could get things moving on the Palestinian side." The goal of negotiations would be the creation of a Palestinian "state with provisional borders," with the actual borders to be agreed on in future talks between Israel and Palestine. In his memoir, *Man in the Shadows*, Halevy writes that his blueprint also called for a reorganized Palestinian security service and a reformed financial system under the prime minister. Halevy's account of his role in the meeting was disputed by Danny Ayalon, who said in an interview that it was he and Dov Weisglass who were assigned the Palestinian portfolio. But an American who was present largely backed up Halevy's story. The White House national security press office was unable to find a record of the session.

The idea of easing Arafat out of power had previously been raised by Terje Roed-Larsen of the UN and the Europeans, a senior U.S.

official said. What was unusual about Halevy's presentation was that an
official from the Sharon government was offering a constructive way to
"get things moving on the Palestinian side." Ordinarily, proposals aimed
at renewing negotiations met resistance from the Sharon government.
Despite pressure from his right flank simply to "get rid of Arafat,"
Sharon had agreed to Halevy's approach of letting new leadership
"evolve," according to the Mossad chief.

Halevy recognized that neither Israel nor the United States could
accomplish this on its own. "Halevy, as I recall, was pretty realistic. He
understood that Arafat would not cede any real power easily, and that
we would have to mobilize key international players, and especially
moderate Arabs, to have any chance of making this work," the U.S. official said.

Even in the State Department, famed for clinging to the status quo,
the idea of finding an alternative to Arafat was being welcomed at high
levels. "Yasser Arafat is of course one of the biggest failures of the twentieth century, I think," said one official who was there at the time, himself a strong advocate of a negotiated end to the conflict. "He could have
had his state ten times over if he had ever said yes to something, and
stopped being a terrorist and a maniac. So part of the problem was that
the State Department stayed in love with Yasser Arafat for too long."

The problem was how to do it. People knowledgeable about Palestinian politics knew that a heavy-handed move by the United States
or Israel against Arafat could well backfire and rally the population to
his side, as had happened with the siege of the Muqata. If the administration wanted to adopt Halevy's suggestion and encourage new
leadership to "evolve," it needed to proceed surgically. Instead, Bush
chose a blunt instrument.

Reform of the Palestinian Authority and weakening Arafat and the
Fatah old guard held wide appeal among Palestinians, even those for
whom Arafat remained a symbol of national struggle. For years, organizations funded by the United States and the Europeans had worked to
build a functioning parliament and government, develop a constitution,
and promote a responsible press. Having witnessed democracy at work
in Israel, Palestinians were widely considered to be more ready than

most Arab societies to adopt the system. Even old-guard veteran Mahmoud Abbas, then No. 2 in the PLO, said at the time that elections must
be held and major reforms implemented immediately, according to the
Palestinian newspaper *al-Ayyam*, whose editor was an Arafat adviser. But
Abbas stressed that Palestinians would not accept a state without borders and without President Yasser Arafat. He said: "We will not accept
an alternative leadership as long as we are alive."

Despite the corruption in his regime and his stubborn grip on the
levers of power, Arafat himself was less of a dictator than Israelis typically pictured him. His double game on violence was a clumsy effort to
avoid alienating the West while not losing influence to a generation of
young Fatah leaders or falling out of step with a population that backed
"resistance" in all its forms. His infuriating inability to make decisions
stemmed in part from a need to consult widely and gain consensus
among a variety of factions.

Internal Palestinian pressure for an end to corruption and cronyism
tended to rise during periods of relative quiet and subside when the
conflict with Israel intensified. Arafat's support rose when Israel laid
siege to his dilapidated compound. The usual voices for reform were
badly weakened by the curfews, blocked transportation routes, economic woes, and damage that accompanied Operation Defensive
Shield. "[O]rganized civil society has been decimated by the April
incursions into the West Bank," Palestinian pollster Khalil Shikaki
told a Brookings Institution forum. A year and a half of violence had
broken down Palestinian social cohesion, leading to fears of instability. "As long as Arafat remains there, most people believe that there is
a Palestinian Authority, that there is some law and order," Shikaki
said. Pressure for reform from outside, particularly from the United
States, drew Palestinian suspicion as an obstacle in the march to sovereignty. Even among reformers, an end to the Israeli occupation took
precedence.

IF BUSH RECOGNIZED this reality, he wasn't swayed by it. During May
and June, a variety of actors inside and outside the U.S. government
competed to influence Bush's next step in the Middle East. On one side

were the State Department, the Israeli "peace camp," Europeans, and Arab allies seeking a renewed peace process. If Arab leaders couldn't prevent the United States from attacking Iraq, they at least wanted to lower the regional flames beforehand. On the other side were the Pentagon's civilian leaders, who saw the Israeli-Palestinian conflict through the prism of the war on terror, and members of Cheney's staff. They didn't believe Israeli-Arab peace was possible without deep, systemic change in Arab society that would be set in motion by the removal of Saddam Hussein. Sharon, for his part, wanted to crush terrorism and evade pressure to enter a peace process. The two sides squared off in a tense, exhausting process of drafting a presidential statement that ultimately became a landmark speech.

Bush dropped broad hints of where he was headed. Already determined to topple Saddam Hussein, he remained committed to a Palestinian state, but only one that was solidly democratic and free of terrorists. On May 2, he set firm guidelines suggesting an overhaul of Palestinian leadership was necessary in the Palestinian government. "Such a state cannot be based on a foundation of terror or corruption," Bush said after meeting with European Union leaders. "A Palestinian state must be based on the principles that are critical to freedom and prosperity: democracy and open markets, the rule of law, transparent and accountable administration, and respect for individual liberties and civil society."

Bush tried to keep Arab leaders in the loop, calling the crown prince and Egyptian president Hosni Mubarak before meeting with Sharon at the White House on May 7. Despite Israeli charges that the Saudis were funding terrorism, Bush stood by Abdullah, telling the press pool, "We had the Saudi crown prince stand up and talk about peace and the need for a peaceful solution."

Sharon did not find Bush in a good frame of mind: "The president's frustration with this issue and the absence of any hope that it was going to improve was pretty potent," recalled a senior U.S. official who was there. Sharon didn't help matters by coming in with a detailed dossier, which he plowed through, reading from index cards. Bush, who preferred an informal exchange, showed signs of impatience, the official said.

None of the tension showed publicly. No one could erase a growing impression that the United States and Israel were colluding against Arafat, particularly when unnamed Israeli officials said as much. The day after the Bush-Sharon meeting, Israel Radio reported that the two leaders "reached an understanding whereby Arafat must play only a symbolic role, and a temporary government headed by somebody else must be formed." In an indication of how the U.S. demand for reforms was being interpreted in the Arab world, commentator Abd-al-Wahhab Badrakhan wrote in *al-Hayat* that "the Palestinians, Arabs, and anyone with a sensible mind will understand what they mean, namely, that the triumphant American-Israeli duo are imposing their conditions on the defeated Palestinian. . . ."

As Bush and Sharon met the press in a televised photo op, cable networks used a split screen to show the grim scene of a suicide bombing that had just occurred in the Israeli town of Rishon Letzion, close to Tel Aviv, killing fifteen and injuring dozens more. Sharon cut short his visit and returned to Israel instead of spending the next day in New York. Before leaving, he blamed Arafat for the bombing and vowed a tough response: "Our sincere efforts to make progress on political tracks were met by further proof of the true intentions of the man who heads the PNA. Anyone calling for millions of shaheeds is guilty. Anyone incessantly inciting his people is guilty. Anyone financing terrorism is guilty. Anyone dispatching terrorists is guilty. Guilty! . . . "We will act to destroy anyone seeking to destroy us," he said, and concluded, "Israel will fight, Israel will triumph, and when victory is achieved, Israel will make peace."

Bush kept on consulting just about every leader with a strong interest in the region—with the important exceptions of Arafat and Syrian president Bashar al-Assad—but he was losing faith in Middle East diplomacy, at least the kind practiced by the State Department. Soon, he would deliver a death blow to Powell's plans for a conference and put any thought of peace negotiations on indefinite hold.

Pressure for Bush to deliver a major address on the Israeli-Palestinian conflict came from Powell and the State Department. Vice President Cheney opposed the idea. Rumsfeld initially sided with Cheney but ended up yielding and playing a major role.

Rarely has a presidential foreign policy speech absorbed so much of an administration's time and energy as the one that ultimately came to be identified by its date: June 24, 2002. It would become the administration's most important reference point for the Israeli-Palestinian conflict. Because Bush dealt regularly with just a small circle of officials, mostly in the White House, and answered questions mostly in brief photo ops, and because top aides were reluctant to talk candidly to reporters about the Middle East, his speeches became the most reliable guide to his thinking.

While regional leaders went to the Oval Office or Camp David in hopes of influencing Bush, the State Department and Pentagon engaged in a tense tug-of-war with competing priorities that went through thirty drafts and left participants drained and exhausted. The State Department's Near East officials and their White House ally, Flynt Leverett, wanted to put more flesh and bones into Bush's "vision" of a two-state solution. They believed Palestinians needed to be given what Leverett called a "credible political horizon" as an incentive to control the terrorists in their own midst and thereby make Israelis secure enough to want to negotiate. "We don't believe it's credible to move forward in an incremental way without a clear understanding of the endgame," a senior official told the *Baltimore Sun*.

It wasn't enough, for them, to talk about a "viable" Palestinian state when Israeli and Palestinian views of viability were starkly different. Sharon spoke of Israel's keeping all of Jerusalem and half of the West Bank and using bridges and tunnels to connect Palestinian areas. Palestinians demanded a full end to the Israeli occupation, which in their view meant gaining Gaza, all of the West Bank (or its territorial equivalent with land swaps), and the predominantly Arab neighborhoods of East Jerusalem, including the Muslim shrine Haram al-Sharif. At the State Department, officials tried to develop language that would cite the June 1967 Green Line as the basis for negotiations. They knew that many Israelis had come to realize that this was the price of a deal.

THOSE ADVOCATING A specific U.S. peace plan got surprising support from Kenneth Adelman, a friend of Cheney's, outside adviser to the Pentagon, and a Reagan-era neoconservative hawk. In an op-ed for the

Washington Times coauthored with former Representative Stephen Solarz, a liberal Democrat, Adelman wrote that "the United States should now prepare, and publicly present, a comprehensive peace proposal." The outline: an Israeli withdrawal roughly to its 1967 borders with the West Bank and Gaza Strip, two capitals in Jerusalem, a nonmilitarized Palestinian state, and a U.S.-led international force providing security to both states.

Civilian policymakers in the Pentagon approached the speech from the opposite direction, making a collision inevitable. They were determined not to reward Palestinian terrorists. Regime change in Iraq was their top priority for the region, but they also opposed a new peace process that would require Israeli concessions.

Unlike Middle East debates in past administrations, the Pentagon under Bush was granted a strong voice in shaping policy. The department's point man was Douglas J. Feith, the undersecretary for policy, an energetic bureaucratic warrior who had a passionate interest in the subject. A fluent and prolific commentator and Georgetown-trained lawyer, he had long been associated with the hard-line Center for Security Policy and held views similar to those of right-wing Israeli leaders. He was a prominent U.S. critic of the Oslo accords, which he believed required Israel to yield territory and get nothing tangible in return. In 1995, he played a key unofficial role in GOP legislation requiring the United States to move its embassy in Israel from Tel Aviv to Jerusalem. In an op-ed in the *Baltimore Sun* that year, he put forward a Middle East doctrine comparable to Ronald Reagan's slogan for dealing with the Soviets: peace through strength. "When Israel appeared vulnerable, it did not achieve peace, or even peace talks," he wrote. "Only after being forced to acknowledge the strength of Israel's position—its military power, its enduring ties to America, and, since the end of the cold war, our unchallenged global predominance—did some Arab powers abandon rejectionist positions and start negotiating. If Israel's antagonists bow to unpleasant realities and lower unrealistic expectations, the peace process may produce not merely signing ceremonies but real peace."

On May 8, 2002, the day after Sharon's visit to the White House, Feith told the American Jewish Committee in a speech that the campaign of suicide bombing against Israelis at the time was "the most salient problem on the antiterrorism agenda at present."

"[A]s to the suicide bombers' political hopes, we must ensure that terrorism is not seen as a winning strategy. This is today's immediate challenge: for example, we have to make it understood that the Palestinian homicide bombers are harming, not helping, their political cause."

Feith took a dim view of what he viewed as a self-contained "cottage industry" of U.S. diplomats and Middle East specialists, so-called peace processors. He thought they engaged in "groupthink." What occurred during the 1990s, he believed, was less a peace process than an Israeli "withdrawal process" benefiting a Palestinian regime that remained hostile and violent. Feith's paternal grandparents had been killed by the Nazis, along with seven of their children. In a home shadowed by the Holocaust and the phony peace of Munich, Feith learned early on about the danger of placing too much faith in diplomacy. He thought the character of regimes was more important to peace than formal agreements. Reflecting on the arms-control "process" of the late twentieth century, he believed history showed that rolling back communism and establishing democracies in Eastern Europe was a much safer bet than trying to strike a deal with the Soviet Union. He welcomed what he understood to be Bush's similar attitude.

"The president's view was that the nature of the Palestinians' leadership and the nature of their political institutions are crucial to whether peace is possible." Bush, he said, "does not buy the idea that the key to peace can lie in the hands of leaders who operate above any law, without human rights considerations—that the key to peace is to have a thug cracking down on the other thugs. It's absolutely inconsistent with his idea of what produces peace." Approaching the end of his consultations on the Middle East, Bush invited Egyptian president Hosni Mubarak to Camp David in early June. Mubarak arrived intending to press Bush to set a timetable for peace talks that would bring a peace agreement and a withdrawal by Israel from occupied territory as soon as two years hence. Palestinians would not halt the violence unless they saw a clear path to a peaceful settlement, he believed, and the United States had to play a leading role.

The two leaders spent a relaxed evening, joined by the First Lady. The next morning they met privately and in a larger group with staff and diplomats. Mubarak figured prominently among the trusted allies of Bush's father, and the president treated him with deference. When the two leaders, wearing open-necked shirts and jackets, faced the press amid the thick Catoctin Mountain greenery, Bush praised the Egyptian's experience and friendship for the United States. But when Mubarak droned through a lengthy prepared statement in Arabic, pausing for translation, Bush grew noticeably impatient, drumming the rostrum with his thumbs. As his own remarks made clear, Palestinian reform and a change in its leadership had to be a first step.

When a reporter asked whether Arafat could pursue the necessary reforms, Mubarak insisted, "Look, we should give this man a chance. . . . If he's going to deliver, I think everybody will support him. If he's not going to deliver, his people will tell him that."

Bush politely disagreed: "The president believes that the chairman— if you notice, he didn't say he's going to deliver—should be given a chance to deliver. And that's an interesting point of view. I also happen to believe that there is plenty of talent in—amongst the Palestinians, and that if we develop the institutions necessary for the development of a state, that talent will emerge."

By the time Sharon returned to the White House three days later, the president accepted the Israeli view that Palestinians had to reform their government before any serious moves toward a peace process could begin. "At the present time, we don't yet see a partner," Sharon said, and Bush agreed: "And so, first things first, and that is, what institutions are necessary to give the Palestinian people hope and to give the Israelis confidence that the emerging [Palestinian] government will be someone with whom they can deal."

Sharon adviser Danny Ayalon recalled: "They all agreed that it has to be phased out in stages, first of all the end of incitement and violence and terrorism; then reforms over the Palestinians so they build political institutions, reform their security apparatus, unify the forces, change some of the personalities, change the practices; of course, economic and financial transparency and all that—so [as] to create a trustworthy partner with whom then we can negotiate with give-and-take, all the way up to a state, possibly."

But Bush added another piece to the puzzle that was less welcome to Sharon, saying, "It is very important for people to understand that as these steps are taken, as this—people work together to achieve the institutions necessary for peace, that there is a political process on the horizon as well." Spokesman Ari Fleischer said Bush believed "that you have to have progress on both the political front and the security front, and the two go hand in hand."

Speech drafts went back and forth to the National Security Council offices from the State and Defense departments. In Foggy Bottom, officials recognized that Bush wanted to break new ground and dispense with what one called "ritualistic recitation of peace process truisms." They knew that as far as Bush was concerned, there was no prospect of a return to peace negotiations if Arafat was going to be involved; that a way around Arafat would have to be found, and new institutions developed. But demonizing Arafat would be counterproductive, State Department officials believed. "I just thought it's a mistake to over-personalize because, again, [Arafat] loves being the center of attention and you make a martyr out of him," said one senior official.

They also argued that if the Palestinian people were going to be persuaded to jettison Arafat and promote new leaders, they needed a strong incentive. The message should be, "If you switch horses, here's what you can expect," a participant said. State Department officials were intent on providing a "political horizon" that was as specific as possible to show Palestinians the reward that awaited them if they made the right moves. "You've got to say what we believe in, and not just stop dealing with Arafat. What is it we want, what are we asking for, and what are we giving to the Palestinian and the Arab world and the European world to make this look like a sensible decision on our part? And the answer to that was, the president has got to put down clearly his vision of a Palestinian state for the Palestinian people. And it had to be with a timeline . . . Arabs always want timelines. They always want something that they can look at on a calendar." The result was inclusion of language that an agreement providing for a Palestinian state could be achieved by 2005.

Besides timing, they wanted to be as specific as possible about what territory the Palestinians had a right to expect, knowing that throughout the Arab world and Europe, the idea of a Palestinian state comprised Gaza, the West Bank, and traditionally Arab East Jerusalem. "There were a lot of different formulations you could have used, which talked about 4 June '67 as a starting point for negotiations; you could repeat the notion of land swaps which had been introduced at Camp David and Taba, as a kind of constructive and creative ingredient in a final-status settlement. There was a sort of degree of empathy, too, that you could project about Palestinian political aspirations . . ." a senior official said.

By the time Feith started receiving drafts, their number had reached the midteens. "We worked on injecting some of our ideas, analyses, into the process. We did it by editing the drafts as they came." Rumsfeld took a strong interest and would go over Feith's proposals. Feith knew changes made in Rumsfeld's own handwriting would get more attention from the White House than the ones he submitted. "So on a number of occasions, I would come in, give him the markup of the speech, and stand at his standup desk with him, and he would have his copy there, and my copy next to him, and we'd go over it.

". . . So he would transfer a whole bunch of comments from my paper to his paper, and then we would fax over his, so they would see his handwriting."

As drafts circulated, senior officials from various agencies met at the White House to argue over them. Ordinarily, Bush would wait for all his subordinates to sort out their differences and present him with their product, which he would then edit to his liking. But this speech was different. The president actually joined one or more of the late drafting sessions, held in the secure White House Situation Room.

"I vividly remember his saying something to the effect that 'I want to change the way people think about this conflict, and about the approach that is needed to make peace,'" Feith said. "He was saying, 'I don't believe you can achieve peace by ignoring certain things that were systematically ignored by the diplomacy of the preceding ten or so years.'

"What became the most radical element of the June 24th speech was the focus on the requirement for a new Palestinian leadership," Feith said.

The president fought attempts to get him to spell out a clear American position on what would constitute a fair and practical settlement on borders, Jerusalem, and refugees. "What State was driving at was getting the president to tell the Israelis that they have to withdraw to such a boundary. But it was more than that. They wanted the president should slice through the Gordian knot and say: Here is what we think the diplomatic result should be on key final-status issues. Boundaries, settlement, Jerusalem, all the stuff that had been debated in the diplomatic process throughout the '90s.

". . . But when he was pushed to be specific on the so-called final-status issues, he said, 'I will not.' That came up explicitly. He got pushed and pushed, including in the drafting session I attended, and he said no. He said something along the lines of: 'We want a new approach based on new thinking.' . . . His view was that we're not going to get people thinking differently if we buy into the standard framework and frame of mind of all the preceding years."

Powell recalled that "the big fight" was over whether the president would be seen as rewarding terrorism. "And my argument to the president was, 'It's not rewarding terrorism. It's rewarding people. It's rewarding people who walk away from terrorism. This speech doesn't give anybody anything. What does it give the Palestinians? You've already said you want them to have a state. It's what you believe. So if you're going to give this speech you've got to really give them something to hope for. Because you're walking away from their leader. We may not think he's much, but they do.' "

In Jerusalem, "We knew that the speech was coming, and we went back and forth, and I talked to Condi many times and told her what are the things that are important to us, what do we think should be stressed," said Danny Ayalon. The points included "the importance of the end of terror; the importance of reforms, to create a partner that is not compromised by terror and corruption; the recognition of Israel as a Jewish state. . . ." While the speech was being drafted, Israel provided Washington with evidence that Arafat had authorized a $20,000 payment to the al-Aqsa Martyrs' Brigades, which had adopted the Hamas and Islamic Jihad tactic of suicide bombings, according to reports in American and Israeli newspapers.

As the address went through its final changes, another prominent Israeli, Natan Sharansky, weighed in.

From his days as a dissident in the Soviet Union and champion of Jews denied the right to emigrate, Sharansky had a wide circle of admirers in the United States. Senior officials, Democrat and Republican, sought his views on the prospects for democracy in the former Communist empire. After he became an Israeli politician with a base among the large immigrant population, these contacts continued. One of his admirers was Cheney, with whom Sharansky spoke two weeks before President Bush was sworn in to his first term. "I made my usual mantra about linkage between democracy and human rights and security and how it was important also for the Middle East, to use this formula. . . . His reaction—and Cheney is not one who reacts with many words; in fact he reacts more by meaningful silence—but I would think his meaningful silence was very positive, very understanding."

The weekend before Bush was to deliver his Middle East speech, Sharansky and Cheney were both attending an American Enterprise Institute conference. Sharansky had heard from the prime minister's office that Bush would give "a last chance to Arafat—that he has to behave." Sharansky asked for time alone with the vice president. "And I said to Cheney that I feel very frustrated—because in fact it was a betrayal. He looked at me almost in amazement. 'But your side already agreed with the speech; it's Arafat that we have the problem with.' I said, 'Look, I'm not speaking for my government. We have Shimon Peres; you have Powell. We have our own disagreements, you have your own. But as a citizen of Israel, and one who believes in these ideas which your president proclaims, just at the moment of such—every day another terrorist attack. There is no doubt we get reports of . . . how Arafat is making clear, he's not giving orders but he's giving a green light . . . and the president of the United States, who is leading against world terror, is saying to him, 'Behave yourself.'"

"He said, 'What do you think needs to be said?'"

Sharansky replied: "This leadership, which is all based on terror, has to go. And there must be a leadership which believes in democratic reform. But it's not enough. . . . You have to demand . . . 'Lead the reform.' He put it down. . . . He said he would see the president on the twenty-second." This was what State Department Chief of Staff Lawrence Wilkerson called Cheney's "fourth bite of the apple" in influencing presidential decisions. Another official said Cheney was arguing about the speech up until the morning it was delivered.

Feith noted with satisfaction that when Bush stepped into the Rose Garden on June 24, he was flanked not just by Powell and Rice but by Rumsfeld—a reflection of the Pentagon's role in the speech. Cheney was absent. Bush opened with an eloquent preamble: "The forces of extremism and terror are attempting to kill progress and peace by killing the innocent. And this casts a dark shadow over an entire region. For the sake of all humanity, things must change in the Middle East.

"It is untenable for Israeli citizens to live in terror. It is untenable for Palestinians to live in squalor and occupation. And the current situation offers no prospect that life will improve. Israeli citizens will continue to be victimized by terrorists, and so Israel will continue to defend herself. In the situation the Palestinian people will grow more and more miserable. My vision is two states, living side by side in peace and security. There is simply no way to achieve that peace until all parties fight terror. Yet, at this critical moment, if all parties will break with the past and set out on a new path, we can overcome the darkness with the light of hope."

Then Bush lowered the boom on Arafat. Though he didn't mention the Palestinian president by name, his meaning was clear to most listeners and became the headline read around the world: "Peace requires a new and different Palestinian leadership, so that a Palestinian state can be born"—one untainted by terror and corruption. To reinforce the point, the United States cut off official contact with Arafat, breaking with European allies and overruling its consul general in Jerusalem, Ron Schlicher. Bush hinted strongly that if Arafat were reelected, the United States would work to cut off aid to the Palestinians.

Powell was chagrined that the State Department's main contribution—the incentives for Palestinians—got lesser media play.

In fact, they were vague: once the required Palestinian reforms occurred, Bush said, the United States would recognize Palestine as a state with provisional borders. The issues of final borders, the fate of Palestinian refugees, and the status of Jerusalem, the president said, could be settled "within three years," an outcome that would finally end the half-century-old Israeli-Palestinian conflict. He called on Israel to halt expansion of Jewish settlements in the West Bank and Gaza, and, as security improved, to withdraw its forces to the positions held in September 2000.

Bush hinted at what Palestinians could expect in a final settlement, saying that "the Israeli occupation that began in 1967 will be ended through a settlement negotiated between the parties, based on UN Resolutions 242 and 338, with Israeli withdrawal to secure and recognized borders."

In published accounts and interviews, both Halevy and Sharansky have identified their ideas in Bush's speech. The president adopted Halevy's suggestion of a Palestinian state with provisional borders in advance of a final settlement. But he rejected Halevy's proposal for encouraging an "empowered" Palestinian prime minister in favor of a verbal blunt instrument similar to Sharansky's suggested "this leadership . . . has to go."

A year later, Bush would embrace Halevy's initial idea after Arafat was pressured by Arabs and Europeans to appoint Mahmoud Abbas as prime minister. But in the immediate aftermath of the president's speech, Arafat dug in his heels and clung to power, nonviolent Palestinian reformers were thrown on the defensive, and valuable time was lost.

A key aspect of the speech was what it left out: it contained no clear direction for implementing the Palestinian reforms demanded by Bush and preparing Israelis to bite the bullet on a settlements freeze, withdrawal of forces, and negotiations. Gone was Colin Powell's idea of an international conference, with nothing to replace it. Aaron Miller, veteran State Department peace broker, reflected two years later, "[T]he June '02 speech really, in my view, made further serious American efforts on the Israeli-Palestinian thing almost impossible. Because it created so many benchmarks that the Palestinians would have to commit to that they'd never get to where they wanted to go. The first half of the speech made it impossible to get to the second half."

His longtime colleague Daniel Kurtzer, U.S. ambassador to Israel, disagreed, in part. "It was a good speech, actually. It would have propelled us forward, but we had let some opportunities slip, so that we were kind of backsliding at this point; we didn't have real traction." One reason, another official added, was that "the battle to get to the twenty-fourth of June was so bruising that people sort of stood back from it." Washington soon concentrated on the coming Iraq War, which, in Powell's words, "sucked the oxygen" from other crises. On the Israeli-Palestinian conflict, it was left to Arabs and Europeans to find a way forward.

12

"[O] N THE VERGE OF PEACE"

■ SUMMER 2002–SPRING 2003 ■

MARWAN MUASHER LIKENED himself to the "Energizer Bunny," the pink symbol of perseverance shown beating a drum nonstop in TV ads for batteries. When the United States let Middle East diplomacy languish, he would come and prod Washington to keep going. As one of Jordan's key peace brokers for a decade, he might also have called himself a glutton for punishment, since his efforts so often met with obstruction or indifference.

Muasher's ready smile and air of equanimity belied a near-desperate urgency. Apart from Israelis and Palestinians themselves, no country in the Middle East felt more insecure as a result of the bitter conflict than the Hashemite kingdom. Located "between Iraq and a hard place," as Prince Hassan bin Talal, brother of the late King Hussein, put it, Jordan survived by maneuvering between the region's hostile forces—chiefly, the United States and Iraq and Israel and the Palestinians. It did so with equal measures of dexterity and denial. Ruled by desert nobility transplanted from the Hejaz, now part of Saudi Arabia, Jordan quietly maintained strategic ties with its neighbor Israel for decades. But in deference to its majority Palestinian population, it didn't sign a formal peace with the Jewish state until 1994, after Israel and the Palestinians reached their own deal. Jordan took money and military aid from the United

States but feared it would be suicidal to acknowledge the presence of any U.S. forces on its barren expanses. Promoting itself as a regional model of modernity and reform, it tolerated political activity by the Islamist Muslim Brotherhood, while keeping a tight leash on the press, and maintained a tough security apparatus that drew allegations of abuse and torture.

Three weeks after President Bush's June 24, 2002, Middle East speech, Muasher was back in the United States to fill in the blanks. U.S.-educated, with a PhD in electrical engineering, he had become intimately familiar with American policymaking in his successive roles as peace negotiator, Jordan's ambassador to Israel and the United States, and then foreign minister. But his small, resource-poor country had little leverage with the United States other than its determinedly pro-Western outlook and discreet cooperation with both the United States and Israel. Unlike the revered King Hussein, Jordan's young monarch, Abdullah II, had limited experience and was a generation younger than most other leaders in the region. He came to Washington as a supplicant. In public, Bush treated Abdullah kindly, as he would an eager-to-please fraternity pledge, telling him "Good job!" at the end of one of their joint photo ops.

Bush, in his speech, had spelled out for Palestinians what was required for them to gain active American support for statehood and an end to Israeli occupation. He demanded that they pick new leaders untainted by terrorism and corruption, reform their government and security structure, and crush terrorist groups. A state with provisional borders would be followed by final-status negotiations, with the aim of achieving an Israeli-Palestinian settlement by 2005. Bush called on Israel to halt its expansion of Jewish settlements and pull its forces out of Palestinian towns. What he didn't offer was any kind of plan. Drained from the infighting over the content of the speech, the State Department was treading water. "I think it's a little unreasonable to expect us to—or anyone right now—to have a precise road map as to how you get there," Secretary of State Colin Powell told Middle East listeners over U.S.-funded Radio Sawa. Condoleezza Rice resisted creating a specific plan, particularly one that simultaneously tackled violence and provided a timeline for achieving a two-state solution.

To the Israelis, the absence of an American plan took them off the hook; they could wait for Palestinians to fulfill Bush's demands. Sharon had no interest in hastening final negotiations with Palestinians over the explosive questions of borders, Jerusalem, and refugees. Referring to Bush's address, Raanan Gissin, a Sharon spokesman, said, "[T]his is a speech, a post-11 September speech, in which it is very clear what comes first. It is not the so-called cessation of occupation, as the Palestinians have been harping time and again, that comes first. First, there has to be a cessation of terror, of violence, of incitement, or at least a major effort on the part of the Palestinians to do so, which they failed to do in the past twenty-one months, and Yasser Arafat has adopted this policy of terror and of violence, and never ceased from it."

WHILE PALESTINIAN MILITANT groups and many Arab and European commentators condemned the June 24 speech as one-sided in Israel's favor, Muasher, along with Saudi and Egyptian diplomats, mined Bush's prose for diplomatic opportunities. They found several parts of the Bush speech they liked: a clear U.S. commitment to a final agreement that took into account the needs of both sides on Jerusalem and refugees; an independent state in three years; an end to the occupation begun in 1967, which they chose to interpret as an Israeli withdrawal to the pre-1967 Green Line, with some modifications; and Bush's calls for an end to settlements, economic siege, and the humiliation of Palestinians. They needed to find a way to make Bush live up to these commitments.

"I want to see a road map. I want to see benchmarks. I want to see a plan that says in March of 2003, the Israeli side will do this and the Palestinians will do this; and in September of 2003, this is where we will be; and in March of 2004, this is where we will be. And I want a plan that is agreed to now," Muasher said at the Brookings Institution. He recognized that a crackdown on Palestinian terrorist groups was an essential early ingredient. Jordan would help restructure Palestinian security organizations.

For Jordan, the continued Israeli-Palestinian conflict was a time bomb. If no final agreement were reached and if fighting and Israeli settlement expansion continued, Jordan could face another large wave of refugees. Officials feared its society and economy would not be able to cope.

With Ahmed Maher, Egypt's foreign minister, Muasher met with Powell and other members of the Quartet in New York. The purpose of the four-party group was to pull the United States together with the UN, Russia, and Europe behind a single strategy for halting Israeli-Palestinian violence and propelling negotiations forward. The Quartet combined the power of the United States, Israel's chief ally, with the international acceptance of the UN, European money, and Russian influence in the Middle East.

In Washington the next day, Maher and Muasher were joined by the Saudi foreign minister, Prince Saud al-Faisal, in a half-hour meeting with Bush. Their visit occurred against the backdrop of a suicide bombing the night before at Tel Aviv's old bus station and an earlier ambush of a bus in the West Bank. Eleven Israelis died in the two attacks, which followed three weeks of strengthened Israeli military presence and curfews in many West Bank cities.

The Arab foreign ministers gave President Bush a *New York Times* advertisement in which one thousand prominent American Jews called for an active Israeli-Palestinian peace process. "Mr. President, this ad represents our views as Arabs," they told him, according to Muasher. The foreign ministers were relieved to find that the president didn't intend to stall. At least five times, they heard Bush say, "I'm serious about this. I'm committed. I want to do it in three years," according to the July 19 account by Muasher at Brookings.

The "road map" was born. For the next six months, the three Arab foreign ministers, along with European and UN colleagues, worked hand in glove with the Near East bureau of the State Department and an ally on the NSC staff, Flynt Leverett. While the Pentagon was mostly preoccupied planning the invasion of Iraq, they crafted a document implementing Bush's "vision." The road map spelled out a series of steps required of both Israelis and Palestinians. It would conclude with negotiations on a final-status agreement that would end the occupation and provide for two states coexisting peacefully. The aim was to reach that goal in 2005. The document was front-loaded with enough Palestinian security measures and reforms to escape an automatic Israeli veto. For Jordan and the Palestinians, the all-important significance of the road map was its call for a final-status solution within a few years.

From an office in the Pentagon, David Schenker, Douglas Feith's specialist on the Levant, tried to apply the bureaucratic brakes, but the document gathered too much momentum to stop.

The diplomats' work was shadowed from the outset by continued violence. On July 31, nine people were killed and eighty-five wounded by a bomb planted in a student cafeteria at Hebrew University's Mount Scopus campus in Jerusalem. Hamas claimed responsibility. Construction worker Muhammad Ouda, twenty-nine, a resident of Silwan, a village neighboring Jerusalem, was subsequently charged.

Bush continued to resist any kind of schedule leading to a political settlement, insisting that Palestinians first develop a responsible security apparatus, produce a democratic constitution, and reform their financial system so that outside aid money would not disappear. But a visit by Jordan's King Abdullah II on August 1, 2002, the day after the Hebrew University bombing, started to change his thinking. During their meeting, Bush said he didn't want to be bound by a certain date. The Jordanians pressed for a timeline of two or three years, with Muasher explaining the purpose of the road map. Bush showed interest and instructed Powell to follow up, according to a diplomat familiar with the meeting.

August 2002 was a pivotal month in the looming U.S. confrontation with Iraq. Four days after the Abdullah visit, Powell met with Bush privately and persuaded him to proceed through the United Nations and attempt to build international support before any military attack. But the administration's hard-liners sought to prevent any active American move toward Middle East peace until after the war. Vice President Cheney explained on August 26 in a speech to the Veterans of Foreign Wars that once regime change occurred in Iraq, "our ability to advance the Israeli-Palestinian peace process would be enhanced, just as it was following the liberation of Kuwait in 1991."

STILL, WITH A major war on the horizon, the United States needed to lower the flame under the Israeli-Palestinian conflict so as to avoid a parallel crisis in the region. This need prompted a new Bush-Sharon standoff in September, when Israeli forces again attacked Arafat's West Bank headquarters in Ramallah. The operation had been launched at Sharon's insistence over the objections of his chief of staff, Moshe Yaalon. The general expected that the White House would demand a halt to the operation as it had in the spring, giving Arafat the impression he was protected by Washington.

Israeli soldiers surrounded the compound, exchanging gunfire with Palestinians protecting Arafat and using bulldozers to turn part of it to rubble. This time, top U.S. officials were truly worried that Arafat could be killed, despite Sharon's earlier pledge to Bush not to harm the Palestinian leader. "I thought what might happen was they'd kill him by accident," a senior official said. Kurtzer was dispatched to Sharon's farm to tell him Bush wanted Israeli forces pulled out. He was careful, as usual, to say that his instructions came from the president.

"What do you expect me to do? Israelis are getting killed," Sharon demanded. Israel renewed the siege a day after a bus bombing in downtown Tel Aviv killed six people and wounded about seventy. Hamas claimed responsibility.

"Well, in this case they got killed by Hamas, but you went after Arafat. Why didn't you go after Hamas?" Kurtzer retorted. Going beyond his talking points, he told Sharon, "I wouldn't be here today if you had gone after Hamas as a result of the terrorist act."

Powell called Sharon that night to reinforce Bush's demand. Nothing happened. A few days later, Kurtzer hosted Sharon for lunch at the ambassador's house in Herzliya. He told the prime minister that the U.S. message hadn't changed. "My sense is that Washington's patience has run out," he told the prime minister. Sharon then dispatched his chief of staff and consigliere, Dov Weisglass, to Washington. "This was the double-check," said Kurtzer. Only when Weisglass returned with word that the White House couldn't be budged did Sharon pull his forces back.

During a White House visit in October, Sharon was given the latest draft of the road map being drawn up by the Europeans, the UN, and the State Department, with a big assist from Muasher in Jordan. The administration was campaigning to line up the UN Security Council behind a resolution paving the way for action against Iraq.

Bush "was kind of in an up mood about moving things forward" and didn't pussyfoot with Sharon, according to Kurtzer. Israelis viewed the road map as a European-led effort. Sharon was "very suspicious," recalled Danny Ayalon. But his top aides—including Weisglass and Efraim Halevy, who by then had left the Mossad to become Sharon's national security adviser—dismissed the importance of the plan.

Terje Roed-Larsen, the UN envoy, tried to get Sharon's team to take the road map seriously. "I had meetings both with Dov Weisglass, the prime minister's chief of staff, and Efraim Halevy, the national security adviser at the time, and they both said, 'The road map—forget it,' because they were both dead sure that Washington would not go for it," Roed-Larsen recalled in 2005. "He told them, 'You're misreading the situation. The road map will become an official document. It will be on your table and you'll have to address it.' I remember [they said] 'Forget it. . . . Let's talk about something interesting.'"

Halevy remembered his conversation with the UN envoy. "I told [Roed-]Larsen the road map would never be accepted by Israel," he said in 2006. "The prime minister gave instructions not to accept the road map as the basis for discussion." Sharon thought the plan "was a real danger to Israel, [to] basic Israeli interests."

"[Roed-]Larsen said to me, 'It doesn't matter what's in the road map. Everybody knows the road map will not be implemented the way it's written. You have to accept it in order to create a basis, and then in all the rest of it, you come up with different solutions. . . . You have nothing to lose by accepting the road map.' . . . I think he even said to me, 'Once you accept it, you can forget it,' or something to that effect." Not all Israelis felt the way Halevy did. Steven Rosen, then a top official of AIPAC, said in an interview: "Israelis weren't really taken by surprise by the road map. They were given draft after draft, as it evolved, in the fall of '02. They chose not to participate in the drafting process because they were in a domestic contest between Sharon and Netanyahu. And Sharon told the administration that, if he was forced to take positions . . . that they would have to be harder-line then they might otherwise be. And so

by mutual agreement, Israel did not participate in the road map drafting process. But it's a little misleading, because in an informal way they
were well aware. I know I had conversations with some Israelis during
that period, and they were clearly steps ahead of the American Jews in
their comprehension of what was going on. And a lot more sanguine
about it."

The Quartet envoys worked on Tony Blair, making two trips to London. While backing Bush on Iraq, Blair believed a strong and simultaneous effort was needed to push forward the Middle East peace process.
For him, this was essential to diminish hostility both in the Arab world
and in his own Labour Party to military action against Iraq. In late September and on October 1, 2002, he made two public calls for "final-
status" talks to start by year's end. Washington quietly dismissed the idea.
When the road map was spelled out to him, "Blair became very enthu-
siastic," Roed-Larsen said. At a meeting with Bush in Prague November 21, Blair told reporters that "the whole world wants to see us now,
having—taken this very firm stand against terrorism, against issues of
weapons of mass destruction, but also try and make sure that we provide the secure future with lasting peace in the Middle East."

Israelis grew alarmed as Europeans pressed to have the road map finished and released in December. Sharon's government had collapsed
after a pullout by the Labor Party, now led by the dovish retired major
general Amram Mitzna, and was headed to elections early in 2003. At
the White House, Elliott Abrams, the national security staffer in charge
of democracy and human rights, but who was involved increasingly in
Israeli-Palestinian affairs, weighed in on the road map. He was worried
that the Europeans and the State Department were watering down the
president's June 24 policies.

Dov Weisglass, Sharon's chief of staff, pressed the White House to
delay releasing the road map. Over Leverett's protests, Condoleezza
Rice was persuaded that releasing the document would look like interference in the Israeli political campaign. Leverett argued to the contrary,
that withholding it meant the United States was interfering in Sharon's
favor. In any event, the Israeli government was in no position at that
point to deal with it seriously. "[T]here was no time for being proactive

and having any initiative when Israel is consumed by a political debate. I think this was the prevailing [view]. And also Israel could not respond to anything like that."

Rice may have surmised that there was no point in antagonizing Sharon, who was bound to win reelection. Dan Kurtzer believed that opinion polls were underestimating Sharon's likely margin of victory. Mitzna lacked staying power, he thought. In a quiet visit to Cairo, he told President Hosni Mubarak that Sharon would get 40 seats in the 120-member Knesset. Sharon ended up with 38.

The Quartet pursued another tack: all agreed that the road map was ready to be presented to the parties "as is," without further changes. The foreign ministers and Annan met with Powell at the State Department on December 20 to cement their agreement. Then they went to the White House and won Bush's endorsement.

"What we agreed there was that not a letter would be changed, not a comma," Roed-Larsen later recalled with satisfaction. Bush, during a photo op, said the road map would not be released because it was "not complete yet." He avoided giving the real reason—that Sharon was opposed to its release. Outside the White House, Per Stig Moeller, the Danish foreign minister representing the European Union, told reporters that the text had been finished except for a section about monitors.

Even though the road map was not officially released, Sharon had in fact been sandbagged by the Quartet. He could not change the text. All Israel was able to do after that was raise fifteen "reservations" and extract a promise from Washington that these would be taken into consideration. But the lack of consultation between Washington and Jerusalem over the road map as it neared completion would have repercussions over the coming months. Rice quietly shook up her Middle East team, placing Elliott Abrams, who had close ties with the Israelis and many key figures in the American Jewish community and among conservatives, in charge of dealing with the Israeli-Palestinian conflict, effectively demoting road map coauthor Flynt Leverett.

Having nailed down their peace plan and a timeline, the UN, the Europeans, and Jordan moved on to their next challenge—sidelining Arafat and elevating a Palestinian "partner" whom Americans would accept and Israel would have no excuse to ignore. Roed-Larsen, through Jeffrey Feltman, acting consul general in Jerusalem, got Rice to agree that the appointment of a Palestinian prime minister would go at least partway toward meeting Bush's demands. Roed-Larsen and Miguel Moratinos, the EU's Middle East envoy at the time, went to see Arafat, still confined to his heavily damaged compound in Ramallah. "We basically said—all of us—'This is your only chance,'" according to Roed-Larsen. "At one point I said, in the presence of everybody, 'If you don't do this, the next thing will be [that] an Israeli soldier will come in this door with a gun in his hand and it will be the end of you. . . . We were all basically telling him, 'You're finished; we don't need to see you; you can just forget us; we will never come back again; you will be totally isolated.'"

Moratinos remembered Arafat's reaction to the pressure campaign. "He screamed at me on the phone. He insisted he did not want [to name Mahmoud Abbas], so I told him . . . 'In the end, Israelis and Americans are going to be right: you would never deliver. You promise to deliver and you never deliver. . . . We cannot stick with you as president.'"

Jordanian officials played the good cop. They told Arafat that since the Americans refused to deal with him, he needed to appoint someone who could be an interlocutor with the United States, so as not to bring the peace process to a halt.

Even though he was being sidelined, Arafat most likely believed he could pull strings from behind the scenes as he had twelve years before, when he controlled the Palestinian delegation at the Madrid peace conference from his headquarters in Tunis. It was widely understood among Arabs and Europeans that major strategic decisions would need his approval.

Mahmoud Abbas, known as Abu Mazen, was the Quartet's top choice. For all of Bush's talk about democratic reform, Abu Mazen was named as a result of diplomatic pressure, not popular will. Long over-shadowed by Arafat's mythical status and scruffy charisma, Abbas had both nationalist and moderate credentials. He was a founding member of the PLO and someone who made quiet contact with the Israeli peace camp years before joining the secret negotiations that led to the

Oslo accords. He made no secret of his view that the prolonged intifada was a disaster for Palestinians. An aide, Maen Areikat, said that early in the uprising, Abbas told a group of Fatah and Palestinian Authority leaders, "You have sent a clear message to the Israelis . . . al-Aqsa is a redline." Now it was time to capitalize and allow a chance for political dialogue, he said.

But it was a measure of Abbas's weak political skills that he failed to persuade the gathering. "He was a minority voice," Areikat said.

Abbas was appointed in March, but it took more than a month for him to be confirmed by the Legislative Council. Still, Arafat stubbornly held on to his acquired levers of power. Here, the Quartet got help from the Palestinian lawmakers. Reflecting the battle fatigue, frustration, and disgust with the PA felt by many Palestinians, the elected parliament staged a rare show of defiance and demanded that Arafat relinquish strong powers to Abbas. This was one of a number of indications from the late 1990s onward that a desire for a more democratic and transparent government had taken root among Palestinians. "When Abbas was first appointed in March, 61 percent of the Palestinian public backed him," pollster Khalil Shikaki later wrote in *Foreign Affairs*. "The people expected him to deliver what Arafat could not: political reform, economic progress, an end to corruption, a return to negotiations with Israel, and the enforcement of security and a cease-fire."

Soon, the Palestinian Authority had the beginnings of a changed government, with Salam Fayyad, a respected former IMF official, as finance minister and Mohammed Dahlan—a longtime Gaza strongman, reared in Khan Younis, who had worked with the CIA and U.S. negotiators—as minister of state for security. The lineup was acceptable to the Quartet, the White House, and Israel. But with the exception of Fayyad, it hardly represented the "new leadership" demanded by Bush the previous June. Whatever his merits, Abbas had been part of an "old guard" that over the previous decade bred cynicism among Palestinians with its lack of transparency and crony capitalism. Abbas's large villa on the outskirts of Gaza City drew envious looks from fellow Palestinians. A U.S. official who knew him in the late 1990s remarked, "He lives very well." (In 2005, a Bush administration official who championed the road map indicated this was of little concern to the Quartet. Of the Palestinian leadership generally, he said, "They all live well.") How effectively Abbas would separate himself from the rest of the old guard became an open question.

The well connected Dahlan, for his part, had a long record of contact and negotiations with the United States and Israel, as well as a reputation for using forces under his control to buttress his political influence. In April 2002 testimony before the Knesset Foreign Affairs and Defense Committee, Defense Minister Benjamin Ben-Eliezer said he had offered control of the Gaza Strip to Dahlan.

Having become a trusted aide to Arafat toward the end of the Palestinian leader's exile in Tunis, Dahlan was given a powerful role after the PLO set up a government in Gaza: control of the Palestinian Preventive Security Service (PPSS), responsible for heading off internal threats to the Palestinian Authority. Among those threats, during the Oslo years, were violent attacks against Israelis, since these undermined the Palestinians' continuing interest in upholding the peace accords. The PPSS was part of a multipronged security apparatus that practiced many of the dark arts long favored by other police services in the developing world. In 1997, Human Rights Watch (HRW) reported, based on the testimony of victims, "Most branches of the security forces have engaged in abusive conduct." Four years later, HRW described a continued involvement by the various services in "torture of detainees, arbitrary arrest, prolonged arbitrary detention, the imposition of the death penalty, and carrying out of executions after grossly unfair trials, the failure to bring to justice those responsible for vigilante killings, and the impunity of security forces and other officials who commit serious abuses." The PPSS also gained authority to collect various fees from Palestinian businesses, according to Israeli critics, in the process becoming a virtual protection racket.

Israelis recognized Abu Mazen as an improvement over Arafat but were torn on how to react. Moshe Yaalon, army chief of staff, argued that Israel's strategic situation had improved following the U.S. invasion of Iraq and the strong pressure put on Palestinians as a result of the 2002 invasion of the West Bank: "The best way to encourage Abu Mazen is to make the Palestinian people support him. And what I recommended is to ease the situation with the Palestinians, and when they will enjoy a better situation, they will be able to compare what they faced when they used terrorism and what they might face if they [ended] terrorism.

"Shabak [Shin Bet, domestic security service] managers thought another way. [Avi Dichter] didn't want to take risks. And the defense minister accepted his attitude. . . . I thought it was a tactical mistake. We are not the side to be blamed because of Abu Mazen's failure. . . . Anyhow, I thought that Abu Mazen in the end would fail because Arafat would not allow him to gain power. But we should gain some more time to enjoy the cease-fire."

Dov Weisglass, Sharon's chief of staff, asked Roed-Larsen if Abbas would be independent enough of Arafat to crack down on terror: "Will Abu Mazen be empowered?"

Roed-Larsen recalled: "And I said, 'That's a meaningless question, because only you can empower him.' And then he asked me, 'What can we do?' And I said, 'Leave Gaza. And then you show that Abu Mazen succeeds at the negotiating table, but Arafat is a failure because he speaks through the barrel of a gun. . . . You can have Arafat marginalized by doing this for Abu Mazen."

THE QUICK INITIAL American victory over Saddam Hussein's military provided the Middle East with a chance to pause and catch its breath. Soon, the postwar looting in Baghdad would give way to an intractable insurgency, turning Iraq into a nightmare. But the momentary vacuum prompted widespread uncertainty about Bush's next move. Israeli hardliners had their suggestions, which found an echo among like-minded figures in Washington.

"Israel's first postwar challenge is to convince America to stand firm against pressure from Europe and the Arab states to adopt the road map. The Palestinians must first be pressured into combating terror and revamping their system. Only then can a real process with Israel begin," wrote Major General (reserves) Ya'akov Amidror, former head of the IDF's National Defense College, in an essay for the Jerusalem Center for Public Affairs. ". . . Israel's second postwar challenge is to convince the

United States not to stop after Iraq. Otherwise, here in the Middle East the Hezbollah will continue to flourish, the Iranians will retain their missiles and their weapons of mass destruction, and Syria will remain as the capital of terrorism."

In mid-April, Dov Weisglass and other Israeli officials came to Washington to lobby for changes in the road map, which Sharon disliked. They had to settle for presenting a series of reservations, which the Bush administration promised to take into consideration. The deal struck in December among members of the Quartet was holding. Still, hardliners continued trying to shape the postwar agenda.

From his influential perch at the American Enterprise Institute, a crucible of neoconservative ideas, former House Speaker Newt Gingrich launched a preemptive strike against State Department intentions of shifting the United States' focus to the Arab-Israeli peace track. The United States now had the chance "to apply genuine economic, diplomatic, and political pressure on Syria," he argued in a speech attacking Colin Powell's department. He went on to criticize the diplomatic quartet comprising the United States, the UN, Europe, and Russia, sponsors of the road map. This grouping represented "a deliberate and systematic effort to undermine the president's policies procedurally by ensuring they will consistently be watered down and distorted by the other three members." It was "a clear disaster for American diplomacy."

The hawkish Center for Security Policy went further: "The Bush administration is obliquely serving notice on Syria that it could be the next country liberated in the war on terror," a brief from the center stated. "Few steps would do more to create an opportunity for a real, just, and durable Arab-Israeli peace than to accompany the liquidation of Saddam's support for suicide bombers and other forms of terror with the elimination of the Syrian/Lebanese base of operations of and much of the support for the Palestinian Islamic Jihad."

Opening a new front against other rogue regimes was not a total fantasy. "Yes, the planning was done. Yes, I was briefed on the planning," said Lawrence Wilkerson, Powell's chief of staff at the State Department. Military contingency plans existed "for both Syria and Iran," he said. "We were a little bit shocked that planning had proceeded to the point where they were actually briefing." When Defense Secretary Donald Rumsfeld, after the Iraq invasion, delivered harsh warnings to Syria, "those of us in the know were very worried that we were going to cross the border. . . ."

The administration rebuffed a spring 2003 overture from Tehran's Foreign Ministry, conveyed by Switzerland, for broad talks with the United States. Flynt Leverett, who by then had left his job as Middle East expert on the National Security Council staff and would soon be leaving the government, told a Council on Foreign Relations interviewer in 2006 that the message "basically laid out an agenda for a diplomatic process that was intended to resolve on a comprehensive basis all of the bilateral differences between the United States and Iran." Besides its nuclear program, the differences included Iran's support for terrorist groups, opposition to any Arab-Israeli peace process, and refusal to accept Israel's right to exist. If Iran were serious, the talks presumably could include recognition of Israel.

One of the consequences of the two-decade freeze in U.S.-Iranian relations is that the United States has had to rely on the accounts of intermediaries to glean Iran's intentions, and can't be sure how much authority to attach to any particular overture. In this case, however, there was no effort even to follow up on the approach.

"We got instructions at the State Department that we would tell the Swiss, in our official response to their offer, that they had overstepped their bounds," Wilkerson told me in 2006, his voice cracking with anger. He attributed the rebuff to Vice President Cheney.

THE "ENERGIZER BUNNY," Marwan Muasher, had his work cut out for him when he headed for Washington at the end of April 2003. Worried about Iraqi instability, Jordan wanted American troops withdrawn as soon as possible, with Iraq's army left intact and a representative government put in place. Muasher also pressed in every forum provided to him—including an interview on the high-profile NBC *Meet the Press* and the *New York Times* op-ed page—for a resumption of peace efforts, with release of the road map as the top priority. He told NBC's Tim Russert that "there is certainly a huge anti-U.S. feeling now in the area, but it does not stem from Saddam Hussein. I think that it also stems from the need to deal with the other problem on our hands, the Arab-Israeli conflict." King Abdullah, interviewed on CNN, said, "If we don't move quickly, then everybody in the Middle East will say, well, this [the Iraq War] is just part of an agenda and there's a list of who's next."

Bush finally released the road map on April 30. A senior administration official said, "When the document came out, it was viewed very negatively by the American Jewish community and the Israelis." The official tried to persuade them: "I don't quite get it. I don't understand why you think this is so bad." For the present, Washington's policy sights shifted from further military adventures in the war on terrorism and toward a Middle East political horizon. As American troops struggled unsuccessfully to stabilize Iraq in the face of Iraqi insurgents and Arab terrorists drawn in to fight the occupying U.S. enemy, there was less talk in Washington of a "pivot" by U.S. forces to topple the regimes in Damascus and Tehran. The Bush administration, in fact, was getting alarming news from Iraq. "We had the CIA station chief writing a cable within thirty days, saying, 'This is a dire situation you've gotten yourselves in, folks, very bad, and it's going to get a lot worse,'" said Lawrence Wilkerson.

As Iraq deteriorated, the Middle East conflict began to look like an issue where the United States could score a badly needed success. In Israel, Sharon sounded a more moderate theme following the appointment of Abbas as prime minister. "Despite all the victims, cracks appeared in the Palestinian belief that Israel could be defeated by force. That's the reason for the first signs that perhaps an arrangement is possible. I don't intend to miss this opportunity," he said in an interview with Ynet, the English-language Web site of *Yediot Ahronoth*. Skeptics were unconvinced of a change. Zeev Schiff, the respected national security commentator for *Haaretz*, viewed Sharon's moves skeptically: "Israeli policy today is focused more on two main aims. One of them is to make a good impression in Washington, but the major objective is to do everything possible so that Israel will not be blamed for the failure of the current move, at the center of which is the road map. That is, so that the failure will be perceived as the Palestinians' handiwork."

But Sharon continued to surprise. On May 26, 2003, he told the Likud Party in a speech broadcast on Israel Radio, "To keep 3.5 million people under occupation is bad for us and them," and said he was committed to finding a solution. "This can't continue endlessly. Do you want to remain forever in Ramallah, Jenin, Nablus?"

Marwan Muasher allowed himself a flight of optimism: "We are on the verge of peace," the Associated Press quoted him as saying. Three days later, Jordan issued official invitations to Sharon and Mahmoud Abbas to join President Bush and King Abdullah at a summit in Aqaba, on the Red Sea. At a press conference, Muasher noted that both Israel and the Palestinians had accepted the road map. He did not mention Israel's multiple reservations. "We believe that this is a very positive development. We also believe that the United States and the U.S. president are serious, which is what made Israel accept the road map."

13

Riding Herd

RICHARD ARMITAGE'S RASPY voice reached John Wolf on the second hole of the Columbia Country Club outside Washington just before Memorial Day, 2003. He told Wolf that Secretary of State Colin Powell wanted to talk to him the following Tuesday about going to the Middle East. "Rich, why?" Wolf asked Powell's deputy and close friend. "Talk to the secretary," Armitage said. Wolf put away his cell phone and whacked his ball with a 9 iron straight onto the green. An omen? he wondered as he caught up with his golfing companions. His remaining sixteen holes were a disappointment.

Two and a half weeks later, Wolf, a trim, boyish-looking veteran diplomat of fifty-four, arrived in the Middle East as the third Bush administration envoy to attempt to curb Palestinian terrorism, loosen the Israeli grip on the West Bank and Gaza, and move Israeli and Palestinian leaders toward peace negotiations. The cease-fire brokered by CIA director George Tenet in the spring of 2001 had quickly broken down. Retired Marine General Anthony Zinni tried in late 2001 and again in 2002 but ultimately failed, his efforts undone by the horrendous Park Hotel suicide bombing and Israel's violent reoccupation of the West Bank.

Before and during the invasion of Iraq in the spring of 2003, Bush had promised his closest ally, Tony Blair, and friendly Arab leaders that he would launch a new peace effort between Israel and the Palestinians once the war was over. With the end of major combat, Bush set out to fulfill his pledge. The United States would help finance and train a restructured Palestinian security apparatus that, in cooperation with Israel, would lock up terrorists and detect and prevent acts of violence against Israelis. Israel, in turn, would pull back its forces to the positions they held before the intifada erupted in late September 2000 and ease the siege that had shattered the Palestinian economy. In charge of a team of American monitors (dubbed "the Wolf pack" by a Washington reporter) Wolf would, in Bush's words, "ride herd" on the process.

Entering Powell's stately office early that last Tuesday in May, Wolf still wondered why he had been chosen. "You know I don't know anything about the Middle East," he told the secretary. Wolf's three decades in the foreign service had ranged widely, from early postings in Australia and Vietnam and Pakistan to ambassadorships to Malaysia, the Asia-Pacific Economic Forum and the Caspian Basin. He was well-known in international security circles. He served twice under John Bolton, a driven neoconservative who was relentless in his pursuit of rogue states and UN improprieties. In the early '90s, Wolf helped craft the UN Security Council resolutions that authorized the first Gulf War and later imposed severe economic and weapons sanctions on Iraq. In the George W. Bush administration, Wolf was assistant secretary of state for arms control, focused heavily on North Korea and Iraq's suspected weapons of mass destruction. He became estranged from his boss over Bolton's treatment of another subordinate and intolerance of dissent. Wolf was the one who delivered U.S. intelligence—much of it vague or flawed, as it turned out—to guide the chief UN weapons inspector, Hans Blix, in an aborted search for Iraq's banned weapons. (Unlike Bolton and many others in the administration, Wolf came to respect the intractable Swede.)

Powell dismissed Wolf's misgivings about his lack of expertise on the region, telling him energy and tough negotiating skills were more important. "I later heard that he described me as his 'junkyard dog,' whatever that means." As with Zinni, Powell wanted someone who could bang heads together. Meeting with Bush at the White House before setting out, Wolf pointed out once more that he didn't know the Middle East.

The president told him, in essence, that this was a good thing. Previous efforts had been based on what had failed to work in the past. Now the administration had a new vision and a new policy and had talked about an independent Palestinian state. Look forward toward the vision, Bush told him.

"In a way, I think the U.S. leadership team probably didn't want somebody who was going to be drawn into long and Talmudic discussions about what did and didn't work at Taba and Camp David, the interim agreement, Oslo, Camp David One. Whatever. That wasn't my job," he reflected later.

At least on the surface, the "U.S. leadership team" seemed to be on the same wavelength after more than two years of infighting. Bush pronounced himself cautiously optimistic about making headway and, in contrast to the first two years of his administration, willing to spend time and political capital. Unlike the Zinni mission, this wasn't just "Powell's baby." Bush took charge publicly and stayed on top of it. Powell and National Security Adviser Condoleezza Rice were assigned to make it "a matter of the highest priority."

ELEVEN MONTHS HAD passed since Bush, in a landmark speech on June 24, 2002, called on Palestinians to elect new leaders untainted by terrorism and corruption as a necessary first step toward a two-state solution of the Israeli-Palestinian conflict. The speech opened the way for Europeans and diplomats from moderate Arab states to develop the road map peace plan, which Bush formally released on April 30, 2003, after the Iraq invasion was completed and Mahmoud Abbas, a respected Palestine Liberation Organization veteran, had been installed as the new Palestinian prime minister.

Bush's new involvement reached a high-water mark during a pair of summits on his way home from the annual Group of 8 meeting—at Sharm el-Sheikh, Egypt, with Arab allies, and then at Aqaba, Jordan, with Sharon, Abbas, and Jordan's King Abdullah.

The choice of Aqaba for the three-way summit reflected Jordan's leading role in developing the road map, its deep and historical connection to the Palestinians, and the fact that its ties with Israeli leaders continued to withstand the strains of bitter regional conflict. The summit, however, would turn out to be the high point of Jordan's role as a peace broker. In coming months, moderate Arabs and Europeans would be increasingly sidelined in Middle East diplomacy. And Jordan encountered opposition in its bid to help Palestinians develop a professional security force that would crack down on terrorism. As Marwan Muasher, foreign minister from 2002 to 2004, later recalled in an e-mail exchange: "Jordan was indeed involved in trying to develop an effective Palestinian security force. One of the ideas was to send the Badr Brigade, a Palestinian force of about two thousand people who were previously part of the Palestinian Liberation Army, and who had been in Jordan for decades, to the West Bank to beef up the security forces. Both the Palestinians [at least Arafat] and the Israelis objected. Sharon did not want to send more Palestinian security forces into the West Bank, and Arafat was worried these forces were too close to Jordan."

At Aqaba, both Sharon and Abbas made important new rhetorical concessions to the other side: noting how Palestinians had suffered from occupation, Abbas added, "At the same time, we do not ignore the suffering of the Jews throughout history. It is time to bring all this suffering to an end." He also said of terrorism, "Such methods are inconsistent with our religious and moral traditions and are dangerous obstacles to the achievement of an independent, sovereign state we seek. These methods also conflict with the kind of state we wish to build, based on human rights and the rule of law."

Sharon said, "The government and people of Israel welcome the opportunity to renew direct negotiations according to the steps of the road map as adopted by the Israeli government to achieve this vision.

"It is in Israel's interest not to govern the Palestinians, but for the Palestinians to govern themselves in their own state. A democratic Palestinian state, fully at peace with Israel, will promote the long-term security and well-being of Israel as a Jewish state. . . . We can also reassure our Palestinian partners that we understand the importance of territorial contiguity in the West Bank for a viable Palestinian state. Israeli policy in the territories that are subject to direct negotiations with the Palestinians will reflect this fact. We accept the principle that no

unilateral actions by any party can prejudge the outcome of our negotiations. In regard to the unauthorized outposts, I want to reiterate that
Israel is a society governed by the rule of law. Thus, we will immediately
begin to remove unauthorized outposts." His speech contained two
loopholes: the road map "as adopted by the Israeli government" could
be interpreted to include fourteen Israeli "reservations" to the document;
territories "subject to direct negotiation" suggested that parts of the West
Bank or East Jerusalem could be taken off the table.

Bush was pleased enough with the summit to invite reporters to his
Air Force One cabin for an unusually lengthy and relaxed midair briefing, further placing his personal stamp on the peace effort. Describing
a three-way meeting with Sharon and Abbas, he said, "What I wanted
to do is to observe the interplay between the two; did they have the
capacity to relax in each other's presence, for starters. And I felt they did.
In other words, it was—the body language was positive. There wasn't
a lot of hostility or suspicion." He called Abbas "a partner in peace,"
and said, "I've spent enough time with Ariel Sharon to know he's the
kind of guy, when he says something, he means it. I'm getting the same
sense about Prime Minister Abbas."

Still, the Aqaba meeting could not have been easy for Sharon. Bush
had spent twice as much time listening to Arab leaders as to him.
Sharon had previously shown with his Czechoslovakia outburst how sensitive he was to signs of U.S.-Arab collaboration. The White House stood
solidly behind the road map, which Sharon "loathed," according to his
national security adviser. Bush had stopped in Egypt and Jordan but,
despite being in his third year of office, had yet to visit Israel. And a year
after Bush sided with Sharon in cutting off contact with Arafat, a new
Palestinian leader was gaining international support and making a
favorable impression on the president. Abu Mazen, moreover, had
already won the admiration of a number of Israelis for his perceived
commitment to nonviolence.

Worse, Israelis—particularly the military leadership—thought the
Americans were being given a snow job by the Palestinians about what
it would require for them to confront the militant groups.

"We thought that the United States should force Abu Mazen to act immediately against the terror organizations. But Abu Mazen and especially Dahlan convinced the president that they need more time to reorganize the troops, the security apparatus, etc. . . . It was ridiculous," Yaalon said.

"In Aqaba [Dahlan] came with a PowerPoint demonstration. He showed a ninety-day plan to reorganize the troops and then to deal with the terror. And I was shouting. I lost my voice. . . ."

Sharon's meeting with Bush at Aqaba brought up sore points. Referring to notes from the session, a senior administration official reported, "Sharon did a lot of complaining about the Palestinians, obviously about security, about the number of attacks and [the Palestinians'] inability to deal with it."

The president "pushed back several times," according to the official. "'What about the positive side? What about what they are trying to do? . . . What can you do to help?' . . . And Sharon kept repeating, 'He's got to act against terror.' The president said, 'I agree with you, but we've got to help him. We've all got to help him. . . . I'm not asking you to take risks to your security. I'm asking you, how can you help him succeed?'" The import of Bush's remarks, the official said, was, "Complaining isn't a policy."

Bush also raised the problem of settlement outposts, which the United States had repeatedly demanded be demolished. According to one account, Bush accused Sharon of failing to keep an earlier promise to take them down. Sharon renewed the pledge to dismantle what Israelis referred to as unauthorized outposts.

A senior official who was present during the Bush-Sharon session said his notes don't mention another exchange that, if it occurred, casts a shadow on the state of the relationship at the time. It was described later privately to a well-known U.S. Middle East expert in Washington. The exchange involved so-called natural growth within settlements to make room for expanding families. U.S. policy called for no expansion of settlements, period. The Middle East expert was told Sharon's comments infuriated Bush.

Raanan Gissin, a longtime Sharon adviser, believes the exchange occurred. "He said it several times, not just that one time. He said it several times. Maybe in Aqaba he made it very clear. . . . He mentioned,

'What do you want to tell them, not to have any babies, not to give birth?' . . . He said, 'What do you want? Do you want that we send them all to conduct abortions?' You know, because it's a sensitive issue with Bush anyway," Gissin said with a slight chuckle. "He was just stating very clearly something that Israel cannot do. The relationship . . . was very clear. When Bush wanted to know something, the prime minister would tell him."

Sharon got his point across, according to Gissin. The issue of natural growth "was never raised again," he said.

Two other important regional players—barred from the two-day festivities—had reason to seethe, with consequences that would become evident later. One was Arafat, eating and sleeping in the same small room amid the ruins of the Muqata compound while Abu Mazen represented the Palestinian people on the world stage.

"I think for Arafat the meaning was very clear," Abington said of the Abu Mazen appointment as prime minister. "The U.S. put heavy pressure on the Palestinian Authority to create the position of prime minister and that was a means of getting around Arafat, getting around the Arafat problem. Everyone knew it. Arafat knew it and deeply resented it."

The other uninvited leader was Syrian president Bashar al-Assad. Bush rubbed it in, telling his press pool that during the Sharm el-Sheikh meeting, "We also spent a lot of time talking about Syria, and the mutual concern about Syria and the desire to convince Syria to shut down terrorist offices inside—in Damascus. So there was a very helpful discussion. I think it was very helpful for Prime Minister Abbas to hear that."

While the United States was holding out the prospect for Palestinians of a resumption of peace talks if they halted violence, al-Assad got the cold shoulder from Washington. No one even mentioned renewing the Israeli-Syrian peace track. Sharon flatly opposed yielding the Golan Heights, the widely understood price for peace with Syria. At the time, the chief pro-Israel lobbying arm in Washington—the American Israel Public Affairs Committee—was giving high priority to getting a new anti-Syria bill—called the Syrian Accountability Act—through Congress. Al-Assad, who clung to the conceit that no peace could be made without Syria, had ways of acting out. Leaders of the most militant Palestinian groups were headquartered in Damascus.

THE AQABA SUMMIT might have set the stage for Wolf to arrive on a high note, had the violence subsided even slightly. Instead, it got dramatically worse. Four days after Aqaba, the three main militant groups, Hamas, Islamic Jihad, and the al-Aqsa Martyrs' Brigades, staged a joint attack on the Erez crossing, the heavily guarded crossing point from Israel into Gaza used by civilians, diplomats, journalists, and Palestinian VIPs. This was a well planned attack aimed at the Israeli military, and therefore all the more unnerving to the top brass. Four Israeli soldiers were killed. "Another solider was killed in a separate incident. Such attacks can be seen only as direct challenges to Palestinian prime minister Abbas, who has been working to achieve a cessation of all forms of violence by Palestinian groups," UN Undersecretary General Kieran Prendergast told the Security Council.

Two years before, Sharon had shown remarkable restraint after the atrocious Dolphinarium bombing, bowing to an international effort to secure a cease-fire. But not this time.

Israel struck back with the attempted assassination of Abdel Aziz Rantisi, a top Hamas leader in Gaza, using helicopter gunships. He wasn't badly injured, but three others died, including a woman and her three-year-old child. Israel was roundly criticized by the UN, Europe, and Bush, who inserted a biting statement into public welcoming remarks for the president of Uganda: "Before we begin our discussions I do want to say something on the Middle East. I am troubled by the recent Israeli helicopter gunship attacks. I regret the loss of innocent life. I'm concerned that the attacks will make it more difficult for the Palestinian leadership to fight off terrorist attacks." Crucially, he added: "I also don't believe the attacks help the Israeli security." This was a rare breach of White House custom. Even when criticizing Israel, the White House usually avoided second-guessing Israeli security judgments. The statement suggested Israeli motives other than self-defense were at work. Fervent supporters of Israel were furious and let the White House know. "I thought that criticism was bizarre and ill-conceived and counterproductive," Gary Bauer, the evangelical Christian president of American Values, told me. "I did an e-mail to our followers around the country and expressed my extreme disappointment with what the president had said, and I said that if you agree I'm sure the White House would be interested in hearing from you—because I know that my list is made up overwhelmingly of people that have voted for the president twice.

"When I came in the next morning I wasn't quite sure what to expect because I know my list is extremely pro-Bush and I was being critical. But what I found when I came in was just an astonishing number of e-mails and faxes very thoughtfully written, for the most part—many of them from people who when they wrote the president said, 'Mr. President, I was your county chairman in this county in Nebraska,' or 'My wife and I ran your campaign in northern Georgia and we're looking forward to working for your reelection and so you can understand how disappointed we were when we saw you criticizing the government of Israel for doing no more than we would do under the same circumstances.' And that was a case where the tone of the White House did change over the following twenty-four hours and I'd like to think that it was at least in part because of some of those messages that I'm sure the president heard about. . . . I did hear later from people that the White House had gotten a lot of feedback that was negative and they went back to the drawing board."

In the region, the violent cycle continued over the next three days, with a horrendous suicide bus bombing in Jerusalem that killed seventeen people, drawing condemnation by Bush, and more Israeli air strikes in Gaza, including the assassination of Yasser Taha, a member of the Hamas military wing, together with his wife and two children, three and five. All told, the three days left twenty-three dead.

The White House was buffeted by crosscurrents. Stung by Bush's criticism of Israel, the leading pro-Israel lobby group, AIPAC, said the Jewish state "will and must take the responsibility to fight terrorist organizations" and "it should be the policy of the U.S. to support" such actions. On June 25, the U.S. House of Representatives voted 399 to 5 to express solidarity with Israelis and support their right to fight terrorism, undercutting White House criticism of the assassinations.

On the House floor, Majority Leader Tom DeLay said, "Mr. Speaker, today Israelis will wake up and go to work. They may drive their children to day care or have lunch with their friends. Israeli children will go to school and play with their classmates. We do not know which ones and we do not know where, but soon some of them will probably die. A bright light will flash, a terrifying concussion will bloom through the air, and in an instant fear, blood, panic, pain, and death. And somewhere in Gaza, violent men will laugh. If this is not evil, nothing is."

In Paris, meanwhile, Quartet envoys heard a proposal from Roed-Larsen to push the road map rapidly in a new direction. "I produced a paper proposing a Gaza withdrawal as a way to leapfrog the road map forward. . . . So I put it on the table for everybody . . . and then the answer I got back from Washington was that this was a very good idea but it was totally unrealistic."

Roed-Larsen also sent copies to Eiland and Dahlan. To Israelis, it may have been read as an ominous sign of the continued pressure they could expect from the international community; to Palestinians, it may have raised what were, at the time, exaggerated expectations. Dahlan pressed Roed-Larsen to pursue an Israeli withdrawal of some kind. "It's not even necessary to give us the whole of Gaza. If they leave three settlements, Abu Mazen will be a success," Roed-Larsen quoted him as saying.

Far from gaining territory, Palestinians were losing it piecemeal. In late June, the special rapporteur for the UN Human Rights Commission, John Dugard, arrived for a firsthand look at the separation barrier. Israel refused to deal with Dugard, viewing his organization as irredeemably biased. But his assessment of the barrier's likely impact was similar to an earlier report by B'Tselem, an Israeli human rights group, and to what U.S. officials were learning. The barrier, he said, "incorporates substantial areas of the West Bank into Israel. Over 210,000 Palestinians will be seriously affected by the wall. Palestinians living between the wall and the Green Line will be effectively cut off from their farmlands and workplaces, schools, health clinics, and other social services. This is likely to lead to a new generation of refugees or internally displaced persons."

Against this backdrop, it fell to Wolf to fulfill a mundane but necessary assignment: prodding Israelis and Palestinians through the detailed first phase of the road map. "I didn't want people to get confused about what I was there to do." He told them, "If you don't go through here [phase one], you won't get to there [peace and statehood]. . . . You can't get to the future if you don't go through the present."

His no-nonsense assignment of tasks to each side impressed Saeb Erekat, the veteran Palestinian negotiator. "This man wanted to cut a long story short. This man wouldn't lecture us, and he didn't want to be lectured to."

Wolf "came to my office, opened his briefcase, put a paper on the table, 'One, incitement; two, media; three, tunnels; four, smuggling. Are these your obligations, Dr. Erekat?' 'Yes, those are my obligations.' 'I expect them to be done in two weeks' time.' So I go to Abu Mazen and Abu Amar [Arafat] and say, 'This man knows his job—I can't beat around the bush.' And I know that he went to the Israelis with a similar list."

The envoy's immediate focus was controlling violence in Gaza, where Israeli settlers felt under threat and where Qassam rockets were being fired on nearby Israeli communities. "Israelis had a sort of neuralgic sense about the rockets. One rocket almost took out the power plant [north of Gaza] and that would have taken out the power for a third of Israel. And . . . the prime minister's farm was not far away."

"But it was more symbolic. . . . If the Palestinians couldn't control Gaza, how were they going to control the West Bank? And it was a place where Dahlan was supposed to have some authority." Meeting with senior security officials of both sides, Wolf worked out "commitments and obligations of the Palestinians, commitments and obligations of the Palestinians and Israelis engaged together, and commitments and obligations of the Israelis. We had nine baskets of those things. And we evaluated each one every week." Besides security, the Palestinians were to institute important reforms in their government and reduce incitement to violence in the media. How seriously Wolf was taken by the Israelis was quickly called into question by the fact that as he got down to work, Dov Weisglass, Sharon's chief of staff, and Avi Dichter, head of the domestic security service Shin Bet, were holding high-level meetings in Washington, according to the *Forward*. Yaalon, for his part, declined to comment on Wolf personally during a 2006 interview but said slowly: "Generally speaking, about American envoys, they are too naive to really understand the situation. And I met all of them." The one exception he mentioned was Tenet.

On separate occasions later, Yaalon and Dichter conveyed their attitude toward Palestinian security cooperation in similarly colorful ways. Yaalon invoked the acronym IBM for the Arabic expressions *"Inshallah"* (God willing); *"buchra"* (tomorrow morning) and *"Maalesh"* ("What can we do?"). Dichter spoke of the "Yanni culture," the Arabic expression *"yanni"* conveying vagueness and uncertainty.

Wolf was intent on getting the two sides to meet their obligations in parallel—"Both wheels have got to turn for the bicycle to go forward." But the Israelis didn't accept that. Instead, "they all responded to the prime minister, and the prime minister, either directly or through Dubie [Dov] Weisglass, had a specific line. And that line was that 'we'll act when the Palestinians have shown that they're taking actions to stem terrorism.'" Washington didn't object.

"The fact of the matter is, though, that their commitments and their obligations weren't really conditional. They chose to interpret them as conditional and we chose to let them—or people in Washington came to accept them as conditional, notwithstanding what we used to tell the Israelis." Nevertheless, Wolf's first two weeks brought progress. After a long, explosive, three-way U.S.-Israeli-Palestinian meeting, agreement was reached on shifting security responsibility at various parts of Gaza from Israel to the Palestinians. "The result was that the arrangements that they put in place actually permitted movement north to south and south to north. And back and forth." The lifting of Israeli restrictions and checkpoints brought a quick improvement in Gaza life. Palestinians also assumed security responsibility for Bethlehem on the West Bank.

"There was such a huge change in the tone of Gaza between mid-late-June when I first went there and mid-late-July, after they had been able to travel for a few weeks: stores were open, people were in the street, produce on the sidewalks, kids playing in the street. I was reporting to Condi on things that were going on and I said, 'There are even kids playing in the street.' She said, 'Is that good?' I said, 'Of course, yes, because their parents aren't afraid to let them out of the house.'" Salam Fayyad, the new finance minister, applied his informal index of economic activity—how late do the stores stay open?—and noticed they were still selling as late as 11 PM or midnight. He told Wolf he was encouraged. At the UN, Roed-Larsen gave the Security Council an optimistic update: "Regular meetings are occurring between the Palestinian and Israeli prime ministers, and Palestinians and Israelis meet frequently at the ministerial level to discuss such issues as security, prisoners, incitement, economic development, investment, and health. Credit for this progress should go first to the leaders of Israel and the Palestinian Authority. They deserve to be commended for their courageous pursuit of the peace process."

Israel demanded that Abbas and Dahlan confront militant groups preemptively, arresting leaders responsible for past terror attacks and disarming them. Abbas, fearing civil war, instead proceeded with Egyptian help to persuade the groups to halt attacks on Israelis. How and when they were to be disabled as paramilitary organizations was never specified. The United States accepted this as a temporary tactic while Dahlan built up his forces. Israeli officials believed the militants had agreed to the truce out of exhaustion and would use a period of quiet to rebuild their forces. While Israelis refrained from targeted killings at the outset, Yaalon made clear to Colin Powell during a visit to Washington how unhappy he was with the delay in a serious crackdown by Palestinians: "I said, 'It is a mistake; we will pay for it.' The Palestinians succeeded in cheating the Americans, escaping a confrontation with terrorism, earned time, and I said, 'At the end of the day they will not do anything. We should force them immediately to operate.' They had the capability."

Abbas continued to be persuasive with Bush during his first visit to the White House as prime minister on July 25. Standing next to Abbas in the Rose Garden, Bush criticized the Israeli separation barrier, even adopting the Palestinians' name for it, which Israelis said was incorrect and misleading. "I think the wall is a problem," Bush said. "It is very difficult to develop confidence between the Palestinians and Israel with a wall snaking through the West Bank." Abbas seized on the public appearance with Bush to make demands that would resonate at home and shore up his weak position. He called on Israel to free thousands of Palestinians imprisoned during the intifada, lift the siege on Arafat at his compound in Ramallah, pull Israeli troops back from Palestinian areas, and remove checkpoints blocking freedom of movement to jobs and schools.

Israel quickly announced it would free 540 prisoners. By the time Bush met with Sharon four days after Abbas's visit, the president's tone on the separation barrier had softened. Sharon was eager for the issue not to drive a wedge between him and Washington and instructed Dov Weisglass to conduct quiet negotiations with Rice over the route.

A senior Bush administration official, speaking in the summer of 2005, traced Abbas's demise as prime minister to his July White House visit. "Arafat couldn't stand the idea that he was barred from the White House and this guy was there with all that limelight. . . ." The official didn't mention that in the zero-sum equation that infuses the Israeli-Palestinian conflict, the White House attention lavished on Abbas complicated Sharon's life. If Abbas progressed in instituting reform and controlling terrorism, either with a crackdown or with his preferred quiet "*hudna*," or truce, he would then be in a strong position to demand final-status negotiations.

Wolf considered Abbas to be something of a hero, "in that he was the first Palestinian at that level to make clear that you couldn't achieve a Palestinian state with the use of violence. I think he was sincere and I believe he remains sincere," Wolf said in 2005. "He was very clear. He said, 'I am sure that I can get at the negotiating table what I can't get on the battlefield. Violence won't get us there. It will simply bring the wrath of the Israelis down on us. But I'll be stronger at the negotiating table than they are.' He felt like he had more international political support and even a historic opening. That is, there was supposed to have been a Palestinian state on the West Bank and Gaza. And the fact that the Jordanians and the Egyptians gobbled it up in 1948 didn't change the terms of reference."

Another hero, in Wolf's eyes, was Salam Fayyad, the finance minister: "Fayyad was beginning to give structure at least to the economic processes that the Palestinians pursued—a budget, the accounts on line, breaking up the petroleum monopoly, the cement monopoly, direct deposits—a whole series of things. . . . He was one of the smartest, most effective financial officials I've dealt with." For a brief period, the Palestinian information minister, Nabil Amr, also began fulfilling another commitment. Wolf noticed "a spike downwards in incitement."

The missing link was the man Wolf was counting on to gain control of Palestinian security, the seasoned negotiator and Gaza strongman, the one who had impressed Bush with his PowerPoint—Mohammed Dahlan. He was, Wolf found, "a lot of talk, but not much action—a big disappointment for me. Everybody said he had all these enormous capabilities to do things in Gaza, and nobody told the story better than he did, and yet, when push came to shove, time after time, he fell short with the constant excuse that 'I need to have equipment, I need to have this, I need to have that.' I think he was spending most of his time positioning himself for some future role and not spending enough time in the role that he had taken on then." (According to *Haaretz*, he was already preparing a bill. Rebuilding the Palestinian police posts destroyed by Israeli forces would cost $250 million and take three years, he said.)

About the Israelis, Wolf said, "I sometimes thought the Israeli military may have had a sense of what needed to happen. . . . I think there's a sense in the Israeli military that this is corrosive, that having young soldiers out on checkpoints playing tough with civilians—men, women, and children—doesn't fit the fabric of Israel's military, of what a soldier should do. But they're very disciplined, and they will do what needs to be done in order to implement the policies of the elected government. And I think at least at the top—I mean, some of them were much tougher and harder-line than others—but I don't think anybody thought that being an occupying force . . . [was] necessarily what they joined the military for." Of the military leadership, "All of them, under certain or different circumstances, could have been helpful, creative."

Israel made a modest show of dismantling settlement outposts as Bush had demanded at Aqaba. According to the UN, of the sixty outposts then existing, Israel dismantled eight. One was rebuilt; another twelve were begun, of which five were dismantled. So, two and a half months after Aqaba, the total still stood at sixty. More significant was the expansion of existing settlements. In a briefing to the Security Council, the UN reported that Israel had approved bypass roads for three West Bank locations and was discussing incentives for new Jewish residents "in the Jordan Valley, East Jerusalem, and elsewhere." In Gaza, where Wolf was concentrating his efforts, Israel announced it would build a number of new housing units at one settlement and expand the land area around another.

Meanwhile, checkpoints, closures, and curfews hobbled the West Bank's economy. Construction of the separation barrier continued apace, trapping thousands of Palestinians on the Israeli side, cut off from communities and jobs, the UN reported.

July turned out to be the high point of Wolf's mission. The informal truce began collapsing with an August 8 Israeli raid on what officials said was a bomb-making factory in a Nablus refugee camp that killed two Hamas activists and two civilians. Four days later, two Israelis were killed and more than a dozen injured in a pair of suicide bombings in Rosh Ha'ayin and the West Bank settlement of Ariel. Then, on August 14, Israel killed an Islamic Jihad leader in Hebron.

Wolf was back in the United States on ten days' leave to attend a wedding but had left behind "homework" for the Israeli and Palestinian security teams: "We gave them each eight or nine different things that they were supposed to do, the most important of which was to reach agreement on the transfer of authority for West Bank towns and cities," he said. On the morning of August 19, Danilo Turk, UN assistant secretary-general for political affairs, warned the Security Council that violence was rising: "The terrible cycle of violence and revenge must not be allowed once again to gather momentum." As he spoke, the security talks neared agreement on the plan to shift security responsibility to the Palestinians in Qalqilya, Jericho, Ramallah, and Tulkarem. This would have replicated the same kind of withdrawal that had brought Gaza back to life. By that evening, the deal was set, and the two sides were preparing to sign it.

Shortly after 9 PM, Raed Abdel Hamid Masq, a twenty-nine-year-old schoolteacher and mosque preacher from the West Bank town of Hebron, pressed his way into the middle of a crowded, two-section, accordion-style bus then nearing a poor Jerusalem neighborhood named

for the prophet Samuel. The bus was filled with Orthodox Jews returning home from the Western Wall. Masq, who according to some reports
was dressed to blend in with the worshippers, triggered a powerful
explosive. Altogether, twenty-three people died, including at least five
children and Lilach Kardi, twenty-two, eight months pregnant, who had
gone to pray for an easy birth. More than one hundred were hospitalized. Both Hamas and Islamic Jihad claimed responsibility, but Hamas
released a videotape of the bomber, who said he was retaliating for
Israel's killing of a Hamas leader in Hebron. Abdel Aziz Rantisi, however, denied knowledge and claimed Hamas was still adhering to the
truce, suggesting a split in the movement, according to a 2006 book by
Matthew Levitt, written while he was a senior fellow at the Washington
Institute for Near East Policy.

Wolf cut short his leave in the United States, arriving in Israel the next
afternoon. For the next several hours, he pushed Dahlan to take strong
action against militant groups in the territory he controlled—Gaza. "All
that evening—almost from the time I got to my hotel room until probably midnight or later, I was back and forth with Weisglass and the Israeli
military talking about what would be enough to prevent them from beating the bejesus out of the Palestinians, which they were preparing to do.
And I sort of laid out a list of four or five things that I was going to talk
about: stopping the rockets; establishing checkpoints; picking up arms
that were being carried openly on the street; dealing with the bomb-
making factories; and closing down the tunnels."

Israel didn't wait long. Late the next morning, August 21, a rocket
from an Israeli helicopter gunship struck a car in Gaza City, killing a
prominent Hamas spokesman, Ismail Abu Shanab, and two body-
guards. A U.S.-trained engineer who taught at Islamic University, Abu
Shanab had been a Hamas liaison with Abbas's government and was a
strong advocate of maintaining Palestinian unity. In soft-spoken English,
he had explained Hamas positions and ideology over tea with Western
journalists in the tidy sitting room of his home in Gaza City. Defending
suicide bombing against civilian targets during an interview in March
2000, six months before the intifada erupted, he said that most Israelis
could not be considered civilians, since all were expected to serve in the

army and remain on reserve duty. Lacking powerful weapons, he said, "[w]e can do at least something which can create the fear inside Israelis and not let them live peacefully on our ground. We tell them, 'We do not fear all your weapons. We have people, individual weapons. [A suicide bomber] can do what you can't deter." Shortly before his death, he had appeared on Al Jazeera to say that without "resistance," "the Palestinian people will become an easy morsel in the mouth of the occupation."

As Hamas vowed to avenge the assassination, Israeli troops moved into Tulkarem and Jenin and sealed off the old-city neighborhood in Nablus. Wolf pressured Dahlan to mount a show of force against the militants—starting with a crackdown on rockets being fired at Israel from northern Gaza. That night, he made serial calls from his hotel to both Palestinians and Eiland and Weisglass. "Yeah, we're just starting to move now, we've got the cars, we're moving them," Dahlan said, according to Wolf. Israelis saw no sign of Palestinian security forces moving. Wolf demanded to know what was going on. "Oh, yeah, we're just moving. We've done this, got a couple of hundred people," Dahlan repeated.

"Well, when dawn came they had a handful of people that they had moved up to the north. And the excuse then was, 'Well, we don't have any weapons, and we only had two cars.' . . . Get a life. Guns could not have been a big problem in Gaza. Two cars? I think he said they had to rent cars to get people up to the north. That's a little bit . . . that was depressing, so we kept pushing them: 'Move people, stop the rockets, deal with the rockets.'

"And the Israelis were sort of hands on the controls to drive into Gaza. So we kept holding them back. Dahlan kept saying, 'I'm doing it. I'm in the process.' What about roadblocks? What about tunnels? In the end, if you remember, he identified two tunnels and he poured some cement down the top of them. The Israelis were not too impressed by that. . . . In the end . . . nothing of the five tasks was dealt with."

Dahlan "wasn't prepared to use force, or use a show of force, in order to do that to which the Palestinian Authority and the prime minister and he committed."

After that, Wolf said, "it was just a question of watching the air go out of the balloon." Officially, Wolf's mission continued well into the fall, but for all practical purposes it was over.

Saeb Erekat could often be quick to blame the Israelis—and only them—for a breakdown in the peace process. But when he was asked what had derailed Wolf's bid to secure a cease-fire, he mentioned both the suicide bombing in Jerusalem and the assassination of Abu Shanab. "These two acts killed me, killed Wolf, and killed Abu Mazen's government that year."

Something else worked against Wolf's efforts: according to Matthew Levitt's 2006 study of Hamas, "in August 2003 Palestinian authorities shut down several Hamas-run charities suspected of financing terrorism. But the PA neglected to assume responsibility for the humanitarian services provided by these charities, and the international community failed to offer its assistance to facilitate the PA's ability to do so. This had a radicalizing effect on a great many Palestinians, including those stripped of badly needed support and others angry on their behalf." The harsh resumption of violence aggravated the power struggle between Abbas and Arafat. Abbas was unable to wrestle control of Palestinian security forces away from Arafat. Members of the Fatah central committee "old guard," including longtime Arafat adviser Hani al-Hassan and Farouk Kaddoumi, the PLO foreign affairs chief, resisted giving away powerful portfolios to the Palestinian Authority under Abbas. Kaddoumi said, "We reject any foreign decision seeking to undermine Arafat's standing."

The prime minister came under increasing personal threat as well. He resigned from office and public life on September 6.

"In words, he [Arafat] gave all his powers to Abu Mazen, but Abu Mazen started doing what he was supposed to do and Abu Mazen—if you speak to him he will tell you the same—drew the conclusion that if he continued he would have been killed. So Abu Mazen came to me and said, 'I have to resign. This is leading nowhere. I'm out of politics,'" Roed-Larsen recalled. Erekat said, "Unfortunately we allowed ourselves to be the hostages to extremists."

IN WASHINGTON, DEFEATISM set in, both at the White House and the State Department. A top State Department official said, "If [Arafat] was unwilling to turn over the reins of the security organizations then there would be no progress. That I believe and I came to understand it pretty well."

Europeans, moderate Arab leaders, and UN officials pressed the Bush administration to remain active, with no luck. Meeting with Jordan's King Abdullah at Camp David, Bush signaled he was prepared to wait indefinitely until the Palestinian government took serious action against terrorism: "And, hopefully, at some point in time, a leadership of the Palestinian Authority will emerge which will then commit itself 100 percent to fighting off terror. And then we'll be able to consolidate the power necessary to fight off terror. And when that happens, the world will come together to provide the conditions for hope. . . ."

The proximate cause of the Wolf mission's collapse was the August 19 suicide attack and paralysis in the Palestinian leadership. But Wolf knew that wasn't the whole story. Israeli and American leaders played a part.

"In this case, the Israelis never stopped doing the things that they were obligated to stop, or did the things that they were obligated to do. Really, almost none of them. And the Palestinians did virtually nothing. I mean, both of them did virtually nothing," he said in the living room of his apartment in Philadelphia, where he had moved as president of the Eisenhower Fellowships. "It's not, one did more or less than the other. The Palestinians on the finance side were doing some things that constituted institution-building and transparency. On the incitement side, they drove media incitement way down. They rejected violence. They did very little on the security side. They did take responsibility for Gaza, but they didn't do very well with it.

"The Israelis did take down some outposts, but they didn't stop the creation of new outposts. They took down some few checkpoints, but they periodically reinstituted ones like the one at . . . just outside Ramallah. The checkpoint between Ramallah and the university that was a major, major inconvenience for Palestinians with no apparent security benefit, except for added controls. So the net number of checkpoints taken down was never a very large number and they never really stopped the expansion of settlements. They certainly made it difficult whenever they transferred funds to the Palestinian authorities, even though it was the Palestinians' own money—you know, customs receipts. Security cooperation between the two was episodic—sometimes it worked and sometimes it didn't and it was always subject to the vicissitudes of the political situation.

". . . There were two red lights. One was Arafat and the other was Sharon," Wolf said. He recommended going public with each side's shortcomings in a ninety-day report but was turned down. "We did hold the Palestinians accountable. We kept talking about the need to reduce violence." With the Israelis, "in private we were quite firm. But since we were only firm in private, and there was never any publicity given to that, and even where we did talk about our unhappiness about the fence route, for instance, we never found a way to pull the Israelis up short. . . . In the end, the Israelis I think are masters at sort of absorbing the words but focusing on whether or not there's anything to come after the words. . . ."

What might have made Arafat cooperate can't be known. Terje Roed-Larsen himself got so disgusted with Arafat's lies and failure to act on promises that he refused to see him after Abbas resigned. But the United States entered the summer of 2003 blind to important Palestinian realities. One was increasing pressure on Arafat—from his public and the Palestinian parliament—to relinquish some of his power and allow for reform of his government. This was evident before Bush's June 2002 speech. Public pressure from Washington may have been counterproductive.

A second reality was the Palestinians' reverence for Arafat as a symbol, even among many who despised his autocratic and corrupt regime. As Roed-Larsen told the Security Council, Arafat "embodies Palestinian identity and national aspirations. He is far from irrelevant." Boycotting him and tolerating Israel's decision to keep him under virtual house arrest at the Muqata not only fed Arafat's resentment but caused the Palestinian public to rally around him, to the detriment of Abbas and the reformers.

"Instead of weakening him . . . the siege only made Arafat stronger at home and more able to resist reform. The young guard grew reluctant to criticize him for fear of being linked with Israel and the United States. The internally driven and externally supported reform campaign soon lost steam. Instead of strengthening Palestinian moderates, the Bush administration's insistence on PA regime change stung them like a slap in the face," Khalil Shikaki, the respected Palestinian public opinion pollster, wrote in *Foreign Affairs* the following year. Egyptian president Hosni Mubarak told the Italian daily *Corriere della Sera*: "One may harbor reservations about him [Arafat]—we ourselves harbor several—but he is the only man who can make concessions in the peace process. Thus no prime minister will be able to govern without Arafat's support."

Arafat might not have been able to flash a "red light" had Abbas been strengthened politically. But for that to happen, the Palestinian public needed a tangible sign that Abbas could deliver, in Roed-Larsen's view. Privately, the UN envoy urged a pullout from Gaza. "This was an historical opportunity and it was squandered," he said in 2005. Before the Security Council he tempered his language: "I am afraid, viewing the situation with hindsight, that we moved too slowly and with only incremental steps at the initial stages of implementation. What was necessary were bold steps that could have produced support on both sides for the process."

The red light from Sharon was caused by his apparent desire to stall and to avoid the further steps along the road map—a settlement freeze and, eventually, negotiations over a peace settlement and ending the occupation, steps that would force him to reveal or change his own redlines. Only Bush could have corrected that—by being consistently firm on the steps required from Israel, patient in explaining the benefits to be gained from entering negotiations with a flexible partner—Abbas— who was firmly committed to peace, and reassuring him that the United States would remain deeply and sympathetically involved.

Aaron Miller was at this point out of government but watching the administration's moves attentively. The Bush administration, he said, "understood how hard this was going to be, and realized that if they were going to succeed it would have required an unbelievable amount of effort. And already preoccupied with Iraq, I think they made a calculation—and the weakness of the Palestinians, which was to come full circle that September, when it was clear Abu Mazen couldn't do the job—basically decided, 'It's just too hard for us.' "

Wolf didn't mention another red light, but it was faintly visible: Syria. The United States refused to engage Syria or help it renew peace talks with Israel until Damascus stopped supporting Palestinian and Hezbollah terrorism. A senior U.S. official explained in 2005: "The Syrians to this day, in my view, don't get it, in terms of the fundamental world shift that took place after September 11 . . . they don't understand, things really did change. They keep believing you can go back to—or we or the Israelis—can go back to a world which we understand that the flame of violence will be adjusted up and down while the peace process, with active U.S. brokering, proceeds. That isn't going to happen. It wouldn't have happened had there been, I think, a Kerry victory; it certainly isn't going to happen in this administration. But Syrians don't understand that. Because it requires a change in their worldview; they don't do that very easily." Continually snubbed by Washington, President Bashar al-Assad saw little benefit in restraining the Palestinian militants—or Hezbollah—over whom he had influence. From his standpoint, Abbas would, if encouraged, obtain a separate peace with Israel, leaving Syria once again to wait indefinitely for the return of the Golan Heights.

Wolf, his mission effectively aborted, took his wife for lunch at Saeb Erekat's house in the ancient oasis town of Jericho. A bedroom window looks out on the biblical Mount of Temptation, where Christ is believed to have wrestled with worldly temptations.

"I'm leaving," he told Erekat, who replied, "Mr. Wolf, I don't think you'll come back." September 29, three weeks after Abbas's resignation and the effective end of Wolf's mission, marked the third anniversary of the intifada, which had begun mostly with exchanges of rocks and rubber bullets and now featured suicide bombs, Qassam rockets, helicopter gunships, and F-16s. Four days earlier, the Israeli human rights group B'Tselem issued a press release headlined grimly: "Three Years of Intifada—Data." It listed the casualties: 548 Israeli civilians, including 99 minors, killed by Palestinians. In addition, 246 members of the Israeli security forces killed by Palestinians; 2,201 Palestinians, including

398 minors, killed by Israeli security forces. In addition, 32 Palestinians, including 3 minors, killed by Israeli civilians. Of the Palestinian fatalities, at least 207 were killed in targeted assassinations, including at least 84 bystanders. In those assassinations carried out by the Israel Air Force, at least 131 Palestinians were killed, including 65 bystanders. In assassinations carried out by ground forces, at least 76 people were killed, including 19 bystanders. In addition to the casualties above, at least 41 Palestinians, including 5 minors, 8 newborns, and 11 women, died following delays in access to medical treatment. And 129 Palestinians carried out suicide attacks.

14

Holy Land

WHEN SONDRA OSTER Baras visited evangelical churches in the United States to seek their support, she did so "as an Orthodox Jew," sometimes the first one her hosts had ever met. She dressed as she would at home in Samaria, in the northern West Bank: she wore a modest long skirt, loose-fitting blouse, and a hat that covered most or all of her hair. Although she avoided participating in church services, Baras frequently accepted invitations to stay overnight with the families of church members. Sitting down with them at the dinner table, she would pull out a paper plate, plastic knife and fork, and the simple but reliably kosher food she had brought with her, such as lettuce and tuna. While family members dined on home-cooked fare, she joined in their conversation and ate her own meal.

"I have always felt only comfortable," she said in a 2006 interview.

"The only time I ever was made to feel uncomfortable was when I was someplace in Florida, not in the Miami area but a place where there's much fewer Jews, at a Hadassah meeting. I was invited by the Hadassah meeting because there were a few Christian ladies in the area who were supporters, and because they loved Israel they joined Hadassah [the Women's Zionist Organization of America].

"But the Hadassah group is clearly a Jewish group, full of women who don't keep kosher, don't know anything about Judaism except that they joined Hadassah. And I came there and it was completely *treyf*, it was not kosher, the Hadassah meeting—I couldn't eat anything. But I was prepared and I brought a sandwich. And I sat there and I took out my sandwich and these ladies looked at me like, 'What are you doing?'"

"And I said, 'I keep kosher, so I can't eat this food.'

'Oh, you do?'" Baras's voice rose an octave on the last syllable, mimicking surprise and disdain.

"And that was from Hadassah Jewish women!" Baras exclaimed. "And I never, ever had a response like that among Christians . . . on the contrary: to them, I'm giving them a peek into what Jesus was like."

Sondra Oster Baras, a mother of five approaching middle age, was an unofficial ambassador from the Jewish settlements in the occupied territory—the biblical lands of Judea and Samaria—to Christian congregations of the United States and Europe. That made her a key figure in an alliance between Orthodox Jewish nationalists in the West Bank and evangelical, fundamentalist Protestants who worked to preserve Israel's grip on the territories claimed by Palestinians. That alliance, in turn, was part of the growing, politically potent collaboration between American evangelicals and hawkish conservatives, religious and secular, in Israel and among supporters of Israel in the United States.

But Baras was also an example of something all too rare in a region torn by religious and ethnic conflict, where holy shrines become bloody battlegrounds, historical narratives are a zero-sum game, and believers of different faiths engage in an ongoing in-your-face competition: mutual respect among practitioners of different faiths. By educating her Christian audiences about biblical sites and the kosher dietary rules Jesus would have followed, she was working to erase religious barriers erected by centuries of ignorance. Hers was a demonstration of how two deeply committed groups can overcome their mutual isolation and sharp cultural and religious differences to find a basis for joint action.

During the Bush-Sharon era, this alliance between Jews and U.S.- and Europe-based evangelical Christians grew in parallel with hatred and fear among Muslims, Jews, and Christians in the Holy Land itself and estrangement between the United States and much of the Muslim world. While President Bush advocated and demonstrated religious tolerance from the White House, the absence of any serious effort to control the Israeli-Palestinian conflict allowed sectarian hatred to fester. The bitterness was exacerbated by continued expansion from 2001 through 2005 of the same Jewish settlements in the West Bank that Sondra Baras promoted. Meanwhile, radical Islamists among the Palestinians deepened their collaboration with Iran, disregarding centuries of discord between Persians and Arabs and between Shia and Sunni Muslims.

Rather than a territorial dispute subject to compromise, the Middle East conflict increasingly became a religious war pitting claims to the biblical Land of Israel against claims to an Islamic *waqf*, or endowment, on the same land. And this war was waged against the backdrop of a larger regional struggle involving the United States, Iraq, Iran, and Syria.

THE JEWISH-CHRISTIAN alliance that drew in Sondra Oster Baras was born as much out of fear as of a search for common religious ground. Threatened both by Palestinians and an international community insisting that Israel trade most of the occupied West Bank for peace, the settlers reached out for allies. Their most natural supporters were American Orthodox Jews. But the Orthodox represented a minority of American Jewry. Most Jews in the United States belonged to Reform or Conservative congregations that tended to support a territorial compromise between Israelis and Palestinians.

Reaching beyond their Orthodox brethren, settlers found new American soul mates among the growing ranks of politically active evangelical Protestants who shared their reverence for the storied lands of the Bible and, like the Orthodox settlers, believed the territories were bestowed on the Jews by God. This fervent pairing reinforced the political strength of each group. Settlers exerted continual pressure on Israeli governments not to yield land to the Palestinians. Evangelicals played a key role in realigning the U.S. Republican Party and its leadership in the House of Representatives behind support for the Israeli right wing and worked to prevent or dilute White House pressure on Israel. Some analysts believed that because of their sheer numbers, in the tens of millions, evangelical Christians exerted an influence on the U.S. policy on behalf of Israel that equaled or even exceeded that of the traditional, largely Jewish, pro-Israel lobby.

The settlers' and evangelicals' combined efforts did not prevent Ariel Sharon from carrying out, with strong backing from Bush, the August 2005 Israeli withdrawal from Gaza and four small West Bank settlements. But it took Sharon's combination of tactical savvy and security credibility to confront the settlers. Even so, he realized he could not make further moves without jettisoning his own Likud Party and starting a new one. After he was incapacitated by a stroke in January 2006, chances of a successful showdown with the settlers diminished. "Israel has become hostage to the settler movement," Philip Wilcox, president of the Foundation for Middle East Peace, wrote in the foundation's October 2006 Settlement Report.

Sondra Baras worked to enlist Christians in the battle to strengthen the settlements both politically and in their quality of life. She encouraged churches to "adopt" individual settlements, invited members to tour the biblical sites that resonate with both Christians and Jews, and urged them to contribute to community playgrounds, schools, or emergency facilities needed to help settlements thrive and stay secure. Articulate and well educated as well as committed, she was ideal for the role. As the Israel director for Christian Friends of Israeli Communities, an organization begun in 1995, she helped to welcome thousands of visitors and raise hundreds of thousands of dollars a year.

UNTIL RELATIVELY RECENTLY, the world of Orthodox Judaism in which Sondra Baras grew up seldom mixed with the world of evangelical Christianity. When members of the two faiths did sit down with each other, they did so uneasily. Jews historically have eschewed proselytizing members of other faiths and tended to be wary of evangelicals, whose faith calls upon them to spread the teachings of Christ. In the United States, Jews, as an often-persecuted minority, felt threatened by any Christian encroachment on the secular authority of the state and by evangelicals' attempts to influence public education.

*   *   *

FOR BOTH BUSH and Sharon, strongly religious constituencies with conservative political views formed an important part of the political base that propelled them into office. Bush courted evangelical Christians on behalf of his father in 1988, when George H. W. Bush competed in Republican presidential primaries against Christian broadcaster Pat Robertson, who sought to enlist evangelicals in a political crusade. The younger Bush reached out to them again when he himself ran for president in 2000. A self-described born-again Christian who testified that faith and prayer had changed his life, he held a natural appeal for many evangelicals. His chief speechwriter during his first term, Michael Gerson, was himself an evangelical Christian.

Bush did not fit neatly into the evangelical mold. A practicing Methodist from a family of Episcopalians, he belonged to the established "mainline" Protestant tradition. Many Methodists voted Democratic and held comparatively liberal positions on American social issues and tended toward a less literal reading of the Scriptures than did evangelicals. Their missionary work abroad deemphasized conversion to Christianity in favor of social-welfare and humanitarian efforts. In Middle East policy, Bush straddled a rift in attitudes between mainline and evangelical Protestant denominations. As the Israeli-Palestinian conflict worsened, that rift grew deeper.

Bush drew praise among conservatives and evangelicals for not restraining Israel's attacks on Palestinian targets and for tolerating measures, such as house demolitions and assassinations of Palestinian militants, that U.S. officials had criticized in the past. At the same time, Bush sided with mainline Protestants in backing Palestinian rights to a viable and contiguous state. He favored a rapid resolution to the conflict once terrorism ended and a reformed Palestinian government emerged and consistently opposed the expansion of Jewish settlements in the occupied territories.

Elliott Abrams, who in late 2002 became the Bush White House's chief point man for the Middle East, viewed mainline Protestant denominations with suspicion. Before joining the administration, he wrote in the online journal *Beliefnet*, "The almost unblemished, unwavering record of hostility to the state of Israel on the part of mainline Protestant denominations has made it into a new century. . . . They have almost always been anti-Israel, pro-PLO stalwarts." He suggested that their attitude might stem from anti-Semitism. He was eager to foster communication between American Jews and evangelical Christians—provided that the issue of Christian efforts to convert Jews was set aside.

One mainline denomination—the Presbyterian Church USA—outpaced the others in threatening to withdraw investments from companies, such as Caterpillar, the bulldozer manufacturer, that it viewed as aiding a harsh Israeli occupation. After a furor, the church backed down.

Sharon wasn't himself religious, but for three decades he was Israel's most effective and consistent political champion of religious Zionists who sought to make Israel's control of the West Bank permanent by expanding Jewish settlements. As an adviser to then Prime Minister Yitzhak Rabin, starting in 1977, and then as minister of agriculture, defense, and infrastructure and as prime minister, he planned, oversaw, and maintained what author Gershom Gorenberg has called an "empire" of settlements and roads that crisscrossed the West Bank and the military bases required to protect them. At least in the early period under then Prime Minister Menachem Begin, Israel's settlement policy included "harassment of the Arab population to encourage them to emigrate, and an elaborate licensing system to discourage them from returning," according to a biography of Sharon by Anita Miller, Jordan Miller, and Sigalit Zetouni.

Most often, Sharon justified his settlement drive on security grounds, particularly when speaking with American officials. The road network designed for the settlements would allow Israeli forces rapid access to the Jordan River Valley in the event of a ground attack from the east, across Jordan. Settlements erected on West Bank hills allowed Israel to command the strategic high ground above its flat and narrow coastal region, home to its main population centers and industry.

SETTLEMENTS BUILT NEAR Arab towns prevented outward expansion of those towns and contiguity among them. Similarly, the sparsely populated Netzarim settlement in the Gaza Strip afforded Israel a stronghold overlooking the Gaza coastline to protect against the importation of

Palestinian weapons. A ring of settlements around Arab neighbor-hoods in Jerusalem would protect Israel's capital. In his autobiography and in conversations and interviews with Israeli journalists, Sharon also played up Jewish historical and religious ties over two millennia to places like Shiloh or Bethel: he particularly cited Hebron, containing the tomb of the patriarchs Abraham, Isaac, and Jacob, and their wives Sarah, Rebecca, and Leah. He vowed to keep Israeli control over all of Jerusalem, including its traditionally Arab eastern sector, preventing Palestinians from establishing their own capital in Arab-populated East Jerusalem.

THE MOVEMENT TO claim the rugged heartland of biblical Israel began with Gush Emunim, or Bloc of the Faithful, launched by Yeshiva students under the spiritual leadership of a Jerusalem rabbi, Zvi Yehuda Kook. After establishing a settlement in the southern West Bank called Kiryat Arba, the young religious pioneers moved on to claim a hilltop outside Nablus, facing off against soldiers dispatched to remove them. The area was rich in Jewish history. It was there that Abraham was said to have received a promise from God, "To your descendants will I give this land," where Joseph was sold into slavery by his brothers, and where the children of Israel returned to live after fleeing from Egypt. The settlers found a willing and eager government sponsor in Ariel Sharon, who had achieved celebrity status from his actions in the 1973 Yom Kippur War.

With the blessing of Rabin's successor, Menachem Begin, who believed in settling the Land of Israel, the religious drive of Gush Emu-nim and like-minded settlers combined with Sharon's determination and tactical skill to become an unstoppable force. While Sharon was minis-ter of agriculture in the Begin government, a pattern developed that would be repeated for decades: settlers would camp at an outpost, liv-ing in small mobile homes, and over time build permanent structures. Wells and roads would follow. The rapid pace that turned outposts into solid communities was accomplished with various legal and budgetary sleights of hand that were winked at by successive governments. Despite stated policies against expropriating privately owned Arab property for the settlements, the Israeli Peace Now organization, years later, found that 40 percent of settlement land was in fact owned by Palestinians.

In the early days, coexistence seemed possible between settlers and nearby Palestinian townspeople and villagers. Rafi Blumberg, a Baltimorean who moved to the Judean settlement of Kiryat Arba and married and raised four children, could buy a used refrigerator in downtown Hebron nearby. His brother-in-law Noam Livnat, one of the original settlers of Elon Moreh in the Samarian hills, ventured into the bustling Nablus market, though warily and usually armed. Once, a merchant allowed him to take home a box of eyeglass frames so his wife, Rivka, could choose the one she liked.

TENSIONS GREW AS the Palestinian population began to see the expanding settlements and their road networks eating up land that they required for a future state and confining them to enclaves. Jews, for their part, became more assertive and provocative in asserting their right to dwell anywhere in the Land of Israel. In the mid-1980s, Arab neighborhoods in and near the Old City in East Jerusalem became the target of a covert Israeli government acquisition effort. Owners would be pressured to sell, or the property would be declared by authorities to be owned by "absentees." According to Peace Now, "The primary player orchestrating this policy was Ariel Sharon. . . ."

A small Jewish enclave in Hebron's old city was born amid violence in 1980, when six yeshiva students were gunned down in a terror attack near a onetime Jewish hospital that had been taken over by a group of Jews. The new settlers claimed to be reviving the community of hundreds of Hebron Jews that was wiped out in the bloody Arab riots of 1929, in which sixty-seven Jews were killed and the rest relocated. They carved out a neighborhood of several hundred Jews surrounded by tens of thousands of Palestinians. Their homes stood cheek by jowl with a busy Palestinian market and the Cave of the Patriarchs, sacred to both Jews and Muslims.

As the new settlement grew, Hebron became a crucible of rage, revenge, and bloodshed. Jews and Muslims struggled continually over the shrine, where Muslims had worshipped for centuries at a fortresslike structure known to them as the Ibrahimi Mosque. The most explosive moment came in 1994, when a doctor from the nearby suburban settlement Kiryat Arba, Baruch Goldstein, entered the shrine during dawn prayer and sprayed worshipers with gunfire, killing twenty-nine Palestinians. In 1995, Nahum Hoss, thirty-four, was killed in a sniper attack on a bus filled with Jews outside Hebron. In March 2001, a ten-month-old baby girl in a stroller, Shalhevet Pass, was killed by a Palestinian sniper; her father, a yeshiva student, was wounded in the legs.

Hebron was hardly the only source of violence between settlers and native Palestinians. In the early 1980s, an underground of Jewish terrorists carried out attacks on Palestinian mayors and conspired to explode buses and destroy the Dome of the Rock on Jerusalem's Temple Mount/Haram al-Sharif before being rounded up by Israeli security services. Later, at a hilltop settlement called Tapuah, a group of angry activists kept alive the spirit of Meir Kahane, a militant rabbi who, before his assassination in 1990, advocated expulsion of Arabs from the territories. Elsewhere, settlers damaged Palestinian shops and disrupted olive harvests, an important source of Palestinian income.

Tucked away off a side street in Balata, a village on the outskirts of Nablus, stood a tiny, domed, stone-walled building destined to join the annals of religious bloodshed. Balata residents claimed the structure venerated a nineteenth-century Muslim cleric, Sheik Youssef, who was said to have healed the sick by reading them verses from the Koran. Though not a full-fledged mosque, it drew worshippers: childless couples would go there to pray for children. Families would take their sons there for the ritual of their first haircuts.

To Israelis, the site was known as Joseph's Tomb. Jewish veneration derived from the biblical description of how Joshua, who led the Jews back into the land of Israel after Moses led them from Egypt, took the bones of the patriarch Joseph and buried them in Shechem, the biblical name for Nablus. After Jews began erecting settlements in the Samarian hills in the late 1970s and '80s, they took over the shrine, built a yeshiva, and held services on the Sabbath and holidays. To protect

Jewish worshippers and students, the Israeli army put up heavy concrete fortifications and tall fences.

The expansion of settlements, met by increasing Palestinian unrest, required Israel to send more soldiers to the territories to protect settlers and hunt for Palestinian militants, impose more curfews, and set up more checkpoints. These steps, in turn, merely deepened the Palestinian sense of living under a hostile occupation.

Alongside the strikes, stone-throwing riots, and sporadic killings of the first Palestinian intifada in 1987, a change occurred within Israel proper. A growing movement of Israeli liberals and leftists demanded an exchange of land for peace with Arab states and an end to Israeli control over the West Bank and Gaza. Their campaign put the issue of settlements squarely before the Israeli public. Settlers, particularly in the more remote, religious communities of the West Bank, became increasingly cut off in their way of life and attitudes from the mainstream of Israeli life centered in the coastal region. Many Israelis came to share the U.S. government's view that the settlements were a major impediment to peace.

Yet if the settlers became separated from the rest of Israel, they retained enough clout in the Knesset and within the bureaucracy to keep expanding their enterprise. By the time the second intifada broke out in September 2000, the growth of settlements, and land confiscation associated with it, had placed 40 percent of West Bank territory out of reach to the Palestinians for development.

The World Bank concluded that a viable Palestinian state could theoretically be formed combining the remaining 60 percent of the West Bank and the Gaza Strip—provided, however, that there was an absence of conflict, Israeli-Palestinian cooperation, and foreign aid.

But the violence of the intifada sharply altered that picture. Security measures imposed by Israel to protect its own population, the West Bank settlements, and the settlers' access to Israel proper ended up strangling the Palestinian economy. By August 2005, Israel had installed 376 checkpoints and other obstacles to Palestinian movement inside the West Bank, sharply restricted Palestinians' access to Israel, and blocked most

travel between Gaza and the West Bank. High Palestinian unemployment, in turn, increased militancy among the population, prolonging
Israel's need for security measures.

The result was that as long as the conflict continued, the options available for territorial compromise became fewer, leaving a stark choice: if
Palestinians were going to have a functioning state, the bulk of the settlements would have to be abandoned so that the checkpoints and
obstacles to Palestinian movement could be lifted. Otherwise, Israel
would have to find a path to peace that didn't include a Palestinian state.

This second path was the one Sondra Baras and her allies wanted
pursued: no Palestinian state; denial of any right of return for several
million Palestinian refugees, requiring their resettlement in other countries; and a new process of building cooperation between settlers and
Palestinians living in the territories. "Then [with] people who are native
to this region, lived here, built businesses, let's start from the ground up—
see if we can work together," Baras said.

IT WAS JUST before the first intifada in 1987 that Sondra Oster Baras
and her husband, Ed, moved to Karnei Shomron, a settlement west of
Nablus, joining a group of Orthodox Jews from the United States and
Canada in building a new neighborhood. Raised in an Orthodox home
in Cleveland, Sondra had taken up religious studies in Jerusalem before
transferring to Barnard College in New York. After obtaining a law
degree from Columbia, she practiced law briefly in the city before moving to Israel and joining the bar. By then, settlers numbered about
eighty thousand, a fourth of them in the heart of the West Bank. As the
intifada spread, Karnei Shomron joined in the broader defiant determination among settlers to claim the land as theirs.

While raising a young family, Sondra Oster Baras used her advocacy
skills as a spokeswoman for the settlement movement and began being
quoted by English-language newspapers and wire services. She became
involved with Christian Friends of Israeli Communities (CFOIC) from
its founding in 1995 under the name Christian Friends of Israel Community Development Foundation. Founder Theodore T. Beckett, a

Colorado developer, had the idea of enlisting Christian congregations to adopt individual settlements. At the time, the settlement movement felt besieged by the Labor government headed by Yitzhak Rabin and, following his assassination in 1995, by Shimon Peres. The government slashed funding for the settlements and pursued a peace process with the PLO that the settlers feared would lead inexorably to Palestinian statehood. One of the earliest "adoptions" linked the large Faith Bible Chapel in suburban Denver to Ariel, the largest Jewish settlement, deep inside the West Bank.

In 1998, Baras opened an Israeli office for CFOIC and became its director. Over the next six years, she would visit American churches in Florida, Wisconsin, Kentucky, and elsewhere, meet noted evangelical leaders and broadcasters, and be interviewed on U.S. television programs, among them the Lehrer *NewsHour* on public TV and Pat Robertson's *700 Club*. CFOIC billed itself as the "only Christian organization to focus exclusively on the communities in the heartland of biblical Israel." But it was just one organization among many linking the religious settlers' ideology with the beliefs of Protestant fundamentalists widely known as Christian Zionists.

Various scholars have traced Christian interest in the return of Jews to biblical Israel to the early nineteenth century or even earlier, in Europe, and particularly Britain—before the spread of political Zionism among Jews. A key British proponent at the time was the Seventh Earl of Shaftesbury, himself an evangelical.

In the United States, the growth of Zionism among fundamentalist and Pentecostal Protestants derived in part from a literal reading of the Old Testament, which taught them that Jews were God's chosen people and were promised the Land of Israel. This reading gave their reverence for the Holy Land a different character from that of other Christian denominations, which for centuries had viewed it primarily as the place where Christ lived, preached, and was crucified. The main Christian churches of Europe and the Middle East had long since staked their own claim, acquiring substantial property and maintaining a strong institutional presence in the form of churches, convents, monasteries, educational institutions, and hospitals. Also, unlike the Roman

Catholic, Orthodox, Anglican, and Lutheran churches, the smaller fundamentalist Protestant sects did not have strong historical ties to Palestinian Christians, some of whom trace their tradition to the earliest followers of Christ.

Free of these ties and institutional pressures, fundamentalist Protestants could give unfettered support to the central claim of religious Zionism: that Jews had the primary right to settle the God-given territories in the West Bank and Gaza, even if this meant depriving Palestinians of a state.

Ties between Israel and evangelical Christians inevitably exposed potential sources of religious friction. One of these was a powerful drive among evangelicals to "save" non-Christians through conversion. Another was a belief by many fundamentalists in New Testament prophecies that foretold an apocalyptic clash between good and evil leading to the Second Coming of the Messiah. According to these prophecies, an ingathering of all the world's Jews to Israel is a prerequisite of the final drama. However, the Jews' ultimate salvation would depend on their acceptance of Christ.

Sondra Oster Baras smoothed over these sources of tension, focusing on shared beliefs rooted in the Hebrew Bible. Because of her own acceptance of the Bible as the literal truth, she was able to understand American fundamentalists' way of speaking and they to understand hers. "Secular people get the heebie-jeebies when you mention God. . . . If I go on television today and I say, 'I'm living in the Land of Israel because God gave this to my ancestors Abraham, Isaac, and Jacob, and I am a child of Abraham, Isaac, and Jacob; therefore, this land is mine,' OK?— I'm going to have someone writing an article about how I am a fundamentalist radical person who is going to be out to conquer the entire Middle East up until the Euphrates because I believe it's mine because God gave it to me. And that's not what I said. And that's not what I meant. And I would never ever start a war or conquer or anything. But I do believe that the basis of my right is because God promised it to us in the Bible. And that's the same thing that happens in the States with some of these pastors—on this issue, on abortion or any other issue. They're talking from a very absolutist point of view because that is what they believe. That does-n't mean that they're going to go and kill or do something very extreme against someone who doesn't agree with them. Because your beliefs are absolute it doesn't mean you're intolerant of some-one who doesn't agree with you."

When confronted on her tours of the United States by Christians who either wanted to convert her or present "end times" prophecies from the New Testament, Baras wasn't the sort to flinch. "That is probably the most difficult challenge I face," she said of the Christians' impulse to convert. "That is *the* challenge, because many of the same people who love us, love us to death, so to speak. They are so concerned for our souls that they want us to accept Jesus, which is, for them, the only path to sal-vation, which of course I don't agree with.

"So it is definitely a challenge, and it's a challenge that I will not com-promise on. When I come and meet with Christians, I come as an Orthodox Jew. When I introduce Christians to our communities, they are meeting Jews who are proud of their faith and don't feel any need to adopt somebody else's. . . . One of the most important things that we're doing is this process of enabling Christians to come alongside Jews without trying to convert them.

". . . That doesn't mean that most Christians don't believe Jews need to be Christian. They do. . . . Do they feel that they as Christians are the ones who have to see that happen, or are they willing to let God take care of it? And if they're willing to let God take care of it, then we can each respect the other's faith."

Orthodox Jews and fundamentalist Christians share some beliefs in biblical prophecies, Baras noted. "We believe that everything written in the Hebrew Scriptures, if we're talking about the prophets, Jere-miah, Isaiah, Ezekiel, Amos, any of the ones that are talking about redemption and the after days, we believe the Jews will all be gathered into Israel. In fact we believe that the six million Jews who are now liv-ing in Israel, the vast majority of whom were ingathered into Israel from various exiles just in the last fifty years—this is exactly what the prophecies were talking about. So we agree with that. We agree the Messiah is coming; . . . we agree at some point there will be peace on earth. We agree that God will be . . . the God of the whole world and everyone will pray to him.

"We don't agree on who the Messiah is and whether he's been here before or not. . . . I know what they believe and they know what I believe. But we stick to the stuff we agree on and we agree to disagree and leave it out of the discussion."

She wasn't always able to avoid problematic subjects. "The level of awareness and understanding among my audiences is very varied. For some people I'm literally the first Jew they have ever seen in their life.

"I have met Christians who don't know that Jews don't believe in Jesus. They can't imagine why, because he's in the Bible. . . . And they're shocked. And I will give a whole talk and then they'll start quoting me something, and [asking] how do I relate to that? And if they're quoting me something from the New Testament I will say that as an Orthodox Jew, we don't read the New Testament. It's not part of our Bible and I don't relate to that at all—it's not part of what we believe in.

"And some people find that very shocking, like they had no idea. That might raise a question like, 'Really? You don't believe this?' I'll say, 'You know, I don't, but that's OK,' and leave it at that."

BARAS'S OUTREACH TO American evangelical Christians requires a kind of tolerance and mutual acceptance that will have to spread more broadly among Jews, Christians, and Muslims—religious and secular— if the Holy Land is to achieve its peaceful potential. But opportunities for this to happen diminished as hostilities mounted between Israel and the Palestinians. A fleeting chance occurred in late March 2000, during the visit of Pope John Paul II to the Holy Land. The pontiff tried to offer a meaningful message for everyone. At the Western Wall, while devout Jews worshiped nearby, he leaned forward and prayed: "God of our fathers, you chose Abraham and his descendants to bring your name to the nations. We are deeply saddened by the behavior of those who in the course of history have caused these children of yours to suffer, and asking your forgiveness, we wish to commit ourselves to genuine brotherhood with the people of the covenant." At Yad Vashem, the Holocaust memorial, he said the Church "is deeply saddened by the hatred, acts of persecution, and displays of anti-Semitism directed against Jews by Christians at any time and in any place."

John Paul also reminded the world of Palestinians' suffering and empathized with their struggle to build a homeland. "Be not afraid!" he exclaimed from a pulpit in Bethlehem, Jesus's birthplace. He toured a depressed refugee camp and called on political leaders to work for "the justice to which Palestinians have an inalienable right."

The pope's pilgrimage left Israelis, Palestinians, and local Christians feeling somehow uplifted and comforted. Yet the region's pain was evident throughout the trip. Jews wanted John Paul to apologize for the Vatican's silence during the Holocaust, which many viewed as a manifestation of centuries of prejudice; Palestinians, overwhelmingly Muslim, wanted him to bolster their struggle against prolonged Israeli occupation and champion the rights of the dispossessed. And the area's beleaguered Christian minority of Palestinians, Israelis, and expatriates wanted him to cement their claim to an important presence.

The seven-day visit saw occasional heavy-handed Israeli efforts to demonstrate that they were in charge of Jerusalem, as well as offensive statements by the top Muslim cleric in the Holy City, Sheikh Ikrima Sabri, who told journalists that he believed that the number of six million Holocaust victims was exaggerated, and said Israel "considers its pain more important than anyone else's." Such affronts to historical and religious sensitivities are not rare. In July 2000, when Yasser Arafat was prodded to negotiate the future of Jerusalem at Camp David, he astounded and enraged Israelis and Americans by insisting that the Jewish Temple had not even existed in the Holy City. Two months later, Ariel Sharon deeply offended Muslims by walking onto the Haram al-Sharif/Temple Mount plateau surrounded by security men. Recalling the triumphant words of an Israeli colonel, Motta Gur, when Israel captured Jerusalem in 1967, Sharon declared, "The Temple Mount is in our hands and will remain in our hands."

Sharon's provocative move was one of the sparks igniting the al-Aqsa intifada, which drew its name from the eighth-century "furthest mosque" on the Haram. The uprising was in part a religious conflict from the start, with Palestinians fighting not only against Israeli occupation but to assert their own claim to Jerusalem and other shrines. Early targets of riots and gun battles were the Israelis guarding Joseph's Tomb outside Nablus. An Israeli border policeman slowly died when Palestinian rioters prevented help from getting to him. Having protected the tiny shrine for years, the Israeli army cut its losses and withdrew under fire. Palestinians ransacked and set fire to the building. Israeli mobs firebombed mosques inside Israel.

Israeli soldiers may have drawn more rocks and bullets in the early months of the intifada, but the religious settlers living on the hilltops and driving on the roads deep in the West Bank were frequent victims of deadly assaults. In October 2000, a U.S.-born rabbi who lived in Elon Moreh outside Nablus, Hillel Lieberman, thirty-eight, was found shot to death in a cave in the West Bank. He had apparently left home on foot, intending to rescue Torah scrolls from Joseph's Tomb a day after it was overrun. Even Palestinians who deplored the attacks against civilians inside Israel viewed the settlers as illegal occupiers and thus fair game for attack.

At Sondra Oster Baras's settlement of Karnei Shomron, in June 2001, fellow resident Michael Baris described how he played a daily game of roulette against Palestinian snipers and drive-by gunmen on his sparsely traveled route to work: before leaving home, he would say a prayer, strap on a twenty-two-pound, $1,500 flak jacket, and grab an army helmet and a pistol. En route, he would push his aging Subaru past 80 miles per hour and flip on a dashboard GPS system so he could be located in case of trouble.

The threats to settlers' lives only strengthened the support they received from American Christians-and Israeli gratitude. Addressing a crowd of Christians at the Feast of Tabernacles on October 2, 2001, a year after his provocative visit to the Temple Mount, Prime Minister Sharon said, "We know your friendship. We appreciate your friendship. We need your friendship."

Baras told the *San Francisco Chronicle* in 2002 that contributions to the settlements had doubled since the start of the intifada. Christian-Jewish ties deepened as well. Yechiel Eckstein, an Orthodox American rabbi and president of the International Fellowship of Christians and

Jews, joined Ralph Reed, former head of the heavily evangelical Christian Coalition, in launching a "Stand with Israel" ad campaign. As regular tourism slumped because of the violence, Israel's right-wing tourism minister, Benny Elon, claimed that three hundred thousand evangelical Christians visited in 2002, one of the bloodiest years, according to *Jewish Week*. He and Gary Bauer, an evangelical who headed the group American Values, launched an ad campaign to attract more.

THE RELIGIOUS SETTLERS in the Land of Israel would need all this Christian help when George Bush and Ariel Sharon united against the movement, in the process defying many members of their respective political bases. Bush, despite his political dependence on evangelical Christians, never backed the settlers, particularly the defiant builders of new West Bank outposts, which he pressed Sharon to dismantle. After hearing strong Palestinian complaints about the separation barrier that Israel was building in the West Bank, he pressured Sharon to adjust the route so it came closer to the Green Line and didn't cut so many Palestinians off from their farms and jobs. The change meant putting most of the eighty thousand hilltop settlers in the heart of the West Bank outside the barrier, cutting them off from Israel. This was one in a series of signals to the settlers from Sharon, their longtime champion, that the settlement enterprise had reached its limit.

Then came Sharon's plan for a total dismantling of settlements in Gaza, home to thousands of religious Jews, and Bush's agreement that Israel was entitled to keep "existing major Israeli populations centers" beyond the Green Line. Again, the smaller religious settlements on the hilltops were excluded.

Sondra Oster Baras alerted the settlers' Christian friends to this betrayal, as she referred to it. Her April 19, 2004, message, affixed to the organization's Web site, didn't pull any punches:

"Over sixty years ago, Jews were forced to leave their homes and businesses and were forcibly transported to ghettos, concentration camps, and death camps. The goal of the Nazis was the complete extermination of European Jewry. They nearly succeeded. Today, our own government of Israel is seriously considering the forcible evacuation of eight thousand Jews from their homes and farms. Of course, no one is trying to exterminate us, but we are being asked to leave what we believed were permanent homes." Over the next fifteen months, Christian Friends kept up the angry messages, while joining public demonstrations against the disengagement. Baras traveled to the United States on visits to churches. As disengagement neared, she joined tens of thousands of West Bank settlers who converged on the area around Gaza to show support for their brethren about to be dislodged from homes and farms. In one lengthy journal entry, she described attempting to reach the Gaza settlements herself and encountering long waits for clearance at checkpoints and rude treatment from Israeli authorities: "They looked at me as if I were a criminal." She did not mention that Palestinians regularly encounter such treatment.

The settlers failed to stir up enough of a groundswell among prominent American evangelicals to interrupt the withdrawal from Gaza. Christian broadcaster Pat Robertson was a notable exception, saying on his network that the withdrawal would bring divine judgment. Later, he apologized for saying that the stroke that Ariel Sharon suffered was God's punishment. The prevailing view among leaders of the Christian Right, most of whom were strong supporters of Bush and Sharon, was that the disengagement was Israel's business. On the Christian Friends' Web site, Margy Pezdirtz, the organization's special projects coordinator, vented her frustration that Christians did not put up more of a fight alongside the settlers: "Need I remind my Christian brothers and sisters, that Genesis 12 is very powerful and very much alive today? Destruction looms for America and will be coming soon, to a location near every one of our homes. . . ."

Pezdirtz's biblical reference, to a verse in the book of Genesis, is one frequently cited by evangelical and fundamentalist Protestant supporters of Israel. In the verse, God tells the Jewish people: "I will bless those who bless you, and curse those who curse you." By tolerating the uprooting of Jews from part of the Land of Israel, in her view American Christians were harming Israel and would face God's judgment.

* * *

THE ISRAELI PULL out from Gaza in late summer 2005, and Sharon's subsequent incapacitation by a stroke in January 2006, raised the stakes for West Bank settlers and for their Christian Right supporters. Polls regularly showed a majority of Israelis in favor of a land-for-peace trade. Ehud Olmert won election to replace Sharon after pledging to withdraw from most of the West Bank—preferably as part of a peace settlement, but unilaterally if necessary. Such a substantial withdrawal would mean uprooting tens of thousands of settlers.

Baras vowed not to go gently. "I will definitely protest," she told me. In the United States, the settlers' supporters among leaders of the Christian Right set out to make sure any American support for a further disengagement in the West Bank would be more difficult to attain than during the summer of 2005. They mobilized early in 2006 to bring pressure on the White House and Congress not to encourage a major Israeli withdrawal. John Hagee, who commanded a large following from his television ministry and as pastor of the Cornerstone Church in San Antonio, Texas, formed a new nationwide organization, Christians United for Israel, and vowed to enlist support in every congressional district.

Soon after Ehud Olmert was elected to succeed Sharon, Hagee wrote to him opposing any further Israeli withdrawal. In public comments, Hagee referred to the Book of Joel in saying that any attempt to divide the Land of Israel would invite the wrath of God. Speaking to the March 2007 policy conference of the AIPAC, Hagee scoffed at the land-for-peace equation that has long been the basis of Middle East negotiations, calling it appeasement of Israel's enemies.

Along with their fervent support for Israel and their lack of any connection with Palestinian Christians, some members of the American Christian Right departed from Bush's stated policy in their harsh criticism of Islam as a religion—and not just Muslim extremists.

Robertson, in an interview with the *Jerusalem Post*'s Christian edition that he posted on his Web site, said, "The goal of Islam—if you carefully read the Koran and what they believe—is world domination. That used to be the goal of atheistic communism, but nothing is as virulent as what is believed by Islam. . . . This is a supernatural struggle. It is either the God of the Bible or the moon god of Mecca they call Allah."

John Hagee, interviewed by Terry Gross on the NPR program *Fresh Air*, said, "Those who live by the Koran have a scriptural mandate to kill Christians and Jews. The Koran teaches that." He acknowledged that not all Muslims followed such a mandate: "There are Islamics who want peace, but they don't have center stage."

Gary Bauer, president of American Values, criticized President Bush's outreach toward Muslims: "He continues to speak glowingly of Islam, describing it as a religion of peace, in spite of all the evidence around the world that it's not a religion of peace at all." Jerry Falwell, in a CBS interview, referred to the Prophet Muhammad himself as a "terrorist."

In contrast, Sondra Oster Baras recognized the importance of the Holy Land to both Christians and Muslims. "Oh, sure. There are many Christians from the United States who tell me, 'Oh, I love Israel and I wish I could live here.' And I say to them, 'Well, Israel is a Jewish country. With rare exception, in order to become a citizen of Israel you have to be Jewish.' And you know what? They say, 'You're right. Israel is a country God gave to the Jewish people.' I say, 'But this is a land that's holy to you. You can come whenever you want, and visit and pray and make a pilgrimage to whatever you consider holy. And I say the same thing to the Arabs.

"If Arabs want to turn it into a third Mecca, if they want to come and do pilgrimage, fine. That doesn't mean they can live here. They can pray here. Of course they can pray here; they pray here now. The problem is when the Arabs controlled this country they didn't allow Jews to pray. Jews were not allowed access to any of our holy sites. We don't say that. I mean every Friday just come and visit the Temple Mount—every Friday and see how many Arabs are coming into *our* holiest site to pray because they consider it their holy site."

FROM ITS BIRTH as a Jewish state, Israel has extolled religious freedom, something honored in the breach in much of the Middle East and denied to Jews over centuries in Europe. In practice, a tension has always existed between allowing the Holy Land's rich tapestry of faiths to flourish and welcome pilgrims, and the powerful Israeli drive to assert its own sovereignty, particularly over areas it captured in the 1967 war. This tension has grown more acute since the start of the second intifada. Israel often sharply restricted Friday worship at the Haram al-Sharif/Temple Mount complex to women and to men above a certain age, citing security fears. During periods when it imposed total closure on the occupied territories, it barred worshippers from the West Bank from entering Jerusalem. The aim has been to keep out militants and unruly youths who, in past years, have hurled rocks on Jewish worshippers at the adjacent Western Wall or, as in late September 2000, battled Israeli security forces.

RESTRICTED ACCESS TO Jerusalem holy sites has not been limited to Muslims. In 2004 and again in 2006, Representative Henry Hyde, the Illinois Republican who chaired the House International Relations Committee, complained that construction of the Israeli separation barrier in and around Jerusalem was restricting Christians' access to their shrines. "Local Christians view the barrier as something that is seriously damaging religious freedom in the Holy Land, impeding their access to important holy sites and tearing at the social fabric of Christian life by destroying the important linkages between Jerusalem and Bethlehem," Hyde told a House panel in June 2006. "I've been unable to understand how the currently routed barrier in Jerusalem, which rips asunder the existential poles of Christian belief, the Nativity, and the Resurrection, and encloses 200,000 Palestinians on the Jerusalem side of the barrier, will improve the security of Israel's citizens."

Sometimes an Israeli leader will resist what at times is a powerful Israeli drive to dominate Jerusalem. One was the late Defense Minister Moshe Dayan. Arriving at the Haram/Temple Mount just hours after Motta Gur uttered his famous "The Temple Mount is in our hands," Dayan ordered the blue-and-white Israeli flag taken down from atop the Dome of the Rock, according to Gershom Gorenberg's account in *The End of Days*. After Israeli forces demolished the Palestinian Mughrabi neighborhood and uprooted its residents to create a wide plaza in front of the Western Wall, Dayan made a crucial decision: he allowed the Muslim *waqf* to continue overseeing the shrines atop the man-made plateau on the other side of the wall. This left the third-most-sacred site in Islam, containing the Dome of the Rock and al-Aqsa Mosque, in Muslim hands. Israel's rabbinate reached a religious consensus that Jews should not tread on the Temple Mount, so as not to disturb the purity of the holy site. Undoubtedly, Dayan's and the rabbis' moves eased some of the shock felt throughout the Arab world over what became known as "the fall of Jerusalem" and perhaps averted a new crisis.

The "status quo" in Jerusalem is a fragile thing. No living city remains static in its ethnic makeup and property ownership. In Jerusalem, the combination of Israeli occupation, as much of the world sees it; expansion of Jewish settlements in the Muslim Quarter; and encroachment of Muslims in the Christian Quarter add an undercurrent of tension.

Dayan's decision did not stop Jews with messianic beliefs from coveting the plateau as the site where they hoped to erect a third temple and thereby hasten the "end times" and the coming of the Messiah. Gershon Salomon, who was among the soldiers on the Mount at the time of its capture in 1967, became the leader of a movement called the Temple Mount Faithful and periodically led marches to the site. The Temple Mount Faithful also linked up with sympathetic American Christian Zionists centered at the Fellowship Church of Casselberry, Florida.

MORE THAN AT any time in the last three decades, religion has become central to the conflict, a result of the rise of political Islam throughout the Arab world, the political strength of religious Israeli settlers, and the influence of Israel's evangelical Christian supporters. But if one can somehow remove the hatred, desire for revenge, and absolutist dogma from the vision of each side, it might be possible to find a basis for some common ground among Jews, Muslims, and Christians—and even between the poles-apart claims of Jewish settlers and Hamas.

Reaching such an understanding would require adherents of each faith to recognize the importance that others attach to holy places. Whether Arafat believed the Jewish Temple existed in Jerusalem was beside the point. In matters of religion, truth lies in the heart of the worshiper, not in facts. Father Jerome Murphy-O'Connor, a leading expert on Holy Land shrines at Jerusalem's École Biblique, cheerfully dismissed the historical validity of several places where pilgrims throng. The site of the Last Supper was likely wrong, he said; the Mount of the Beatitudes was a "complete fake." But he made the point that accuracy wasn't all that mattered: "A place is important because it was visited by thousands of pilgrims. No place is holy in itself. Places are made holy by veneration."

A place where mutual religious respect could start, oddly enough, would be in Hebron at the Tomb of the Patriarchs, or sanctuary of Abraham, and the thousand-year-old structure that has served at various times as a synagogue, church, and mosque. For the present, this shrine stands as a symbol of irreconcilable conflict between Muslims and Jews, requiring a heavy security presence. As with other sites that are sacred to more than one faith, each side fears the other wants to gain exclusive access.

But the tomb also represents something else: the birthplace of the belief in a single God and the common Abrahamic heritage that Jews and Muslims share with Christians.

Christianity and Islam each superimposed the teachings of a new holy figure—Jesus and Muhammad, respectively—on the history, and the lessons derived from it, that forms the basis of Judaism. The prophets of the Hebrew Bible are also considered prophets by Christians and Muslims. Islam, which originated hundreds of years after Christianity, incorporates Jesus as one of its prophets.

The land where all this history occurred, the hills and valleys trod by the prophets and tilled by their people, is considered the Land of Israel to Jews, the Holy Land to Christians, and by Islamists as a Muslim endowment. Looking at Hebron as ground zero of a shared religious heritage provides a way to look at the whole disputed territory surrounding it. If the concept of shared heritage were accepted and the claims of the three faiths somehow merged, the land could be considered the sacred inheritance of the descendants of Abraham. Jews, Muslims, and Christians would be required, collectively, to conserve it for future generations. The temporal states of Israel and Palestine would exercise political power and custodianship over areas within it that each controlled.

*   *   *

AN HOUR SPENT in Jerusalem's Old City can leave eyes blurred and ears pounding from the sights and sounds of a striking religious diversity: Hasidic Jews in old-world black suits, rocking in prayer; Franciscan friars in brown robes, tied at the waist with white rope, and sandals; the muezzins' loud call to prayer; church bells, chants. But similarities soon become obvious. Jewish rabbis and Muslim imams are invariably bearded, as are Eastern Orthodox clerics. Rabbis and imams also wear one form or another of headgear; the crocheted skullcap favored by many Jewish settlers can barely be distinguished from the cap worn by an imam from an Arab village; skullcaps worn by Catholic cardinals differ from Jewish *kippot* only by their scarlet color. Orthodox Jewish women and observant Muslim Palestinian women both wear modest loose clothing that hides their figures and keep their heads fully covered. Traditional Catholic nuns' habits resemble the veils and floor-length dresses worn by Muslim women.

Jordan's Prince Hassan bin Talal spent years studying the common philosophical threads of Islam, Judaism, and Christianity, and promoting interfaith understanding through organizations like the World Conference of Religions for Peace. In a 2006 commencement speech at Brandeis University, Hassan, brother of the late King Hussein, offered an example of the three faiths' shared intellectual roots: "It so happens that Moses Maimonides, one of the greatest Jewish thinkers of the last millennium, and the celebrated Muslim sage Ibn-Rushd [Averroës], were both born in the town of Córdoba, in Andalusia, what is now southern Spain, during the Islamic caliphate. By expanding on the knowledge of the ancient Greeks, it was Ibn-Rushd, an Arab Muslim, who helped to ensure that philosophical giants like Aristotle became one of the foundations of the European Enlightenment. Maimonides wrote almost all his books in Arabic and was openly influenced by the great Muslim thinkers who came before him. And so, in turn, the spiritual creativity of Thomas Aquinas, a towering icon in the history of Christianity, was heavily indebted to Maimonides and Ibn-Rushd. By standing on the shoulders of giants, these great thinkers furthered the collective wisdom of humanity. Looking back on this age of intellectual exchanges between these three wise men—one Jew, one Christian, one Muslim—we might ask: we have come so far in science and medicine, but what about ethics and humanity? And more importantly, can we really have a clash of civilizations when all our civilizations are built upon the same edifice?"

Rabbi David Rosen of the American Jewish Committee, a colleague of Prince Hassan's in the World Conference of Religions for Peace, wrote in a 2003 essay: "Few religions have as much in common as Islam and Judaism." While Muslim societies tended to accord Jews second-class status, the real clash between the two religions developed with the end of imperial rule and the growth of nationalism, he noted. Rosen made a ringing plea for "the enlightened voices of religion within these traditions . . . to work together not only to be greater than the sum of their different parts but also to provide the essential alternative testimony—i.e., that of interreligious cooperation and mutual respect." Rosen was among Israeli and Palestinian signatories from all three faiths of the January 2002 Alexandria Declaration, which sprang from an interfaith conference in Egypt. Among other things, the declaration called for "a religiously sanctioned cease-fire, respected and observed from all sides, and for the implementation of the Mitchell and Tenet recommendations, including the lifting of restrictions and return to negotiations."

Sondra Oster Baras began her own interfaith dialogue with her outreach to American evangelical Christians who shared her political goals. She did so for a compelling reason: preservation of the West Bank settlements. She also recognized Muslims' right to visit and worship at their holy shrines. When I asked Baras if she could imagine remaining in Samaria under Palestinian, rather than Israeli, rule, she replied, "If the Palestinian Authority were Canadian, then I wouldn't have a problem. These guys are murderers. They're thugs. They kill. I think if we were left behind, we would be dead. Literally. And that's the problem."

At the root of the clash of civilizations in the Holy Land is fear. There are both tangible fears—of threats to one's own survival; of the loss of one's home or livelihood; of denial of access to holy places—and imaginary ones. The tangible fears can be addressed through a genuine peace process that addresses the needs of a majority of Israelis and

Palestinians. The imaginary fears are born of ignorance, of the kind that in another era might have made Sondra Baras cringe at a Christian's attempt to convert her or persuade Rabbi Rosen that any Muslim secretly hated him. These fears will require more effort to abate; adherents of different faiths will need a compelling reason to make the first step, such as the promise of a richer religious life for all. As Prince Hassan told his audience at Brandeis, "Turning bloody conflict into broad-minded coexistence takes some imagination."

15

SIDESHOW

THIS WAS NASSER AL-QIDWA'S moment. For years, the round-faced Palestinian envoy with shrewd eyes and caustic tongue had made the customs and rules of the United Nations work in his favor. Competitive, quick on his feet, equally at home before a microphone or in a hushed tête-à-tête, he deftly enlisted Arab, European, Russian, and third world support for resolutions and special sessions intended to advance the Palestinian cause and pressure or embarrass Israel. Even though he only had "observer" status, because Palestine was not recognized as a country, he was usually treated like a representative from a UN member state—and not an insignificant one. Although he was a nephew of Yasser Arafat, his job security derived as much from ability as from family ties.

Now, on a chilly February morning in 2004, al-Qidwa was in the Hague, making the Palestinians' case before the International Court of Justice, the highest legal body in the UN system and often the final arbiter of the patchwork of treaties, conventions, and customs known as international law.

If al-Qidwa and his team proved persuasive, the court might strike a serious legal blow against "the wall," the separation barrier of fences, walls, and trenches that Israel had begun to erect in the West Bank in mid-2002, during the bloodiest period of the uprising that had begun two years earlier. The court's decision, depending on how expansive it was, could also cast a dark legal shadow over Israel's occupation of Palestinian land.

The hearing in the Hague opened a major new battle in an important but often ignored aspect of the sixty-year Israeli-Palestinian conflict: a competition between the two sides for international legitimacy. The conflict is usually seen as the ebb and flow of violence and diplomacy; when negotiations collapse, violence escalates. But each side's struggle for acceptance by the world at large permeates everything from the vocabulary they adopt to major political decisions and military tactics. Each wants to be accepted and recognized first as a sovereign nation. Beyond that, each seeks acceptance of its claims to territory, religious sites, a right to self-defense, and, perhaps most important, a historical narrative that attempts to justify all the rest.

The hearing also focused attention on an aspect of the Israeli-Palestinian conflict that was largely ignored by Washington: the relevance of international law to the conduct of each side. From President Bush on down, U.S. officials routinely used harsh adjectives in condemning suicide bombings, but there's one description they avoided: they did not call them war crimes, which, as deliberate attacks targeting civilians, they surely were. Neither did the United States threaten Palestinian leaders who abetted, tolerated, or failed to act to prevent such attacks with prosecution under international law. By the same token, the United States also failed to cite international law or possible war crimes in criticizing Israel for instances of indiscriminate or excessive force, collective punishment, or extrajudicial killings. And since the Jimmy Carter presidency, the United States had stopped describing the expansion of Jewish settlements in occupied territory as illegal, a view held by most of the world. The avoidance of any mention of international law was a major American blind spot. It diluted the importance and meaning of international law, deprived the United States of a legitimate form of pressure and an important diplomatic tool, and possibly even contributed to the rising bloodshed.

Standing before the fifteen black-robed judges in the paneled Great Hall of Justice, al-Qidwa read from a well crafted script. He avoided the bombast he had indulged in while denouncing Israeli practices before the General Assembly or Security Council or in his frequent letters to the secretary general.

In New York, his speeches and letters were peppered with words like *colonialists, racists, vicious, insane, fascist,* and outbursts against "the shame of the century" or "one of the biggest war crimes of its kind in modern history."

Not at the Hague. Here, the Palestinian diplomat delivered a passionate yet disciplined argument: The "wall," far from being a security measure as Israel claimed, amounted to an illegal and destructive annexation of Palestinian territory that would make a two-state solution to the conflict, and thus peace, virtually impossible to achieve.

For al-Qidwa, the hearing was a career high-water mark; for Palestinians, it was a moment of renewed self-respect in their conflict with Israel. For the United States and Israel, it was a missed opportunity both to enhance the prestige of a new generation of educated, moderate Palestinian leaders and to influence the shape of international law.

From 1991 to 2000, tense negotiations interspersed with crises dominated Palestinians' relations with the Jewish state. Through their own and others' mistakes and miscalculations, Palestinian leaders failed to use this period effectively to secure statehood. Among other faults, they failed to persuade the Israeli public that they truly sought peace, failed to make a persuasive case with the Americans for their claims, and failed to prepare their own population for compromise.

After 2000, violence and terrorism took the lead. Over the next two and a half years of intifada, Palestinian society and governance slid backward. At first, militant leaders had encouraged rock-throwing teenagers to confront Israeli soldiers and get wounded or killed, stoking a culture of martyrdom that inspired a desperate young generation even as it destroyed families. Then the Muslim resistance groups Hamas and Islamic Jihad and the secular al-Aqsa Martyrs' Brigades concentrated on the more lethal suicide bombings, drawing support from a population driven to fury and despair.

By the fall of 2003, the Israeli-Palestinian conflict had become a contest between Palestinian bombers and Israel's attack helicopters and fighter jets. Law and order broke down in Palestinian cities; radical forces and gangs were ascendant. And what had this brought the Palestinians? Seemingly endless suffering and worldwide condemnation. Many educated, Western-oriented Palestinians were dispirited, realizing that the conflict was alienating actual and potential supporters in the outside world and empowering extremists in the territories—all while drawing an ever-harsher Israeli response.

But if neither violence nor negotiations could secure what Palestinians claimed to be their rights, what would? This is where al-Qidwa saw his chance. Making the most of the lopsided support for the Palestinians and often blatant hostility toward Israel at the United Nations, he pursued a nonviolent path to advancing the Palestinian cause. He did so by building up a case in international law against a range of Israeli tactics: the continued Israeli occupation of lands captured in 1967; expansion of settlements; the annexation of East Jerusalem; and assassinations.

Born in the Gaza Strip in 1953 and raised in Egypt, al-Qidwa joined his uncle's Fatah movement as a teenager in 1969. Although he trained as a dentist at Cairo University, most of his adulthood was devoted to Palestinian activism. For more than a decade, he was a leader in the General Union of Palestine Students, the same organization that Arafat led in the 1950s, and attained senior posts in both Fatah and the Palestine National Council. He arrived at the UN in 1986 as an alternate observer, the No. 2 Palestinian diplomatic post, and became permanent observer in 1991. Few Palestinian leaders were more Westernized than al-Qidwa, who married a Frenchwoman and had American-born children. Unlike the Palestinian Authority leadership jobs, al-Qidwa's position predated the Oslo agreements between Israel and the PLO and was based on the unique relationship between the UN and the Palestinian national movement.

The late 1980s, when al-Qidwa came to the UN, marked a low point for Israel diplomatically. Its invasion of Lebanon in 1982 had stirred international outrage, particularly after the massacre of Palestinian refugees by a Lebanese militia allied with the Israelis. The Palestinians enjoyed growing Arab, third world, and European support and had not yet alienated the Persian Gulf states by supporting Saddam Hussein.

Al-Qidwa rarely won a victory in the Security Council, which had the power to make binding decisions for all the nations of the world and decide matters of war and peace, and never succeeded in winning approval of any measure that would punish Israel. The United States regularly used its veto power as a permanent member of the council to block adoption of anti-Israel resolutions. Instead, al-Qidwa turned to the General Assembly. Its resolutions were nonbinding, but not meaningless: in sum, they amounted to a voluminous paper trail showing the world's view of Israeli conduct.

"Al-Qidwa used to say, 'Israel might control the situation in the area, but in the UN, I am the boss,' or 'I can do what I want,'" said Israeli legal adviser Alan Baker. Whether or not the Palestinian used those words, the charge reflects how Israelis viewed him. He got under their skin.

The UN and Israel were born at roughly the same time, and the world body as a whole was an early champion of the idea of a Jewish state coexisting alongside an Arab state in Palestine, a concept rejected by the Arabs. Yet Israel, the state of a people cast out or ignored by other nations, never accepted the world body's authority over its actions even as it built a democracy based on the rule of law.

The United Nations' involvement in the Israeli-Palestinian conflict grew gradually. After 750,000 Palestinians fled or were driven from what became the state of Israel in 1948, the United Nations created and funded a special refugee agency to look after their basic humanitarian needs. The agency, the United Nations Relief Works Administration (UNRWA), set up schools and health clinics at refugee camps in Israel, the West Bank, Gaza, Jordan, Syria, and Lebanon, enabling the camps to grow into permanent towns and cities. UNRWA could justly take a share of credit for the Palestinians' becoming one of the best-educated populations in the Middle East.

After Israel captured East Jerusalem, the West Bank, and the Gaza Strip in the 1967 war, the plight of the Palestinians drew increased attention at the UN, and Israel came to be seen less as a struggling young state surrounded by enemies than as a colonial-style oppressor. This attitude was particularly strong in the General Assembly, the one global forum where small third world countries could band together as a power bloc. But the Security Council itself rejected Israel's annexation of East Jerusalem and the acquisition of land by force.

Over the next two decades, as the Soviet bloc sought greater influence among Arab states and the third world, a network of overlapping UN committees and agencies would take shape, all devoted in some way to monitoring the plight of Palestinians under Israeli occupation. In 1975, the General Assembly adopted a resolution that to Israel and its supporters became a symbol of the world body's hostility toward the Jewish state and, in the view of many, its blatant anti-Semitism. The resolution stated that the assembly "DETERMINES that Zionism is a form of racism and racial discrimination." It remained on the books until it was repealed by a U.S.-led campaign in 1991.

The various institutional committees, groups, and mechanisms set up to support the Palestinians included the International Day of Solidarity with the Palestinian People; the Division for Palestinian Rights within the UN secretariat; the "special information program on the question of Palestine" in the UN's Department of Public Information; and the Special Committee to Investigate Israeli Practices Affecting the Human Rights of the Palestinian People and Other Arabs of the Occupied Territories. The United Nations Commission on Human Rights assigned a special investigator, or rapporteur, to probe the treatment of Palestinians in the occupied territories. Besides the staffs assigned to these various bodies, the Office of the Secretary General was frequently called in to conduct fact-finding inquiries and prepare reports, further increasing the amount of time and attention the UN bureaucracy devoted to the "Question of Palestine."

Israel, for its part, became increasingly isolated at the UN and excluded from decisive forums like the Security Council and the regional groupings where the council's nonpermanent members were picked. The fact that this seemed to repeat a centuries-old pattern in the treatment of Jews by many countries did not make the experience any less bitter for Israel. The United States could be counted on to insulate Israel from punishment by the Security Council, but condemnation by the General Assembly became routine.

So deep was Israel's distrust of the UN that the United States deliberately kept the world body removed from the Arab-Israeli peace process through the 1990s, although the land-for-peace Security Council resolutions remained the main legal pillars of the process.

The collapse of negotiations at Camp David in 2000 and the subsequent eruption of the al-Aqsa Intifada brought the UN back into the picture. As worldwide alarm mounted over the rising bloodshed, the Security Council called for monthly briefings from senior officials of the secretariat.

Al-Qidwa was ready to assume a more prominent role. He kept up a steady drumbeat of letters alerting the Security Council and secretary general to Israeli "war crimes" and "relentless military campaign against the Palestinian people." He enlisted Arab states to seek special sessions of the council and General Assembly, crafting resolutions that, if nothing else, served to isolate Israel and its superpower protector. "I did feel isolated," the Israeli ambassador at the time, Yehuda Lancry, told me. Lancry was reminded of a biblical story of the sorcerer Balaam, with whom God intervened to deliver a blessing, rather than a curse, to the Israelites:

"I see them from the mountaintops, gaze on them from the heights; they are a people who dwell apart. . . ."

Lancry added: "This has been almost for the last six decades the situation of Israel in the United Nations—dwelling alone, under the protection of the United States. In this respect I felt that the United States was really the emissary of God."

While they dueled in public, Lancry and al-Qidwa were amicable in private. Lancry recalled in a 2006 interview, "He was a strong adversary. But he was also—he was a nice man. . . . We were able to sit, to have lunch, to discuss, to have fun between us, in spite of the bitterness of the clashes. And when the intifada started I saw him crying during the delivery of his statement. We were at the third or fourth day of the intifada, with some forty-five Palestinians killed, and three Israelis." When a suicide bus bombing killed Lancry's eighteen-year-old niece, Noa Shlomo, in April 2002, al-Qidwa approached the Israeli envoy to express his sorrow. Lancry considered the gesture "very decent, very correct."

A U.S. veto became the norm rather than the exception as Washington's attitude toward the intifada hardened after the terrorist attacks of September 11, 2001. Eventually, the administration took the position that it would oppose any resolution that criticized Israeli actions unless the measure also condemned terrorism and cited the groups responsible, whether Hamas, Islamic Jihad, or the al-Aqsa Martyrs' Brigades. Al-Qidwa would later claim that he kept on good terms with U.S. ambassador John D. Negroponte and other American diplomats, in part by trying to steer clear of UN debates over Iraq. "It's one thing if they oppose you; it's different if they fight you," he said of the Americans.

The tougher American posture meant Palestinians also lost ground with the Europeans, who had long been fairly reliable supporters. The British government under Prime Minister Tony Blair, determined not to clash publicly with Washington, would not back a measure the United States flatly opposed. "Basically the British commitment was to be only one step ahead of America, not two steps," al-Qidwa said. Still, the Palestinians could count on consistent support from France, Russia, China, much of Africa, and the Muslim world.

By the fall of 2003, al-Qidwa seemed to be the one Palestinian leader with a purpose and a plan. Each fall, world leaders gather in New York for a new session of the United Nations General Assembly, which takes on the atmosphere of a convention. Al-Qidwa swung into gear, using his many allies and the multiple levers of the UN apparatus. His main target that fall and winter would be "the wall."

Dubbed a "security fence" by Israel, the barrier of electrified fences and concrete walls had been started reluctantly by the Sharon government, under strong pressure from a public desperate for protection from suicide terrorists. One of the earliest decisions setting it in motion came in the aftermath of the March 27, 2002, bombing at the Park Hotel in Netanya, the deadliest suicide attack to date. The idea stemmed from the concept of firmly separating Israelis and Palestinians. That concept began to get serious attention during the Labor government of Yitzhak Rabin in the early 1990s and was later considered seriously by Ehud Barak. Its supporters noted that few suicide bombers managed to infiltrate Israel from the Gaza Strip, which was sealed off. Inevitably, the new barrier could not be erected along a route that would protect all the far-flung Israeli settlements in the West Bank; at the same time, it would be politically treacherous for Sharon to put the fence along the Green Line. First, this would leave all West Bank and East Jerusalem settlers outside the wall, and thus still vulnerable to terror. Second, placing it along the Green Line would also appear to be caving in to the Palestinian view of where the border should be, even if the fence was not intended to be a border. The Israeli security establishment sought to carve out a route that protected the maximum number of Israelis while keeping as many Palestinians outside of the wall's confines as possible. Whether or not the barrier was effective in keeping terrorists out of Israel proper, it undoubtedly gave Israelis a greater feeling of security.

Palestinians viewed the "wall" as a land grab and as part of a scheme to push Palestinians into defined enclaves. In early September 2003, the separation barrier drew increasing attention in and around the United Nations. The Committee on the Exercise of the Inalienable Rights of the Palestinian People, an officially sanctioned UN body, led off before the arrival of world leaders with a large conference of civil society groups, its second in two years. A major theme was the need to mobilize worldwide action against the construction of the separation wall by Israel. Speakers included leading officials of nongovernmental organizations active in aiding the Palestinians, as well as Naomi Chazan, a well-known left-wing Israeli politician, and Cindy Corrie, the mother of Rachel Corrie, who had been crushed to death six months earlier by an Israeli bulldozer while protesting the demolition of Palestinian homes.

The September 8 report of the UN special rapporteur concluded that the "evidence strongly suggests that Israel is determined to create facts on the ground amounting to de facto annexation," which the report characterized as "conquest in international law . . . prohibited by the Charter of the United Nations and the [1949 Geneva Convention relative to the protection of civilian persons in time of war]."

On September 15, Special Coordinator Terje Roed-Larsen, an architect of the diplomacy that led to the 1993 Oslo accords, whose views carried considerable weight with world leaders, gave the UN secretariat's regular monthly briefing to the Security Council, telling members: "We remain concerned by the continued construction of the West Bank security fence or separation wall. . . . People are separated from farms, schools, and livelihoods and are having their lands confiscated. . . . It makes the establishment of a viable Palestinian state more difficult and the hope of peace more distant, and it undermines any Palestinian prime minister's efforts to muster popular support."

Israeli and American supporters of the fence, in turn, promoted its value. But they failed to persuade the Bush administration that the barrier should be built inside the West Bank, land that Palestinians considered theirs. In a rare display of unity between the State Department and the White House, the administration decided to deduct almost $300 million from loan guarantees to punish Israel both for erecting the fence on Palestinian territory and for continually expanding settlement outposts in defiance of the road map.

President Bush was frustrated with the ongoing conflict. He reminded subordinates that he had stuck his neck out and spent political capital at the Aqaba summit with Ariel Sharon and Palestinian prime minister Mahmoud Abbas in June 2003, and all for naught. Although he blamed Yasser Arafat for Abbas's political collapse, he felt Sharon wasn't helping, either.

For al-Qidwa, the main event that fall was still to come. On October 1, he sent a lengthy letter to Kofi Annan complaining about the expansion of the "conquest wall." Israel, he said, was confiscating thousands of *dunams* of Palestinian land in violation of the UN Charter and Geneva Convention and in a way that threatened to preempt a two-state solution and entrench Israel's annexation of East Jerusalem.

Eight days later, the Arab League demanded a Security Council meeting and floated a proposed resolution that declared the barrier illegal and said it should be dismantled. U.S. envoy Negroponte cast a veto—his second in three weeks on a resolution aimed against Israel. Still, he implicitly criticized the barrier: "We have repeatedly urged Israel and the Palestinian Authority to avoid actions that can lead to a further heightening of tension in the Middle East and to think carefully about the consequences of their actions. In addition, senior United States administration officials are engaging directly with Israel on the matter of the fence."

Al-Qidwa, seated in the council chamber, vowed not to let the matter rest. Turning their attention to the General Assembly, Palestinians and their allies debated a new gambit: seeking an advisory opinion on the wall's legality from the International Court of Justice (ICJ). At first, al-Qidwa opposed such a move, fearing that if it failed and the court ruled against the Palestinians, their legal position would be weakened.

"The concern was that the judgment would be nuanced [and could] be interpreted as an endorsement of the wall," said Amjad Atallah, a lawyer and adviser to the Palestinians. Court watchers, however, believed there was a strong likelihood they would prevail. So a second resolution circulated in the General Assembly.

Al-Qidwa would later claim a share of the credit for what he called "a masterpiece of diplomacy." Alarmed at the prospect of pulling the ICJ into the Israeli-Palestinian conflict, the Europeans took charge of crafting a compromise. Their version dropped an explicit reference to the ICJ. But it made certain that the barrier would remain a live issue by requesting periodic reports on the barrier from the secretary general, with the first one due in a month. Al-Qidwa also negotiated wording that would later allow him to revive the ICJ proposal: upon receipt of the first report, "further actions should be considered, if necessary, within the United Nations system."

The Israeli government began to feel increased pressure, not just from the outside world, but from highly respected members of its own security establishment. On November 14, four former leaders of Shin Bet, the Israeli internal security service, gave an interview to the mass-circulation *Yediot Ahronoth* newspaper expressing fears that the country was headed toward a catastrophe because of its actions toward the Palestinians. Several of them criticized the separation barrier.

"It creates hatred, it expropriates land and annexes hundreds of thousands of Palestinians to the state of Israel," said Avraham Shalom, who headed the agency from 1980 to 1986. "The result is that the fence achieves the exact opposite of what was intended." A few days later, in a major policy statement, the European Union declared that it was "particularly concerned by the route marked out for the so-called security fence in the occupied West Bank and East Jerusalem. The envisaged departure of the route from the 'Green Line' could prejudge future negotiations and make the two-state solution physically impossible to implement. It would cause further humanitarian and economic hardship to the Palestinians."

The statement continued, "Thousands of Palestinians west of the fence are being cut off from essential services in the West Bank; Palestinians east of the fence will lose access to land and water resources. In this context the EU is alarmed by the designation of land between the fence and the 'Green Line' as a closed military zone. This is a de facto change in the legal status of Palestinians living in this area which makes life for them even harder. Hence, the EU calls on Israel to stop and reverse the construction of the so-called security fence inside the occupied Palestinian territories. . . ." On November 16, Pope John Paul II weighed in with his own criticism of the barrier, saying the Middle East "does not need walls but bridges" and calling it "a new obstacle" to peace.

This growing opposition to the barrier came at an inconvenient time for the Bush administration, which was trying to repair diplomatic damage from the war in Iraq and enlist international help in stabilizing and rebuilding the country. The White House sought a face-to-face meeting with Ariel Sharon and dispatched Elliott Abrams to meet him in Rome, where Sharon was visiting. Neither disclosed what was discussed, but others familiar with the meeting said Sharon used the lengthy discussions to broach his idea of a major withdrawal of Israeli settlers and forces from Gaza. Looking forward to Italian food, Abrams was disappointed to learn that Sharon had requested Israeli dishes from the Italian hotel staff. At one point a waiter brought in a plate containing various kinds of meat, including a pink variety that Abrams, who usually avoided pork and shellfish, recognized as ham. "What do you suppose that is?" he asked Sharon, who replied: "Sometimes it's better not to ask."

Bush, on a state visit to Britain that same week, chastised Israel succinctly, preparing the ground for the $300 million loan penalty. The president owed a huge political debt to Blair over the war in Iraq and recognized that the stalled peace process was causing political problems for his friend. "Israel should freeze settlement construction, dismantle unauthorized outposts, end the daily humiliation of the Palestinian people, and not prejudice final negotiations with the placements of walls and fences," Bush said. At the same time, he implicitly warned Palestinians anew that their society had to change before the United States would help them gain statehood. "Achieving peace in the Holy Land is not just a matter of the shape of a border. As we work on the details of peace, we must look to the heart of the matter, which is the need for a viable Palestinian democracy."

That same day, in a five-minute special meeting of the UN Security Council held despite Israeli objections, the United States joined in approving a unanimous resolution that put the council's imprimatur on the road map, binding Israel and the Palestinians to its requirements under international law.

Al-Qidwa publicly praised the council's action but had more dramatic steps in mind. He renewed his lobbying effort to seek an advisory opinion from the International Court of Justice (ICJ). Over the next week, he gathered support for a resolution asking the ICJ: "What are the legal consequences arising from the construction of the wall being built by Israel, the occupying Power, in the Occupied Palestinian Territory, including in and around East Jerusalem, as described in the report of the Secretary-General, considering the rules and principles of international law, including the Fourth Geneva Convention of 1949, and relevant Security Council and General Assembly resolutions?"

Al-Qidwa went into the debate December 8 certain of adoption by a large majority. "What is happening is the enslavement of the whole Palestinian people, who are being increasingly cantonized by the Israeli fascist colonial occupier. . . . It is the shame of the twenty-first century," he told the General Assembly. But he got nowhere near the number of votes usually cast for a Palestinian resolution. The vote of ninety to eight, with seventy-four abstentions, was a victory for the Palestinians but showed the assembly to be deeply divided on taking the issue into the World Court. European and UN diplomats had spent months on end working and reworking the road map into a document acceptable to Arabs and Americans and had won partial acceptance from Israel. Now a new complication had been introduced. Among the many countries that abstained were some, like Russia, to whom the Palestinians regularly looked for support.

In Washington, the Bush administration, so often divided on Middle East issues, was of one mind in opposing the Palestinians' legal move. "There were no disagreements inside the U.S. government. We thought the whole thing was a mistake from start to finish," a senior administration official said. "We were against the resolution in the UN, we were against taking it to the ICJ. . . . We thought, 'No good will come of this; this will not bring us closer to peace.'"

For Al-Qidwa, the stakes were high. He set about assembling a team of legal heavyweights, reaching into the tiny elite of international law experts who had appeared before or were knowledgeable about the World Court. He operated virtually on his own, with little, if any, guidance from the semidestroyed Palestinian headquarters in Ramallah, where Arafat was holed up. The resulting team included a distinguished international lineup from Christian, Muslim, and Jewish faiths. It drew academics from Oxford and Cambridge, a noted international lawyer from Belgium, a former ICJ staff lawyer from the Netherlands (Pieter Bekker), as well as Palestinians and an Egyptian. The team boned up not only on the issues but on the judges, trying to ascertain which ones would be more likely to favor them and which ones would lean toward Israel. They learned, for instance, that the American judge Thomas Buergenthal, was a survivor of the Nazi Holocaust who had spent his childhood in concentration camps, and that the maiden name of Dame Rosalyn Higgins, the British judge, was Cohen. After hiring his team, al-Qidwa didn't interfere in their work. "We never received instructions from Ramallah or from him," said Bekker.

Early procedural decisions by the court encouraged the Palestinians and signaled that the court was eager to take up the case. On December 19, the judges put the case on a fast track, despite Israel's plea that it take more time, and split the case into two parts—one to weigh the question of jurisdiction, and the second to consider the substance.

The court also declared that the Palestinians could submit written material and participate in oral presentations by virtue of their observer status at the UN and cosponsorship of the resolution seeking the advisory opinion. This was a major political breakthrough for the Palestinians; it marked another milestone in their long march toward international acceptance as a nation. Court documents, such as UN documents originating in the General Assembly, referred to Palestine as if it were a state, based on the declaration of statehood by the PLO in 1988. Security Council resolutions, in contrast, mentioned Palestine in the context of the council's "vision" of two states, as did the Bush administration; they referred most often to "the parties," or the Palestinian Authority.

In Jerusalem, these preliminary decisions, a "ridiculously hectic" schedule for the case—plus UN documents submitted to the court that made scant mention of terrorism—persuaded Israeli Foreign Ministry lawyers that the court would not give them a level playing field, one official recalled later. The upcoming drama in the Hague was overshadowed by Sharon's decision to pull Israeli forces and settlers out of the Gaza Strip, a move that was widely viewed as a tectonic shift in his own thinking. But behind the scenes, officials treated the court case as a looming crisis. The Jewish Telegraphic Agency summed up the import of the case: "Never before has Israel been forced to defend before an international tribunal a specific project in the territories it captured in the 1967 Six-Day War."

Defensive almost from the outset, Israelis complained that the court had adopted Palestinian terminology (the "wall") in describing the barrier. Then they challenged the participation in the case of one of the judges, Nabil Elaraby, a former Egyptian ambassador to the UN. Israel cited his "leading role" in the same General Assembly emergency session that produced the request for an advisory opinion and his past involvement in Palestinian autonomy talks. The Israelis also found an interview Elaraby gave to the semiofficial Egyptian newspaper Al-Ahram that they claimed showed anti-Israeli bias. In it, he expressed the view that the Israeli occupation of Palestinian territory was illegal. He also described what he said was an Israeli strategy of creating "facts on the ground" in the occupied territories to gain time. The court voted to let Elaraby hear the case anyway, but the American judge, Buergenthal, dissented, saying the interview showed at least the appearance of a bias against Israel.

Dov Weisglass, Sharon's consigliere, took charge of coordinating Israel's response. A key question the government faced was the extent of Israel's participation. Justice Minister Yosef Lapid argued that Israel needed to participate fully in the case and mount a strong defense. Lapid, who was born in the former Yugoslavia, survived the Holocaust in wartime Budapest and immigrated to Israel at age seventeen in 1948, was well-known in Israel as a figure of irascible independence. A trained lawyer, former *Maariv* correspondent in London, TV talk show veteran, and author of several books, he was the leader of Shinui, a centrist political party that stuck to a moderately hawkish line on security issues while fighting tooth and nail against the influence of Israel's Othodox religious establishment in the country's domestic affairs.

Lapid had worried that the barrier would be condemned internationally because it cut too deeply into the West Bank and publicly expressed the fear that Israel could be made into an international outlaw state like South Africa. He called for the barrier to be moved closer to the Green Line, saying this would allow it to be built faster and at lower cost. But he was also in favor of a full-throated Israeli case in defense of the barrier before the ICJ. For one thing, he argued to Sharon and other government colleagues, this would allow Israel to name a judge who would join the panel. An ICJ rule states: "When the Court does not include a judge possessing the nationality of a State party to a case, that State may appoint a person to sit as a judge ad hoc for the purpose of the case." This rule wouldn't automatically apply in an advisory-opinion case, but Israeli lawyers believed the court would permit an Israeli judge.

Lapid believed having a judge on the court would give Israel the chance to "win some points" when the judges discussed the case privately. "If you're one of the justices, at least he can supply information or viewpoints," Lapid said in a telephone interview in September 2005. He wanted Israel's revered chief justice, Aharon Barak, to take the ad hoc seat. Lapid and Alan Baker, who spoke with Barak about it, both said later that the justice probably would have agreed to serve if asked.

"There were two or three vociferous debates in the cabinet," over having Israeli representatives take part in the hearing, according to Baker.

"I was invited to present the reason against appearing." Lapid's view was backed by a senior international lawyer in the Justice Ministry, Shavit Mattias. Most other ministers, along with Baker and a second Justice Ministry lawyer, Irit Kahan, were opposed.

In the end, the government decided against participating, fearing that this would lend legitimacy to the Palestinians' tactics. "What the Palestinians wanted to do since Durban was to have Israel dragged before a tribunal and declared the ultimate international outlaw," Baker said. "This would have given credence to that tactic of the Palestinians." The government also decided not to seek to appoint an ad hoc judge, fearing the Palestinians would be granted the same privilege.

Early in January, Baker flew to Washington to coordinate strategy with the Americans, including State Department Legal Adviser William H. Taft IV. The Bush administration was sympathetic, having opposed the Palestinian move in the General Assembly to seek an opinion from the World Court.

"We were in full agreement on the basic strategy—that neither of us will ignore the ICJ," Baker recalled. Like Israel, the United States decided not to appear for an oral argument, although Baker believed that, had Israel requested it, the United States would have sent a representative to the court to explain its position. Both governments also decided not to argue about the merits of the case, but merely to try to persuade the court not to take it.

Learning of Baker's trip, al-Qidwa pressed the Americans to meet with the Palestinian side and sent Bekker to Washington, where a State Department lawyer met with him outside the building. "The Israeli government having 'briefed' the U.S. government, the Palestinians requested a similar opportunity. We were not trying to sound out the Americans on U.S. and Israeli strategy. The Americans seemed eager to know what Palestine was going to argue in its written statement. At the same time, the Palestinians were interested in convincing the Americans not to file a written statement that was unhelpful to the Palestinians," Bekker related in an e-mail. Bekker learned little of the U.S. legal strategy; he was told the administration hadn't decided whether to file a brief.

Two more procedural decisions by the court in mid-January seemed to favor the Palestinians: the judges allowed both the Arab League and the Organization of the Islamic Conference to participate.

Israel prepared a hard-hitting brief, bristling with outrage at the General Assembly for failing to consider the carnage caused by Palestinian terrorism, and calling the request for an advisory opinion a "travesty." It forcefully challenged the court's jurisdiction, arguing that the assembly exceeded its authority in making the request for an opinion. This intruded on the purview of the Security Council, Israel said. Israelis argued that even if the court decided it had jurisdiction, it should avoid becoming involved in a "tainted" exercise that amounted to abuse of the whole advisory-opinion procedure. Israel also said the case would interfere with the "road map" peace process and would in fact involve the court in deciding a significant part of the Israeli-Palestinian dispute, which should be left to negotiations. Further, Israel argued that the court didn't have enough information to render an opinion and that since "Palestine" wasn't a state and would not be allowed to bring a case before the court on its own, it didn't have the "standing" to participate in the case.

Baker, the foreign ministry's legal adviser, showed a draft of the Israeli brief to the State Department. "I think we urged them to tone it down," recalled Taft. In an interview with an AIPAC publication, Baker warned that the case could pose a threat to the United States and other countries: "If it becomes evident that any particular political matter such as this can so easily be sent for an advisory opinion to the ICJ, just by having a majority of the General Assembly send it, theoretically, any hot political matter could go to court. [For instance] the legal status of the prisoners in Guantanamo Bay, or the legal consequences of actions by allied forces in Iraq, or the legal consequences of China's policy toward Tibet, or the legal consequences of fences being built by India in Kashmir, or the legal consequences of Russian actions along the border with Georgia."

Americans opted for a less confrontational approach toward the court than Israel adopted. Like Israel, the State Department decided not to argue the merits of the case. But unlike Israel, the department did not challenge the court's right to hear the case. "We filed a brief—it was not too extensive—that argued that the court ought to decline to take the case. We were respectful of the court, but we tried to point out that the road map was ongoing, and if the court was going to get into this it should not prejudice that effort," Taft told me.

"There was also a very important principle: that jurisdiction over a dispute that's a focus of two parties can only be established by consent of those parties," said Taft. He sent a copy of the brief to the Office of Legal Counsel at the Justice Department. "They just said, 'Fine.'"

In their brief, State Department lawyers gently reminded the World Court judges of the principle that countries had a right to decide whether to submit issues to the court for a decision. They also argued that the case risked politicizing the court and interfering with the peace process. The court, they said, should particularly avoid expressing an opinion on final-status questions—borders, settlements, the status of Jerusalem—that ought to be resolved in negotiations. The American desire to keep the court out of the Middle East conflict was consistent with a U.S. policy going back decades; the United States claimed the lead role as peace broker and tried to keep both the Europeans and the United Nations on the fringes.

To Israel's satisfaction, none of the world's major powers sent representatives to the court session. Turkey, which had been expected to appear on behalf of the Palestinians, dropped out at the last minute. Its appearance would have been ticklish, since it maintains close military ties to Israel, has often been accused of violating the rights of its Kurdish minority, and sought to avoid ICJ jurisdiction over its dispute with Greece in the Aegean.

An American international law expert, Ruth Wedgwood, wrote an essay urging the court to take note of the countries that chose to participate. "The conspicuous absence of the major states from the hearing on the Israeli fence now being held in the Hague—all of Europe, the United States, Russia, Japan, and China—should be taken by the International Court of Justice as a sign of the dangers of going forward," Wedgwood wrote in an essay published on the Web site of her agent, Benador Associates. "Interference with the road map peace process, the implicit challenge to the authority of the Security Council, the one-sided characterization of the human equities at stake, and the unavailability of necessary fact-finding make this dangerous ground for the court. We should preserve the integrity of international courts for circumstances where they can make a genuine contribution. This is not such a case."

If the Israelis hoped to get support from the Western countries that had abstained in the General Assembly, they would be disappointed. None challenged the court's jurisdiction. Among countries submitting briefs, Australia, Canada, Britain, France, and Germany joined the United States in urging the court not to hear the case. All stressed that the court shouldn't become embroiled in a dispute that ought to be settled by negotiations, and that the case could interfere with the delicate process of implementing the road map, which had been unanimously endorsed by the Security Council and was widely seen as offering the best route back to the peace table. Britain argued that an advisory opinion could interfere with the work of the Security Council, which had primary responsibility for the Middle East and would end up being used inappropriately as an enforcement tool against Israel, and said the court would not be able to collect all the necessary facts, particularly involving the security threats faced by Israel.

But deep in the European briefs, these arguments that helped Israel clashed with a conviction that the barrier was illegal and with a strong urge to see it torn down. Germany lumped the wall's construction together with the continued violence and terror as a "major obstacle" to peace. France went further to undermine the Israeli case, in a brief written by attorney Ronny Abraham, who was later tapped to be a judge on the ICJ. The French brief repeated the consensus European argument against hearing the case almost as a form of boilerplate, apparently assuming that the court would reject this advice. With that out of the way, France's brief proceeded to instruct the court in detail on how it should go about concluding that the barrier was illegal. Then it went on to discuss what consequences should flow from this, not only for Israel but for other states, including dismantlement of the wall and restitution for Palestinians whom it had damaged.

Baker recalled, "The French ambassador came to me to explain. He said, 'It was much worse before I persuaded them [Paris] to weaken it.'"

Likewise, Japan, which had abstained along with the European countries when the General Assembly voted, submitted a short brief that said Israel's construction of the barrier within the West Bank could not be justified.

Ireland, which held the European Union's rotating presidency, was not content merely to relay the EU belief that an advisory opinion would be inappropriate. Dublin also submitted a separate ten-page brief that undercut the EU argument that an opinion would interfere with the peace process. Not only was the wall illegal, the brief said, but "Ireland believes that the wall amounts to an obstacle to the peaceful resolution of the conflict and the establishment of a viable Palestinian state." It went on to agree with the Palestinians that the wall's purpose was to "protect Israeli citizens illegally settled in the occupied Palestinian territory. . . ."

Israeli officials knew that even if they didn't participate in the court hearing at the Hague, they needed to mount a major public relations offensive to justify the barrier and blunt the potential damage from an opinion that went against them. Although the ruling would not be binding, it could encourage countries to impose sanctions on Israel. Israeli diplomats in major U.S. cities sent opinion pieces to local newspapers defending the fence. Later, the Ministry of Foreign Affairs developed a special Web site devoted to the barrier. Government public affairs specialists prepared a PowerPoint presentation that support groups in the United States could download.

As the hearing approached in February, an Israeli businessman offered cut-rate tickets to Israelis who would participate in pro-Israeli demonstrations at the Hague. Zaka, an ultra-Orthodox organization whose members perform the grim task of collecting bodies from streets and sidewalks after a bombing, arranged to fly the wreckage of a blown-up bus to the Hague. The government made plans to send twenty or thirty terrorism victims, first to the Hague, and then to make the case for the barrier in other European cities. The Jewish Agency helped organize student delegations from Israel, France, England, Germany, Poland, Belgium, and the Netherlands.

The fractious and beleaguered Palestinian leadership looked to the hearing to lend respectability to their cause and overcome the West's disgust at the wave of terrorism that the leaders were unable or unwilling to control. A distinguished lineup of legal brainpower gathered in the Hague to argue alongside the Palestinians, including professors of international law at Oxford and Cambridge, the Graduate Institute of International Studies in Geneva, the Free University of Brussels, and Yale.

"The thing was scripted," recalled Texas-born Stephanie Koury, a young member of the team. "Their guidance was, 'Keep it simple; stick to the facts, and use sources that are unquestionable.'" She herself was allotted ten minutes. At one point during preparations, team members feared Israelis may have gotten an early look at their strategy. In January, Koury and two other lawyers on the Palestinian team were returning to Ramallah from a planning meeting in Geneva when they were stopped at Ben-Gurion Airport in Tel Aviv, according to Koury. While they were detained, Israeli security agents confiscated documents in their possession, including drafts of their legal arguments. The papers were returned to them twenty to thirty minutes later.

For the session's opening day, the leaders planned a speech by Arafat over radio and television; the sounding of sirens, church bells, and prayers from mosques; a five-minute traffic halt; an hourlong work stoppage at ministries and stores; and popular demonstrations coinciding with what Palestinians expected would be a series of sympathy rallies in Europe and the Middle East. For a brief period in mid-February 2004, it looked as if the intifada's center of gravity were shifting away from terrorism.

But this notion was shattered during rush hour on Sunday, February 22, the start of the Israeli workweek, when a Palestinian from a village outside Bethlehem blew himself up on a crowded bus in Jerusalem, killing eight people and scattering glass and body parts across a two-block area. No more compelling evidence of Israel's self-defense needs could be presented than the scenes of panic and grief that always accompanied such attacks. "If anyone had any doubts of the need for the fence, today's crime against humanity speaks louder and better than any deposition," said Raanan Gissin, adviser to Israeli prime minister Ariel Sharon, according to CNN. At the time of the attack, Malcolm Hoenlein and other leaders of the Conference of Presidents of Major American Jewish Organizations were in Jerusalem's Inbal Hotel being briefed by Chief of General Staff Lieutenant-General Moshe Yaalon, around the corner from where the attack occurred.

The bombing was claimed by the Fatah-linked al-Aqsa Martyrs' Brigades, who identified the bomber as Muhammad Za'al, twenty-three, from the village of Husan near Bethlehem, although Palestinian television aired what it said was a statement by the group denying responsibility. An embarrassed Palestinian leadership in Ramallah issued a statement condemning both the bombing and its timing, noting that it "took place prior to the meeting of the International Court of Justice and amid this international campaign in support of the Palestinian rights." It complained of "this recklessness, carelessness, and lack of responsibility towards our cause, people, rights, and blood."

Interviewed on Al Jazeera, Hamas leader Abdel Aziz Rantisi sneered at the ICJ case and at those in the Palestinian leadership who were attaching such great importance to fighting the separation barrier. "It is as though those you are referring to had expected the International Court of Justice to set up a scaffold to execute Sharon," he told an announcer. "There are hundreds, if not more, of resolutions in the archives of the United Nations and the UN Security Council that serve the Palestinian interests and Palestinian cause. What have they done [for] us? What benefit have they brought us?"

The opening day of the ICJ hearing, the Israeli mass-circulation *Yediot Ahronoth* carried a public appeal to the court from Fanny Haim, whose husband, Yehuda, was among those killed by the suicide blast: "Do not judge my country; do not restrain it from preventing additional people from becoming victims. Today, I am burying my husband; don't you bury justice."

Snow flurries swirled through the Hague as more than one thousand pro-Israel demonstrators gathered in a square near the Peace Palace, an ornate, century-old, redbrick structure set in a handsomely landscaped park. Many carried photos, supplied by the Israeli embassy, of people killed by terrorists, along with Israeli flags and banners calling for an end to terrorism. Silently, they filed past the skeleton of a bus destroyed in a January 29 bombing in Jerusalem. Demonstrators included Jews and Christians, students and terrorism victims, two U.S.

congressmen, and activists, such as leaders of B'nai B'rith International. Israel also made officials available to the Western media for interviews, including Daniel Taub.

Pro-Palestinian demonstrators gathered in the same area later in the day for a rally that featured Azmi Bishara, an Arab member of the Israeli parliament. Thousands of Palestinians participated in anti-barrier marches throughout the West Bank and elsewhere in the Middle East. Soldiers fired tear gas to keep marchers near Jenin and Tulkarem from getting too close to the barrier, and to disperse stone throwers in Bethlehem and the Jerusalem suburb of Abu Dis.

The demonstrations drew media attention away from the early stages of a hearing inside the Peace Palace. Fifteen black-robed, white-bibbed judges entered the paneled Great Hall of Justice to take their seats on a raised dais as sunlight filtered into the chamber through soaring stained-glass windows. The rest of the judges sat silently as Presiding Judge Shi Jiuyong of China described the background of the case, entitled, "Legal Consequences of the Construction of a Wall in the Occupied Palestinian Territory," and read the list of participants in the hearings. Then he offered the floor to al-Qidwa, stumbling over the pronunciation.

The Palestinian, dressed in a dark suit and tie offset by a white shirt, rose and shot quick glances at judges to his right and then his left, his moist dark eyes gleaming in the light. Speaking smoothly in fluent, slightly accented English, he opened with a brief declaration: "I stand before you as a representative of the Palestinian people, the indigenous people of the land, who for too long have been denied the right to self-determination and sovereignty over their land and half of whom remain refugees.

"The Palestinian people have been subject to a military occupation for almost thirty-seven years. They have been dehumanized and demonized, humiliated and demeaned, dispossessed and dispersed, and brutally punished by their occupier," al-Qidwa said, before quickly shifting to the specific topic of the separation barrier. "This wall is not about security. It's about entrenching the occupation. . . . This wall, if completed, will leave the Palestinian people with only half of the West Bank within isolated, noncontiguous, walled enclaves. It will render the two-state solution to the Israeli-Palestinian conflict practically impossible."

He continued, speaking in a blunt staccato. Since 1967, he said, Israel had transferred four hundred thousand illegal settlers to the territory and was continually trying "to change the status, physical character, nature, and demographic composition of that territory. . . ." Since the Oslo peace process began, the number of settlers had "doubled . . . doubled," he emphasized.

Al-Qidwa quickly dispensed with Israel's justification for the barrier—that it prevented Palestinian suicide bombers from killing Israelis. "Israel claims that the construction of the wall is a temporary defensive measure to prevent suicide bombings and provide security for Israel. This is not true, and the proof is simple. If this were in fact the case, then Israel would have constructed the wall on its territory along the Armistice Line of 1949. . . . If Israel wanted a wall for security, it could construct it on its territory and raise it to eighty meters rather than eight meters if it wished." This glib statement sidestepped the fact that hundreds of thousands of Israelis lived on the West Bank—legally or not—and were threatened by terrorism.

Al-Qidwa was followed by Koury, one of a group of young, Western-educated lawyers in Mahmoud Abbas's Negotiation Support Group whose energy, brains, and commitment were beginning to sharpen and enliven Palestinian diplomacy. For Koury, briefings on the separation barrier had become a specialty. Eight months earlier, she had briefed Condoleezza Rice, President Bush's national security adviser, on the route of the barrier, and then did the same for Elliott Abrams.

Looking stylish in a black suit with burgundy blouse as she stood at the Hague podium, she hesitated in a brief moment of nervousness at first as she peered at the judges through black-rimmed spectacles but quickly gained her footing. Using slides of pictures of the barrier and maps, she described the route of the wall and then concentrated on its impact on the lives and livelihoods of West Bank Palestinians. "Because of these conditions, Palestinians are leaving the area," she said.

The presentation continued with a succinct argument by a Cambridge professor on why the court should accept the case; a scholarly survey of international law governing occupied land territory; a biting analysis on how these laws should be applied to the Palestinian territory;

and, finally, the Palestinians' view of what the "legal consequences" should be. Jean Salmon, a Belgian international law professor, said these must include a halt to the wall's construction, a return to the status quo ante, including moving out Israelis who had settled close to the barrier, and compensation to Palestinians harmed by the wall. He also demanded criminal prosecution of anyone who violated international law in connection with the wall. Other countries should be required to cooperate in bringing about an end to the violations. If Israel persisted in building the wall, the Security Council ought to "take the necessary coercive measures," Salmon said.

Three hours after it began, the presentation ended—for the most part, the Palestinians had wasted little time.

Beyond the legal arguments, the presentation by al-Qidwa and the lawyers he had assembled carried important symbolism. For more than a decade, Yasser Arafat had drawn sneers for his pretensions to statesmanship—by flaunting his title of "president," travels to world capitals, and his personal plane, helicopter, and uniformed honor guard—at a time when statehood remained just a dream, when his government was corrupt, and Palestinians themselves lived with poverty and humiliation. Now, in the rarefied precincts of the Hague, a world away from Arafat's broken-up headquarters and the bloodied battlegrounds of terror, stood Palestinian representatives whose comportment and careful preparation suggested they belonged there. If so, maybe they deserved, as well, "a place among the nations."

For the first time, a live webcast of a hearing before the ICJ was being made available to viewers worldwide on the court's Web site. In Jerusalem, the Palestinian presentation drew grudging admiration. In Washington, Shimon Peres complained during an appearance before the Washington Institute for Near East Policy. "I wonder about the whole idea of an international court, maybe just for genocide, because how can one nation that didn't fight, that doesn't suffer from terror, judge a nation that is all the time suffering from it?"

Both Palestinians and Israelis expected the ICJ to accept jurisdiction. "[T]he ICJ had never before refused to entertain a request for advisory opinion from the General Assembly," member Pieter Bekker said in a

2005 e-mail. Palestinians also had reason to be optimistic about the opinion itself, he said. "We took the 'less is more' approach, aiming for a confirmation by the ICJ that the Fourth Geneva Convention is applicable de jure to the OPT (Occupied Palestinian Territories). Everything else (i.e., Israel's obligations under international humanitarian law embodied in the Fourth Geneva Convention) would follow from such a confirmation. Given that the UN Security Council, the General Assembly, and the International Committee of the Red Cross had confirmed many times that the Fourth Geneva Convention is applicable de jure (and not simply de facto), it was to be expected that the ICJ would follow the position taken by these organs."

But when it came, nearly five months later, the opinion jolted both sides. As expected, the court accepted jurisdiction and found no reason not to render an opinion. Dismissing Israeli arguments, it found that the Fourth Geneva Convention applied to the occupied territories east of the 1967 Green Line, along with various human rights conventions. As to the barrier, the court said the route chosen for it "gravely" infringed on Palestinian rights in a way that couldn't be justified by military or security requirements. Israeli right to self-defense, it said, is irrelevant as a justification for the wall, since Israel is not being attacked by another state, the court ruled. In short, the barrier violated international law.

The court said Israel should not only dismantle the wall but undo any legislation connected with it and pay compensation or return property to those whose land or belongings had been seized or damaged. Other countries must not recognize the changes caused by the barrier or in any way help its construction. The General Assembly and Security Council should "consider what further action is required to bring to an end the illegal situation." Finally, it said the UN needed to encourage a negotiated solution "on the basis of international law" that would lead to a Palestinian state existing alongside Israel in peace.

"I didn't expect all that we got, frankly," Koury said.

The case marked the first time that any international court had ruled "on a prominent aspect of the problem in application of the rules of international law," as Bekker would later write in the *Cornell*

International Law Journal. It also marked the first time that an international court would affirm that the territories are, in fact, occupied, rejecting Israel's designation of them as "disputed."

The ICJ found that the Israeli settlements in the territories violate international law. "Perhaps the most remarkable aspect of the ruling is the fact that the ICJ explicitly condemned the settlements that Israel has established in Palestinian territories occupied by it since 1967," Bekker wrote. An added plus for the Palestinians was that most of the court's findings were approved by a 14–1 vote, with only the American judge, Thomas Buergenthal, dissenting.

That lopsided vote, however, masked deep disagreements over the reasoning behind the judges' conclusions, particularly over the threat faced by Israel and the Jewish state's right to defend itself. Elaraby, the Egyptian judge, was unsparing in his criticism of Israel, suggesting that Israel had only itself to blame for the terrorism it faced. "Throughout the annals of history, occupation has always been met with armed resistance. Violence breeds violence. . . . I wholeheartedly subscribe to the view . . . that the breaches by both sides of the fundamental rules of humanitarian law reside in 'the illegality of the Israeli occupation regime itself.' Occupation, as an illegal and temporary situation, is at the heart of the whole problem. The only viable prescription to end the grave violations of international humanitarian law is to end occupation."

Higgins's position was significant. In her opinion, there is nothing in the text of Article 51 of the Charter of the United Nations that stipulates that self-defense is available only when an armed attack is made by a state. Judge Higgins also failed to understand the ICJ's view that an occupying power loses the right to defend its own civilian citizens at home if the attacks emanate from the occupied territory—a territory which it has found not to have been annexed and is certainly "other than" Israel. However, she did not vote against the ICJ's opinion on this issue, both since she was unconvinced that nonforcible measures (such as the building of a wall) fall within self-defense under Article 51 of the Charter, and since the building of the fence, even if it can be seen as an act of self-defense, would need to be justified as necessary and proportional. Those justifications, according to Judge Higgins, had not been explained.

The Dutch judge, Pieter Hendrik Kooijmans, along with Buergen-thal, said the court had ignored the Security Council's new approach to terrorism, which allowed "individual or collective self-defense without making any reference to an armed attack by a state." Buergenthal argued further that since the area beyond the Green Line was not part of Israel proper, "attacks on Israel coming from across that line must therefore permit Israel to exercise its right of self-defense against such attacks, provided the measures it takes are otherwise consistent with the legitimate exercise of that right."

In a strong rebuke of his colleagues, Buergenthal wrote that the court should not have taken the case and that its sweeping conclusions could not be justified given the limited amount of information it relied on.

But reading over the opinion, al-Qidwa drew deep satisfaction from a nugget in Buergenthal's ninth paragraph.

There, in a nutshell, was the Palestinians' case—and the American judge agreed with it: Referring to a paragraph of the Fourth Geneva Convention, he wrote: "I agree that this provision applies to the Israeli settlements in the West Bank and that their existence violates Article 49, paragraph 6. It follows that the segments of the wall being built by Israel to protect the settlements are ipso facto in violation of international humanitarian law. Moreover, given the demonstrable great hardship to which the affected Palestinian population is being subjected in and around the enclaves created by those segments of the wall, I seriously doubt that the wall would here satisfy the proportionality requirement to qualify as a legitimate measure of self-defense."

On two key questions—are the settlements illegal; and are sections of the wall built to protect the settlements illegal—the court was unan-imous: yes.

In Jerusalem, the advisory opinion hit Israeli legal circles like a sub-terranean earthquake. "We were quite taken aback by the opinion," said Alan Baker, speaking by telephone from his new post as Israeli ambassa-dor to Canada. He was surprised that the relatively balanced views of Hig-gins and Kooijmans hadn't made more of an impact on their colleagues.

"It was as if they ignored completely the brief we filed and accepted the Palestinian-Egyptian-Arab League presentation. On a long list of claims—settlements, humanitarian law, human rights—it was as if they approved the legal case put forward by the Arabs, completely ignoring our claims." Although Israel had limited its argument to the question of jurisdiction and judicial propriety, its lengthy brief included material on its security concerns.

"Israeli leaders expected to lose the case, but said they were unprepared for such a sweeping condemnation of their presence in the West Bank, criticism of Jewish settlements, and the near-total rejection of the threat their nation faces from suicide bombings and other attacks," reported Peter Hermann of the *Baltimore Sun*.

When a bomb exploded July 11, two days after the ruling, at a Tel Aviv bus station, Sharon told his cabinet, "What the judges refused to see, the Palestinians quickly showed them this morning—murder and the wounding of innocent civilians." He said the decision "sends a destructive message to encourage the terror and denounces countries that are defending themselves against it." Finance Minister Benjamin Netanyahu, writing on the *New York Times* op-ed page, was defiant: "Because the court's decision makes a mockery of Israel's right to defend itself, the government of Israel will ignore it. Israel will never sacrifice Jewish life on the debased altar of 'international justice.'" Shinui Party Leader Yosef Lapid, meanwhile, felt vindicated in having urged Israel to participate in the case. "I still think I was right. It would have had a different outcome," he said in 2005.

Netanyahu was mistaken. Israel couldn't ignore the advisory opinion. As Israel grew and dealt with the rest of the world in deeper and more complex ways, its government increasingly realized it couldn't thumb its nose at international law. Israel was increasingly dependent on trade and markets for its technological and scientific breakthroughs to ensure its continued prosperity. Thus, it needed the protection of certain clauses of international law—particularly those governing commerce and copyrights. Israel also was party to two bilateral international peace treaties and various world conventions.

The Bush administration, despite having backed Israel at the World Court, continued to have concerns about the separation barrier's impact on Palestinian lives—and its downright ugliness. In August

2004, attorney Daniel Seidemann, a strong advocate for Palestinian legal rights, took Elliott Abrams, the National Security Council's main point man for the Middle East, on a tour to show him the route of the barrier through Arab neighborhoods. He warned Abrams that the barrier could radicalize Palestinians in East Jerusalem. He also described the potential impact of Israel's plan to erect new Jewish neighborhoods between Jerusalem and the expanding settlement of Ma'ale Adumim, thus imposing another barrier to the contiguity of a future Palestinian state.

Israeli attorney general Menachem Mazuz named a team to study the ramifications of the World Court advisory opinion. The next month, the team recommended that the government consider applying the Geneva Conventions formally to the West Bank and Gaza. Israel had previously said it operated according to the conventions but wouldn't apply them because the territory was disputed, rather than occupied. Mazuz suggested that the ICJ opinion had created "a new legal reality for Israel" and its "negative repercussions" should not be underestimated, according to a report by the U.S. Institute of Peace.

It fell to Israel's Supreme Court, the most respected pillar of the state's democratic traditions, to decide what impact the ICJ ruling would have on Israeli actions. This court faced a tough task: it had to explain how the continued existence of the barrier squared with Israel's commitment to the rule of law. The court's room for argument was further restricted by the fact that it had already ruled on the separation barrier in June. Its decision said the wall, in principle, was legal, but the route it took had to be weighed carefully against the hardship it imposed on the Palestinians. As a result, it had ordered the government to change parts of the route to ease the impact on Palestinians.

It took the Israeli high court more than a year, but in September 2005, it offered an explanation: "What is the basis of this difference between the two judgments?" the Israeli justices asked, comparing its own previous ruling with the ICJ's. "The answer to that question is that the main difference between the legal conclusions stems from the difference in the factual basis laid before the court." Because of a "severe oversight," for which Israel itself may have been partially responsible, the ICJ had failed to consider a substantial amount of evidence showing a security and military necessity to erect the barrier, the court found. Instead, it drew its facts almost entirely from the UN secretariat and UN reporters. These reports paid hardly any attention to the terrorist threat faced by Israelis and also contained inaccurate descriptions of the impact on Palestinians, according to the Israeli court.

Aharon Barak, who wrote the opinion, effectively zeroed in on what several ICJ judges concluded were gaps and deficiencies in the Hague ruling, particularly when it came to Israelis' right to self-defense. But to satisfy himself that Israel could continue building the wall and comply with international law, he had to tiptoe around the fact that the ICJ had declared the barrier illegal in part because it was protecting illegal settlements, in addition to residents of Israel proper. He accepted without question that the sole purpose of the wall was security and therefore said Israel could confiscate West Bank territory to build it. Thus, he disregarded concerns repeatedly expressed by U.S. officials that the route could prejudge Israel's final border, as well as the acknowledgment by Israeli officials that politics played a part in the route. Peres, at his February 23, 2004, appearance in Washington, said, "[T]he line of the wall was a mistake. I think it should never become pregnant with political appetites. And I'm very glad that the present government is correcting it."

Since the wall was intended to preserve public safety and protect lives, it was perfectly legal for it to protect the lives of settlers, even if they were in the area illegally, Barak wrote.

In truth, both courts glossed over inconvenient truths. The Hague judges failed to look at the wall from a practical standpoint: yes, it imposed a hardship, but it also could reduce the need for lethal counterattacks by Israel. Israeli justices ignored a history of settlement expansion and land confiscation intended to annex parts of the West Bank to Israel.

For al-Qidwa and the Palestinian leadership, the ICJ opinion posed a new challenge: how could they use it to gain a durable political advantage over Israel? Since it was advisory, there was no automatic enforcement. And since Israel had no intention of halting the building of the fence, the Palestinians needed to find ways to make sure others respected it—if not the Israelis.

Al-Qidwa took the first logical step, working with his allies in the General Assembly to produce a new resolution following up on the ICJ opinion. He won overwhelming support, including from Europe, for getting the secretariat to tally the damage incurred by the construction of the separation barrier and sound out the signatories of the Fourth Geneva Convention for a new conference focused on Israel's failure to comply: "The debate has been concluded. We believe that it is time for implementation, for compliance, and, at a later stage, for additional measures," he said during General Assembly debate on the resolution. In a burst of hyperbole, he said of the advisory opinion: "We believe it is the most important development within the United Nations system since the partition plan," the 1947 resolution calling for a Jewish and an Arab state in Palestine.

"Thank God that the fate of Israel and of the Jewish people is not decided in this room," retorted Dan Gillerman.

U.S. representative James Cunningham signaled that al-Qidwa would have trouble moving beyond the General Assembly. Explaining why the United States opposed the resolution, he said the ICJ ruling had failed sufficiently to address Israel's right to self-defense, was based on outdated information, and was ill-advised to begin with. If a conference of the Geneva Convention signatories were held, the United States would not participate, he vowed. Left unsaid but clear was the threat that if al-Qidwa tried to introduce a similar measure in the Security Council, the United States would veto it.

The next month, al-Qidwa played a major role at a conference of the 115-member Non-Aligned Movement in Durban, South Africa, emerging with a statement that welcomed the advisory opinion and detailed its most significant findings. The statement also urged members to impose sanctions against Israeli settlements by preventing "any products of the illegal Israeli settlements from entering their markets consistent with the obligations under international treaties, to decline entry to Israeli settlers, and to impose sanctions against companies and entities involved in the construction of the wall and other illegal activities in the occupied Palestinian territory, including East Jerusalem."

From there, momentum created by the ICJ opinion slowed dramatically. The following January, Kofi Annan promised to open a registry of damages resulting from the building of the wall, in keeping with the assembly resolution. His announcement meant he would create a new UN agency, with a board and technical and legal experts, that would document the confiscation of land, destruction of orchards, citrus groves, olive groves, and wells, and the seizure of immovable property, and decide on categories of damages. A month later, Annan's spokesman said Israel had not indicated whether it would cooperate. By late October, there had been no public announcement that the registry had begun.

In July 2005, Switzerland, in its capacity as depository of the Geneva Conventions, told the General Assembly in a letter that it had complied with the request that it contact the signatories to the Fourth Geneva Convention. There would not be a conference of signatories, as the Palestinians had hoped, and, "There is currently no expectation that Israel will agree to dismantle the barrier, or ensure that it is built entirely along the Green Line," the Swiss government said. It proposed instead the formation of two "dialogue groups," one with Israel, the other with the Palestinian Authority, reporting to the Quartet, but said "the parties concerned" didn't support this idea.

In discussions with the Swiss, the Palestinians mapped out a campaign of escalating pressure they hoped would be brought to bear on the Israelis, starting with regular demands from countries that are close to Israel. If this didn't work, the Security Council and Western countries should step in. Imports from settlements should be banned, and companies that assist in building the separation barrier should face sanctions. Finally, they called for "the adoption of measures by the High Contracting Parties with a view to ensuring Israel's compliance with its obligations under the Fourth Geneva Convention, especially as regards the punishment of grave breaches."

"The case has potentially huge ramifications," attorney Amjad Atallah said in the fall of 2005, referring to potential legal pressure that could be used against Israel. "The Palestinians simply haven't capitalized on it yet."

There was reason to doubt they ever would; in fact, the alarm felt by Israel when the ICJ ruled may have been unwarranted. By then, the whole center of gravity had shifted in Middle East politics. Israel's plans to withdraw military forces and settlers from the Gaza Strip had come to dominate any discussion of the Israeli-Palestinian conflict by the international community, overwhelming any follow-up action. Arafat died, to be replaced by Mahmoud Abbas, who rejected violence and campaigned for president on a platform of nonviolence and negotiations, and actively courted support from the United States.

Meanwhile, a sea change occurred at the United Nations. Enough corruption and malfeasance had been uncovered in the Iraq oil-for-food scandal to discredit the institution and batter the heretofore clean reputation of Secretary General Kofi Annan. The man who insisted in 2001 and thereafter that solving the Israeli-Palestinian conflict had to be the international community's top priority was, by mid-2004, fighting to salvage his reputation. Annan's actions became more cautious, apparently out of a desire to avoid giving more ammunition to his critics, and he took steps that made him appear more sympathetic to Israel, like arranging a daylong seminar on anti-Semitism in August 2004.

The oil-for-food scandal produced the worst crisis in U.S. relations with the United Nations since the period when North Carolina Republican Jesse Helms presided over the Senate Foreign Relations Committee and withheld payments to the world body. Once again, "reform" became the watchword of American dealings with the UN. One of the prime examples cited by American diplomats of what needed to be changed was the world body's approach to "the Question of Palestine," particularly what American and Israeli officials complained were biased, redundant, overlapping, and expensive agencies, meetings, and reports—all geared toward criticizing or complaining about Israel. U.S. officials charged that these various bodies "perpetuate the notion that only one party to the Middle East conflict has rights but does not have any of the accompanying responsibilities."

In the fall of 2005, under the aggressive leadership of the outspoken and determined conservative John Bolton, who became the American permanent representative in August, the United States resumed a campaign to cut back agencies devoted to the Palestinian question—which together cost the UN $3 million a year.

Al-Qidwa left the Palestinian mission to the UN in March 2005 to become foreign minister in the new cabinet headed by Prime Minister Ahmed Qurei. Ostensibly, this was a promotion. In fact, it may have removed him from a forum where his talents and contacts were most effective in advancing the Palestinian cause. His new domain was an office building in Ramallah with a lobby that needed paint and showed dusty footprints on the black-tiled floor.

Interviewed in June 2005, al-Qidwa regretted the failure by the Palestinians to follow up on what he considered their greatest triumph in a decade at the United Nations.

"Here we should have been working in a much more serious way in all fields," he said, citing possible sanctions against companies or individuals involved in the security barrier. "We started—we went to the [Non-Aligned Movement] meeting. Then things started to change. There were the U.S. elections. The political situation here changed. Several events occupied everybody."

Al-Qidwa, in fact, had been yanked off his perch at the UN to confront an unpleasant reality. For three and a half decades, the "Question of Palestine" had been a major preoccupation of the United Nations; drawn days on end of heated rhetoric in New York, South Africa, and other venues; consumed untold hours of behind-the-scenes diplomacy; and produced scores of resolutions. The legal underpinnings for its demand that Israel end the occupation of the West Bank seemed to grow stronger by the year. And what had all this achieved for the Palestinians? At the United Nations, they seemed almost to dwell in a separate universe—where they were recognized, even celebrated—while on the ground, their lands and livelihoods were shrinking.

On September 15, 2005, Prime Minister Sharon climbed to the rostrum of the General Assembly, the chamber where al-Qidwa's biting rhetoric used to be heard so frequently and where the Palestinians—representing the last peoples on earth to live under a form of colonialism—so often got their way. It had been a great couple of days for Sharon, who drew public praise from Bush for his "courageous decision to give peace a chance" by withdrawing from Gaza, and who continued his rapprochement with the Muslim world by getting introduced to the president of Pakistan and meeting with the foreign minister of Indonesia.

"Israel will know how to defend itself from the horrors of terrorism. This is why we built the security fence," Sharon told the assembly, whose members had overwhelmingly and repeatedly denounced the barrier, "and we will continue to build it until it is completed, as would any other country defending its citizens. The security fence prevents terrorists and murderers from arriving in city centers on a daily basis and targeting citizens on their way to work, children on their way to school, and families sitting together in restaurants." As long as Palestinian militants kept dispatching suicide bombers and Israel retaliated, the real universe that the Palestinians occupied would remain one that was dominated by Israel and the United States. The United Nations and international law would be a sideshow.

By October 2005, American hostility toward the barrier had all but dissipated. Sharon had won President Bush's admiration by facing down internal opposition and then successfully carrying out the Israeli withdrawal from Gaza. The administration was inclined to believe Israeli claims that the barrier's purpose was only one of security. A senior official said, "Any democratic state has to protect innocent citizens from being murdered. I sympathize with those who say it's a terrible thing, it's an ugly thing, it places a great burden on Palestinians. I then say, 'Well, what would you then have them do? What are they supposed to do? People are being murdered.' This is a product, essentially, of suicide bombers, and an inability of Palestinian security forces to cope with the problem."

Nasser al-Qidwa's moment had passed. But the United Nations General Assembly remained a valuable forum for the Palestinians to air their grievances and assert their legal claims. Even in 2006, with a government controlled by the militant Hamas movement, and with U.S. permanent representative John Bolton aggressively working to support Israel, the Palestinians continued to get strong backing for their annual slate of resolutions—and kept the Europeans mostly on their side. And they won a new mandate—for a UN probe of civilian deaths in the Gaza town of Beit Hanoun. Israel isolated itself anew by denying access to the inquiry team, led by famed South African cleric and antiapartheid activist Desmond Tutu.

By trying to separate the UN and international law from Middle East diplomacy, the United States did neither itself, nor Israel and the Palestinians, a favor. It isolated itself within the world body, prevented Israel from gaining the full international acceptance many of its leaders craved, diminished the authority of international justice, kept Palestinians from facing international sanctions for acquiescing in terror and crimes against humanity, and ignored a forum where some of the most talented Israeli and Palestinian diplomats could engage in creative compromise.

16

A New Chance

■ LATE 2003 ■

"GOOD EVENING. RAMADAN KAREEM." George
W. Bush's expressive eyes roamed the State Dining Room as he stood to
welcome American Muslim leaders, visitors, and ambassadors with a
customary wish for a generous (kareem) holy month. Letting his gaze fall
affectionately on people he recognized, he paid gracious tribute to a religion that wasn't his: "America is a land of many faiths—and we honor
and welcome and value the Muslim faith." The occasion was an Iftar,
the festive meal breaking the daylong fast during Ramadan, in late October 2003. Since the start of Bush's campaign against terrorism two years
earlier and the subsequent U.S.-led invasion of two Muslim nations, the
Iftar had become an important part of the administration's affirmation
to Muslims that the United States was not at war with their beliefs.

The White House placed Ziad Asali at the president's table, and not
by accident. Asali was president and founder of the American Task
Force on Palestine, an organization headquartered two blocks from the
White House that campaigned for Palestinian statehood. His honored
seat at the Iftar was meant to show that Bush remained committed to a
cause that burned throughout the Muslim world: Palestinian statehood.
As the president reminded Asali more than once when they met, "I'm the
first president to mention Palestine by name. I didn't say 'a Palestinian

state' or 'Palestinian rights.' I mentioned it here at the White House and at the United Nations."

That a gesture toward the head of a small, Washington-based organization was chosen as the way for Bush to reassert his commitment to Palestine spoke volumes about how far relations had sunk between the United States and the actual Palestinian leadership by the fall of 2003. More than a year had passed since the White House had blocked all contact between American officials and Palestinian president Yasser Arafat. After lauding Prime Minister Mahmoud Abbas as an agent of nonviolent reform in the Palestinian Authority, meeting with him in Jordan, and then welcoming him to the White House, Bush had watched as Abbas failed to wrest power away from Arafat and resigned within just a few months. Arafat then tapped as Abbas's replacement the speaker of the Palestinian parliament, Ahmed Qurei, while retaining a grip on cabinet selections and the multipronged security apparatus. While low-key and moderate, Qurei lacked Abbas's clear commitment to nonviolence and was less independent of the longtime Palestinian leader.

Bush told others that he had wasted political capital in the summer of 2003 to support Abbas and get a new peace process started with a reformed Palestinian government—only to have the effort collapse amid a resumption of terror and retaliation. He chose to blame Arafat. "Unfortunately, they [the Palestinians] have a poor leadership, untrustworthy, and they need to put an end to terrorism," Asali recalled Bush saying at the Iftar. Among his advisers, the preferred view was that the ploy designed by the UN, the Europeans, and the State Department to work around Arafat and loosen his grip over the Palestinian Authority had been too clever by half and had failed.

"[O]ur view was that one of the things that happened was that Arafat couldn't stand the idea that he was barred from the White House and this guy [Mahmoud Abbas] was there with all that limelight, and got rid of him," a senior administration official, whose views often reflect the president's, said. "Fundamentally, I think there was a one-word answer: Arafat. The president said in his speech that Palestinians needed new leadership. Clearly he meant that you're not going to solve this with Arafat. And . . . so we tried to work around Arafat, by creating the position of prime minister, filling it with a good man—the international community pressured the Palestinians to do it—and it was done: they created the position, the PLC did it, he selected Abu Mazen. But it was not possible to make progress. You still had essentially the same power structure, that is, you had Arafat and his security setup. We blamed him."

This view might have been more widely shared had the United States itself made more of an effort during Abbas's brief tenure in 2003. But the intense focus on halting violence against Israelis, with little that was tangible for the Palestinians in return, exposed Abbas to charges that his peaceful, pragmatic approach was a sellout to the Americans and Israelis.

"I think we probably could have, during that period, done more in terms of economic assistance to the Palestinians," a senior official acknowledged. "We probably could have pushed harder on the security side in terms of providing visible support to the Palestinians to rebuild their services and also pushing for a little bit more generous Israeli attitude toward what the Palestinians were trying to do. I'm not sure . . . in the end that that would have produced a different result, but it certainly would have helped."

Like Bush, Abbas spilled political capital with public gestures to Israelis. At Aqaba, he acknowledged the suffering of Jews throughout history and renounced terrorism against Israelis "wherever they might be. Such methods are inconsistent with our religious and moral traditions and are dangerous obstacles to the achievement of an independent, sovereign state we seek." Ziad Abu Amr, a Gaza-based politician and scholar who was active in Abbas's government, scoffed at the notion that Abbas failed simply because Arafat pulled the rug out from under him. "That's not true. He was very forceful in challenging Arafat. I was in the cabinet and I remember how we took decisions. Arafat in most cases was kept in the dark. . . . [T]he people who let Abu Mazen down were the Israelis and Americans."

After Abbas became prime minister, "I helped negotiate a truce between Hamas and our position. It lasted for fifty-one days," Abu Amr said. "What did the Israelis do? Even if there was no truce, if you were interested in progress, you would have given a lot of concrete gestures, goodwill, confidence-building measures, tell the Palestinians, through the new prime minister, that Israeli troops would redeploy from three cities, five cities. That did not happen. You would have released prisoners, you would have removed some of the roadblocks. You would say, 'OK, we're going to put a freeze on settlement activity. Give him a chance.'"

The collapse of Abbas's government opened a diplomatic vacuum. The United States stopped trying to mediate between Israelis and Palestinians. Instead, the White House used direct channels to the Israelis in a bid to ease the plight of Palestinians. These two-way negotiations mostly involved details and incremental steps, nibbling around the edges of the conflict, but they set an important precedent and a format for what would occur a few months later.

The White House pressed Israel, without success, to dismantle new outposts on occupied territory that Israeli settlers continued erecting in defiance of international opinion and even of Israeli law. Condoleezza Rice negotiated with Ariel Sharon's chief of staff, Dov Weisglass, in an attempt to alter the route of the Israeli separation barrier, then under construction in the West Bank. The resulting route hewed more closely to the Green Line, but that wasn't the Americans' main concern, according to Israeli ambassador Danny Ayalon. "[I]t wasn't so much whether it was on the Green Line or not. For them, the most important issue was not to infringe upon Palestinian lives. So, humanitarian considerations, not to separate kids from school, farmers from their land, workers from their workplaces. . . . [W]e were quite specific in saying that this is not a political boundary." The United States and Israel also worked out a symbolic penalty for the encroaching fence and settlements—a cut of $289.5 million in loan guarantees to Israel—that would not badly damage the Israeli economy.

Such steps did nothing to address the overall conflict. Outside the Washington-Jerusalem channel, impatience mounted for a major new diplomatic push to fill the void. The week before the White House Iftar, Kieran Prendergast gave the United Nations Security Council a gloomy assessment in the monthly report on the Israeli-Palestinian conflict delivered by UN officials: "Instead of moving forward, we are seeing backward movement, away from a peaceful settlement and away from the negotiating table," said the undersecretary general for political affairs. Israelis and Palestinians could not advance on their own, he stressed: "The level of trust between them is too low, and the lines of communication too weak. This makes it imperative that the international community reassert its role in Middle East peacemaking." Prendergast's sharp challenge was clearly aimed mainly at the United States, whose role was crucial as the most powerful member of the Quartet and the only nation with strong leverage on Israel.

At the Iftar, Ziad Asali used the chance of a conversation with Bush to urge him to resume an active role in trying to end the Israeli-Palestinian conflict. This wasn't their first or last meeting, or the only time he tried to make the case with Bush. Asali's style is low-key. A physician born and raised in Jerusalem, he was a pillar of the Palestinian American establishment, soft-spoken and courtly. He valued high-level access. He avoided harsh criticism of the administration, preferring think tank seminars and quiet contacts with senior officials to hard-hitting press statements. He held no brief for Yasser Arafat and accepted as a given the United States' close strategic ties to Israel. Asali thought the armed intifada, with its suicide attacks on civilians, had been a catastrophe for the Palestinians—particularly after the shock that terrorists administered to the American psyche on September 11. "I don't think the Palestinian leadership understood—like Arab leaders, Muslim leaders, states in general— understood the significance of September 11 and what it meant," he said in an interview in 2006. Palestinians could have escaped with their national cause intact had they spurned Islamic terrorism and stuck to passive resistance, he felt. Instead, the leadership failed to control the violence. But there was a second part to the tragedy: "Really and truly, Sharon was determined to paint the Palestinians as terrorists."

With Bush, Asali argued that an administration effort to resolve the conflict would improve U.S. standing in the world. At one point in their conversations, Asali told Bush that if he managed to achieve a solution that had eluded a half-dozen of his predecessors, "You could get the Nobel Peace Prize."

"I don't want the Nobel Peace Prize," Bush retorted. "I want peace."

Like other Palestinians who have met with Bush, Asali came away convinced that the president meant it. He was also impressed by Bush's knowledge of the details of the conflict. Ghaith al-Omari, a U.S.-trained lawyer and negotiator who had worked with both Abbas and the Americans during the spring and summer of 2003, had the same impression of Bush. He remembered most vividly "a very strong sense of sincerity." Over time, "his knowledge of the issues has greatly increased."

At the 2003 Iftar, Bush recognized that Palestinians were competent and talented and deserved a country of their own, Asali recalled. Some of the president's respect for Palestinians no doubt stems from his forty-year friendship with a Yale classmate, Jerusalem-born Muhammed Saleh, a businessman and inventor who went on to become vice president of Timex, the watch manufacturer.

"He was even-handed . . . in terms of compassion, in terms of ordinary people, in terms of just basically recognizing Palestinians as people who deserve a democracy, who deserve peace, who deserve to get to hospitals without having to go through checkpoints," a senior U.S. official said.

Bush's meetings with moderate, well schooled, well mannered Palestinians may have increased his contempt for Arafat's tolerance of corruption and terrorism. They also may have blinded him to the difficulty any Palestinian leader would have in quelling the population's violent impulses. Even though a consistent majority backed a two-state solution to the conflict, the hatred and bitterness toward Israel led a consistent majority to believe that violence was the only way to achieve it. Bush, however, viewed the violence and terror in black-and-white terms and demanded a decisive Palestinian leader who could end it.

Whatever impact Asali had on Bush's thinking at the late-October Iftar, Bush clearly wasn't ready to go out on a limb again with Arafat still in power and the Palestinian leadership in disarray. With his own reelection campaign looming, he had less political capital to spend on what could prove to be a useless diplomatic venture. And he had a growing problem coming from a different direction. The unruly insurgency in Iraq was turning into a vicious jihad that threatened the whole enterprise. The toll in blood and treasure was rising. "There's been— obviously, it's tough," Bush told a roundtable of British journalists

November 12. "We lost Italian police today. These killers are—they're hard-nosed people. They'll kill because they want to intimidate. They want us to leave. That's their goal. They've got different ambitions. Some would like to see a Taliban-type government, that would be the mujahideen-type people. Some want to revenge the loss, the defeat in Afghanistan. They would be your al-Qaida types. And the Baathists, of course, want to get back in power." International security analysts were offering a grim prognosis on the global campaign against terrorism. Far from striking a new blow against Islamist extremism, the American occupation of Iraq, they warned, was providing al-Qaida with a powerful propaganda tool in its holy war against the West, injecting new energy into the worldwide network even though many of its key operatives were in jail or dead and its top leadership was on the run.

Sympathetic though Bush was to the Palestinians, an initiative to fill the diplomatic vacuum would have to come from elsewhere. But at the time, impatience was mounting in the Middle East and in Europe. Others were developing their own initiatives. With European funding, Israel's perennial peace activist Yossi Beilin, a former minister now far from the center of power, had teamed up with a longtime Palestinian negotiator, Yasser Abed Rabbo, in a shadow negotiating process to frame an Israeli-Palestinian agreement. The two aimed to demonstrate that a realistic agreement could be achieved even amid the bitter tensions of the intifada. They produced a detailed, line-by-line blueprint. Separately, Ami Ayalon, a former director of Shin Bet, the Israeli domestic security service, joined the Palestinian president of Al-Quds University in Jerusalem, Sari Nusseibeh, in a statement of principles called the People's Voice. While only a page long, it was similar in its main outline to the Beilin-Abed Rabbo effort: two states; a division of territory roughly along the 1967 Green Line, including a division of Jerusalem to create the capitals of two states, and a right of Palestinian refugees, or at least the vast majority, to return only to a Palestinian state.

The plans spoke to a growing fear among the Israeli public that without a separation from the Palestinians, their country was headed toward becoming a binomial state that in just a matter of years would have an Arab majority. Neither proposal grabbed large-scale public support.

The "virtual" agreement hammered out by Beilin actually offended many in Israel who felt only an elected government should conduct such negotiations, according to surveys analyzed by Tel Aviv University's Steinmetz Center.

But a lackluster popular response in Israel did not diminish the threat that Sharon saw in the two plans. Both drew wide media attention. Ayalon joined three other former Shin Bet directors in a caustic interview with *Yediot Ahronoth* about the Sharon government's military approach to the Palestinians. The four warned that the country was headed for disaster unless Prime Minister Sharon reversed course and moved quickly to settle the conflict with the Palestinians. "We are taking sure, steady steps to a place where the state of Israel will no longer be a democracy and a home for the Jewish people," Ayalon was quoted as saying.

Drafters of the two peace plans took their proposals on the road to Europe and the United States, where they were widely hailed for a constructive effort to correct the absence of a peace process. The Beilin-Abed Rabbo agreement, dubbed "the Geneva Initiative," drew encouragement from British prime minister Tony Blair. This was no surprise, given that one of its drafters, a committed young lawyer named Daniel Levy, was the son of Lord Michael Levy, a British pop-music magnate and Labor Party fund-raiser who doubled as Blair's special Middle East envoy.

In Washington, Deputy Defense Secretary Paul Wolfowitz met with Ayalon and Nusseibeh and praised their initiative in an October 30, 2003, speech at Georgetown University, linking it to broad American strategy: "Clearly, one huge factor in our relations with the Muslim world, as well as one of the greatest obstacles to peace in that region, is the continuing conflict between Israelis and Palestinians. It is clear that the solution of this conflict can only come through political means. President Bush has made it clear the importance that we attach to Israeli-Palestinian negotiations. . . . Right now there is a significant grassroots movement that has already gotten some 90,000 Israeli signatures and some 60,000 Palestinian signatures in support of principles that look very much like the road map favoring a two-state solution. I had the privilege last week of meeting with the two organizers of that petition, Sari

Nusseibeh, a Palestinian, and Ami Ayalon, an Israeli. One of the keys to achieving peace is to somehow mobilize majorities on both sides so that the extremists who oppose it can be isolated."

Such praise from a prime architect of the administration's war on Iraq and "New Middle East" strategy, and a neoconservative to boot, was obviously significant, even if it didn't reflect the views of the White House or even of his own boss, Donald Rumsfeld. A week later, Colin Powell sent a letter praising the drafters of the Geneva Initiative. Carefully written to avoid an endorsement, it told them, "Projects such as yours are important for sustaining hope and understanding."

The trend of outside initiatives worried Sharon. In an interview later with his friend Uri Dan, recounted in *Ariel Sharon—An Intimate Portrait*, the prime minister said, "We risked an avalanche of new 'suggestions' from the international community. We couldn't stand by and do nothing, arms folded."

Any talk of final-status negotiations with the Palestinians was anathema to Sharon at that point. "He didn't believe that this generation was mature for final status. He thought that the relations between the peoples—Israel and the Palestinians—had not reached the point where there could be a real reconciliation. Therefore the time had not yet come to make those real, major, final-status concessions, which could be made if the atmosphere and the mutual acceptance and mutual accommodation was ripe," according to Efraim Halevy. "To come to final status without this mutual acceptance, we would be giving real estate and all the other advantages for hollow commitments on the part of the Palestinians. What did the Palestinians have to offer us? Nothing. Goodwill, that's all. Because they had nothing to give us. We had territory. . . . If we don't believe in their goodwill, they'll take the territory and they'll say, 'OK, now we go on.' And he [Sharon] didn't think they were mature for acceptance. They were not mature for acceptance. And of course the rub of it all was that they would have to accept that the refugee problem would be to all intents and purposes [set aside]. Which they were not willing to do."

Sharon viewed the Geneva Initiative in particular as "a mortal danger to Israel," according to Halevy, who by then had left his position as head of Israel's National Security Council. "The Geneva Initiative accepted the right of return. And the Geneva Initiative on Jerusalem was a travesty, it was horrendous, it was shocking." While paying lip service to the road map so as not to anger the Americans, Sharon actually loathed it, according to Halevy.

Ten months after a resounding reelection victory, Sharon's second term was also being threatened from another quarter. In Israel, three criminal investigations dogged his family: one into campaign funding during his 1999 race for leadership of the Likud Party; a second into an allegedly illegal loan to pay off a 1999 contribution; and a third into an alleged bribe from a resort developer. None would produce charges against Sharon during his remaining time in office, although his son Omri ultimately pleaded guilty to falsifying documents and perjury in the 1999 case.

Sharon was in a bind and needed a way out. Washington was prepared to encourage moderates among both Israelis and Palestinians but didn't have a plan. Interviewed by David Frost on the eve of his London trip, Bush had little to say that was new.

Q: And in—one of the reasons that people say, in the Arab world—obviously there was your landmark speech last week—but in the Arab world, that you won't really be able to address the balance against America until the United States is seen not to tilt towards Israel in the Middle East. What do you think about that?
THE PRESIDENT: *I think about that—I think it's an excuse, because America—I am the first president ever to go to the United Nations—*

Q: And say, two—
THE PRESIDENT: *Two states side by side in peace.*

Q: Two states.
THE PRESIDENT: *No president has ever said that. And I said it, and I said it with conviction, because I believe it is in Israel's interest that there be a peaceful Palestinian state, and I know it's in the Palestinians' interest. However, to achieve a peaceful Palestinian state—the emergence of a peaceful Palestinian state,*

a state where people are willing to risk capital, a place where people are willing to develop an economy, there must be a focused effort to defeat terror. And there hasn't been with the current Palestinian leadership. I went in and embraced, in Aqaba, Jordan, Abu Mazen. And the reason I did so, David, is because he came to the Oval Office, and he said, "I will join you in the fight against terror; we're not going to allow the few to destroy the hopes of the many." As well, I could sense in his talk, in his feeling, that he has—he's got great trust in the Palestinian people. In other words, given the chance, the Palestinian people will develop the habits of democracy, and out of that will come a great state, a peaceful state. And I trusted him. And we were working with him. We were making good progress. And I was working with Ariel Sharon. I gave a speech on June 24, 2002, which says, all of us have responsibilities, and you, Israel, have a responsibility.

Q: Do you think Ariel Sharon could ever emerge as a man of peace?

THE PRESIDENT: *Yes, I do. I believe he wants peace for his people, I truly do. I mean, he's a man who has presided over suiciders, where he has to go to the funerals of women and children, because some cold-blooded killer is trying to destroy the hopes of all the people in the region. And it's—yes, I believe so. And I believe he believes in a Palestinian state. I've asked him, in the Oval Office, I said, "Listen, am I out there by myself on a Palestinian state, or will you support it?" He said he will. But both of us understand, as do a lot of other people, that for a state to emerge, there must be a focused effort to get after the Hamas killers, for example, who want to destroy the hopes of the people that believe in a Palestinian state. And there hasn't been that effort. Let me finish my Abu Mazen story, if you don't mind. I embraced the guy. And I believe that he is a—I believe he's a partner with whom we can work. And he's shoved out. Progress is being made, and he is shoved aside by the old guard. And that's unacceptable behavior. It's just unacceptable.*

Bush himself showed impatience with both sides when, in London, he delivered a speech at the Guildhall, mostly about Iraq and the Middle East: "Even after the setbacks and frustrations of recent months, goodwill and hard effort can bring about a Palestinian state and a secure Israel. Those who would lead a new Palestine should adopt peaceful means to achieve the rights of their people and create the reformed institutions of a stable democracy.

"Israel should freeze settlement construction, dismantle unauthorized outposts, end the daily humiliation of the Palestinian people, and not prejudice final negotiations with the placements of walls and fences."

But the White House didn't think diplomatic progress was possible at that point. Instead, it looked to Sharon for answers on what to do next. Sharon needed a breakthrough that would counter the unofficial peace initiatives. He knew, according to his adviser and spokesman Raanan Gissin, that "the world would not accept the lack of a political process. It was better for us to take an initiative, rather than having to face Geneva."

A combination of Sharon's tactical shrewdness, Palestinian dysfunction, and a lack of American drive to launch a peace process gave the prime minister an insurmountable advantage—provided he did not just stand still.

While Bush was in London, the White House dispatched Elliott Abrams on an unannounced trip to meet with Sharon, who was then on an official trip to Rome.

By then, Abrams had spent almost a year as the National Security Council's point man for the Middle East. A highly intelligent lawyer and a capable manager, he was one of the youngest-ever assistant secretaries of state during the Reagan presidency when his role in the Iran-contra scandal derailed his government career and subjected him to four years of investigation by Congress and a special prosecutor. He eventually pleaded guilty to withholding information from Congress and was pardoned by the first President Bush. A neoconservative by inclination and family ties—he was a son-in-law of movement tribunes Norman Podhoretz and Midge Decter—he shared Paul Wolfowitz's passion for spreading democracy, a passion he carried with him when he returned to government in George W. Bush's White House. He also admired Ariel Sharon and shared much of his outlook. He was among the conservative American authors who sarcastically inserted quotation marks whenever he mentioned the "peace process." Writing at the time of Sharon's election as prime minister, Abrams compared his political comeback to Winston Churchill's:

"[O]ne is reminded of what happened to Winston Churchill in World War I. He designed and championed the British campaign in Gallipoli in 1915, and it proved to be a huge disaster: forty-three thousand British troops were killed, and Churchill was forced to resign as first lord of the admiralty. Yet twenty-four years later, when his nation found itself in a crisis threatening its survival, Great Britain turned to Churchill again.

"Israel continues to face mortal peril, surrounded by enemies who wish its destruction. When Ehud Barak reached out for peace through concessions and compromises so great they threatened the nation's security, they were rejected out of hand by the Palestinian Authority. It has become clear to the great majority of Israelis that their Arab neighbors—today, as in 1948, 1967, and 1973, the years of Israel's major wars—continue to want not peace but victory, not compromise but surrender, not a Jewish state but another Arab state in Israel.

"So Israelis have chosen a leader who all along knew, and said, that the road to peace lies through strength instead of weakness, and firmness rather than unilateral concessions. Ariel Sharon gauged Israel's security situation far better than the Labor Party's leaders, and for this he has been rewarded with a landslide electoral victory. Americans who regret—who even denounce—this outcome should stop a moment and wonder what Israeli voters now know that they themselves still do not."

Such views, echoing those of Israel's right wing, spelled doom for a diplomatic approach to solving the Israeli-Palestinian conflict in the eyes of some foreign-policy veterans. Brent Scowcroft, for one, thought the promotion of Abrams reflected Rice's lack of understanding of the conflict. Speaking of his onetime acolyte at the White House, he said in an interview, "Had Condi understood the region more, she never would have accepted [the appointment of Abrams]."

For Rice, however, the choice of Abrams could be seen to offer important advantages: it gave her a conduit both to the Sharon government and to influential American conservatives among American Jewish leaders and evangelical Christians, with whom he had worked for years. A good listener, Abrams was someone who could catch flak and understand their thinking. At the time, conservative Jews, Christians, and Israelis were in an uproar over Bush's endorsement of the road map. For

balance, Rice could rely on Bill Burns and other State Department officials as a channel to Palestinians and the Arab world.

Abrams himself was far from being the inflexible figure suggested by
his tough prose. Ghaith al-Omari, a U.S.-trained lawyer who was an aide
to Mahmoud Abbas during the latter's short tenure as prime minister, said
he worked closely with Abrams at the time. "He struck me as someone
with whom you can definitely talk about everything, open to listening but
very hard to convince. But ultimately someone you can work with very
well. . . . You can't bullshit him. He's smart, and unless you have a very
strong case, a very strong argument, you're not going to pull a fast one
on him. But if you deal with him honestly and directly he's a good person to deal with. We disagreed a lot . . . but he was always a very honest
person to talk to and he spoke his mind. . . . He was always seen, among
the Palestinians, as someone who is close to the kind of hard-line policies, but not in a way that made him impossible to deal with."

"The United States agreed to help us on condition that there was a
process and that something happened," Sharon told Uri Dan. He scrutinized various options in search of a potential breakthrough, according to his son Omri. "The problem was there was not someone on the
other side to talk with. . . . Nothing moved. Nothing changed." American proposals by George Mitchell and George Tenet had been
attempted, but "nothing actually happened," the younger Sharon said
in a 2006 telephone interview.

An early indication of the strategy Sharon would seize came in a trial
balloon floated by Deputy Prime Minister Ehud Olmert, the broadly
pragmatic former mayor of Jerusalem. In an interview with *Haaretz* editor David Landau published on November 15, 2003, Olmert said,
"There is no doubt in my mind that very soon the government of Israel
is going to have to address the demographic issue with the utmost seri-
ousness and resolve. This issue above all others will dictate the solution
that we must adopt. In the absence of a negotiated agreement—and I
do not believe in the realistic prospect of an agreement—we need to
implement a unilateral alternative." His formula called for incorporating into Israel the maximum number of Jews from the territories; keeping the number of Palestinians to a minimum; not withdrawing to the

1967 border; and not dividing Jerusalem. Large settlements such as Ariel would "obviously" be carved into Israel.

Sharon was publicly silent on Olmert's proposal. But Olmert's friend Yosef Lapid, then head of the Shinui Party in the Knesset, believes Olmert was "the man [Sharon] sent into the first line of fire." When Abrams arrived in Rome, the prime minister floated the idea in an effort to gauge the U.S. reaction, according to Raanan Gissin, his longtime spokesman.

Abrams raised the possibility of negotiations with Syria, according to Dan's account. Given Abrams's own negative attitude toward the Syrian regime, it's unlikely that he did so with much enthusiasm.

"I stated that I was ready to undertake such discussions if the Syrians ceased supporting terrorism, which wasn't the case and still isn't," Sharon told Dan. "I emphasized, however, that it was better to concentrate, above all else, on a single problem, that of the Palestinians."

As Sharon later told Dan, he used the meeting to describe in broad terms a plan to withdraw Israeli forces from Gaza and evacuate the settlements there. Gissin, who said he was briefed afterward, recounted: "He pointed out to [Abrams] that in light of the stalemate and the peace process not moving forward, this disengagement was a means to restart the peace process."

"A means to restart the peace process" may have been the way Sharon pitched the idea to the Americans. Dov Weisglass, a top Sharon adviser, gave it a far different—and, some believe, more honest— interpretation in a revealing interview eleven months later. "The significance of our disengagement plan is the freezing of the peace process," he told *Haaretz*. "It supplies the formaldehyde necessary so there is no political process with Palestinians. . . . Effectively, this whole package called a Palestinian state, with all it entails, has been removed indefinitely from our agenda." Yosef Lapid, the Shinui leader, said Weisglass was mainly intent on weakening resistance to disengagement on the Israeli Right.

Sharon's move was well-timed. Efforts by Russia, a member of the diplomatic Quartet that had drawn up the road map, were beginning to eat away at excuses for inaction on the diplomatic front. A day or two after the Sharon-Abrams meeting, the UN's Prendergast delivered a withering commentary during the secretariat's monthly briefing to the Security Council: "It is true that it has been a month of relative quiet. But that quiet has been met not with positive steps, but with inaction. Everyone has waited for others to act. The government of Israel has waited for the Palestinian Authority to form an empowered government and for terrorism to end. The Palestinian Authority has waited for Israel to halt military operations and take steps to ease the closures that have so deeply damaged Palestinian life, for the international community to lead the parties toward peace, and for its own political wrangling to end. And we, the international community, have waited for the parties to make progress on their own, despite the accumulation over the years of compelling evidence that they are incapable of making peace without international intervention. The period of inertia, excuses, and conditionality in Middle East peacemaking must end."

Two hours after Prendergast's briefing, U.S. ambassador John Negroponte ended weeks of resistance to a Russian-drafted resolution that put the Security Council squarely behind the road map. Israel opposed the draft, with Sharon lobbying Russian president Vladimir Putin during a visit to Moscow not to push it. The resolution calling on Israel and the Palestinians "to fulfill their obligations under the road map in cooperation with the Quartet and to achieve the vision of two States living side by side in peace and security," passed unanimously. Negroponte explained the American shift by citing the formation of a Palestinian government under Ahmed Qurei: "One specific reservation we had at the time the Russians put it forward, was that there was no Palestinian government. A Palestinian government has now been formed, and the conditions became somewhat more propitious."

Speaking to Al Jazeera, Palestinian negotiator Saeb Erekat said, "The fact that Russia went to the Security Council shows clearly to the world that the road map has been neglected and the Quartet committee's role should be activated through mechanisms for implementation, timetables, and monitoring teams on the ground."

Sharon, however, had already begun a move that would push the Quartet to the margins. If Sharon won American backing for his new disengagement plan, it would put him—not the Quartet, not the Security Council, and not even the United States—back in the driver's seat in deciding what moves Israel should make in relation to the Palestinians. And Sharon would not have to stop with this disengagement. He hoped, Gissin said in a 2005 interview, that it would be the first of a series of moves "to ensure a Jewish majority in the Land of Israel."

The disengagement was still too vague to win an American endorsement. But after the Rome meeting, the White House showed little enthusiasm for outside peace initiatives. In early December, Yossi Beilin and Yasser Abed Rabbo arrived in Washington to publicize the Geneva Initiative. Bush allowed Colin Powell to proceed with plans to meet with them, despite strong objections from Israel, but the pair's request to meet with Rice and her deputy, Stephen Hadley, was turned down and a meeting with Wolfowitz at the Pentagon was scrapped.

The session at the State Department confirmed for Daniel Levy, a drafter of the Geneva Initiative, that the administration's divisions on the Middle East had not disappeared. Powell "could not have gone more out of his way to generate the atmospherics of warmth and supportiveness," recalled Levy. Abrams, who attended, wore a "chilled" look, he noted.

When Jordan's King Abdullah met with Bush at the White House December 4, he found little inclination on the president's part to assume an active role in advancing the road map or trying to jump-start a peace process. Abdullah told the *NewsHour*'s Jim Lehrer, "[T]he president has certain capital that he can expend on to the peace process. And it is up to the rest of us, the international community, Jordanians, and even many people in Washington, to create the circumstances so that when the president gets engaged, we actually can move the process forward. At the moment, there is nothing tangible—the president can give his support—but you know, it's a presidential card as he said to me several years ago, and when you use that, you can only use it sort of once. And we have to make sure that all the ducks are lined up in a row, so to speak."

Sharon officially unveiled the disengagement plan December 18 in a speech to a security conference in Herzliya, north of Tel Aviv. "The unilateral steps which Israel will take in the framework of the disengagement plan will be fully coordinated with the United States," he pledged. A new process of negotiation between Jerusalem and Washington was about to begin. Sharon would prefer to negotiate with the Americans than the Palestinians, according to Gissin.

Dov Weisglass and a second Sharon adviser, Shalom Turgeman, rushed to Washington to open talks with the White House but had few answers for the skeptical Americans. At first, the Israelis talked just about withdrawing from Gaza, with perhaps part of the West Bank to be evacuated later on. Condoleezza Rice told them, "You have some ideas, you have some support, but you still don't have a plan," according to Giora Eiland, who was then chief of planning for the Israeli Army.

The Israelis returned with a written plan. The Americans had two concerns: that the plan not be seen as inconsistent with the road map, and that it include withdrawal from at least part of the West Bank, so as not to look as though Israel was giving up Gaza only to tighten its grip on the most fought-over territory: the West Bank and East Jerusalem. Stephen Hadley and Rice both insisted on this.

Israel considered four options: not to evacuate any of the West Bank, which would cost them U.S. support; evacuating four tiny northern West Bank settlements; evacuating a more significant part of the West Bank; and evacuating a "very large part of the West Bank," according to Eiland. The four-settlement idea would be relatively easy, since some settlers in the region were already prepared to leave in exchange for government compensation. The Israelis were prepared to withdraw from more territory, depending on what they could get from the Americans.

Negotiations soon focused on how much territory Israel would give up, and how much Washington would give Israel in return for withdrawal. Israelis wanted the United States to endorse as many of their final-status demands as possible. Most important were a rejection of Palestinian refugees' right to return to their original homes inside Israel and protection of large settlements close to Jerusalem and the Green Line.

The Americans never mentioned Bush's campaign for reelection in the upcoming November 2004 elections, Eiland said, "but we did understand it was quite a sensitive year."

A senior Bush administration official described the talks: "[W]hat's on the table on the Israeli side, once they've decided to get out of Gaza, is, 'What can be done on the West Bank?' What's on the table on the American side is, 'If the Israelis do something on the West Bank, what is the compensation for it?' And I mean here not money . . . it's the ideological compensation. It's political compensation."

In effect, the White House was negotiating on behalf of the Palestinians—and the Arab world—with only Israelis and Americans in the room. Bush himself did not appear to be particularly concerned about the territorial boundaries that were a burning issue to Israelis and Palestinians. He told Ziad Asali at one point that such matters would be settled in final-status talks and that the U.S. would support whatever division of land the two sides worked out between themselves. At London's Guildhall, he said, "Achieving peace in the Holy Land is not just a matter of the shape of a border. As we work on the details of peace, we must look to the heart of the matter, which is the need for a viable Palestinian democracy."

The U.S.-Israeli talks at the White House were not a secret—it's hard to keep secrets from the Israeli press—but their substance was kept under wraps. If it occurred to the administration to acquaint Palestinians at any point with the terms being discussed, there was no sign of it. Partly, this was the Palestinians' failure. While the PLO had a strong diplomatic presence at the United Nations, its representative in Washington, Hassan Abdul Rahman, was relatively ineffective. Emissaries from the Palestinian Authority were seldom authorized to speak for the leadership. But unofficial talks with well connected Palestinians or Arab governments might have averted a subsequent backlash.

In early 2004, Elliott Abrams and a colleague, Rob Deneen, met with Ghaith al-Omari, a former Abbas aide, and Salah Abdel Shafi, an economist and entrepreneur from a prominent Gaza family, both of whom were in Washington to promote the Geneva Initiative. Deneen told the pair that while the Israelis were regularly knocking on his door for a variety of reasons, he seldom heard from Palestinians. He suggested they get their act together. Although Abrams refused to discuss the Geneva Initiative, their friendly talk extended well beyond its allotted half hour. Word of Sharon's planned disengagement had already become known, but Abrams said the administration had received "no information whatsoever" about the proposal, according to Abdel Shafi.

Among Palestinian moderates, the Sharon disengagement plan generated a mixture of relief and alarm. On one hand, "People felt that anything would be better than what they have . . . the way we were looking at it was that this would be very dangerous on a number of levels. Obviously it would be kind of the last nail in the coffin of bilateralism . . . make it very hard to go back to negotiations, and also that it would very much strengthen the Hamas political line. Our line has always been, negotiations are the way forward. Hamas would be able to spin such a unilateral withdrawal as a result of their 'resistance.' Which is actually what they did."

If the Palestinians could not supply anyone appropriate to speak with, Jordan could. While Jordanians could not negotiate on behalf of the Palestinians, they at least might have been a go-between. But the terms of the emerging deal were kept from Jordan, as well. Numerous others could have been used, including envoys for the European Union and the UN.

Sharon, however, was selling the disengagement to his cabinet and to the country as a unilateral measure, one necessitated by the absence of any "partner" on the other side. Involvement of the Palestinians in any way would have undercut his argument. He also preferred not to deal with any foreign government other than that of the United States. Washington didn't object.

Not only were U.S. allies in the Arab world kept in the dark, but so was the British ambassador, David Manning, who had previously served as Tony Blair's foreign-policy adviser and, before that, as Britain's ambassador to Israel.

A senior administration official involved in the talks with Israel said the United States was aware that Sharon was prepared to consider, under certain conditions, relinquishing more of the West Bank than he eventually did—a "very large part of the West Bank," as Giora Eiland had put it. The official said nevertheless that the White House obtained an appropriate deal—one that would allow a return to the peace process once the disengagement was complete. "I think if you look back at the whole process of negotiation in the Middle East, where we ended up is the right place to be. Now, could Sharon have done more? We didn't think so," the official said.

The U.S.-Israeli negotiations ended just before Sharon arrived in
Washington in April to get Bush's official endorsement for the disengagement plan. He stuck with his early offer to give up Gaza and four
northern West Bank settlements. In exchange, Bush backed two important Israeli demands for what should be included in a final settlement
with the Palestinians: refugees would not be allowed to return to Israel,
but only to a Palestinian state; and Israel would be able to keep major
settlements in the West Bank and not be required to return to the 1967
borders.

"The realities on the ground and in the region have changed greatly
over the last several decades, and any final settlement [between Israel
and the Palestinians] must take into account those realities and be
agreeable to the parties," Bush said in a statement with Sharon at his
side. One of those realities is the "existing major Israeli population centers," Bush said, referring to the large settlements. He said it is "unrealistic to expect that the outcome of final-status negotiations will be a
full and complete return to the armistice lines of 1949," which formed
Israel's de facto border until 1967. On refugees, Bush said, "It seems
clear that an agreed, just, fair, and realistic framework for a solution to
the Palestinian refugee issue as part of any final-status agreement will
need to be found through the establishment of a Palestinian state and
the settling of Palestinian refugees there rather than Israel." A year later,
Bush would effectively commit future administrations to the same position by repeating it and adding, "That is the American view."

A furious reaction from Palestinians might have been predicted: not
only was Bush not pressing or even encouraging Israelis to negotiate
with them, but he was trading away what they considered to be valuable cards that they were holding for final-status negotiations. Briefing
reporters at the White House, a senior administration official seemed
taken aback by the pointed questions prompted by the Bush-Sharon
agreement, spelled out in an exchange of letters between Israel and the
White House. "I think you guys are missing the news here. . . . I mean,
the news here is that the Israeli government, headed by Ariel Sharon,
has decided to pull out of Gaza and to abandon settlements—not only
on Gaza, but also on the West Bank—and that is an opportunity for us

now to move the Palestinians, because what he's doing is opening the door for a pathway to a Palestinian state."

Jordan, alarmed by the White House concessions to Israel, tried to contain what its officials viewed as a damaging blow to any future peace process. Jordanian diplomats persuaded the White House to prepare a new letter—this one to King Abdullah—stressing that a final-status settlement would have to be agreed on by both Israel and the Palestinians.

Still, White House enthusiasm for the disengagement plan was undiminished. Over dinner with Scowcroft, Condoleezza Rice cited the planned Gaza pullout as good news—a first step in a larger withdrawal from the territories. "Condi—that's bad news," Scowcroft argued. "My judgment is, from Sharon's perspective, this was the last step, not the first step. He's pulling out of Gaza not as a favor to the peace process but because it's unsustainable for Israel to try to protect eight thousand settlers in a sea of hostile Palestinians. He's doing it for his own purposes. When he does that, finishes the wall, then he says, 'I'm done.'"

17

Palestinians Turn the Page
■ NOVEMBER 2004 ■

YASSER ARAFAT HAD eight days left to live when George Bush won reelection in 2004. In some respects the post-Arafat era had been under way for some time. Over three years of Israeli-Palestinian violence, the enigmatic liberation fighter who summoned "martyrs by the millions," and who vowed to lead Palestinians to statehood and raise their flag atop the mosques and churches of Jerusalem, had shrunk in importance. His claim to be the only undefeated Arab general was an empty conceit. He had lost control of the street and the guns to militants and gangs. His very survival was purely a matter of strategic calculation by Israel, which could control his movements, arrest him or expel him at will. The pockets of West Bank and Gaza territory he once controlled were reduced now to the Muqata, his partially destroyed headquarters in Ramallah. Palestinians had mostly given up on his ability to deliver either freedom from Israeli occupation or responsible governance. Holed up in a few badly ventilated rooms, he grew sick and weak. By several accounts, his mental capacity declined as well.

Still, the seventy-five-year-old known to his followers as Abu Ammar (Abu means "father;" Ammar can mean "rebuilding") still had unrivaled potency as a symbol of the Palestinians' hopes and grievances.

That symbolism lent a shred of dignity to Arafat's final days. France dispatched a plane to fly him to a military hospital outside Paris, where doctors labored unsuccessfully to treat a blood illness of undetermined cause. Arafat's subordinates patched up their quarrels with him, his volatile wife, Suha, and each other, arranging a solemn military funeral in Cairo ("Borrowed pageantry for a stateless president," as the BBC put it), burial at the Muqata, and an emotional eulogy: "Yasser Arafat closed his eyes to this world, his noble heart ceased to beat and his pure soul passed into its creator's mercy, but he will continue to exist as long as our great people exist," the broadcast tribute read. "He was the leader of their armed and political struggle and he was the leader of their mighty march towards building their national identity anew in their home-land." Israel kept a discreet distance from the arrangements while firmly rejecting any notion of burying Arafat in Jerusalem and imposing a complete closure throughout the territories as a precaution against riots.

It was symbolism, as well, that prevented other politicians from mounting a strong internal challenge to Arafat while he lived. One man who could have matched the old man in charisma and political dexter-ity, Marwan Barghouti, was in an Israeli prison serving multiple life sen-tences for murder. Now, with Arafat's death approaching, the Palestinian leadership arranged a transition generally accepted as legitimate: the speaker of parliament would become interim president; Mahmoud Abbas would assume leadership of the Palestine Liberation Organiza-tion, the dominant political body; and elections would be held in sixty days to choose Arafat's successor as president.

Low-key moderates who eschewed violence were ascendant. A pow-erful opportunity beckoned to Israel and the United States to put their relations with the Palestinians on a new footing and move resolutely toward negotiations and peace. No longer could it be argued that the top leader on the other side was unwilling to end the conflict or discourage violence. As Bush celebrated his election victory, European and Arab leaders urged him once again to intervene publicly. Tony Blair, his clos-est ally, called peace in the Middle East "the single most pressing politi-cal challenge in our world." Bush didn't reject these appeals, but his own priority at the moment was changing his cabinet. On November 10, with Arafat just hours away from death, Bush fired Colin Powell, the man who presumably would have led any peace effort, and got ready to replace him with Condoleezza Rice. According to *Soldier*, Karen DeYoung's biography of Powell, Bush's decision was relayed to the secretary of state in a phone call from White House Chief of Staff Andrew Card, who told him, "The president would like to make a change."

In a brief exchange with reporters the same day, Bush was asked if he saw an opening for peace under a new Palestinian leader. "I do," Bush replied but then reverted to standard "talking points" that put the onus on Palestinians to reform. He gave no hint that he would lead a peace effort. "There will be an opening for peace when leadership of the Palestinian people steps forward and says, 'Help us build a democratic and free society.' And when that happens—and I believe it's going to happen, because I believe all people desire to live in freedom—the United States of America will be more than willing to help build the institutions necessary for a free society to emerge, so that the Palestinians can have their own state." Asked if he wanted Powell "to stick around to lead your efforts to revive the Middle East peace talks," Bush indicated otherwise: "I'm proud of my secretary of state; he's done a heck of a good job."

That evening, Bush hosted the annual White House Iftar, the meal breaking the daylong fast during the Muslim holy month of Ramadan. Speaking to distinguished American Muslims and diplomats from throughout the Middle East and Asia, he read his prepared greeting at a rapid clip, mentioning neither Arafat nor prospects for peace. "I want to acknowledge our secretary of state, Colin Powell," Bush said, then mumbled something like, "I appreciate his great service." When Powell's name drew polite applause, Bush somewhat incongruously gave a brief, warm grin. Once again, Ziad Asali, head of the American Task Force on Palestine lobbying group, had a privileged seat at Bush's table. Part of the dinner conversation was dominated by the recent U.S. presidential election. (Asali hadn't voted, he later told me.) But half the talk was taken up with the Israeli-Palestinian conflict. "I brought up the question of Jerusalem," Asali said. At the time, Israel was erecting a wall that would separate Arab populations in East Jerusalem from the West Bank. "I said I'm concerned that the changes in Jerusalem may foreclose the option" of meeting Palestinian demands for a contiguous state with its capital in the Holy City's Arab neighborhoods, Asali told me. "It would be a problem for the viability of a state." Bush replied that it was too early to talk about that.

Bush praised Abbas and asked Asali if the United States had helped doom Abbas's tenure as prime minister in 2003 by appearing too friendly toward him, giving him "a bear hug," in Bush's words. Asali replied that the problem for Abbas was that neither the United States nor Israel had matched its words with enough tangible support and said, "There was no relief for his people on the ground." Looking ahead to Abbas's return to power, he urged Bush to adopt a new tack—more concrete action and less talk.

At 9:30 PM Washington time, Arafat died. Having come to despise him in life, Bush was not about to praise him in death. A statement in the president's name omitted any final judgment on the leader who had forced the world—through terrorism and peacemaking—to recognize the Palestinian struggle. It said simply, "The death of Yasser Arafat is a significant moment in Palestinian history. We express our condolences to the Palestinian people. For the Palestinian people, we hope that the future will bring peace and the fulfillment of their aspirations for an independent, democratic Palestine that is at peace with its neighbors. During the period of transition that is ahead, we urge all in the region and throughout the world to join in helping make progress toward these goals and toward the ultimate goal of peace." Powell, suddenly a lame-duck secretary, struck a sharply different note, recognizing what Arafat had meant for Palestinians. He called Arafat "a significant figure in the history of the region and the world," adding, "and we know that, in the eyes of the Palestinian people, Arafat embodied their hopes and dreams for the achievement of an independent Palestinian state." At 7:30 the next morning, Asali got a call from the White House asking if he wanted to be part of the official American delegation to Arafat's funeral. George Salem, a Palestinian American attorney in Washington, was also invited. In contrast to other nations that sent heads of state or foreign ministers, the American delegation was led by a midlevel official, Assistant Secretary of State Bill Burns.

In Israel, Prime Minister Ariel Sharon sounded open to a change of direction by Washington now that Arafat was dead, while not giving up his own demand that the Palestinian leadership actively prevent terrorist attacks on Israelis and avoiding any initiative of his own. BBC monitors translated his remarks to the Prime Minister's Conference for Export and International Cooperation, as relayed by Israeli media: "I do want to reach an agreement," Sharon said, "and we will reach one; we are on the verge of a new era.

"If a different leadership emerges after the Arafat era, a serious and responsible one that carries out the commitments they made in the road map, namely the cessation of terrorism, violence, and incitement; the disbandment of terrorist organizations; and the implementation of government reform, the situation will then warrant the coordination of various moves and even the resumption of political negotiations with that leadership. . . . Israel is a peace-seeking country. I hope the Palestinians will soon come to their senses so that we can resume the negotiations with them. But as long as bona fide steps are not undertaken against terrorism, and as long as terrorist infrastructures are not disbanded, there will be no change in Israel's policy." Another account of Sharon's remarks, by Diana Bahur-Nir of Ynet, also hinted at a change in Israel's planned disengagement from Gaza, depending on Palestinian behavior: "I hope Palestinians will soon come to their senses so we can resume the negotiations with them. As long as they do not do so, Israel will continue to carry out the DP [disengagement plan] according to the planned timetable." According to Israel Radio, Sharon told a ministerial committee "that Israel must not make even the slightest concessions to the Palestinians now. We must not embrace them now, Sharon said, because concessions and hugs could legitimize terrorism and force Israel to take political steps before terrorism stops." To prevent Arafat from being seen as a freedom fighter, the station reported, "Israel will seek to portray him as an international strategist of terrorism."

Once again, Sharon was weighing tactics in the event that Israel came under new international pressure to enter a peace process with the Palestinians. But this didn't mean he would block the new process if Bush were determined. And he had his own reason to reach out to the new Palestinian leadership: to make sure the Israeli withdrawal from Gaza occurred without violence and didn't hand the terrorists a victory.

Sharon must have known by then that tough action against militants by Palestinian security forces was unlikely. Denuded by three years of Israeli attacks on its infrastructure, Palestinian security forces were so badly weakened that they couldn't control the chaotic, emotional mob that rushed to the helicopter returning Arafat's body to Ramallah.

Ami Ayalon, the former chief of Israel's domestic security agency who went on to launch a peace initiative with Sari Nusseibeh, the Palestinian head of Al-Quds University in Jerusalem, went to see Sharon after Arafat's death. He wanted the prime minister to bolster Abbas and other Palestinian moderates. He later recounted the visit to the *Jerusalem Post*'s David Horovitz: "I told him, 'OK, there was an obstacle, but he's gone now. Why don't you go to Abu Mazen and negotiate. Tell him, "We're going to leave [Gaza]. But if you want the settlements, take them. If you want to house refugees there, fine."' But this zero-sum game? That if we see smiling Palestinians, it's an Israeli failure? Come on."

If the new Palestinian leadership was ill-equipped, militarily and politically, to launch a major crackdown on terrorist groups, it nevertheless could move ahead on democratic reforms demanded by President Bush. These were widely seen as an important, but not the most important, element of the Israeli-Palestinian conflict. The International Crisis Group warned in December 2004, "While international support for Palestinian reform is welcome, it ought not come at the detriment of simultaneous moves on the political front, lest the new Palestinian leadership rapidly lose whatever legitimacy elections will bring."

An impressive start came with Palestinian presidential elections on January 9, 2005. Mahmoud Abbas, campaigning on a platform of securing statehood and peace through negotiations rather than violence, was elected with 62 percent of the vote. He also negotiated with Hamas over a cease-fire, or *hudna*, in which Hamas would refrain from violent attacks on Israelis. Fearful of a Palestinian civil war, he hoped to draw Islamists into the political mainstream. Ziad Abu Amr, a U.S.-educated Palestinian lawmaker who helped negotiate the *hudna*, believed giving Hamas a stake in the Palestinian government would moderate the group's actions, even if it did not alter Hamas's formal refusal to recognize Israel.

"[W]e may not be able to convince Hamas to recognize Israel as a partner, but Hamas may become, and I think it is going to become part of an authority, a state, political entity that recognizes Israel," Abu Amr told a Brookings Institution forum on February 1, 2005. "So if they want to oppose as a party that principle, this is their privilege. The Muslim Brotherhood in Jordan, they are in the parliament. At one point they were in the government and they do not recognize Israel. But if they want to become part of the state, they have to be bound by the imperatives and by the parameters and the laws of the state. And I think this is what is happening right now."

But Abbas's continued political strength, and his success in maintaining the cease-fire, did not depend on him alone. He needed tangible progress on relations with Israel—if not full-fledged negotiations, then an easing up of the siege on the occupied territories and release of some of the thousands of prisoners in Israeli jails. His margin of victory in the elections was misleading, since Hamas had boycotted the vote. At the municipal level, Hamas was showing increasing popularity, as well as a strong political organization.

Ariel Sharon, likewise, was changing his own government to make sure he kept a majority of the Knesset behind him for his planned withdrawal from Gaza. To counter strong right-wing opposition to the disengagement, he brought the center-left Labor Party into his governing coalition. But he still faced a potential revolt within his own Likud Party.

Both Sharon and Abbas had a lot to gain if the coming withdrawal went well. Sharon could win broad approval for Israel internationally, strengthen his hold on the Israeli political center, and be free of the military, financial, and moral burdens of the Gaza Strip. Abbas could gain freedom for more than a million Palestinians and economic aid and investment from the West while showing his countrymen that a nonviolent approach brought progress toward an end to occupation. But Sharon's reputation would be damaged if his forces were perceived to be retreating from Gaza under fire. For his part, Abbas would suffer politically if Palestinians regained Gaza but saw that they were losing any hope of getting the West Bank.

At this point, each could have helped the other turn the disengagement

into a lasting success for both and a major step toward peace. Yet each
had demands that were politically difficult for the other to meet: Sharon
wanted to see more than voluntary self-restraint by terrorist organizations;
he wanted them out of business. Abbas wanted prisoner releases and a
viable peace process, ensuring that Israel's withdrawal would lead to a
viable Palestinian state. Both, at that point, had reason to be flexible, provided each man got incentives that would help his domestic political position. Sharon, for instance, was not necessarily wedded to withdrawing just
from Gaza and four small settlements in the West Bank, as called for in
his disengagement plan. That much territory had been agreed on with
the White House in exchange for the understandings reached with Bush
in April 2004. American and Israeli officials told me Sharon would have
been willing to give up significantly more land in the West Bank in
exchange for American support for Israel's final-status positions. The
same proffer could have been put before Abbas. But both leaders would
need help and pressure to break down years of accumulated mistrust and
turn a unilateral Israeli withdrawal into a bilateral peace process.

In Washington, where Condoleezza Rice was gliding through the
Senate confirmation process as secretary of state, the word "opportunity" sprang from the lips of a cross section of officials and politicians.

Supporting Rice, Senator Dianne Feinstein, a Democrat from California, used a floor speech to highlight part of Rice's testimony at her
confirmation hearing. "I was very pleased to hear her statements before
the Senate Foreign Relations Committee in which she said—and let me
quote—'I look forward to personally working with the Palestinian and
Israeli leaders and bringing American diplomacy to bear on this difficult but crucial issue. Peace can only come if all parties choose to do the
difficult work and choose to meet their responsibilities. And the time for
peace is now,' end quote."

In early February, Rice embarked on her first trip as secretary, signaling a new American willingness to engage cooperatively with the
world and repair the diplomatic damage resulting from the Iraq War.
The journey would quickly mark her as one of the most peripatetic secretaries of her era and draw wide media attention. It took her to Berlin,
London, Warsaw, and Ankara, then on to Jerusalem and Ramallah.

As Rice arrived in the Middle East, Prime Minister Sharon and President Abbas were preparing to meet February 8 in Sharm el-Sheikh, the Egyptian Red Sea resort, at the invitation of Egyptian president Hosni Mubarak. This would be the first meeting of Israeli and Palestinian leaders since Arafat's death three months before, and the highest-level meeting between the two sides in years. Jordan's King Abdullah would also be there.

This was a moment crying out for a stronger American and international role than a quick visit by the new secretary of state. In New York, UN secretary general Kofi Annan noted in a statement that despite encouraging signs, the situation between Israelis and Palestinians remained fragile; they needed to be encouraged to deepen their engagement, he said. But the Bush administration wasn't ready to make a significant move. It would be another two years before Rice spoke of "a diplomatic horizon." Right now its main focus was security. Rice named a security coordinator, Army Lieutenant General William (Kip) Ward, to monitor an Israeli-Palestinian cease-fire and train and equip a revamped Palestinian security force.

After Rice's separate meetings with Prime Minister Sharon and President Abbas, a journalist put her on the spot during a press conference at the Muqata in Ramallah, asking her to explain why she wouldn't be participating in the summit. Rice acknowledged that the meeting would be "an extremely important step forward" and then said: "Not everything has to involve the United States, but the United States has to be there when it is needed. We will be very active."

The administration had weighed having Rice join the summit, a senior administration official said. "We did consider it. But as I recall, neither the Israelis nor the Palestinians were pushing for us to attend the actual meeting in Sharm. We did a lot to help prepare for the meeting, and figured it made sense for Sharon and Abu Mazen to try to get off on a solid footing without us in the room, at least at the start." The official added, "I understood very clearly that we would have to be heavily engaged if Gaza disengagement was to succeed, let alone any more ambitious hopes to revive the peace process."

Later, before boarding her plane in Tel Aviv, Rice said, "This is the most promising moment for progress between Palestinians and Israelis in recent years." She was departing "confident of the success of the meeting tomorrow between President Abbas and Prime Minister Sharon." The United States, she said, was "determined to do all that we can to take advantage of this moment of opportunity in the weeks and months ahead." Then she left for Rome, Paris, Brussels, and Luxembourg.

The following day's summit was indeed a success, to the extent that Sharon and Abbas agreed to a truce: Palestinians would stop all acts of violence against Israelis everywhere, and Israel would cease all military activity against Palestinians. Statements from officials around the world lavished praise on the Middle East leaders. But the meeting did not take advantage of the new political landscape in both Israel and the Palestinian territories to move the two sides closer after four years of bloodshed. With American backing, Sharon's course was set: the overarching event of the year would be the Israeli disengagement from Gaza. The Bush administration, insisting on "no shortcuts," refused even to consider quiet Israeli-Palestinian talks on final-status issues—Jerusalem, borders, and refugees.

Speaking in August 2006, eight months after Hamas won a parliamentary majority and took over the Palestinian government, Maen Areikat recalled that moment of promise in February 2005. An adviser to Abbas, he was director general of the Negotiations Affairs Department of the PLO. "Do you recall the Sharm el-Sheikh meeting, February 2005?" he asked me. "Nothing happened. I think if Israel, if Sharon delivered on some of the promises he gave Abu Mazen at that summit . . . believe me, the political map in Palestine would be a much different one right now. Hamas wouldn't be in power. If they helped in releasing prisoners, allowing for a greater freedom of movement, economic conditions improved, Gaza was coordinated better with the Palestinians, it was not turned into a big prison as we anticipated, Hamas wouldn't have scored high in the elections."

18

Hope and Reward

■ SPRING AND SUMMER 2005■

SITTING IN GEORGE W. BUSH'S study at Prairie Chapel Ranch, Ariel Sharon didn't look like a man basking in American admiration. His squat, bulky form barely fit into a swivel chair. His head was turned stiffly leftward as he listened to the president during a photo session. Bush, in contrast, was a picture of youthful relaxation: legs spread, leaning backward and gesturing, he had his own chair positioned so he could face his guest directly.

This was Sharon's eleventh meeting with Bush, and he should have felt more at ease than he appeared. By early April 2005, he had climbed into the tiny elite of world leaders whom Bush considered his partners in a bold gambit to remake the Middle East. The invitation to the cherished Bush retreat in Crawford, Texas, was a gesture of White House esteem for the Israeli prime minister. Sharon's aides liked to tout a fondness for the rural life as something the two leaders had in common, part of their chemistry. Raised in a *moshav*, a farming village, as the son of a pioneer agronomist, Sharon was at home in a pastoral setting. While Bush's spread was not big by Texas standards, Sharon's own Sycamore Farm, near the Negev, was the largest family-owned agricultural property in Israel, a state built on collective enterprise where just a fraction of the land was in private hands.

Part of Sharon's discomfort may have been physical. Aluf Benn, the diplomatic reporter for *Haaretz*, reported in early 2007 that in 2005, "Sharon showed increasing signs of physical deterioration. He had difficulty walking, tired quickly, and told his close associates that his vitality was no longer as it used to be. His aides tried to make things easier for him, to spare him physical effort and to keep his schedule light so that he would be able to rest. At events to which Sharon was invited the distances were carefully measured so that he would have to walk as little as possible."

Still, Sharon seemed to struggle to fit in, showing the same subdued formality he brought to the Oval Office. With his attention to detail, he had made sure to wear correct ranch attire, minus the cowboy boots. His dark trousers matched Bush's; his open-neck blue shirt was just a shade darker than the president's. But despite being indoors, he was still wearing a windbreaker. When they faced the press after their meeting, he made an awkward joke: "Of course, I would be very glad, Mr. President, to have you as a guest on our farm, not only because we are short of labor."

After a career spent planning and building settlements as a way of entrenching Israel's hold on the occupied Palestinian territories, Sharon was poised to evacuate and dismantle twenty-one settlements in the Gaza Strip and four more in the northern West Bank. Bush saw the move as a major step toward his own oft-stated goal of Israel and a new state of Palestine living side by side in peace. With American forces trapped in a deadly struggle against insurgents and holy warriors in Iraq, the planned Israeli disengagement offered one welcome sign of progress in Bush's bid to reform and transform the region. "Prime Minister Sharon is showing strong visionary leadership by taking difficult steps to improve the lives of people across the Middle East—and I want to thank you for your leadership," Bush said at their joint press conference. Sharon's decision, which was causing a rebellion in the right-wing precincts that had long been his political home, put him alongside Tony Blair of Britain, Junichiro Koizumi of Japan, José Maria Aznar of Spain, and Silvio Berlusconi of Italy—each of whom had supported Bush's war in Iraq in the face of strong domestic opposition.

Closeted together, Bush probed Sharon on why he had decided on the pullout from Gaza, and why right then. "I'm just asking you, as one leader to another: what went through your mind? You didn't do it five years before, you didn't do it one year later, you did it then, you did it this way. Why? What was your thought process? I'm just trying to understand better how you got there."

A senior U.S. official, present for the exchange, said, "That elicited a kind of philosophical answer from Sharon about Israel and its security interests [and] Arafat . . . being in control, the political situation, Abu Mazen, Abu Alaa [Ahmed Qurei]. . . . The tone was more of allies thinking through problems with each other." Although his longtime nemesis Arafat had died and been succeeded by Mahmoud Abbas, Sharon continued to insist that there was no reliable negotiating partner on the Palestinian side. Whatever actions Israel was taking that undermined the chance of peace with the Palestinians, including settlement expansion and erection of the separation barrier in the West Bank, these paled in significance next to Sharon's courageous plan to pull out of Gaza, in Bush's view. When Tom Raum of the Associated Press asked Bush during the leaders' joint press conference if he was "satisfied that Israel will do enough, once they pull out of Gaza, to meet the terms of the road map and put it back on track," Bush steered attention back to disengagement. "I've been very clear about Israel has an obligation under the road map. That's no expansion of settlements. I look forward to continuing to work and dialogue with Israel on this subject. We've got—this is an ongoing process. This is a process that's going to take a lot of work to get a democracy stood up on Israel's border. And we look forward to working with Israel. The thing that I want people to understand is that the prime minister of Israel has made a commitment toward the vision of two states living side by side in peace. And I appreciate that commitment, Mr. Prime Minister, and we look forward to continuing to work with you on it."

Sharon's obvious determination to complete the disengagement, despite a full-blown revolt within his own Likud Party and defection of its right wing, won Bush's admiration. "My view of this is, the president admires leadership," said a senior official who watched the two men together. "The president thinks you weren't elected to sit around. . . . You were elected to take risks to achieve goals. That is why he admires Blair. He happens to like him, but he admires Blair, he admires Koizumi, he admires Sharon. And he says this not only to Sharon, he says also to Arab leaders, 'You have to admire Ariel Sharon. He took an extremely tough decision. He knew there would be a heavy political price, and he continues to pay that price. But he doesn't let it daunt him, he keeps going, he's determined to see this through, he's a tough old guy, he's doing what he thinks is right.'" Bush moved close to the high respect for Sharon long held by I. Lewis "Scooter" Libby Jr., the vice president's chief of staff, and Elliott Abrams, the point man for the Middle East on the National Security Council staff.

In Crawford, Bush rewarded Sharon by repeating the language he had used a year earlier, assuring Israel that the United States would not insist on a return to the 1967 borders during negotiations for a final settlement, saying, "New realities on the ground make it unrealistic to expect that the outcome of final-status negotiations will be a full and complete return to the armistice lines of 1949. It is realistic to expect that any final-status agreement will be achieved only on the basis of mutually agreed changes that reflect these realities." When first uttered in 2004, the language produced a storm of protest from Palestinians and Arabs generally, who believed Bush was depriving them of leverage they would need in final-status negotiations. While the context indicated he was referring to Israeli-Palestinian negotiations, his language might also be applied to Syria. Then Bush added a bonus for Israel, saying, "That's the American view." This meant he was committing not just his own administration but the U.S. government, binding future administrations.

After the brief press conference and lunch, Bush took Sharon on a tour of his ranch, driving his pickup truck. According to a colorful tidbit later recounted to the prime minister's friend Uri Dan of the *Jerusalem Post*, "President George W. Bush told Prime Minister Ariel Sharon that prior to their meeting in Crawford, Texas, he had read the chapter in the Bible about 'the spies and that woman.' Bush meant of course Rahav the prostitute who hides Joshua's spies and speaks about the Jews' upcoming victory at Jericho.

"As the president drove around Crawford ranch, Sharon sat along-side him and Sharon's bureau chief Dov Weisglass sat in the back. Weisglass chimed in: 'Yes, and there's also the story about Joshua and the walls of Jericho—how they collapsed before the Israelis. . . .'

"'I haven't yet reached that chapter,' Bush said peremptorily, and switched the subject to the cedar trees on his ranch.

"'When the Jews built the Temple they also used cedars from Lebanon,' Sharon remarked.

"The conversation between Bush and Sharon ranged over a variety of topics: the Bible, history, and current affairs. The major problem in our relations with the Arabs is that the Arab world is not prepared to recognize the right of the Jewish people to its homeland, Sharon reiterated to Bush."

Sharon promised to return to the road map after disengagement. Although he'd resisted the plan at first, Sharon came to see it as a "security blanket," a senior administration official said. The road map was front-loaded with requirements for the Palestinians to meet Israeli security needs.

Sharon's promise was enough to satisfy Bush about an eventual return to the peace process. In the president's view, a "process" was less important as a step toward Palestinian statehood than the disengagement, an end to violence, and Palestinian reforms. He was confident that once the Palestinians produced responsible leaders, reformed their government, and halted terrorism, Israel would accept the idea of a Palestinian state next door. Sharon, after all, was already demonstrating a willingness to dismantle settlements and withdraw from big chunks of territory. Although Israel hadn't committed to further withdrawals, Sharon had clearly signaled that this was where he was headed, in the White House view.

Bush's message to the Palestinians, in essence, was, "Show yourselves capable of having a state that can live in peace next to Israel, and we'll get you a state. Don't worry about where the lines will be drawn. We'll make sure you get a viable country." Prominent Palestinians who met with Bush believed he was sincere. The trouble was, few among the Palestinian population shared Bush's rosy view of Israel's intentions.

Sharon's disengagement plan, in their view, was either a retreat under fire, a distraction, or an efficient redeployment of Israeli forces that would allow Israel to concentrate on holding the West Bank and East Jerusalem. Nothing in their unhappy history of dealing with Israel or with Sharon suggested that Israel would make concessions other than under duress—either from violence or from American pressure. That's why, to Abbas and the people around him, negotiations were essential to restoring Palestinian confidence in the future.

Next to stabilizing Iraq, helping Sharon make disengagement a success became the Bush administration's top priority in the Middle East. Officials had already abandoned their customary squeamishness about getting involved in Israeli politics and actively helped Sharon shore up his government so he could proceed with the withdrawal.

Toward the end of March, Sharon's coalition was endangered. The Shinui Party, whose main reason for being was to weaken the influence of Israel's religious establishment on the state and its claim to state money, had pulled out of the government in September 2004 over a $66 million subsidy for the educational system run by ultra-Orthodox Jews. Now Shas, the powerful ultra-Orthodox party representing Jews of Middle Eastern and North African descent, was threatening to quit over budget cuts in other subsidies.

If the Sharon budget didn't pass by a March 31, 2005, deadline, the government would collapse and with it, the whole disengagement plan. Yosef Lapid, head of the Shinui Party, who supported a two-state solution with the Palestinians, came under renewed pressure to support the government's budget, even though to do so violated his party's principles. Dan Kurtzer, the U.S. ambassador, spoke to Knesset members to impress upon them how much the U.S. government wanted disengagement to proceed. He joined in the effort to persuade Lapid. He didn't call it lobbying. "The USG [United States government] actively supported disengagement, and I met constantly with ministers and Knesset members to explain our thinking," Kurtzer explained in a 2006 e-mail. "We didn't push for specific votes on specific legislation."

Lapid suspected it was the White House that had enlisted U.S. Representative Tom Lantos, a California Democrat, in the pressure campaign. Lantos and Lapid were old friends; both were originally from Budapest, Hungary, and survived the Holocaust as boys. Lantos telephoned Lapid: "Listen, let's fly to London tomorrow and meet there on this subject. You come from Tel Aviv and I'll come from Washington. I want to speak to you on behalf of very high personalities in the government." Lapid told Lantos such a trip wasn't necessary but listened to the California congressman's argument. A second call came from an American official whom Lapid would not identify. "Both said that I must make the budget possible in order not to disturb the peace process. And I told both of them that we had left the government because we disliked the budget, so it would be strange if a party leaves the government because it objects to the budget and then votes for the budget in order to save the government from its own people.

"It weighed very heavily, because suddenly I felt responsible for the fate of the peace process," Lapid said during a visit to Washington in the spring of 2005. "Sharon told me, 'The fate of the Middle East depends on you.' I said, 'No—it depends on you.'" Lapid and his Shinui colleagues didn't want to prevent the disengagement but realized they were now in a good position to bargain with the government. Meeting with Sharon at his farm, they cut a deal: they would support the budget in exchange for 700 million shekels (about $167 million) in added spending for higher education, middle-class tax breaks, health care, and traffic safety. Sharon's budget passed.

With the immediate Israeli domestic hurdle overcome, the Bush administration set about easing Israel's worries on other fronts. A top priority was ensuring that the disengagement proceeded without attacks from Palestinians on Israeli soldiers or settlers. Condoleezza Rice assigned Lieutenant General William E. (Kip) Ward, deputy commander of the U.S. Army in Europe, who had been a brigade commander in Somalia and later commanded the NATO Stabilization Force in Bosnia-Herzegovina, to head a security liaison mission. Its purpose was to streamline and modernize the Palestinian security forces so they could effectively combat terrorism and get Israeli and Palestinian security officials to cooperate.

Meanwhile, the Quartet tapped newly retired World Bank president and prominent investor James Wolfensohn as special envoy in charge of coordinating international efforts to support the disengagement. His job was to help the Palestinians emerge from disengagement on a sounder economic footing, with a better-functioning government, and foster cooperation between Israelis and Palestinians to help the withdrawal go smoothly. A key task was to help Palestinians make appropriate use of the land they were about to acquire from the vacated settlements, amounting to some 25 percent of the Gaza Strip.

All these steps would benefit Israelis, the moderate Palestinian government, and Palestinians generally. But they omitted something big: an answer to the question, "What next after disengagement?" And they showed a White House blind spot both about various Israeli agendas at work in parallel with disengagement and the new Palestinian president's precarious political situation.

UN undersecretary general Kieran Prendergast, delivering a monthly report to the Security Council, noted "a degree of edginess and renewed suspicion" about both Israeli intentions and Palestinian resolve and capabilities. "The pressing challenge for the parties and the international community is to take all possible actions to ensure that disengagement happens, that it happens in a coordinated way, and that it does not become a dead end, but contributes to the momentum for peace."

Israeli officials reiterated their commitment to the diplomatic road map in their meetings with American and European officials. But an interview given to *Haaretz* in October 2004 seemed, for many, a more truthful statement of Sharon's intentions: "The significance of the disengagement plan is the freezing of the peace process," Sharon's chief of staff, Dov Weisglass, said in the interview. "And when you freeze that process . . . you prevent the establishment of a Palestinian state, and you prevent a discussion on the refugees, the borders, and Jerusalem.

"Effectively, this whole package called the Palestinian state, with all that it entails, has been removed indefinitely from our agenda. And all this with authority and permission. All with a presidential blessing and the ratification of both houses of Congress. The disengagement is actually formaldehyde," Weisglass said. "It supplies the amount of formaldehyde that is necessary so there will not be a political process with the Palestinians."

It was no secret to most Palestinians that Israel wanted to be free of Gaza; in every peace negotiation, ending the occupation in the Gaza Strip was among the least controversial issues. The nine thousand settlers living surrounded by close to 1.2 million Palestinians represented a huge financial and military drain for Israel. Once Sharon decided Israel could safely dispense with a strategic position at Netzarim overlooking a future Palestinian seaport, and once he decided to brave the wrath of the settlers and their right-wing supporters, the issue was largely settled. So while Palestinians were glad to see the Gaza occupation end, they didn't share the White House view that disengagement drastically altered the political landscape. Compared with the West Bank, Gaza held little biblical importance. For Palestinians, the West Bank and Jerusalem represented the core of the conflict. They feared—with some justification, given Sharon's past statements—that Israel would continue strengthening its hold on the West Bank by continuing to erect the separation barrier and expanding settlements. (The following January, diplomatic correspondent Udi Segal reported on Israel's Channel 2 that Sharon told him privately he wanted to keep eight settlement blocs in the West Bank—several more than expected—as well as the Jordan Valley.)

Palestinians demanded several commitments to ensure that Gaza would not become a sealed-off prison, choking with a growing, impoverished population. These included agreement by Israel on rebuilding the airport demolished during the intifada by Israeli air strikes; construction of a seaport; passage for Palestinians between Gaza and the West Bank; and easy movement of goods into and out of Gaza.

More important, Palestinians demanded assurance that if Israel were granted a reasonably smooth departure from Gaza, the international community would then focus powerful attention on sponsoring peace talks leading to the two-state solution its leaders so often talked about. For the time being, there was a lull in Palestinian violence against Israelis, brought about by agreement between President Abbas and militant factions. But instead of the cease-fire being the jumping-off point for renewed negotiations, diplomacy was consumed by disengagement—as Sharon intended.

Speaking in Washington while Bush and Sharon were meeting in Texas, veteran Palestinian reformer and moderate Hanan Ashrawi described the challenges confronting Abbas and Washington's expectations:

"He has to build institutions, he has to hold people accountable who have been guilty or found guilty or accused of abusing their position and public funds and public trust and so on. So there are allegations now that are being pursued. And he has to reform the security. And the security system has become the major focus of the American endeavor as well as Israeli demands when it comes to the reform agenda. And he also has to deliver to the Palestinian people's hope that there is a possibility of a resolution. And that there is a partnership and a negotiating process. . . .

"So we have to show that we are democratic, that we can carry out serious reforms in order to demonstrate that we are good little boys and girls and we're worthy of being talked to. And it's extremely difficult if you do not have a political option. Right now, everybody's talking about reform and nation building, but we don't see the opening. We don't see the avenue for a serious, credible, legitimate, substantive political process that would tell the Palestinian people there is light at the end of the tunnel; there is hope that there can be an end to this occupation and there is hope for a two-state solution."

Of the Israelis, she said, "They lost their scapegoat Arafat, but they're very busy transforming Abu Mazen into another scapegoat." Meanwhile, the Palestinian political map was changing, despite Abbas's overwhelming election victory for Fatah. Long the dominant political party in the West Bank and Gaza, Fatah had "lost a great deal in terms of its own base among the Palestinians also because it was seen as the party that adopted the political course of action, the peace plan, and so on, and of course it didn't succeed," Ashrawi said. "The Islamic political parties have gained constituency and support." It wasn't just Palestinians making these points. That same day, Ami Ayalon, retired chief of the Israeli Navy and former director of the General Security Services, was in Washington, speaking at an event organized by the Middle East Institute. Gaza disengagement, he warned, had to be the first step toward a two-state solution. Both sides, he said, believed they had won: Israelis thought the lull in violence meant their demonstration of military strength had succeeded; Palestinians thought disengagement meant an Israeli retreat and a victory for the intifada.

Palestinians appeared to be blind to the benefits that could accrue to them in international, and particularly American, opinion if they made a concerted effort to support a peaceful disengagement and build an efficient, humane administration in the Gaza Strip, thereby proving themselves ready for statehood.

For Israel, there were pluses and minuses to the kind of coordination with Palestinians during disengagement that the international community was seeking. On one hand, Israel clearly hoped to conduct the evacuation of settlers without soldiers or settlers being attacked in the process and without renewed Palestinian violence elsewhere. Settlers might themselves resort to violent resistance, and Palestinian attacks would just make a difficult situation tougher. Palestinian security forces would help prevent such violence. Therefore, coordination with them was essential.

But if the cooperation worked too well, there would quickly be international pressure to use it as a springboard to deeper contacts and negotiations, which the Sharon government wanted to avoid. Good cooperation would also undercut the key rationale offered by Sharon for moving forward with the disengagement unilaterally, without negotiation: that Palestinians were too consumed by hatred to make peace, and that there was no reliable partner on the Palestinian side with whom to negotiate.

What's more, the Israeli government was already drawing accusations from settlers and the right wing of retreating from battle by pulling out of Gaza and getting nothing in return from Palestinians. More concessions by Israel, in the form of approval of a seaport, airport, and safe passage between the West Bank and Gaza, would only add to the impression of giving up something for nothing.

Even though the Israeli military thought it had defeated the armed intifada with its incursions into the West Bank and Gaza and targeted killings of militants, officers recognized that Palestinians had not been defeated psychologically. Thus, their presumed victory held little value as a deterrent against future Palestinian attacks or against other enemies in the region. Outgoing Chief of Staff Moshe Yaalon, who was replaced after he opposed the disengagement plan, said: "We stood firmly for about four-and-a-half years, with more than one thousand casualties, and Israeli society didn't surrender. But the disengagement plan has become their victory.

". . . This was Arafat's idea, that at the end of the day, Israel will surrender. . . . Tactically, militarily we defeated them. Militarily we defeated them. Politically, this is not the case.

"In the end, the Palestinians should understand, should realize, that violence doesn't pay off. If it is not the case, we will go on fighting for years. . . . Sharon at the beginning said, 'I'm not going to do anything unless we reach peace and quiet—for seven days. . . . Then I will go back to the political process.' But in the end he decided to evacuate from the Gaza Strip. Without getting anything, and without causing any price to the Palestinians for this step.

"If we are talking about the disengagement, what we enjoy now is international empathy. It's not a substantial asset," Yaalon said, and would not last indefinitely. "The Israeli principle was 'land for peace.' We gave up land, we didn't get peace. We didn't get anything." In the poisoned, zero-sum atmosphere of the Israeli-Palestinian conflict, a win-win situation didn't exist.

So the stage was set for the most grudging form of cooperation between Israelis and Palestinians over disengagement. Israel entered the talks not eager to give anything more away. Palestinians were suspicious of Israel's long-term intentions. Dennis Ross, the longtime Middle East envoy for the George H. W. Bush and Bill Clinton administrations, urged the United States to step up its intervention in a May 6, 2005, op-ed article in the *Jerusalem Post*: "In the current political climate in Israel it is too much to expect that Israel will do much more for Abbas without seeing more from him. And yet, having produced calm, Abbas's own expectations are that he needs more from the Israelis before he can do dramatically more. If ever a situation cried out for a third party to help out, this is it." He warned that Abbas's position was precarious: "One thing is for sure: if Mahmoud Abbas does not make it, it will be a long time before there is another opening."

The White House understood that long-term economic prospects for Palestinians needed to be improved. But they were not prepared to move to the next step—a peace agreement.

Fixing Gaza required restoring basic law and order so that Palestinian factional rivals weren't shooting and killing each other in battles over political and criminal turf, and restoring a measure of economic hope to a population that had slid into dire poverty during the intifada. General Ward's team quickly came to understand the woeful state of Palestinian security forces. Briefing Congress at the end of June, Ward said, "As you are aware, the Palestinian security sector was fractured and dysfunctional, with separate fiefdoms that were loyal to individuals with—not having any clear lines of authority and unresponsive to any central command. To reform their security sector first required the Palestinians to shift the way they thought about providing security and the role of these security institutions, and that, I believe, sir, has occurred. Translating that into actions on the ground is where the challenge still remains." The security services had turned into a welfare safety net, with just twenty thousand to twenty-two thousand of their fifty-eight-thousand-plus employees actually showing up for work, he said.

Economically, there was no way Gaza would revive—or even survive—on its own. There had to be a connection with Israel, the West Bank, and the outside world. This would require easing and in places dismantling the tight closure regime that barred movement between the West Bank and Gaza; that blocked all but a few thousand Gazans from working in Israel; that made the export of goods from Gaza to Europe unreliable and so costly as to be uncompetitive; and that kept West Bankers confined much of the time in enclaves isolated from the rest of the territories.

Starting in 2004, World Bank officials, led by their country director, Nigel Roberts, tried to persuade Israelis that it would be in Israel's long-term interest to have a thriving Palestinian economy. They argued that if Palestinians had jobs, fewer would be lured into violent extremism. A World Bank report in June 2004 argued that disengagement offered an opportunity to revive the Palestinian economy, but by itself wouldn't accomplish it. A broad-based rollback of the closure regime would be required. Such a rollback, at least at the border, would not imperil Israeli security, the report said, because there were more effective ways of screening the movement of goods and people than the ones Israel was currently using. With a modern, properly managed system at the border, security would be improved, as would the movement of trade.

Israel's National Security Council, headed at the time by Giora Eiland, listened receptively to the bank's arguments. But the plan ran into trouble with the army, which would shoulder most of the security risks from any easing of the restrictions on Palestinian movement. Another problem had nothing to do with security: corruption on both sides of the crossing, in which bribes were used to speed up the movement of goods. Bank officials believed it was most prevalent on the Palestinian side.

In a new report in December, the World Bank warned that for Palestinian economic recovery to occur, "the government of Israel needs to roll back the system of restrictions on the movement of people and goods imposed since the beginning of the intifada—it is these various closures that are the proximate cause of four years of Palestinian economic distress." The bank added that "there are solutions that permit a significant dismantling of closure measures without endangering Israeli security."

The bank wielded a blunt instrument of its own: its assessments had a big influence on whether donors would kick in large sums to help the Palestinian economy. At the time, it was in Israel's interest to have the international community assume this burden. But the bank advised that "it would be a mistake to respond to today's potential opening by efforts to raise large sums of money without addressing the root causes of today's economic crisis."

Whether due to the bank's pressure, the arrival of Wolfensohn on the scene in the spring of 2005, the comparative lull in violence, or all three, Israel did ease the West Bank system of closures and checkpoints during the first half of the year. But for Gaza, the key question of access to the outside world was still unanswered.

Economist Salah Abdel-Shafi was among those Palestinians who shared the American goal of wanting Gaza disengagement to be successful all the way around. Son of Dr. Haidar Abdel-Shafi, one of the Gaza Strip's most respected and independent leaders, he was part of a technical team attempting to plan for disengagement's aftermath. During an afternoon in the late spring of 2005, he sat over coffee on the terrace of Gaza's al-Deira Hotel overlooking the sun-drenched Mediterranean, veering between pessimism and hope. The hotel, partly owned by his brother Khaled, was undergoing renovations to accommodate the journalists and foreign visitors expected to arrive later in the summer to observe disengagement. With luck, more visitors would follow, and tourism would flourish. West Bankers could come to enjoy the sea. Visitors from the Arab world could tour holy sites in the West Bank.

But at the moment, Palestinian planners were having trouble getting information from Israel about the assets that would shortly be turned over to the Palestinians. As for the future, so much depended on the arrangements worked out with Israel. "If the issue of access is not solved, nothing will happen," he said. Without a major increase in work permits allowing Palestinians to hold jobs in Israel, Gaza faced disaster in the short term, he said. "Every year, there are twenty thousand to thirty thousand entrants to the labor market." Because of its longtime economic integration with Israel, Gaza's wage rates were higher than Egypt's, and so its agricultural products and finished goods could not compete in the Egyptian market. This increased Gaza's dependence on the Israeli market and exports elsewhere. Yet delays at the crossing points and the inability of trucks to leave or enter Gaza imposed high additional costs. Still, the outlook was bleak for Gaza's industrial base unless it developed alternatives to its traditional garment and furniture factories. "China is killing our garment and furniture industry."

The World Bank zeroed in on the Karni crossing, the main transit point for goods in and out of Gaza, knowing this could be pivotal to economic survival. Bank officials tried to persuade Israelis to accept new, high-tech screening systems that would speed up movement of shipments while at the same time improving security. Under the existing back-to-back system, a trailer full of merchandise would be driven to the border with Israel at Karni; the goods would then be off-loaded to another trailer on the Israeli side. Instead, the bank proposed that a single trailer be driven to the Karni crossing, then go through X-ray screening to check for weapons or other contraband. Only the tractor would be replaced on the Israeli side, since tractors are harder to screen thoroughly. It wasn't enough to accept the new equipment, however; to save time and money, it had to be used as intended. American officials were persuaded.

By June 30, when he appeared before the Senate Foreign Relations Committee in Washington, special envoy Wolfensohn was "more optimistic now than I was just a month ago . . . my experience in the first sixty days gives me hope that the process of disengagement from Gaza can lead both sides back to the road map." Picking up on the work of his former employees at the bank, he was pressing Israelis and Palestinians to work on solving six crucial matters: border crossings; connecting Gaza with the West Bank; greater movement for Palestinians within the West Bank; rebuilding the Gaza airport and constructing a new seaport; demolition and disposal of houses in settlements to be evacuated; and preserving the settlers' greenhouses. The talks, he said, resembled "a kind of uneasy chess game" between senior Israelis and Palestinians, in an atmosphere "heavy with mistrust."

Palestinians faced their own challenges: getting their fiscal house and bloated payroll in order and creating a long-term development plan for Gaza that would draw substantial international aid. In Wolfensohn's view, disengagement would have to be accompanied by quick-impact job-creation schemes, building infrastructure, and rehabilitating agriculture, to provide "a sense of change and hope."

Back in Washington a month later, Wolfensohn's tone was more urgent. Key issues still had not been solved, with disengagement less than a month away. Speaking of the crossing points, he said during a House subcommittee hearing, "This is not a gift by the Israelis to the Palestinians and it is not something that the Palestinians are asking for just to win a debate. What is necessary here if you want to have enduring peace is not a prison in Gaza and the northern West Bank, but an environment in which there can be movement of goods and people in an atmosphere of respect for the Palestinians." Again, according to a report by the State Department Washington File, he pressed for international funding for a job-creation scheme that "frankly can hold people for six months at least," as well as Palestinian government reforms. He worried about how well Hamas would do in upcoming elections. "You need to have visible hope, because at the time of the elections God knows what will be said."

Wolfensohn said that "it is exceedingly important" that the Palestinian people see that the Palestinian Authority is "an alternative to Hamas, that it can be run honestly, that it will be run honestly and transparently and that it can provide the social services that are needed. . . . Otherwise, Hamas, because of its provision of social services and a better reputation, has the opportunity of gaining political ground, which none of us would like to see."

For the Bush administration, disengagement became the be-all and end-all of its Middle East efforts. Speaking to the American Israel Public Affairs Committee on May 23, Secretary Rice called it "an unprecedented and incredibly delicate opportunity for peace." On another occasion, she called it a "historic opportunity." The administration recognized that it was only the first step on a path back to negotiations between Israelis and Palestinians but feared that if it went badly, or was marred by serious violence, "our progress along that path is going to be very, very difficult indeed," as David Welch, assistant secretary of state for the Near East, told Congress on June 30.

American officials pressed for "coordination" between Israelis and Palestinians on the mechanics of the disengagement, hoping this would restore shattered relationships. Speaking to Israel Radio during a trip in June, Rice laid out optimistic expectations: "[W]hat we hope after Gaza is done is that several conditions will have been met. First of all, that there would be greater trust and confidence between the parties, because they will have worked together on this project. And if it goes as we hope it will, peacefully, orderly, then you have a much different relationship between the parties.

"Secondly, that you will have more capable Palestinian security forces that have demonstrated that they can work in a coordinated fashion with Israel. Third, that you will have stronger political and economic institutions, as well as a viable economic future for the Palestinian people, so the Palestinian people can begin to see that their own authorities can govern and give them a better life."

U.S. officials repeatedly deflected questions about what would happen afterward. Interviewed by Jordanian radio in June, Rice said, "The Middle East has a tendency to get out ahead of itself and to look at what is out there, rather than what is right in front of it." But something "right in front" also escaped the attention of the U.S. administration: how disengagement was playing on the Palestinian street. For many Palestinians, Israel's pending withdrawal represented at least an incremental triumph for the violent intifada. To them, it followed the pattern of Hezbollah's "victory" in forcing Israel to retreat from its so-called security zone in southern Lebanon after an occupation of eighteen years. The political beneficiaries were those who led the resistance—namely Hamas.

The only way that Abbas and moderates in his Fatah party could gain an advantage was by demonstrating that their preferred tactics—bilateral negotiations with Israel and the involvement of the international community—brought added value to the Palestinians. Instead, they got to "coordinate" the withdrawal with the Israelis, which largely meant fulfilling obligations—mostly involving security—that fit priorities set by Israel.

"Our political objective was to show that negotiations work; violence does not necessarily work," said Ghaith al-Omari, one of Abbas's bright, Western-educated aides. "'Coordinated,' the way it ended up . . . we did not get any political benefit from it. Sure, the disengagement was very smooth and safe and secure, and there was no violence from the Palestinian side, etc., etc., but we could not use that to send a political message. We could not capitalize on that politically.

"What we wanted was something like, 'You know what? These are [Sharon's] parameters of disengagement.' Let's add a couple of parameters, so we can tell our people, 'Look—when we negotiated, we got even more.' That's what the administration was not willing to push for." Al-Omari said the Americans explained why: "They said that Sharon has spun this as a unilateral thing. That's how he built his support in Israel. To move it to a bilateral [negotiated] one would expose him to domestic problems," threatening his coalition. Bush "was not going to make him [Sharon] pay for that."

Instead, the Bush administration spent a great deal of senior officials' time on details to help Israel get through the disengagement. And there were a lot of details. Diana Buttu, a Palestinian lawyer involved in the disengagement, recalled: "They forced us to spend weeks focusing on Israeli rubble. I remember there was a visit of Secretary Rice in which she focused on Israeli rubble . . . and there being an agreement on the clearance of Israeli rubble, rather than there being any focus on, 'What is going to be the future of the Gaza Strip? Is it going to be connected to the West Bank? Is there going to be safe passage? Is the airport going to open? What's going to happen to the seaport? . . . Fundamental issues that actually affect day-to-day lives of Palestinians were always put on the back burner and we were told, 'Don't worry; we will get to that; but for the time being we need to focus on the rubble.'"

On July 28, a senior administration official was asked if the United States had a post-disengagement strategy. "We're doing a lot of thinking about postengagement. . . . We don't have a two-page plan. But we talk about it with the Israelis and with the Palestinians. We talk about it amongst ourselves. So, sure. Dr. Rice has been quite emphatic in conversations with other leaders that it is a mistake to focus too much on that question prior to disengagement—first, because there are immensely complicated tasks related to disengagement that need our attention. We shouldn't be talking about next year. We should be talking about what we need to do now—partly because we may argue about next year, and we don't want to argue. We want to get to work on the questions that we have to solve now, like how do you get from Gaza to the West Bank and back after disengagement; also because, what happens after disengagement is dependent upon how disengagement goes. At one end of the spectrum, a smooth, nonviolent disengagement leading to a peaceful and nonviolent Gaza so that you can point to it and say, 'You want to know what a Palestinian state will look like? That's what it looks like." At the other end of the spectrum, disengagement under fire, Hamastan. Today there is not really much law and order in Gaza. If that continues and the PA can't control it, Hamas isn't controlled, that's a very different situation. So how can you really judge, in the summer or worse yet, last spring or winter, what's next, when you don't really know how disengagement's going to go."

Israel and the United States, in fact, presented starkly divergent pictures of Gaza's future. To his people, Sharon presented Gaza as a hopeless basket case that Israel needed to get rid of—fast. At the same time, Americans were challenging the Palestinians to turn Gaza into a pilot project for future statehood: peaceful, well-governed, fulfilling its economic potential. But as for the important questions that would have a major impact on Palestinians—like "How do you get from Gaza to the West Bank and back after disengagement"—these remained unanswered as disengagement got under way, even though the top White House point man for the Middle East, Elliott Abrams, spent two weeks beforehand in the region.

Declaring "The day has arrived," Sharon addressed his nation on August 15, the eve of disengagement: "Gaza cannot be held onto forever. Over one million Palestinians live there, and they double their numbers with every generation. They live in incredibly cramped refugee camps, in poverty and squalor, in hotbeds of ever-increasing hatred, with no hope whatsoever on the horizon. It is out of strength and not weakness that we are taking this step. We tried to reach agreements with the Palestinians which would move the two peoples towards the path of peace. These were crushed against a wall of hatred and fanaticism. The unilateral disengagement plan, which I announced approximately two years ago, is the Israeli answer to this reality. This plan is good for Israel in any future scenario. We are reducing the day-to-day friction and its victims on both sides. The IDF will redeploy on defensive lines behind the security fence. Those who continue to fight us will meet the full force of the IDF and the security forces. Now the Palestinians bear the burden of proof. They must fight terror organizations, dismantle its infrastructure, and show sincere intentions of peace in order to sit with us at the negotiating table."

The speech highlighted a key flaw in disengagement, from the standpoint of any hope to get back into a peace process: to make his case for a unilateral withdrawal without peace negotiations, Sharon was promulgating an attitude toward the Palestinians that fed Israeli pessimism: the Palestinians were enemies, almost irredeemably so and, beyond that, incapable of improving their own situation.

After watching Sharon's speech from Washington, Condoleezza Rice told the *New York Times* she thought "it was really remarkable statesmanship. And I just think we have to sometimes pause and think about what this means. It means that the father of the settlement movement, the Likud, Israel is ceding territory. And then, if you look at the other side of that, of course, it is also giving to the Palestinians an opportunity to breathe freely in Gaza, to live without the shadow of settlers and the Israeli army and to begin to build the institutions that are, I think, ultimately going to be the institutions for statehood."

Disengagement in fact went forward amid powerful emotion, as Israelis watched Jews being removed from homes they had occupied for a generation, noisy protests and pockets of obstreperous settler resistance, but no serious violence. There was also no Palestinian violence, continuing a lull that had existed for some time, reflecting both good security coordination and a general Palestinian sense that any Israeli withdrawal was a good thing.

With relief, a senior administration official noted that the debate in the Israeli press had exaggerated the political crisis that would confront the country. "[I]f you think back to the claim of civil war, that thousands of people in the IDF would disobey orders—none of the terrible predictions came true." One man—Sharon—got nearly all the credit. "There were real challenges time after time after time, hurdles that he had to jump, that he got through and got over all of them.

"Looking back, it's hard to see how anyone could have done this but Sharon. Nobody on the Right would have, and nobody on the Left could have. It's an extraordinary achievement for him . . . twenty months of absolutely firm leadership, just bulldozing his way forward. And that won a lot of admiration here," Bush included. "His reaction was one of admiration for a political leader who adopts a policy and sees it through despite the fact that it was pretty costly politically."

Praise for Sharon didn't come just from Washington. The reception that Sharon received in September at the United Nations General

Assembly in New York, the annual convention of world leaders, amounted to a hero's welcome compared to the treatment usually accorded Israel by the world body. Israel routinely faced condemnation not only in the assembly but in various UN subgroupings. Now, in the wake of his withdrawal from Gaza, Sharon got a public handshake from Pakistan's leader, Pervez Musharraf, met with Jordan's King Abdullah, and enjoyed a general thaw in the Muslim world's attitude toward the Jewish state. Qatar's foreign minister said Arab nations should recipro-cate Israel's Gaza pullout, according to the Associated Press.

Back home in Jerusalem, the situation was less bright: Sharon faced a bitterly divided Likud Party and a strong challenge to his leadership from former Prime Minister Benjamin Netanyahu, who called the Gaza withdrawal a mistake. At the UN, President Bush offered Sharon encouragement during a quick meeting, according to a senior official: "You'll win, because Israelis, too, will respond to strong and deter-mined leadership." But a tactical disagreement during the meeting foreshadowed a coming crisis: Sharon opposed allowing Hamas to compete in Palestinian parliamentary elections slated for January 2006. In a meeting with *New York Times* journalists, he threatened to withhold cooperation on logistics, such as lifting checkpoints, that would allow a large number of Palestinians to vote in the West Bank. Bush decided that the question of who should participate was one that should be left up to the Palestinians.

One thing the two men did not address—one that might have made a crucial difference to Palestinian moderates in the coming election— was how to fulfill the stated commitment of both the United States and Israel to get new traction on the road map. While disengagement was under way, Rice spoke glowingly to the *New York Times* about a poten-tial new spirit of cooperation between Israeli and Palestinian officials. If the withdrawal occurred successfully, "You would hope that confi-dence and trust between the Palestinians and the Israelis is also grown up because they had to have practically daily contact and meetings at every level of government in order to be able to pull this off. And if they indeed do, I think you will have created conditions and a level of trust that is unparalleled between the Palestinians and the Israelis."

But when Bush and Sharon met in New York, according to an official who was there, "We talked mostly about the follow-up to disengagement and the political situation in Israel," not about the question, "What next?"

"The president does believe that Sharon is committed to a two-state solution," the American official said. "The president's view is that Sharon has reached that conclusion and will not deviate from it. . . . The question of, 'OK, how do we get from the end of disengagement to there?' is one that we need to have more discussions with the Israelis about—and with the Palestinians. In part . . . pieces of the answer are clear—the need for Israelis and Palestinians to cooperate on Palestinian economic development; the need for there to be a link between the West Bank and Gaza; the need . . . for the Israelis to move back in the West Bank, out of the main cities. Have greater mobility for the Palestinians. The problem is, of course, security. And we're not going to impose deadlines on those things that are unrelated to security."

In Gaza, Hamas shrewdly used the Israeli withdrawal to its political advantage. Ghaith al-Omari noticed a Hamas banner. Translated, it read, "Four years of resistance beat ten years of negotiations."

"For the Israelis, this was a very specific operation. The operation was, 'We want to get out of Gaza.' So there was no particular interest in the IDF or political instruction in the IDF to continue the coordination afterwards," al-Omari said. "On the Palestinian side, the central control that [Interior Minister] Nasser Youssef had over the forces was always questionable."

Al-Omari said the Israelis stopped showing interest in security coordination. "They stopped returning our phone calls; they stopped helping us with things. . . . I remember some meetings with [Defense Minister Shaul] Mofaz. We were asking for ammunition; it was clear that we would have to go confront Hamas. And even at some point we did confront Hamas. There were some confrontations. We had a meeting with Mofaz. We asked for ammunition and weapons. They went back to their traditional concept of coordination, which was basically, 'Here— do this.' We had to go to meetings and get instructions. It was hard for us to operate in these kinds of circumstances. There was no particular interest on the Israeli side. On the Palestinian side, unless you have a specific mission that you're coordinating around, it's hard to coordinate in the abstract."

19

UNFULFILLED WISH
FALL–WINTER 2005

PRESIDENT BUSH'S TONE was reassuring: don't worry, he told the cluster of young aides to Palestinian president Mahmoud Abbas. Bush said he was intent on creating a Palestinian state during his presidency. Borders? Again, they shouldn't worry; Jerusalem would be a problem, as would connecting Gaza to the West Bank. But the borders had already been figured out. Bush recognized that Palestinians couldn't have a viable state if it looked like "Swiss cheese."

The young Palestinian officials were in Washington in early October 2005 to prepare for Abbas's visit to meet with Bush on October 20. The red-carpet treatment they received included a brief meeting with Secretary of State Condoleezza Rice and a longer one with Undersecretary Karen Hughes, who was about to report to Bush about her first trip to the Middle East as the official in charge of repairing the United States' battered image in the Arab and Muslim world. Then, an additional session with Assistant Secretary David Welch was interrupted by one of Rice's assistants: "The president would like to see you."

"The president of what?" asked Abbas's communications adviser, Diana Buttu, according to an account by Glenn Kessler of the *Washington Post*. Besides Bush's own desire to send a signal of strong support to Abbas, whom he liked and admired, the high-level entrée given to the

Palestinians was a measure of Hughes's coming to grips with the conflict. At every stop on her recent tour, the Abbas aides were told, one issue was consistently highlighted by the people she met with: Palestine. It was almost as though Palestinians themselves had taken charge of her schedule. Hughes didn't need a trip to the region to learn how anger over the Israeli-Palestinian conflict resonated throughout the Muslim world; State Department experts had been making the point for several years.

The new generation of Palestinian officials impressed Bush in much the same way as had Salam Fayyad, the finance minister who had straightened out the Palestinian Authority's murky, corruption-prone accounting and curbed Yasser Arafat's access to easy cash. The circle around Abbas was reform-minded, Western-educated, fluent in English, and determined to gain Palestinian rights through peaceful means rather than violence. Other members of this same generation had persuaded the International Court of Justice that the Israeli separation barrier being erected in the West Bank was illegal. But their technocratic skill and sophistication tended to leave Americans with a distorted, benign picture of the challenges confronting Abbas as he tried to lead a people wracked by poverty, hatred, and disillusionment after five years of conflict and crushing restrictions.

Six weeks after Israel had dismantled Gaza's Jewish settlements and three weeks after all its soldiers had left, the situation in the Palestinian territories was getting worse, from the top down. Abbas himself was indecisive and unable to exert full control over his government or its security services. His office didn't operate professionally. The Palestinian Authority was splurging beyond its means on salaries, building up a deficit.

More important, Abbas had little to show Palestinians for nine months of cooperating with Israel and the United States in allowing Israeli settlers and soldiers a relatively violence-free exit from Gaza, which was completed with the withdrawal of the last Israeli soldiers in late September. No Palestinian prisoners had been released from Israeli prisons, no peace talks had begun. Gaza was turning into the "prison" that many Palestinians had feared, and the inmates were killing each other. Borders with Israel and Egypt were closed most of the time, trapping 1.3 million Palestinians inside and squeezing their economy. During a Hamas rally in the Jabalia refugee camp, a mishandled explosive device went off, killing nineteen people. Embarrassed, Hamas tried to blame Israel, and the next day fired thirty rockets into the Israeli town of Sderot, just outside the closed-off Gaza Strip, wounding five Israelis.

Israel had warned that once it was out of Gaza, it would respond harshly to attacks emanating from there. Now it acted, sealing off not only Gaza but the West Bank and launching four days of air strikes in Gaza. As Ibrahim Gambari, the new undersecretary general for political affairs, told the UN Security Council, "Israeli F-16 fighter jets repeatedly flew low over the Gaza Strip. The consequent sonic booms caused widespread fear among the population, and medical officials in Gaza reported negative effects on children and pregnant women. In the West Bank, the Israeli military killed three suspected militants on 29 September and arrested hundreds of others. That series of arrests constituted Israel's largest since Operation Defensive Shield in 2002."

Hamas, meanwhile, began retaliating for the cooperation with Israel that Palestinian security services had displayed during disengagement; the services claimed to have prevented seventeen terrorist attacks against Israel. "On 2 October, a Palestinian police commander and two civilians were killed in clashes with Hamas militants, and more than forty people, including many children, were injured. On the following day, Palestinian police broke into the compound of the Legislative Council, firing into the air in protest at their inability to deal with militant attacks," Gambari told the Security Council.

Determined to prevent civil war, Abbas hoped that enlisting Hamas in the democratic process, with legislative elections scheduled for late January 2006, would restore a semblance of Palestinian national unity. Here he had Bush's support; rejecting Israeli arguments, the president insisted that Hamas be allowed to campaign for parliament. In his meeting with the young Palestinian officials, he suggested that election to office might domesticate the Islamic movement, even though U.S. officials would refuse to deal with any group that posed an armed threat to Israel.

Time was running out for Mahmoud Abbas to regain the political advantage for his Fatah party or surrender credit for Israel's withdrawal to Hamas and the other armed factions who claimed a victory for "resistance."

Bush registered concern about Fatah's long-term political strength during his meeting with Abbas's aides and with Abbas himself. Turning to Buttu, a Canadian Palestinian lawyer with a PhD from Stanford, he asked her if she was a member of Fatah. She told him she wasn't; neither was Ghaith al-Omari, a U.S.- and British-trained lawyer who was Abbas's director of international relations. Bush wanted to know why. Buttu told him she wasn't part of the political system, didn't understand what the goals of Fatah were anymore, and didn't think the party had a political program.

That's a problem, Bush said. Meeting two weeks later with Abbas, Bush worried aloud that Fatah wasn't able to appeal to the smartest members of a young generation that wanted to help build the country. Bush, however, demurred on the one thing that Abbas's supporters hoped would give him a political boost: strong American support for renewed peace negotiations with Israel. Abbas's main selling point to his constituents was that he could achieve more through negotiations and support from the international community than militants could get through violence.

Bush's statement that Gaza's future borders had already been fixed struck one listener as an indication that "there are no more negotiations." A second sign was Bush's reaction when Maen Areikat introduced himself as the head of the Negotiations Affairs Department in the PLO. Bush remarked dismissively that Areikat must have had little to do over the previous five years.

Just before Bush's meeting with Abbas, a senior administration official said in an interview that the administration still hadn't grappled with the question of how to move from disengagement to Palestinian statehood. The question of, "'OK, how do we get from the end of disengagement to there?' is one that we need to have more discussions with the Israelis about—and with the Palestinians," this official said. When Abbas arrived, Bush seemed to be stuck in a rhetorical time warp, as if the resumption of violence since disengagement had not occurred.

"The Gaza withdrawal is a magnificent opportunity to help develop trust. It's an opportunity to develop trust between the Palestinians and the Israelis. And after all, the world watched strong cooperation between two willing governments to help good disengagement of Gaza, which is a—right now, I guess, we take it all for granted," Bush told reporters in his joint appearance with Abbas on October 20. He went on to disappoint Abbas by backing away from his previous timetable for creating a Palestinian state: "I can't tell you when it's going to happen. It's happening. And the reason I can't is because there will be moments of progress, and there will be moments of setback."

Rather than press for negotiations, which would require persuading Sharon of their merits or pressuring him to cooperate, Bush focused on economics as a bridge to Palestinian statehood. He was deeply interested in the project undertaken by newly retired World Bank president James Wolfensohn. The Australian-born investment banker and philanthropist exuded can-do optimism and a commitment to laying a foundation for Palestinian prosperity, which he believed would foster peaceful relations between a future Palestine and Israel.

"I talk to Jim Wolfensohn a lot. Now, there's a practical man," Bush told Al Arabiya television. Indeed, Wolfensohn felt welcome in the Oval Office. "In all honesty, his treatment of me has never been anything but impeccable," Wolfensohn said of Bush.

In his large corner office at the Wolfensohn Family Foundation, high above Manhattan's Avenue of the Americas, Wolfensohn kept a framed picture of one of his meetings with Bush—evidence, in his view, of how seriously the president took his role. Although Secretary of State Rice was traveling at the time, the photo included most of the administration's national-security pantheon: Vice President Cheney, Deputy Secretary of State Robert Zoellick, Chief of Staff Andrew Card, National Security Adviser Stephen Hadley, Deputy National Security Adviser Elliott Abrams.

"These meetings would take an hour," he said in a December 2006 interview. And despite the large, high-powered attendance, "it was basically a discussion between me and the president." Bush, he said, was "absolutely on top of the issues. . . . I was surprised."

Wolfensohn's access wasn't limited to the Oval Office. Having led the World Bank for ten years, he could get in to see heads of government throughout the Middle East and Persian Gulf with a phone call. First names of world leaders tripped off his tongue: Tony [Blair], Jack [Straw], Arik [Ariel Sharon]. When he made the case for substantial international aid to help build a Palestinian economy, it carried credibility.

At the July 2005 summit in Gleneagles, Scotland, of the G-8, where the group of seven advanced industrial democracies plus Russia, Bush gave Wolfensohn the floor. Despite terrorist bombings in London that pulled Blair back to his capital, Wolfensohn's presentation before the world leaders lasted a full hour and brought commitments for $3 billion a year for three years.

"He [Bush] allowed me to make the case for what was necessary and then gave me tremendous support. I had thought he would present it all, but he was very gracious and let me do the whole thing. I had the advantage of knowing all the leaders. It was more or less a gathering of friends."

Wolfensohn and his staff of fifteen, drawn from all the members of the Quartet, set up shop at the American Colony Hotel in East Jerusalem, the favorite gathering spot for expatriates. They drew on previous work by the World Bank to identify the most important impediments to Palestinian economic prosperity. Along with the need for Palestinian reforms and budget tightening, the main problems were the security barriers erected by Israel: hundreds of checkpoints in the West Bank; no free movement for Palestinians between Gaza and the West Bank; long delays or outright closure at borders between Gaza and Israel, preventing the movement of goods in and out; a closed or restricted border with Egypt; and no airport or seaport.

These were political problems, not technical issues. Wolfensohn realized early on that Israeli security and Palestinian economic prospects were closely connected and had to be tackled simultaneously. "I don't think that we can succeed without the security issues. And frankly I don't think security will succeed unless there is hope," he told the Senate Foreign Relations Committee on June 30, 2005. In an interview in late 2006, he said, "My task was fundamentally to try and give hope through the economics. But you couldn't make economics work. But you couldn't make economic decisions unless you knew about the politics. So it wasn't that I was trying to extend my mandate. It was that you couldn't just separate economics from politics. So you immediately became involved in the whole of the issue."

Wolfensohn had ready access to Mahmoud Abbas. Relations with Sharon initially were tense. Sharon tended to regard with suspicion anyone who represented Europe or the United Nations; Wolfensohn represented both through the Quartet. But that changed over time into a relationship of trust, Wolfensohn said. "He decided I was straight and I wasn't trying to manipulate him. I also decided he was being straight to me . . . [he] gave me access whenever I needed it."

"I actually believe he wanted me to work with him on withdrawal to make sure there was a peaceful basis on which there could be an ongoing Palestinian community in Gaza that would be able to sustain itself," Wolfensohn said. Though Sharon showed no love or regard for the Palestinians, "he was very constructive with me."

But neither Wolfensohn's relationship with Bush nor his access to Sharon translated into full cooperation from subordinates. Wolfensohn suspected the friction resulted from his ability to operate outside the boundaries that constrain American diplomats. Although he was asked by Bush and Rice to assume the role of special envoy, Wolfensohn actually represented the Quartet. He believed that the EU's foreign policy chief, Javier Solana, and its commissioner for external affairs, Benita Ferrero-Waldner, persuaded Washington to appoint him.

In representing the Quartet, Wolfensohn was for the first time pulling the United Nations and Europe into a process where, since the early 1990s, Americans and Israelis had held sway without any challenge. Before then, Europeans had the feeling that "we were the checkbook of the process" and that "the Quartet was a fiction," as a French diplomat put it in 2005. Now, members of the Quartet, not just Secretary Rice, got regular briefings from Wolfensohn.

He traveled independently. "For me, going to the Gulf countries, going to Saudi Arabia—anywhere—was not a novel thing where I had to get the American consul to get me a date. . . . I would have my own meetings. I wouldn't take the American ambassador or the European ambassador. . . . I was keeping no secrets from Condi, but I didn't want a lot of stuff around the system being the subject of e-mails intercepted by ten other governments."

Well before disengagement got under way, Wolfensohn insisted, "We're going to have to deal with the question of what happens the day after." He recognized that Gaza could turn into a prison and knew that it had to be linked not only to the West Bank and Israel but to Egypt and the world beyond. Designs were developed for a permanent Gaza-West Bank passage that would carry either rail or trucks. "It was pretty exciting to think there was a possibility of a three to four million [population], viable Palestinian state linked with Egypt and linked to the Arab world with an airport and a seaport."

But Israelis and Americans were concentrating on making sure the event itself went smoothly. As a result, none of the impediments to movement were resolved before disengagement.

Eager to give a quick boost to the Gaza economy, Wolfensohn and the World Bank seized on the opportunity afforded by the acres of greenhouses on the Jewish settlements that were to be vacated. Drawing from some of Gaza's best water sources and using modern irrigation and growing methods, the settlers had developed high-quality fruits, vegetables, spices, and flowers worth tens of millions of dollars a year. The produce was sold in Israel and exported to Europe. As well as a source of income for settlers, the greenhouses employed several thousand Palestinian workers.

Before leaving, the settlers balked at turning over the greenhouses intact to Palestinians without additional compensation—beyond the Israeli government payouts to settler families who were being uprooted. Palestinians, for their part, refused to use their own foreign-aid money to pay the settlers. "The idea that they were going to give more money to settlers who were already compensated just made me irate," said Diana Buttu, an Abbas aide who was involved in the negotiations.

As the settlers started to dismantle the greenhouses, Wolfensohn reached out to fellow philanthropists in the United States. In a week, he raised the $14 million needed to "buy" the greenhouses from the departing settlers: $3 million to $4 million from American Jews, $500,000 that Wolfensohn himself committed, and the rest from a single donor whom he wouldn't identify. Palestinians put up millions more, mostly through a public-private development company, to refurbish the greenhouses and start growing peppers, cucumber, cherry tomatoes, strawberries, and beans.

After the Israeli pullout, a wave of Palestinian looting damaged some of the greenhouses, a sign to some in the West of Palestinian ingratitude and backwardness. The *New York Daily News* reported, "A week after they descended like locusts on the greenhouses that Jewish settlers nurtured in Gaza, looters continue to pillage what should be a prize asset for a fledgling Palestinian state." Wolfensohn said later that looters damaged a "trivial" 5 to 10 percent of the project, "and it could be fixed very quickly." By mid-November, crops covering five hundred acres were ready for harvest and export.

"The tragedy is that things were working beautifully. I went over there and saw the fruits and everything. . . . I was there, tasting the tomatoes," he recalled. "They were about to grow everything. And it was wonderful."

But three months after disengagement, the larger task Wolfensohn hoped to accomplish—opening up Gaza to the West Bank, Israel, and the wider world—was stymied by an Israeli-Palestinian impasse. Hundreds of checkpoints severely restricted movement of Palestinians in the West Bank. Gaza's borders with Israel and Egypt were still mostly closed; movement between Gaza and the West Bank was still blocked; and nothing had been done about rebuilding the airport and starting work on a Gaza seaport.

The history of Israeli-Palestinian negotiations shows that no single problem in their complex relationship can be solved in isolation. Each is bound up with Israeli fears about security and Palestinian demand for sovereignty.

All pieces of the puzzle had to fit. Gaza's economy couldn't improve without access to the outside world—particularly to Israel and the West Bank—at least in the short term. Israel wouldn't permit that unless it could guard against infiltration of militants and weapons. Palestinians were unenthusiastic about serving as Israel's proxy enforcers unless they had confidence about gaining a viable state. They wouldn't gain such confidence without active political engagement intended to produce an Israeli-Palestinian peace agreement.

The most urgent problem was opening up the main Gaza crossing point at Karni. Here the question of Israeli security was complicated by corruption—on both sides of the border, Wolfensohn found. "The borders were under the control of crooks."

Whatever the state of enmity between Israelis and Palestinians generally, their civilian border officials walked arm in arm, "hands around each other's shoulders. They always seemed very cozy to me. The net result was trucks didn't get through and when they did, drivers and the people told you they'd made massive bribes," Wolfensohn said. "I cannot believe they [the payoffs] were not split."

By the time Secretary of State Rice arrived in the region in mid-November, Gaza was becoming a pressure cooker. And with an agricultural harvest at hand, the greenhouse operators and other Gaza farmers had no way to export fresh produce. Addressing the Israeli Council on Foreign Relations on November 14, Wolfensohn vented his frustration with the stalemate, hinting that he would walk away. "We've been discussing [these points] for twenty weeks and have yet to reach finality," he told the group, according to a report by Joshua Brilliant of UPI. "If you want to blow each other up, I have a nice house in Wyoming, and in New York and in Australia and I will watch with sadness what you're doing. If you . . . try and make things move forward . . . I'll be in it up to my ears in trying to help because I think it's worth doing, but the fundamental decision that has to be made is not mine," he said.

During Rice's visit, Elliott Abrams and David Welch took over the negotiations Wolfensohn had been mediating for months. "I was not included in any meetings that Welch and Abrams had with either Israelis or Palestinians. Palestinians were calling me to say, 'What the hell is going on?'" Wolfensohn recalled. He suspected Israelis wanted only to deal with the Americans and didn't want him in the middle. During a graveside ceremony on Mount Herzl in Jerusalem, marking the tenth anniversary of the assassination of Prime Minister Yitzhak Rabin, Rice asked Wolfensohn to ride back to her hotel with her. He used the chance to press Rice to intervene personally. She was due to leave that day for Jordan and travel on to Asia. "Condi, you can't leave this thing to be resolved by your colleagues," Wolfensohn told her, according to his account. "I've not been in the meetings, but it's not finished. I'm getting complaints from Palestinians." Sharon's chief of staff, Dov Weisglass, sitting in front, didn't react. Rice decided to return to Jerusalem from Jordan that same evening.

Before her return, Wolfensohn crossed Jerusalem to the David Citadel Hotel, where he confronted Abrams about being cut out. "She came back, asked me why I was so rude to Elliott," but agreed that Wolfensohn should be part of the negotiations. Rice and Wolfensohn stayed up most of the night working out what came to be called the Agreement on Movement and Access, which was announced the next morning. "I never saw Elliott or David again during the night."

Although she projects the image of a global strategist, Rice has a genuine talent as a negotiator and mediator, whether bridging gaps in a UN Security Council resolution on Lebanon or cutting through the tangles of a deal between Israelis and Palestinians. "She's very pragmatic. She knows what diplomacy is about," a French diplomat said. "She's good at getting rid of details to get at what's important."

But Rice's nightlong intervention over access to Gaza also underscored the lack of high-level American involvement in making sure disengagement worked well for both Israelis and Palestinians—and moving from there to tackle the bigger questions. "I found it kind of amazing that the secretary would come to Palestine and Israel back in November of last year and put all of her weight behind doing an agreement on borders and access agreements," former Abbas aide Ghaith al-Omari said during a fall 2006 interview. "That has always been one of the sources of frustration that we had with the administration. Yes, they're willing to kind of push for some of the practical things to happen, but either they were not aware or they were not willing to deal with . . . the big political-process issues."

Wolfensohn said he never got an explanation for what happened next, but the period immediately after Rice's visit marked the end of

American cooperation with what he was doing. He noticed "a definite break with the U.S. in terms of the role of the Quartet and the office in Jerusalem . . . and a change in who was running things. The Americans essentially came in and took on all the subsequent negotiations. . . . The office of the Quartet was essentially made less important because of the lack of cooperation of the Americans."

U.S. officials decided that "this was now high policy for the U.S. and there were two elections coming up"—first in the Palestinian territories and then in Israel. "Arik [Sharon] got sick. There was a change in dynamics in Gaza and ultimately the election of a Hamas government. . . . The Americans at that moment didn't want an envoy of the Quartet there."

"Part of my problem was that it was functioning, and functioning quite well. The Europeans, the Russians, and the UN thought they had a voice, which they'd never had before. They were clinging to the Quartet and clinging to me because I was treating the four of them equally," Wolfensohn said. This apparently "didn't suit the Israelis and the Americans."

Six days after Rice brokered the Agreement on Movement and Access, Prime Minister Sharon announced he would break away from his own Likud Party and establish a new party, indicating that he planned further withdrawals from the West Bank, opposed by many in Likud. In the territories, Hamas loomed ever larger on the political horizon, prompting warnings from Washington that an armed terror group could not be part of the Palestinian government if Palestinians were ever going to get a state. A senior administration official explained, "The objective here is clear. You cannot have a democratic state in Palestine with terrorist groups and armed militias roaming around, not under control of the state. You can't have people who fight for power with guns and fight for power at the voting booth. So the Palestinians are going to have to resolve this fundamental contradiction. We are not going to define today how the Palestinians should resolve that. But it's clear to us that it has to be resolved in order to build a democratic state. We will say that to them that you can't let this one go and say, in the first ten years of an independent Palestine we'll deal with that. No. This has to be dealt with sooner than that and really now. Now if they then say we're going

to do x before the parliamentary elections and we're going to do y after
... elections ... we're not going to try to impose an American plan for
how they resolve this problem. All we're going to say to them is, 'Be
under no illusions that this one can be put aside. This one is critical.'"

As for the agreement on access, it did not lead to any broader understandings between Israelis and Palestinians. In fact, only one aspect of
the accord was fully carried out: the opening of the Rafah crossing point
between Egypt and Gaza, supervised by the European Union. The deal
had also specified that "on an urgent basis, Israel will permit the export
of all agricultural products from Gaza during this 2005 harvest season,"
with 150 trucks a day passing through Karni—the main entry and exit
point for goods—by the end of the year.

Israelis accepted new border-security equipment. But getting them
to use it proved impossible. An international aid official said, "The
Americans offered everything. But they were not prepared to push the
Israelis on these issues beyond a certain point. So where there was real
push-back, the Americans tended to retreat. And so they did purchase
these scanners; they did set them up in place, but without having agreement to a new and reformed management system."

Efficient though the new screening devices were, they cut against the
security logic that Israelis believe has served them well for decades. This
logic puts heavy emphasis on personal scrutiny of both people and goods
by security officers, whether at airports, border crossings, or checkpoints.
Machines are considered no substitute for the skills and instincts of a well-
trained officer. Efficiency can't be achieved at the expense of thorough-
ness. Changing this logic would take time and effort. The official said:
"The Israelis would always argue—I think correctly—that this was unique,
so you needed a higher level of security inspection. I think that's right. But
it didn't mean you couldn't do it. It was not unfeasible, with the tech-
nologies available, embedded into a properly managed system."

Whether an energetic, American-led push to open up Gaza would
have generated enough hope among Palestinians to have an impact in
the January 2006 elections can't be measured. Hamas had been gaining support during 2005, and Mahmoud Abbas's Fatah Party was so torn
by internal dissension that it failed to present a single slate of candidates,

with the result that Fatah members competed against each other in some districts, giving Hamas an added advantage.

What is clear is that Gaza remained closed off, depriving Palestinians of a tangible sign of improved well-being as a result of disengagement. Palestinians appeared not to believe—or not to care—that election of a Hamas-led government would mean a cutoff of international aid for the Palestinian Authority. A key Fatah campaign platform—that it could achieve Palestinian rights through negotiation rather than violence—lacked anything tangible to back it up.

"If we say, 'We'll get the international community involved,' Hamas will come back and say, 'Oh, yes, so we can get an agreement like the AMA [Agreement on Movement and Access]? Sorry, that's too little.' . . . The average Palestinian is seeing, it's the same thing—we get a crap agreement, and even then it didn't get implemented," said Ghaith al-Omari, the former Abbas aide. "The fact that we, as moderates, could not come up with any credible message in terms of negotiation, in terms of peaceful means for conflict resolution, did affect our election performance."

By early 2006, it was obvious that all the effort put into speeding up Gaza's imports and exports had come to naught. When the main entry point at Karni was not totally closed off, the old system of slow, cumbersome, inspections prevailed. James Wolfensohn went there to see what was happening with the harvest from the greenhouses of the former settlements, into which he had poured time and his and others' money. He saw trucks lined up, not moving, the border closed or backed up, and fresh produce, which had rotted in the sun, being thrown out.

"The borders got closed because of the terrorism thing. . . . They were worried less about Qassams going over than they were about [Palestinians] taking stuff through. . . . There was some equipment there, and the logic suggested you could get everything done. But there were always problems. The Israeli military and the Americans—we could never get clarity, to be honest with you. I've no doubt that there were Palestinians who wanted to blow everything up. And I don't have any doubt that there was stuff that they were trying to bring through. But the reaction to close everything down and in the course of it to ensure that there was no commercial transfers and that trade was impossible—and then you had crookedness at the borders, straight criminality at the borders—just meant that all the dreams that we had of getting normality there" were shattered.

"It made your heart cry when you saw, half the way from the truck centers, people just dumping produce that had been there in the sun for three days. See, the trucks were lined up and you had fresh produce three days earlier which had just been baking in the sun for three days. So that by the time it was ready to go through, if you managed to get through the normal queue and hadn't paid somebody off to get to the front of the line, your stuff was ruined."

The failure, Wolfensohn said in late 2006, "has led to what you have now, which is 70 percent of the people in poverty, more or less, and massive bribes and increased prices to take account of the massive bribes. The only people who have made out on it are the joint Israeli-Palestinian crooks at the borders."

20

Sharon Immobilized

■ EARLY 2006 ■

ON THE EVENING of December 18, 2005, Ariel Sharon abruptly lost the ability to speak coherently. At 8 PM, he entered Hadassah Medical Center outside Jerusalem, where doctors determined he had suffered a mild stroke. Suddenly, Israelis confronted the fact that their strong-willed, seemingly inexhaustible prime minister, almost a national father figure, was nearly seventy-eight, hugely overweight, and performing a punishing job under constant pressure.

Sharon's sway over public life had been reinforced a month earlier, when he set off a political earthquake by abandoning the right-wing party he helped found—Likud—to form a new centrist party vaguely committed to following up Gaza disengagement with further territorial withdrawals and a "political process" with the Palestinians. He quickly drew prominent defectors from Likud and Labor, including former Jerusalem mayor and deputy prime minister Ehud Olmert and former Prime Minister Shimon Peres. Temporarily named "National Responsibility," the new party soon adopted the name Kadima (Forward), the battle charge for army officers. With elections set for the following March, Sharon was expected to keep enough support in the Knesset to pursue his goal of setting Israel's final borders.

If at that time Sharon was as politically secure as an Israeli leader could hope to be, there was much to preoccupy him on other fronts. Israel's withdrawal had left Gaza more isolated than ever from Israel and the West Bank, fertile ground for Hamas to gather political strength. Hamas was now determined to compete for the first time in legislative elections that were little more than six weeks away. Palestinian president Mahmoud Abbas, faced with a violent split in his own Fatah Party and a growing challenge from Hamas, favored proceeding with the vote—even with Hamas's participation. Israel mounted a strong diplomatic push and enlisted its allies in the U.S. Congress to oppose Hamas's deepening political involvement. But after President Bush agreed with Palestinians and Europeans that Hamas should not be excluded from the elections, Sharon grudgingly gave way. His spokesman warned, however, that Hamas terror suspects would nonetheless be hunted and arrested by Israeli domestic security services. And Sharon continued to hold out against Palestinian electioneering in East Jerusalem.

A long-running police corruption probe, stemming from the 1999 Likud leadership primary that helped propel Sharon into power, was about to derail the parliamentary career of the prime minister's son Omri, his confidant and political problem solver. Omri was awaiting sentence after pleading guilty to providing false testimony and falsifying documents in a probe of illegal campaign contributions. Police were still investigating where Sharon got the money to repay the illegal contributions. The trail led first to a South African businessman, Cyril Kern, and later to an Austrian financier, Martin Schlaff, a large shareholder in a once-popular Jericho casino.

Sharon walked out of Hadassah hospital on December 20, two days after he was stricken, outwardly upbeat. "I can see that you all missed me," he told the waiting press. "I was moved by the great concern shown by the citizens of Israel for my health, and I want to convey to them my deepest gratitude. Now I have to hurry back to work and continue to move ahead. I also want to thank you for showing interest and concern. Thank you." When Udi Segal of Israel's Channel 2 asked, "Mr. Prime Minister, are you not concerned that your stroke will have an adverse effect on your performance?" Sharon said no. Back home, he took a get-well call from President Bush, later recounted to the press by Israeli officials. Bush's precise wording differed in various reports, but all carried the same message: "Allow me to give you some pointers," Bush told him. "First, eat healthy. Second, work out, and third, after reading your busy schedule I must tell you, please spread it out. I got tired just reading it." Bush told Sharon that he views him as a true partner and courageous leader with a vision for peace. "I need you healthy."

A monthly briefing to the UN Security Council the same day showed how far removed any vision for peace was from on-the-ground realities. Delivered by Ibrahim Gambari, undersecretary general for political affairs, it offered a glimpse of crises to come: A Palestinian suicide bombing in Netanya had killed five Israelis. Qassam rockets were being fired from Gaza, reaching the outskirts of the large Israeli town of Ashkelon. Israel had resumed targeted killings from the air and tightened restrictions on Palestinian movement. Poverty was growing in the territories while thousands of new Jewish settlement units were being built. In the north, Hezbollah was rebuilding a position on the border, and Israeli warplanes were repeatedly violating Lebanese airspace.

During Sharon's two days in the hospital, doctors discovered a heart defect that he apparently had always been living with, a small hole known as a patent foramen ovale. They also found several "microbleeds" in his brain, a sign of a disorder called cerebral amyloid angiopathy. Giving him two weeks to recuperate, they scheduled a surgical procedure to fix the heart defect on January 5, 2006. They kept him on blood thinner to prevent another stroke, balancing the medication's protective benefit against the possibility that, with the microbleeds, it could cause additional bleeding.

Sharon didn't take time to rest. David Horovitz, editor of the *Jerusalem Post*, speculated later that Israel's tempestuous political scene wouldn't let him.

"I don't know whether Sharon's doctors told him he would be putting his life at dire risk if he returned to work so rapidly after the first breakdown. But even had they issued the starkest warnings, I doubt that Sharon would have heeded them," Horovitz wrote. "He must have calculated, after all, that to have allowed himself what all the rest of us ordinary folk would have required and been granted—a couple of weeks off, maybe even a month to recuperate—would have been to commit political suicide."

Two days after Sharon left the hospital, police searched the Israeli home of Austrian businessman James Schlaff, whose brother, Martin, was described in Israeli press accounts as a possible source of money used to repay illegal contributions to Sharon's 1999 primary campaign. Police took away documents, paperwork, phones, and computers. They also went to court for authority to examine James Schlaff's computer, which police suspected contained evidence of a $3 million bribe to the Sharon family.

This new dimension to the bribery scandal was not publicly known during the day on January 3, 2006, when Omri Sharon resigned his seat in the Knesset. He chose to do so rather than wait for a court to rule on his right to serve following his guilty plea. That night, information about the search of the Schlaff home, obtained by investigative journalist Baruch Kra, was broadcast in an explosive television news report, triggering newspaper headlines the following day.

Besides continuing to work, Sharon did not confine himself to Jerusalem, which would have kept him close to the hospital. On January 4, the night before the scheduled procedure to repair the small hole in his heart, he was at his beloved Sycamore Farm in the Negev, more than an hour by car from the capital.

"Sharon was watching news on television, became upset, and developed a headache," Louis Caplan of Harvard Medical School, who was in touch with Sharon's doctors, later wrote in the journal *Neurology Today*. Attendants feared aggravating the prime minister's condition by putting him in a helicopter, so Sharon made the journey to Hadassah hospital in an ambulance. He arrived barely conscious, with high blood pressure. Doctors diagnosed a massive brain hemorrhage. Laboring for seven hours, surgeons stopped the bleeding. "His vital signs are stable," a hospital statement said the next morning, "however his condition is still considered to be severe." Later, another operation was performed to relieve cranial pressure and drain blood clots. The next morning, Sharon underwent a third operation. He stabilized, but doctors kept him in an induced coma and on a respirator.

News of Sharon's incapacitating stroke reached Washington late in the day on January 4, 2006. Shortly before the nightly news broadcasts, a White House spokesman said, "Our thoughts and prayers are with Prime Minister Sharon and his family." A lengthier statement from the president said, "Laura and I share the concerns of the Israeli people about Prime Minister Ariel Sharon's health, and we are praying for his recovery. Prime Minister Sharon is a man of courage and peace. On behalf of all Americans, we send our best wishes and hopes to the prime minister and his family."

A statesman's final departure from office in a democracy usually brings a dignified, unhurried transition and a pause to reflect on his or her career. A death in office triggers nationwide mourning; a state funeral brings in the powerful and prominent from around the world. Sharon's stroke ended one of the most dramatic public careers of the post–World War II period, combining military triumph, disgrace, and a long comeback that took him to the pinnacle of Israeli politics. Yet there was no prescribed official ritual for a leader in a coma, unlikely to recover.

By the morning after Sharon's second stroke, it was becoming apparent that he would not resume his job. In Washington, Bush did not mention Sharon during his first public appearance. The White House allowed a press pool into the Roosevelt Room after a meeting at which former secretaries of state and defense were briefed on the Iraq War. Bush delivered a brief summation and thanked the former officials for attending.

In midafternoon, Bush went to the State Department's stately Benjamin Franklin Room to greet university presidents and deliver a brief speech on the need to improve training in languages from the Middle East and South Asian flash points. He opened with a good-natured crack at Secretary of State Condoleezza Rice, who had introduced him to the crowd with lengthy and lavish praise: "Thank you all. Madam Secretary, it's your building, you can give my speech, if you want to," Bush said, drawing chuckles. Then he quickly shifted tone, speaking slowly, looking straight at the audience. "But first, our nation sends our deepest sympathies to Ariel Sharon. He lies immobilized in an Israeli hospital. We pray for his recovery. He's a good man, a strong man, a man who cared deeply about the security of the Israeli people and a man who had a vision for peace. May God bless him." Midway through the tribute to Sharon, Bush had veered from the present to the past tense.

His statement of sympathy finished, the president looked down for remarks and returned to the topic at hand. He made a joke about his own trouble with language. The audience laughed some more.

Sharon survived, but he never regained consciousness. In late May, he was moved to Chaim Sheba Medical Center in Tel Hashomer, east of Tel Aviv, which bills itself as the largest hospital in the Middle East and offers respiratory rehabilitation care. There, doctors hoped at least to wean Sharon off a respirator, if not to pull him from his coma. Periodic infections required intensive care, but each time, his old soldier's body revived. While security surrounding him was heavy at first, Sharon's immobile presence in a respiratory-care unit soon blended into the hospital's routine. His sons Omri and Gilad visited regularly. Omri kept up a vigil during medical crises. By mid-August 2006, visiting the large, well-equipped, and almost uncannily quiet hospital, I was able to walk along the corridor outside Sharon's unit unquestioned, encountering a security agent only when I inquired how to get a message to Omri. The agent passed on the message, and Omri later called.

Some observers expected the sudden end of Sharon's long public career to precipitate a new political crisis, strangling his Kadima party in its infancy. No one in Israel's leadership circles could match his combination of shrewdness, longevity, and military exploits. He was almost certainly the last prime minister from the generation that had fought to create the state of Israel.

But acting prime minister Ehud Olmert moved deftly into the leadership void. Holding the government together, he assumed leadership of Kadima in the campaign for the March Knesset election, running on a platform of further unilateral withdrawal from the occupied West Bank. His brief and comparatively undistinguished military background did not wreck his chances.

Three months after Olmert won the prime minister's office in his own right, he seemed to lose his footing. A summer that brought fierce Israeli-Palestinian fighting in Gaza and a punishing new war in Lebanon convinced many Israelis, as measured by polls, that a vacuum existed at the top.

Epilogue

Squeeze

■ 2006 ■

THE AMERICAN OFFICIAL was contrite: "Now you're
going to tell me, 'We told you so.'" Nabil Fahmy laughed. It was late January 2006, and the militant organization Hamas had just won a sweeping election victory in the Palestinian legislative council elections, gaining
the right to name a prime minister and cabinet and run the Palestinian
Authority. The defeat of Fatah, the preeminent party of the Palestinian
national movement for four decades, shocked Israelis and Americans
and delivered an embarrassing blow to Mahmoud Abbas, the moderate, U.S.-backed opponent of violence who just a year before had won
the Palestinian presidency in a landslide as the Fatah standard-bearer.

Fahmy, Egypt's ambassador to Washington, hadn't predicted the
Hamas upset, but leaders of his government thought it was the wrong
time for the Palestinians to call elections. "We were not at all confident
that holding an election was going to give you the right result. Personally I cannot claim to have drawn the conclusion that they [Hamas]
would win, but given that Cairo felt it was the wrong time to have an
election, you have to give them credit for feeling it's not going to turn
out the way that we want, traditionally, which is Fatah, and the logical
correlation would be, yes, they did expect Hamas to win," Fahmy said
in an interview. He did not mention an added irony: the victory of a

militant Islamist party in the West Bank and Gaza served to underscore President Hosni Mubarak's warning about what would happen if he were suddenly to open up Egypt's political system and allow free elections.

President Bush, who made advancing democracy the central pillar of his Middle East policy, had championed the elections, over the objections of Israeli prime minister Ariel Sharon and his successor, Ehud Olmert. The Israelis had wanted to prevent Hamas from participating, and to make it difficult for the elections to proceed smoothly if they did. ". . . [W]e brought up some arguments against it," recalled Danny Ayalon, Israel's ambassador to Washington and formerly a top aide to Sharon. "The most cogent one was the legal one. That is, based also on the precedent of the Palestinian election of 1996 . . . no illegal armed group that doesn't recognize Israel would be permitted to run. And that was part of the 1995 Oslo agreement. It was just not implemented. We could invoke that clause to prevent it, and unfortunately it was not invoked. Also, there are other examples of elections, whether . . . in Iraq or Afghanistan or Yugoslavia, where armed groups are denied participation in the election. So here we have a unique case against the agreements and against precedents, and they were able to run."

Under pressure from Washington, Israel grudgingly allowed the elections to proceed, albeit with some arrests of Hamas campaigners and inconvenience to Palestinian voters, particularly in Jerusalem, where Israel resists any encroachment on its sovereignty. International observers, led by former President Jimmy Carter, pronounced the conduct of the vote free and fair—even exemplary.

The Bush administration sought to portray the Hamas victory as a Palestinian revolt against the incompetent, corrupt rule of the Fatah-led government. That was doubtless part of the story, but close observers of the Palestinian political scene knew that the American explanation was too convenient. It overlooked the dominant, even overwhelming influence of the Israeli-Palestinian conflict in the political life of both peoples. Just as Israelis turned in fear and despair toward Ariel Sharon in 2001, so did Palestinians turn toward Hamas five years later out of frustration and anger. The Islamic Resistance Movement, as Hamas is formally known, certainly benefited from Fatah's lack of party discipline and internal squabbles. In a number of electoral districts, Fatah members ran as independents against the declared Fatah candidate, diluting the party's strength. This meant that Hamas won a majority of seats without gaining a majority of votes cast. Hamas also bested Fatah with its electioneering skills and capitalized on its delivery of social services. Palestinians also joined in a regionwide trend away from the secularism of the 1970s and 1980s and toward Islam, in part as a backlash against Western policies and cultural influences.

The widespread perception of corruption, cronyism, and nepotism in the Palestinian Authority also hurt Fatah. But a key reason why internal issues of corruption and the need for reform so dominated the campaign was the absence of a peace process that could have brought hope for change. As a result, Fatah lost its single greatest electoral asset, according to Amjad Atallah, director of the Strategic Assessments consulting group, which had worked with the security liaison team led by U.S. General William E. (Kip) Ward. The asset was Fatah's claim that it could negotiate an end to the conflict with Israel. "As far as Palestinians are concerned, final-status negotiations were not on the table during the elections," Atallah said. As a result, the election played to Hamas's strengths: demands for reform, change, and an end to corruption.

"The people were really voting for change. In fact, Hamas tailored its position and called itself the Party for Change and Reform. This is exactly what the public wanted; they have been living in misery for decades; they have, you know, an impoverished economy; they live under occupation with checkpoints and miserable existence in general. The promise of peace that was so high in the air a year ago when Abu Mazen got elected evaporated," Ziad Asali, president of the American Task Force on Palestine and an occasional guest at the White House, said on the television program moderated by Fareed Zakaria, editor of *Newsweek International*.

The absence of a peace process played into the voting in another way, as well: "I think what Palestinians chose last week was a government with a spine. That is, a government that would be capable of facing occupation with strength," said George Bisharat, a law professor and anthropologist at Hastings College of the Law in San Francisco. His and Atallah's comments came in separate talks at the Palestine Center in Washington. Before the election, the *Economist* reported: "More and more Israeli commentators are also beginning to recognize that Israel's attempts to exclude Hamas—such as a mass arrest of its candidates, targeted killings of a few of its fighters, and a clumsy attempt to prevent or restrict voting in East Jerusalem because of Hamas's participation—have only added to the movement's credibility. Warnings from America and Europe that the PA might lose foreign funding if it includes Hamas, a listed terrorist organization, have had a similar effect."

When the Hamas victory was announced, Danny Ayalon, Israel's ambassador to Washington, was summoned to the White House. "It was a shock for everybody," Ayalon said. He later chalked up the splintering of the Fatah vote among official party candidates and independents, a key factor in the Hamas majority, as a "major, major failure of leadership of Abu Mazen, who didn't deal with politics. And you cannot ignore politics.

"I think everyone was embarrassed. First and foremost it was Abu Mazen who was embarrassed," Ayalon said. "The Arabs were the last ones who wanted Hamas to run." Israeli officials viewed the Hamas election as another in a series of missed opportunities that confirmed once again the Abba Eban axiom that "Palestinians never miss an opportunity to miss an opportunity." Ayalon's successor, Sallai Meridor, told the Washington Institute for Near East Policy, according to an institute summary, that "after the Israeli disengagement from Gaza, Palestinians failed to capitalize on the opportunity to have their own sovereign state, instead choosing to freely elect a terrorist government and use the evacuated territories to mount attacks against Israel."

Postelection collaboration between the White House and Jerusalem was "very close, very intimate," Ayalon said in a January 1, 2007, telephone interview. "First time the results were shown I got a call from Elliott Abrams and we met at length to discuss [it]. There were phone calls between Dubi Weisglass and Steve Hadley, and [Weisglass] came over and we met with Condi and Steve and Elliott. And we said once the results are out, there is no looking back. We have to move forward. . . .

So we decided, we, both the United States and Israel, 'We'll be willing to deal with this representative government provided they just adhere to international law, to the norms of the international community and to common sense.' And this is where the U.S. did a great job convincing the Quartet, if you remember, to come up with this statement saying they would deal with Hamas provided (a) Hamas will renounce terrorism, (b) recognize Israel's right to exist, and (c) they will accept all formal agreements which were signed by former governments of the Palestinian Authority. And this still stands now as the official position of both Israel and the United States, and of course also the Quartet."

In New York and the capitals of the Quartet, the international group comprising the United States, Europe, Russia, and the United Nations that oversaw the peace process, members scrambled over the phone to work out a consensus reaction to Hamas's victory. They decided not to portray the vote as an embrace of terror and militancy. "The Palestinian people have voted for change, but it is the view of the Quartet that their aspirations for peace and statehood, as articulated by President Abbas in his statement following the closing of polls yesterday, remain unchanged. The Quartet reiterates its view that there is a fundamental contradiction between armed group and militia activities and the building of a democratic state. A two-state solution to the conflict requires all participants in the democratic process to renounce violence and terror, accept Israel's right to exist, and disarm, as outlined in the road map," the group said in a statement released by UN secretary general Kofi Annan.

Following Mahmoud Abbas's lead, the Quartet also called "on all parties to respect the results of the election and the outcome of the Palestinian constitutional process so that it may unfold in an atmosphere of calm and security."

Hamas leaders seemed initially to be almost as surprised as everyone else by the prospect that they would now be forming a government instead of agitating from opposition benches and the streets. Suddenly, Ismail Haniyeh, Mahmoud Zahar, and other Hamas politicians in Gaza and the West Bank had increased stature in the movement in relation to the leaders in exile, Damascus-based Khaled Mashaal and Mousa Abu Marzuk. Not only had they secured a solid majority through the democratic process, but they would soon be able to go beyond slogans and turn their organizational skills toward running the Palestinian Authority. Their new stake in the government also presented a challenge: they had something to lose if the Palestinian Authority failed to meet the people's basic needs or fell apart.

Their early moves signaled pragmatism: they reached out to Fatah leaders to explore the formation of a national-unity government. While refusing to recognize Israel, they were prepared to yield responsibility for negotiations to Abbas and the Palestine Liberation Organization, which had recognized Israel in 1993. They also tried to make contact with James Wolfensohn, the retired World Bank president and special envoy for the Quartet.

Hamas picked a cabinet with more of an emphasis on technocratic skill than ideological purity. Several members were well-known to various Western agencies, including the U.S. Agency for International Development and nongovernmental agencies. Of the twenty-four members of the new Hamas-controlled Palestinian cabinet, at least five had received an undergraduate or advanced education in the United States. Another three had studied in Britain, and one in Germany. In addition, the speaker of the Palestinian parliament, Aziz Dweik, had studied at the State University of New York at Binghamton and later earned a doctorate at the University of Pennsylvania. Not all were formally members of Hamas. For instance, Planning Minister Samir Abu Eisheh (PhD, Pennsylvania State University) called himself a technocrat. Finance Minister Omar Abdel-Razek likewise said he was not a Hamas member but an Islamist who believes Muslim teachings "can shape the political and economic and social life of Muslims" and provide life with "very good meaning." Speaking of the government as a whole, he said, "We believe that Islamic teachings are suitable for modern life and are suitable for political, economic, and social systems."

Abdel-Razek took part in a 1992 conference at Harvard's Kennedy School. Until 2004, when he left the economic research center because travel from his home in Nablus had become so difficult, he met periodically with officials from the U.S. consulate in Jerusalem and USAID, he told me.

Eisheh may have kept the closest ongoing ties with the United States. As recently as January 2006, he submitted a paper for the annual meeting of the Transportation Research Board in Washington. He held visiting professorships at Texas A&M and the University of Washington, the latter on a Fulbright grant. On the Web site of An-Najah National University, where he was assistant to the president for planning and development, he lists continuing membership in three U.S.-based professional associations, including the American Society of Civil Engineers. He continued to work closely with Purdue University professor Fred Mannering, a widely published transportation expert. They collaborated in 2002 on a paper about ways to predict demand for cars in developing countries.

Naser al-Shaer, deputy prime minister, participated in an intense six-week study of religion in American history as an international fellow at New York University in 1998. Philip Hosay, the professor who directed the fellowship, recalled him as a "very amiable" academic who took the course seriously and gave no indication of extremism or even of being an Islamist.

A number of American officials, academics, and nongovernmental organizations were quite familiar with members of the new Hamas cabinet. David Sammons, a Purdue University agriculture specialist who spent two years with USAID, had worked closely with the new agriculture minister, Mohammad al-Agha, a professor at the Islamic University in Gaza who had a PhD from the University of Manchester, in the United Kingdom, putting together a curriculum to develop Palestinian water specialists. In a spring 2006 telephone interview, Sammons referred to al-Agha as one of the "top-notch colleagues" on the project.

"One of the things I came to admire was that these individuals really wanted to see this work," Sammons said.

The appointment of these Western-educated cabinet members suggested that the new Hamas leadership was serious about economic progress and developing a well functioning government—two of the very goals set by President Bush, the Quartet, and its special envoy, James Wolfensohn. The Palestinian state they envisioned would be more independent of Israel than in the past, but remain connected economically. As Omar Abdel-Razek explained in an April 2006 telephone interview,

"The World Bank research and every research in that regard has reached the conclusion that the very big and huge and single relationship of the Palestinian economy with the Israeli economy is not healthy, is not in the right direction. So there is a need to reduce the dependence on the Israeli economy and a need to increase ties and economic relations with not only the Arab world but also Europe and the States. Now, when you're talking about reducing the relations with the Israeli economy you're not talking about eliminating it," he said, given the close proximity of Israel and the Palestinians. But the heavy reliance on Israel and its jobs and products "is very unhealthy to our economy. Look, now when they close the border you have a very big unemployment problem and you have a very big poverty problem. . . . Our chances with the Arab world are much better than our chances with Europe or the other places. . . . [Goods] will probably compete better in the Arab world than in Europe. . . . We are thinking about reforming these economic relations. We hope to make changes . . . to increase ties with the Arab world, to increase direct trade, which also saves us some money; it's a complicated formula."

Paul Pillar, national intelligence officer for the Near East and South Asia until 2005 and for many years one of the CIA's top experts on Islamic political movements, drew a distinction between Hamas and global jihadist groups like al-Qaida. "Hamas is interested in gaining and maintaining power in Palestine. They are not apocalyptic jihadists of the al-Qaida sort that talk about waging war on the great Satan and all that kind of crap. They're interested in political power in Palestine. They, like many other organizations, parties, governments have various mantras that are in charters, party constitutions, and so on, which, in their case, as in many other cases, ostensibly take a rather extreme position but which don't necessarily describe what their actual positions and bargaining limits or goals would be," he told me. "It would be politically difficult internally for any Hamas leader to stand up and say, 'OK, we renounce everything we said in our charter about our attitude toward Israel and what our maximal goals are and so on.' . . . I don't think Hamas leadership considers having some manifesto or charter with extreme language in it on the books as being at all inconsistent with making deals— in the first instance with someone like Abbas and in the second instance with the Israelis, even if the deal is not some peace treaty but instead is a *hudna*, a long-term truce. . . . They've spoken about this explicitly, that they would accept, despite all their rhetoric in the charter and whatever about not recognizing Israel, wanting all of Palestine, that they would accept an indefinite truce."

To the White House and Israeli government, however, the possibility that Hamas might succeed in governing posed a danger. According to Ayalon, both governments viewed the leadership in Damascus as the ones calling the shots for Hamas, not Ismail Haniyeh in Gaza. "And unfortunately, they are also being manipulated—or being run—by Iran," he said. "There wasn't [any] daylight," between the approaches of Washington and Jerusalem, he said. "And I would say most of the Europeans agreed." The decision was made to squeeze the Hamas government financially.

"First of all we had to formulate the policy, which was the three [conditions]. Then [we] came up with more concrete issues to make sure that Hamas doesn't succeed and doesn't manipulate the system and use the money—first of all to establish itself and then to use the money for terror. And then it was agreed that we will hold the money. And not only we will hold the money but also the Europeans and others will not funnel any money through Hamas, but find circumventing channels.

"Every political analyst will tell you that Hamas won not because of its own popularity, not because of its own agenda or ideology," Ayalon continued. "It was a protest vote against the Fatah. However, being there in power Hamas [could] continually shore up support and build a real strong political base for the future. And we didn't want that to happen. And this is why we came up with this concrete step with the money and of course nonlegitimacy and political isolation and all that."

Despite some conciliatory gestures toward Abbas and a willingness to enter a long-term truce with Israel, Hamas refused to comply explicitly with the three Quartet demands: renouncing violence, recognizing Israel, and accepting previous agreements between the PLO and Israel. It took partial steps on the first and the third conditions: proposing a truce, and accepting past agreements that it deemed "in the Palestinians' interest," implying that some weren't. Recognition proved impossible for an organization that considered all of Palestine to be an Islamic *waqf*. For Hamas, it would have been a major concession without anything in return.

Fatah refused Hamas's offer to join in a government of national unity. As far as Washington and Jerusalem were concerned, the fate of the Palestinian Authority was sealed: any agency led by Hamas would get neither recognition nor money. Insistence on the three conditions seemed to provide a rationale for what many in Washington and Jerusalem wanted to do anyway: squeeze Hamas with the hope that it would lose power. Had Hamas complied with the conditions, it clearly would have done so under duress and its "recognition" of Israel would have lacked credibility.

Former President Jimmy Carter told the Al Jazeera network that he had urged the Quartet "not to impose any kind of economic sanctions against the Palestinian people, but they decided to do so. When alternatives were proposed by the Arab countries and by the United Nations, the U.S. rejected the alternatives, and [refused] to transfer money to the Palestinians." With American agreement, Israel stopped turning over the $50 million a month in import duties that it routinely collected on behalf of the Palestinian Authority. The Europeans also cut off the aid money that had up until then enabled the authority to meet its payroll.

In Washington, the Bush administration adopted a new legal approach to the Palestinian Authority. "We waited to see what they were going to do with their ministries and so forth, and said, 'OK, Hamas is going to control these ministries.' So we said, 'Here's the deal: Now the Palestinian Authority is a government in which Hamas, a terrorist organization, has an interest. Therefore the entire Palestinian Authority must be treated accordingly as a terrorist entity," according to Treasury Undersecretary Stuart Levey. This meant that no U.S. government official could deal with the ministries. Exceptions were carved out and licenses issued to allow continued contact with the office of President Mahmoud Abbas and with members of the Palestinian parliament who were not part of Hamas. The ban on contact with the Hamas government did not extend to the World Bank or the United Nations. "There was no question but that we were going to treat Hamas as a terrorist entity. The only question was what was the precise scope of what would be forbidden," Levey said.

Meeting with members of Mahmoud Abbas's brain trust soon after the election, Elliott Abrams told them, according to one of those present, "You need to do your best to get rid of Hamas." Dov Weisglass, the former chief of staff to Ariel Sharon who remained an adviser to the new Israeli government led by Ehud Olmert, came the closest of any U.S. or Israeli official to saying that the point of squeezing the Hamas government financially was to punish the Palestinian population and make them face up to the consequences of electing a terrorist movement. "The idea is to put the Palestinians on a diet but not to make them die of hunger," he was widely quoted as saying in February.

James Wolfensohn, still the envoy of the Quartet, "vigorously" opposed the cutoff of outside aid to the Hamas-led Palestinian Authority, he said in late 2006. "I just thought pushing the Palestinians to the wall would only bring about extremism, frankly, and there was a humanitarian issue that was more important than that and that if you wanted to get them on [your] side that the best way to cut violence [was to] give them some hope. . . . Sure, I protested—with everybody. I probably just told anybody that would talk to me what I thought." However, "in the period from January to May, I was clearly a declining force," Wolfensohn said. His time was mostly spent in making sure that emergency food aid was delivered to Palestinians.

Wolfensohn said he received several requests to meet with members of the new Hamas government and "would have been happy" to do so, but "the Americans wouldn't let me."

The official squeeze on Hamas was only part of the pressure directed against Hamas. Despite American, European, and Israeli moves to deprive the new Palestinian Authority of money, private citizens and a few governments in the Arab and Muslim world were ready to pick up at least some of the slack. The coup de grâce that prevented Hamas from being able to run a functioning government was dealt by the private sector—specifically, financial institutions.

The banking community's squeamishness about Hamas had been building for several years, thanks largely to a section of the U.S. Treasury

devoted to halting the flow of money to terrorist groups, drug traffickers, proliferators of weapons of mass destruction, and rogue regimes,
such as those of Iran and North Korea. Led by an attorney schooled in
fighting terrorism while at the Justice Department, Stuart Levey, the
office, known by the initials TFI (for Terrorism and Financial Intelligence), quickly became a model for how to wage war against terrorist
groups and their sponsors without firing a shot. Rather than tanks and
bombs, Levey wielded powerful regulatory tools that could send shud-
ders through the financial world. Increasing globalization and open markets played to his advantage in gaining international cooperation.

A high honors graduate of Harvard College and Harvard Law
School, Levey had years of experience as a white-collar-crime litigator
before joining the Justice Department and then the Treasury. He waged
his legal war against terrorist groups with total enthusiasm, exuding a
consuming energy. "Those who work with me will tell you that I am not
complacent, and not very patient, either," he said in a speech to AIPAC
in May 2005.

By the time of the Palestinian elections, Hamas had already become
a target for both government and private sleuths in the United States.
Treasury and Justice had gone after the group's financial pipeline, shut-
ting down and choking off money sent to several charities operating in
the United States and overseas that maintained ties with Palestinian militants. On July 2, 2004, six families of victims killed or injured in terrorist
attacks in Israel and the occupied territories filed an $875 million law-
suit against Arab Bank, which maintained a branch in New York. The
Jordan-based bank, founded by Palestinians, was one of the largest and
most important financial institutions in the Middle East. The families
charged that the bank was used as a conduit to send money from Saudi
Arabia to Hamas, Islamic Jihad, and other Palestinian terrorist groups.

While the suit made its way slowly through U.S. district court in Brook-
lyn, Treasury took its own action against Arab Bank. In February, regu-
lators ordered the bank to stop accepting new deposits and halt money
transfers at its New York branch, citing inadequate internal controls.
The following August, Treasury levied a $24 million penalty against the
bank for failing to conduct adequate scrutiny of accounts and transfers.

It was hard to exaggerate the impact on a venerable institution that for decades had taken pride both in its probity and its ability to keep up with the financial world's latest trends in services and products. The crackdown was not without irony. The Arab Bank had long-standing ties with the Palestine Liberation Organization's leadership, which opposed Hamas, and had financed a number of job-creating enterprises in the West Bank and Gaza that "undoubtedly contributed to reducing violence, rather than the opposite," its chief officer, Shukry Bishara, told Reuters.

Levey recognized the growing power of Hamas earlier than did many U.S. officials. With the help of Matthew Levitt, an expert on Middle East terrorist movements whom Levey had hired from the Washington Institute for Near East Policy, Levey understood well before the January 2006 elections that Hamas's network of social service agencies had enabled it to boost its political standing among Palestinians. He met with Salam Fayyad, the PA finance minister who was widely respected in Washington, to look for a way that the PA could compete with Hamas.

"One thing that I have tried to do in the Treasury, since I've been here, before Hamas was elected, was talk to the Palestinian Authority, and Salam Fayyad in particular, and tell them, 'Look—you guys are not delivering the humanitarian services in many parts of the territories; Hamas is. We'd like to try to help you fix that.'

"And I remember my first meeting with him [Fayyad]. I think he was surprised because he realized that was the purpose of the meeting, from my perspective, to tell him, 'Look—we want to set up some kind of a mechanism to have charitable money, that we thought could be raised very easily for humanitarian purposes in the territories if there could be the right kinds of safeguards put in place to make sure it ended up in the right place. And if that didn't happen, Hamas was going to get the political credit for delivering humanitarian services in the territories.' . . . No real criticism of him or the Palestinian Authority. . . . It's easy for me to sit here in my nice office and say they should have made this a higher priority. They had lots of problems they were dealing with, but for whatever reason, they never wanted to pursue that with the same intensity that I had hoped, and so it never happened.

"I don't know if that would have changed the outcome of an election,

but certainly Hamas did get the political benefit of delivering social services . . . and it proved itself in the election. . . . They ended up getting
a loyal following from that."

By the time Hamas gained control of the Palestinian Authority in
March 2006, Arab Bank evidently realized the consequences it could
face through even the appearance of cooperating with a group viewed
by the United States as a terrorist entity. With three of the PA's main
sources of revenue—the European Union, American aid, and taxes
gathered on its behalf by Israel—shut off, the Hamas leadership set out
to raise money in the Middle East and Persian Gulf. While unpopular
with Arab governments allied with the United States, Hamas still had
broad support in a region where its attacks against Israelis were viewed
as legitimate resistance against occupation.

But the money solicited by Hamas didn't move any farther than
Cairo. Arab Bank refused to touch it, and other regional banks followed
suit. No financial institution was willing to run the risk of transferring
it to the Hamas-controlled Palestinian Authority.

In Washington, Stuart Levey realized Treasury had made a powerful impact. The fact that the United States and other members of the
Quartet now regarded the Palestinian Authority itself as a terrorist
organization "has made a big difference," Levey said in an interview. But
its importance lay in how the banks reacted. By the time Hamas was
elected, banks wanted to avoid not only the threat of Treasury punishment but the aroma of being used by terrorists.

"Banks said they would not deal with the Palestinian Authority. And
that is where the pressure has come from," Levey said in a late-2006 interview. "Not from the United States' formal sanctions policy. Yeah, that
stopped United States persons from dealing with them. That has stopped
any bank in the United States from sending money to the Palestinian
Authority. But the big deal is that the financial institutions across Europe,
across the Arab world have also voluntarily decided not to do business
with the new Hamas government. People can explain why in two ways:
they can say it's because they're worried about U.S. regulatory action
against them if they deal with Hamas; or you could say that they really
don't want to deal with a terrorist entity.

". . . I think it would have been incredibly difficult to get a multilateral government agreement with this effect—it would have been very, very difficult. And in fact the best evidence of that is that there were governments that were willing to pledge money, but it was the private sector who said, 'No, we're not going to deal with them.'"

"The result has been that . . . the Palestinian Authority doesn't have access to the international banking system and they're trying to run their government by smuggling cash into the territories. Well, you can run a terrorist organization by smuggling cash. You can't run a government by smuggling cash.

"The key financial institutions in the Arab world set an example that everyone else followed," Levey recounted. As it turned out, Treasury didn't have to use the major weapons at its disposal for Hamas to feel the heat immediately.

"Arab Bank is a key financial institution in the Arab world—certainly in the Palestinian-Jordan world. And they have made it very clear that they do not want to deal with Hamas. That has been incredibly powerful. I think these things have a real industry-standard kind of thing that informally gets set up and they've been important in this process."

Levey was struck by how little pressure he had to exert for this to happen. "I've seen press stories that have me twisting the arms of financial institutions all over the world. I'm not going to [say] that I didn't talk to anybody, but by and large this has been a decision-making process that banks have made on their own—in fact, exclusively a decision-making process that banks made on their own. We have not coerced any bank into doing anything.

"Our authorities are very well-known to financial institutions around the world. . . . They know how seriously we take terrorism, they know how seriously we take Hamas, they may well have calculated that we wouldn't hesitate to use our authorities. But we didn't have to have any conversations like that with any financial institution. They are very much aware of this. They are very much aware, if they do business in the United States, of the potential of private lawsuits, which is something I couldn't control even if I wanted to. But that's something that has an impact on the risk calculation of banks that do business in the United States."

Had the banks balked, the U.S. Treasury had at its disposal the financial equivalent of a nuclear option: Section 311 of the Patriot Act. This law allows Treasury to bar access to the U.S. financial system to any bank found to be involved in money laundering.

"When we have used it, it has been very, very powerful," Levey said. "I don't want to suggest that banks only act in certain ways because they're scared of regulatory consequences, but this is a very, very, very powerful tool that I don't think any bank, anywhere wants to have to deal with, particularly if they do business in the United States; it can be quite devastating.

"There was some discussion at the time: 'Oh, do we really believe in democracy? They won the election—why are we trying to put pressure on this government?' The truth is, I don't think there is any inconsistency there. If the winner of an election is a terrorist organization, there are going to be consequences for that. . . . If you elect a terrorist organization, we're going to continue to treat it like a terrorist organization. If that's what you vote for, that's going to be the outcome. I didn't see that as a—it didn't in any way undermine our commitment to democracy. . . . What's cut off is aid, it's that kind of benefit to the government. It's not an entitlement. We'll send aid to governments as a matter of policy, but we're certainly not going to send aid to a government that's controlled by a terrorist organization."

The idea of talking directly to officials in a Hamas-led government—even those who had been educated in the United States and Europe—seemed to strike Levey as a no-brainer: such an idea was simply out of the question. "That are members of Hamas? . . . Members of Hamas are members of a terrorist organization.

". . . The people we're facing are misguided and pursuing an agenda of violence and in my view evil—it's not because they're uneducated or stupid. They're just as smart as we are, and they are educated, that's what makes the whole thing so challenging. The fact that there may be a Hamas person who speaks fluent English and was educated in the United States, well, you know, so be it. At this point it doesn't make any difference.

"The alternative [to the policy] would be what? That we would be allowing people to send money to Hamas? That's not an alternative that

I would be comfortable with, from a legal or moral standpoint, so I think both in terms of it being the right thing to do and in the effect it had, I think it's been exactly the right step that we took."

In late February, before the Hamas government took office, the United Nations' coordinator for the territories, Alvaro de Soto, warned the Security Council of the impact of cutting off outside aid and tax revenue to the Palestinian Authority: "It is through the authority that basic social and economic services and salaries are provided. If those services are not provided and if those salaries are not paid, the humanitarian, economic, institutional, political, and security consequences could be severe. And if the authority—essentially a creature of the Oslo process— is allowed to collapse or is sacrificed, then with it may go hopes of achieving a Palestinian state in a reasonable time frame, for a functioning authority is an essential building block of a Palestinian state. I need hardly elaborate on the consequences of that happening—for the parties, the region, and international security." The World Bank predicted that the steps contemplated by Israel and the international community would produce a deep recession.

With the economy of the West Bank and Gaza already in dire straits after five years of conflict, it took just a matter of weeks before the cutoff of outside funds plunged the Palestinians into a humanitarian crisis affecting practically every aspect of their well-being. Food came in the form of emergency rations, with meat a rarity; fuel became more scarce or unaffordable; hospitals ran short of medicines; and water quality deteriorated. As reports from the territories became more alarming, the Quartet devised a scheme for supplying relief money in a way that bypassed the Palestinian Authority. Nevertheless, the World Bank reported in September that 2006 could shape up as the worst-ever year in Palestinian economic history. As security services loyal to Fatah went unpaid and the Hamas-run Interior Ministry created its own forces, Gaza degenerated into factional and clan-based violence.

It's unknown whether governing and becoming responsible for the Palestinians' plight would have steered Hamas toward pragmatism and moderation. The possibility was never tested, and the Western-educated technocrats were left with a shell of a government to operate from. By midsummer, after militants infiltrated Israel and captured a young soldier, Gilad Shalit, many cabinet members and Hamas legislators were arrested and detained indefinitely.

But if the White House and Israel imagined that punishing the Palestinians would turn them against Hamas, they were wrong. Khalil Shikaki, a respected Palestinian pollster, told Bernard Gwertzman of the Council on Foreign Relations, "The public is highly critical of the performance of Hamas in law and order and on the economy by not being able to pay salaries, etc. But this does not seem to translate into less support for Hamas if and when new elections are held. . . . May was the highest point for Hamas, with close to 50 percent telling us that if new elections were held they would vote for Hamas. This came at the peak of the international pressure on Hamas, but the more international pressure there was the more steadfast the public was in supporting Hamas." In June, the International Crisis Group cautioned against expecting that the poverty and despair in the territories would encourage greater moderation among Palestinians: "Those are the very conditions that helped propel Hamas to power in the first place. . . ."

Levey, in the 2006 interview, sounded matter-of-fact about how Hamas was managing to stay afloat: with smuggled cash from, among other places, Iran. "I suspect that they may be more dependent on Iran," he said. "They're certainly more dependent on entities that are willing to cooperate with them in getting money into the territories surreptitiously."

Ghaith al-Omari, a former aide to Mahmoud Abbas, told the Palestine Center in January 2007 that the West's leverage over Hamas had decreased as Iran's had risen. "What this issue caused by the Treasury does, it doesn't only remove the U.S. from being an interlocutor, a meaningful interlocutor, with any leverage vis-à-vis these players, but it removes anyone else. The Europeans cannot engage in any constructive way; [they] cannot use their leverage. Because of this, the Arabs cannot do that. So, suddenly Hamas is being pushed, totally isolated. The only ones who can engage Hamas in leverage are the Iranians, who don't particularly care. What happens in this particular case is that [Khaled] Mashaal [the Hamas leader in exile] becomes the most important guy because the Iranian money goes there. Anyone who wants anything to get done will have to go to Damascus, kiss the bishop's ring, and get the money. So, it definitely limits the maneuverability that one has to deal with Hamas and with the political system."

Four years after Iran tried and failed to gain a foothold by sending arms to Gaza aboard the *Karine A*, the Islamic Republic—seen as an existential threat by Israel—was now using its oil revenues to nurture an alliance with the Jewish state's closest neighbors. This was one of the realities of the Middle East in 2006. Another was succinctly put by Nabil Fahmy, Egypt's ambassador to Washington: "There's no negotiations, there are targeted killings, there's no control over the Palestinians—they're divided. And it's chaos."

Acknowledgments

OF THE MANY people who contributed to this book, special thanks go to editors and colleagues at the *Baltimore Sun* who over the years encouraged my exploration of U.S. policy in the Middle East. Foreign editors Jeff Price and Robert Ruby drew on their extensive experience in the region to act as tutors, guides, and critics. They routinely improved and polished my stories with sharp questions and skill with a pencil. In Washington, the *Sun*'s bureau chief, Paul West, and his deputy, Robert Timberg, set and maintained demanding standards and strengthened my reporting with their deep knowledge of American domestic politics and national security. Timberg, an accomplished and successful author, gave me the benefit of his own experience. The *Sun*'s editor, Tim Franklin, granted a year's leave of absence, without which this project could never have begun, and the paper allowed me continued access to its knowledgeable librarians and research tools.

Current and former U.S. government officials gave generous amounts of time for interviews. Some of them agreed only to speak on condition that their names not be used, and some who provided useful information and guidance are not directly quoted. Among those who can be identified, I particularly want to thank generals Colin Powell and Brent Scowcroft, former deputy Secretary of State Richard Armitage, ambassadors Martin Indyk, Daniel Kurtzer, Philip Wilcox, Samuel Lewis, and John Wolf, former Pentagon officials Dov Zakheim and Douglas Feith, and Edward Abington, former consul general in Jerusalem, former Senate Majority Leader George Mitchell and his chief of staff on the Mitchell commission, Frederick Hof. I also want to thank members of the National Security Council press staff at the White House, particularly Frederick Jones and Kate Starr, and Price Floyd at the State Department, for their gracious help.

In the Israeli government, Mark Regev of the Ministry of Foreign Affairs, David Siegel, Embassy spokesman in Washington, and their colleagues offered valuable guidance and opened doors to key current and former officials, including ambassadors Danny Ayalon, Zalman Shoval and David Ivry, and Maj. Gen. Giora Eiland.

I am grateful to several Palestinian officials and government advisers who provided important information and recollections, including Saeb Erekat, Nasser al-Qidwa, Maen Areikat and Diana Buttu, as well as to the embassies of Jordan and Egypt in Washington.

This book derived important information, insight and research leads from the work of numerous other journalists who were at key places when I wasn't, and who had access to people I couldn't reach. A great deal was learned from, among others, articles by Peter Hermann and John Murphy, my colleagues at the *Sun* who came after me on the Mideast beat; Ann Lolordo, my predecessor in Jerusalem; Joshua Brilliant, our excellent, plugged-in and indefatigable resident colleague in Israel; the Associated Press and Agence France Presse, and the reporting of correspondents on the scene for the *New York Times, Los Angeles Times,* and *Washington Post.* I owe a large debt to the Israeli press corps. Standouts include Ze'ev Schiff and Aluf Benn of Haaretz, Nahum Barnea and Shimon Schiffer of Yediot Ahronot, and David Horovitz of the *Jerusalem Post.* A number of books on the Middle East and the peace process have been valuable as background and sources. They include *The Iron Cage* by Rashid Khalidi, who also gave me an interview; Dennis Ross's *The Missing Peace,* Gershom Gorenberg's *The Accidental Empire* and *The End of Days,* and Charles Enderlin's *Shattered Dreams: The Failure of the Peace Process in the Middle East, 1995-2002.*

Of the growing body of books on the Bush administration, I benefited particularly from *Soldier,* the biography of Colin Powell by Karen DeYoung, who was a friend and highly respected *Washington Post* colleague of my late wife, Ann Devroy. Karen also provided important advice during the early stage of writing and finding a publisher.

I was extremely lucky to have Eve Bridburg and Esmond Harmsworth, of Zachary Shuster Harmsworth, as my agents. Their professionalism, knowledge of the publishing world, and persistence made an enormous difference in this project. Carl Bromley, my editor at Nation Books, has a gift for language, a keen understanding of the subject of this book, and a shrewd instinct for what to add and what to take out.

This project got its start in the extremely hospitable setting of the Hoover Institution at Stanford, which hosted me as a media fellow in early 2005 and gave me the chance to become acquainted with and interview retired federal Judge and State Department Legal Adviser Abraham Sofaer, Larry Diamond, Amichai Magen and Khalil Barhoum. I am very grateful to Mandy MacCalla for her kindness while I was there.

Without skilled translators, a number of interviews could not have been conducted. I want to thank Mohammed Dawwas in Gaza and Tahsin Alawneh in the West Bank for their professionalism and friendship.

Family and friends offered steady encouragement throughout. Three wonderful women sustained my spirits: Ruth Osterweis Selig, a constant source of strength, encouragement and comfort, as well as an exacting editor; my daughter Sarah, to whom this book is dedicated, who will forever give unique meaning to the words pride and joy; and my sister, Alison Freeman Matthews, whose boundless warmth and good sense are a lifeline.

INDEX